Captain Kidd

ALSO BY SAMUEL MARQUIS

Soldiers of Freedom

Lions of the Desert

Spies of the Midnight Sun

Blackbeard: The Birth of America

Altar of Resistance

The Fourth Pularchek

Cluster of Lies

Bodyguard of Deception

The Coalition

Blind Thrust

The Devil's Brigade

PRAISE FOR *CAPTAIN KIDD*

"A swashbuckling account of privateers, pirates, and pirate brokers on the Caribbean high seas at the dawn of the eighteenth century. With *Captain Kidd*, Samuel Marquis deftly separates the man from the myth in a riveting narrative that includes a compelling cast of characters, cannon fire, sword fights, mutiny, and treasure—all with the fate of empires hanging in the balance. A rollicking tale that proves that true stories are the best ones."

—**Buddy Levy**, bestselling author of
Realm of Ice and Sky and *Empire of Ice and Stone*

"Marquis paints the life of the inimitable Captain Kidd in bold, rich colors. A dashing, absorbing tale."

—**Stephan Talty**, bestselling author of *Empire of Blue Water*

"*Captain Kidd* presents one of the most intriguing tales of all time, with author Samuel Marquis bringing it to life through a blend of Clive Cussler–esque prose and Biblical scholar–level research. You will taste the salty air, feel the cannonballs buzzing past, and not merely hear the explosions, but feel them in your teeth."

—**Keith Thomson**, author of *Born to Be Hanged*

"The name 'Captain William Kidd' has become synonymous with 'pirate,' but few really understand the nuanced and complicated history of the man. Happily, Samuel Marquis has done much to bring the true story to light. *Captain Kidd* is a well-researched and thoroughly readable account of the rise and downfall of this enigmatic character, and is a welcome addition to the world of pirate history."

—**James L. Nelson**, author of *Benedict Arnold's Navy*

"It is hard to imagine that anything new could be discovered about Captain Kidd, the subject of many biographies, but Marquis has done it in a lively and well-researched book. If you enjoy a good read about piracy, this is a book for you."

—**Robert Ritchie, PhD**, former foundation director of research,
Huntington Library, professor of history, UCSD,
and author of *Captain Kidd and the War against the Pirates*

"Samuel Marquis provides the reader with a remarkable impression of Captain William Kidd, one that attempts to reincarnate the real person rather than the caricatured and often enigmatic villain trope created to satisfy the one-dimensional schemes of popular works of fiction and fact. Even readers who might disagree with Mr. Marquis's conclusions will still find much to ponder and enjoy."

—**Benerson Little**, historian and author of *The Golden Age of Piracy* and *The Sea Rover's Practice*

"Marquis has written a fascinating and engaging new study of the pirate Captain Kidd. A must-read for all pirate fans and scholars!"

—**Rebecca Simon, PhD**, historian and author of *Why We Love Pirates*

"Few figures in the history of piracy are as puzzling as Captain William Kidd. He was a married man with a family, a propertied New Yorker, but also a world-roving privateer who broke bad in a big way—or so said the English authorities who put him on trial at the turn of the eighteenth century. Few authors could tell Kidd's complicated story as well as Samuel Marquis. With a beachcomber's eye for detail and a playwright's sense of drama, Marquis traces Kidd's zig-zagging trajectory as he threads his way through history, gaining fame and absorbing blame. How will it end?"

—**Kris Lane, PhD**, professor of history, Tulane University, and author of *Pillaging the Empire* and *Piracy in the Early Modern Era*

"Anchored in rapidly globalizing seventeenth-century seascapes and crewed by some of the most compelling and historically consequential characters that you've never heard of (until now), Marquis takes us on an action-packed voyage to discover the real Captain Kidd and his contributions to the making of America. A Kidd descendant himself, Marquis blends scrupulous attention to personalities, places, and events with a tight chronicle of the dynamic colonial conflicts that transformed the planet and birthed both the United States and the myth of the swashbuckling Kidd."

—**John R. Welch , PhD**, professor of archaeology, Simon Fraser University

CAPTAIN KIDD

A TRUE STORY *of* TREASURE *and* BETRAYAL

SAMUEL MARQUIS

DIVERSION BOOKS

Diversion Books
A division of Diversion Publishing Corp.
www.diversionbooks.com

For more information, email info@diversionbooks.com

Originally published in hardcover by Diversion Books, May 2025
First trade paperback edition, May 2026
Hardcover ISBN: 9781635769685
Trade Paperback ISBN: 9798895151396
e-ISBN: 9781635769692

Design by Neuwirth & Associates, Inc.
Cover design by Jonathan Sainsbury / 6x9 design
Maps by Mapping Specialists

Printed in the United States of America
1 3 5 7 9 10 8 6 4 2

For my ninth-great-grandfather Captain William Kidd—
democratic Caribbean buccaneer; patriotic colonial American privateer and merchant sea captain; New York gentleman and founding father of Trinity Church; loving husband, father, and son; defender of a fledgling nation in the New World; and challenger to the imperial English Empire.

Table of Contents

PART 4: Treasure Fever

PART 5: The Trial of the Century

Cast of Historical Figures
(1689–1701)

COLONIAL AMERICAN NEW YORKERS:

Captain William Kidd: New York privateer, merchant sea captain, and former Caribbean buccaneer born an English commoner in 1654; wealthy gentleman, civic leader, and founding father of Trinity Church; commander of Crown-sanctioned 1696–1699 Indian Ocean expedition to hunt pirates and French merchant ships; known today as perhaps the most famous "pirate" of all time.

Sarah Kidd: Wife of Captain William Kidd; New York she-merchant and socialite; devout Anglican born in England in 1670; previously married to Dutch merchants William Cox and John Oort, both of whom died prior to her union with Kidd; mother of Elizabeth and little Sarah.

Robert Livingston: Scottish-born merchant and New York government official in Indian affairs and supplying English troops stationed in Albany; chief promoter and manager of Kidd's Indian Ocean expedition.

James Emott: English-American lawyer and governor's adviser who served as the Kidd family's legal advocate; staunch anti-Leislerian and supporter of the Madagascar pirate trade; close friend of Captain Kidd and enemy of Governor Bellomont; vestryman and key builder of Trinity Church.

Thomas Clark: Merchant, sea captain, former privateer, and occasional smuggler from Setauket (Port Jefferson), Long Island; served as New York governor's council member and on other city councils, including one to help the poor; vestryman and key builder of Trinity Church; good friend of Captain Kidd; known to his friends by the smuggler's name "Whisking."

Frederick Philipse: Wealthiest merchant in New York province, from 1675 until his death in 1702, from both licit and illicit transoceanic commerce; known as "the Pirate King" for pioneering the Indo-Atlantic Red Sea pirate trade between New York and Madagascar.

NEW YORK ROYAL GOVERNORS:

Richard Coote, First Earl of Bellomont (Governor, 1698–1701): Irish-born Whig nobleman, member of Parliament, and colonial governor of New York, Massachusetts Bay, and New Hampshire; lead sponsor of Kidd Indian Ocean expedition; ousted his predecessor, Governor Fletcher, and led anti-piracy crusade in American colonies.

Benjamin Fletcher (Governor, 1692–1698): Tory royal governor and commander in chief of New York province during King William's War (1689–1697); longtime English soldier who rose to colonel during Glorious Revolution; as governor, enriched New York and lined his own pockets by condoning lucrative Madagascar pirate trade.

Richard Ingoldsby (Governor, 1691–1692): Major-Colonel of English troops in New York province; acting governor from July 1691 to August 1692.

Henry Sloughter (Governor, 1691): Royal governor briefly from April to July 1691 who put down Leisler's Rebellion; friend of Captain Kidd and Frederick Philipse.

Jacob Leisler (Governor, 1689–1691): German-born merchant, New York City militia officer, and leader of Leisler's Rebellion; acting lieutenant governor from June 1689 to March 1691; fiercely anti-Catholic, militant Calvinist Protestant; corrupt, incompetent, and despotic colonial administrator.

ENGLISH CROWN AND EAST INDIAN OFFICIALS:

King William III: Dutch Prince of Orange who became King of England, Ireland, and Scotland from 1689 until his death in 1702; commander in chief of English forces during King William's War; ruled alongside his wife, Queen Mary II, until her death from smallpox in December 1694.

King Aurangzeb Alamgir I: Muslim Great Mughal of India, reigning over most of modern-day India from 1658 until his death in 1707; cracked down on English Crown and East India Company for Anglo-American Indian Ocean pirates or Red Sea Men; nicknamed the "White Snake" because he was born with curiously pale skin.

Colonel Christopher Codrington: English governor-general of the Caribbean Leeward Islands; owner of several of the largest sugar plantations in Barbados, Antigua, and Barbuda; commander in chief of all English forces in the Caribbean; important patron of Captain Kidd from 1689 to 1691.

William Blathwayt: Tory Secretary of War and powerful member of the English Privy Council, the king's cabinet in London charged with colonial administration; wheeler-dealer in imperial patronage in London in the 1690s.

Charles Talbot, First Duke of Shrewsbury: Whig Secretary of State for the Southern Department, responsible for Southern England, Wales,

Ireland, and the American colonies; referred to as the "King of Hearts" by William III; important member of Whig Junto and key backer of Kidd's Indian Ocean expedition.

Admiral Edward Russell: First Lord of the Admiralty and treasurer of the Royal Navy; commander of English fleet, powerful member of Whig Junto, and first earl of Orford in 1697; key backer of Kidd voyage.

Sir John Somers: Member of his Majesty's Privy Council, Lord Chancellor, and Lord Keeper of the Great Seal of England; key member of the Whig Junto and one of the sharpest legal minds in England; key backer of Kidd voyage.

Henry Sidney, Earl of Romney: Womanizing and hard-drinking master general of ordnance under William III from 1693 to 1702; key backer of Kidd voyage.

Sir John Gayer: Knight-General of English East India Company and governor of Bombay from May 1694 to November 1704; in charge of diplomatic negotiations with Great Mughal's court regarding Indian Ocean piracy.

Samuel Annesley: English East India Company president and factor based in Surat, India; principal financial reparations negotiator with Great Mughal's court for Indian Ocean piracy.

NAVAL OFFICERS, PRIVATEERS, PIRATES, AND PIRATE-BROKERS:

Captain Jean-Baptiste DuCasse: French naval commander of 44-gun flagship *Le Hasardeux* who fought against Kidd at St. Martins in 1690; senior captain and governor in French Hispaniola by 1691 and full admiral by 1701.

Captain Thomas Hewetson: English commander of 48-gun Royal Navy ship *Lion* who fought with Kidd against the French at Marie-Galante and St. Martins in 1689–1690; known by the French as a "scélérat cruel" (vicious rogue); good friend of Kidd who testified on his behalf at 1701 trial.

Robert Culliford: English privateer who sailed and fought French under Kidd in West Indies in 1689–1690; turned to piracy in 1690 and became one of the most successful Red Sea pirates from 1692 to 1700, using St. Mary's as a base to attack the Great Mughal's treasure ships.

Samuel Burgess: New York privateer-pirate who served as quartermaster under Kidd in 1689–1690; became merchant captain for Frederick Philipse in the mid-1690s in the lucrative Madagascar pirate–slave trade.

William Mason: Senior privateer officer under Kidd aboard *Blessed William* in West Indies in 1689–1690; returned to piracy with Culliford, Burgess, and Browne on and off in 1691–1692; retired from piracy in 1692 to become maritime adviser and pirate negotiator for East India Company.

John Browne: English-born privateer-pirate who sailed under Kidd in West Indies in 1689–1690; one of the earliest Red Sea pirates, returning to New York in 1693 with a rich haul of treasure; senior seaman and later quartermaster aboard *Adventure Galley* during Captain Kidd's 1696–1699 Indian Ocean expedition.

William Moore: Chief gunner aboard the *Adventure Galley* during Indian Ocean expedition; arrested in 1683 at the age of eighteen for attacking his captain, for which he received a two-year prison sentence; lead mutineer during Kidd pirate-hunting voyage.

Robert Bradinham: Heavy-drinking English chief medical officer aboard *Adventure Galley* and later *November* during 1696–1699 Indian Ocean expedition; lousy physician even when he wasn't inebriated or skulking about belowdecks; turned state's evidence and committed perjury by lying about Kidd to save his own neck.

Joseph Palmer: Seaman aboard *Adventure Galley* and later *November* during 1696–1699 expedition; former Royal Navy reject who turned state's evidence and committed perjury against Kidd to spare his own life.

Richard Barlycorne: Fourteen-year-old Carolina-born apprentice (cabin boy) aboard *Adventure Galley* during Indian Ocean expedition; fiercely devoted to Captain Kidd.

Adam Baldridge: Former Caribbean buccaneer who became "Pirate King" of Madagascar between 1691 and 1697; married chieftain's daughter and set up profitable base of operations with local tribal leaders supplying the pirates of St. Mary's Island and selling enslaved Malagasies to New York and New England trading vessels.

Captain Thomas Tew: Rhode Island gentleman-pirate who in 1693 was the first successful Red Sea raider to plunder the Great Mughal's fantastically rich treasure fleets in the Indian Ocean; Captain Kidd was recruited as a Crown-licensed pirate-hunter to pursue and bring Tew to justice in 1696.

Captain Henry Every: English pirate who captured the *Ganj-i-Sawai* of Aurangzeb's treasure fleet in 1695, taking an astronomical haul and causing a major uproar in India; celebrated in London as the "Grand Pirate," his exploits appeared in London booksellers' shops in the form of *The Ballad of Henry Every* and other colorful works.

Captain Giles Shelley: New York merchant captain working for French Huguenot merchant Stephen Delancey aboard the *Nassau* in pirate-brokering and slave-trading voyages to Madagascar; former Red Sea pirate who lived in the city just down the street from his friend and neighbor Captain Kidd.

Commodore Thomas Warren: Royal Navy commander of 70-gun fourth-rate flagship HMS *Windsor*; sailed from England to southern Africa in 1696 with 93-ship flotilla but lost his way en route and 300 of his men to scurvy; sought to impress 25 to 40 seamen from Captain Kidd, who daringly escaped Warren's fleet during the night.

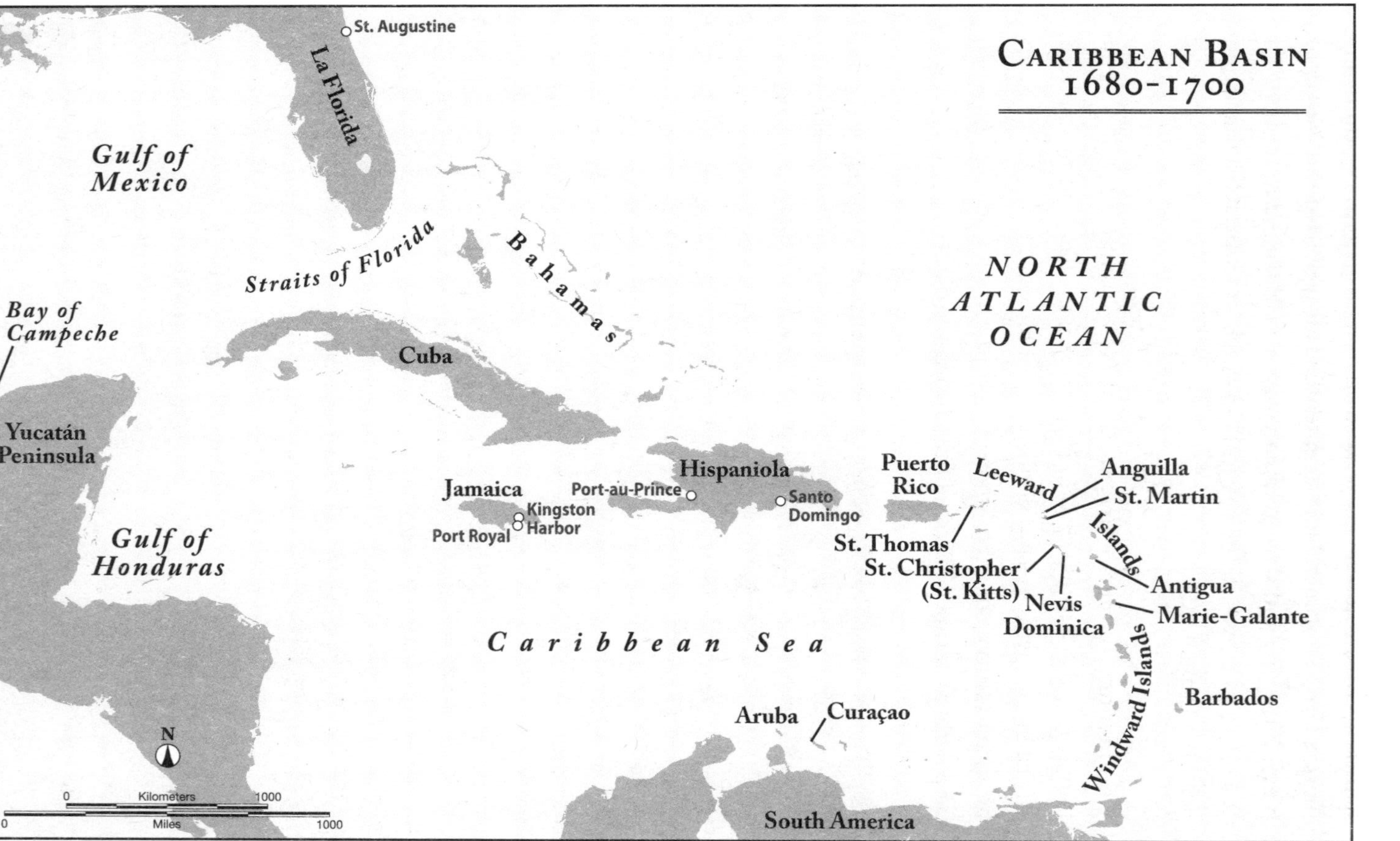
CARIBBEAN BASIN
1680-1700
St. Augustine
La Florida
Gulf of Mexico
Straits of Florida
Bahamas
NORTH ATLANTIC OCEAN
Bay of Campeche
Cuba
Yucatán Peninsula
Hispaniola
Puerto Rico
Leeward Islands
Anguilla
St. Martin
Jamaica
Port-au-Prince
Santo Domingo
Kingston Harbor
Port Royal
Gulf of Honduras
St. Thomas
St. Christopher (St. Kitts)
Nevis
Dominica
Antigua
Marie-Galante
Caribbean Sea
Windward Islands
Barbados
Aruba
Curaçao
N
0
Kilometers
1000
0
Miles
1000
South America

Indian Ocean and Madagascar 1680–1700

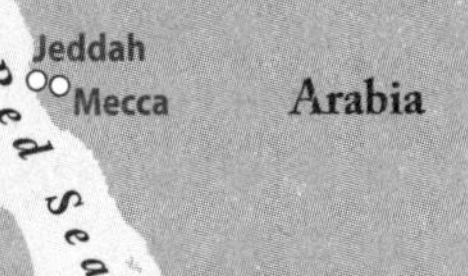

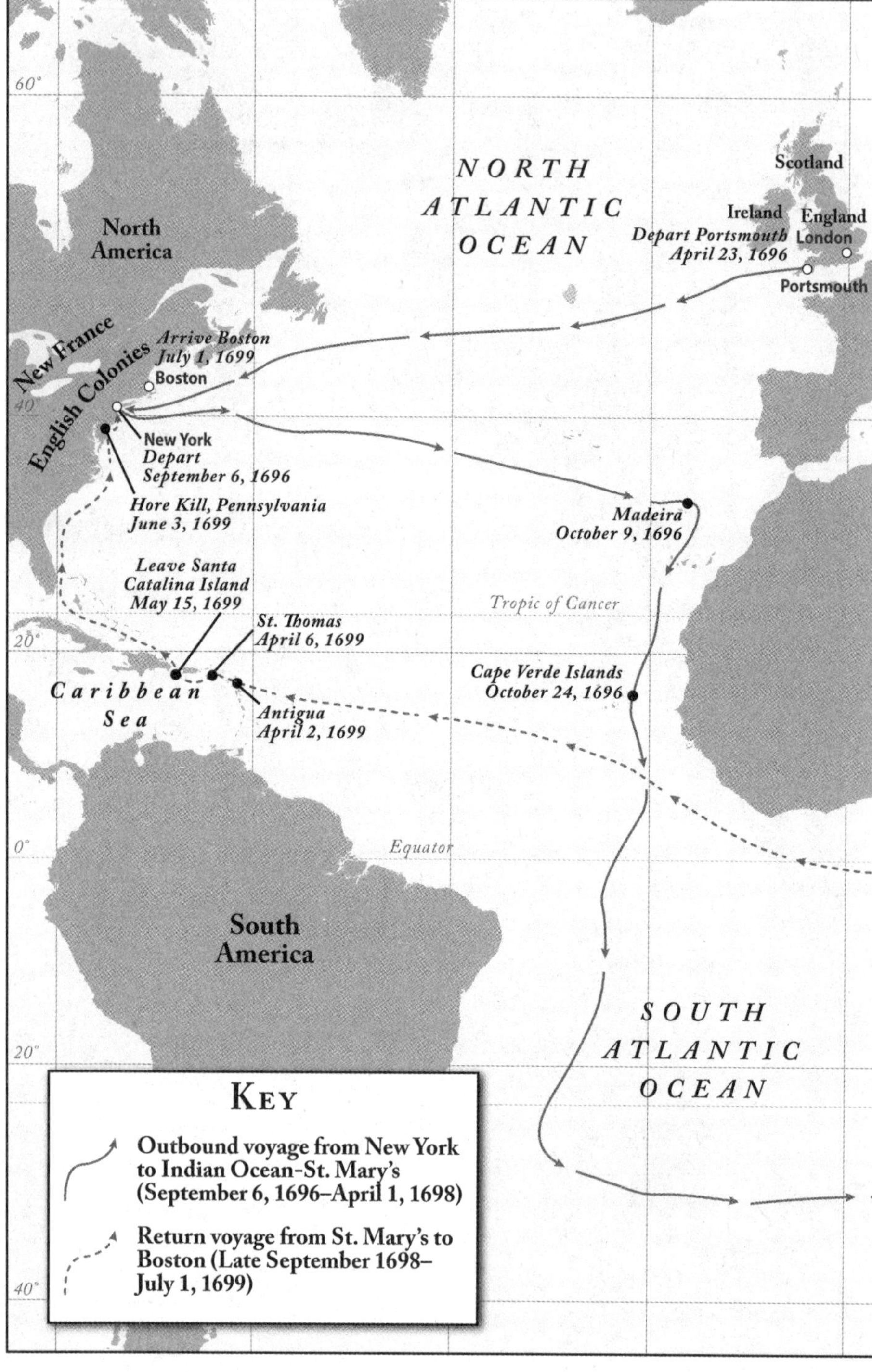
NORTH ATLANTIC OCEAN
North America
Scotland
Ireland
England
London
Depart Portsmouth April 23, 1696
Portsmouth
New France
English Colonies
Arrive Boston July 1, 1699
Boston
New York Depart September 6, 1696
Hore Kill, Pennsylvania June 3, 1699
Madeira October 9, 1696
Leave Santa Catalina Island May 15, 1699
St. Thomas April 6, 1699
Tropic of Cancer
Cape Verde Islands October 24, 1696
Caribbean Sea
Antigua April 2, 1699
Equator
South America
SOUTH ATLANTIC OCEAN
60°
40°
20°
0°
20°
40°
KEY
Outbound voyage from New York to Indian Ocean-St. Mary's (September 6, 1696–April 1, 1698)
Return voyage from St. Mary's to Boston (Late September 1698–July 1, 1699)

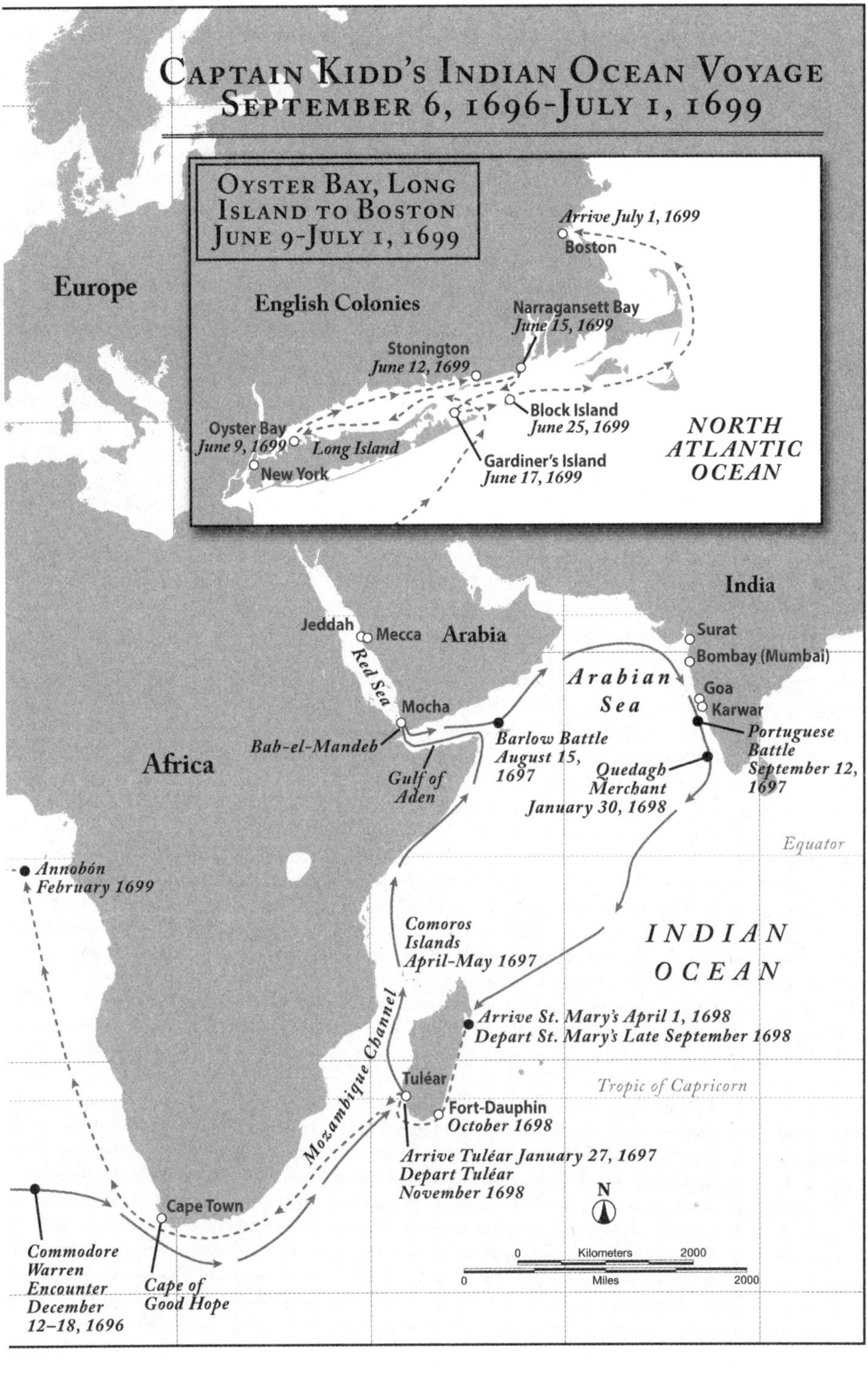

Captain Kidd's Indian Ocean Voyage
September 6, 1696–July 1, 1699

Oyster Bay, Long Island to Boston
June 9–July 1, 1699

English Colonies

Arrive July 1, 1699
Boston

Narragansett Bay
June 15, 1699

Stonington
June 12, 1699

Block Island
June 25, 1699

Oyster Bay
June 9, 1699

Long Island

New York

Gardiner's Island
June 17, 1699

NORTH ATLANTIC OCEAN

Europe

India

Jeddah

Mecca

Arabia

Red Sea

Surat

Bombay (Mumbai)

Arabian Sea

Goa

Karwar

Mocha

Bab-el-Mandeb

Barlow Battle
August 15, 1697

Portuguese Battle
September 12, 1697

Quedagh Merchant
January 30, 1698

Africa

Gulf of Aden

Equator

Annobón
February 1699

Comoros Islands
April–May 1697

INDIAN OCEAN

Mozambique Channel

Arrive St. Mary's April 1, 1698
Depart St. Mary's Late September 1698

Tuléar

Tropic of Capricorn

Fort-Dauphin
October 1698

Arrive Tuléar January 27, 1697
Depart Tuléar
November 1698

N

Cape Town

Commodore Warren Encounter
December 12–18, 1696

Cape of Good Hope

0 Kilometers 2000

0 Miles 2000

PART 1

—

The Making *of a* Sea Captain

–1–
The Caribbean Privateer

On July 29, 1689, beneath a sweltering Caribbean sun, William Kidd scanned the deck of the wooden frigate *Sainte Rose*, taking in the swarthy faces of the dozen French privateers guarding the gunship. The tide was going out and it was time to make his move. He and the seven other Englishmen making up a small part of the man-of-war's predominantly French, 118-man crew had been sailing, fighting, tossing back rum, and swapping stories with these rugged yet jovial Frenchies for the past six months—but that was all over now.

It was time to attack and seize the ship.[1]

He inhaled a deep breath of the salty air of Basseterre Harbor, a stretch of emerald water off St. Christopher's, or St. Kitts as it was better known, situated in the Leeward Islands of the Caribbean. Though his mind and body were on high alert, the veteran sea warrior felt calm and composed as he prepared to give the signal to his men to do battle and take the *Sainte Rose* as a prize.

The plan he, Robert Culliford, William Mason, Samuel Burgess, John Browne, and the three other Anglo-American privateers had surreptitiously agreed to only minutes before called for them to kill or incapacitate every last one of the twelve remaining Frenchmen onboard guarding the 16-gun warship, seize the privateering vessel by force, and sail her swiftly to nearby English-controlled Nevis Island to fight for king and country. With war recently declared between Mother England and France, their Gallic comrades in arms—at this moment smoking their pipes, sharpening their knives, and throwing dice—had transformed overnight from fellow Brethren of the Coast into mortal enemies.[2]

The chain of events leading up to war and the sticky situation in which William Kidd now found himself had begun nine months earlier in the fall of 1688. In a bloodless coup, the Catholic King James II of England had been usurped by his Protestant daughter Mary Stuart and her Dutch husband, Prince William of Orange, who as the nephew and son-in-law of James stood as a viable Protestant alternative for the English throne.[3] In an aggressive military gambit and political power grab, William had "invaded" England and marched to London as a preemptive maneuver to commandeer England's vast financial, naval, and military resources for his planned Dutch alliance in the war against France. Aided by disaffected and high-ranking officers in the English army and navy, the Dutch prince crossed the Channel and landed without resistance at Devon in November 1688. Turning against their Catholic king and siding with the more muscular coalition, many English officers and government officials had defected to join William and his Stuart wife, who vowed to rule as co-monarchs. Meanwhile, James II had fled to France and the court of Louis XIV, the *Roi du Soleil* or Sun King, who offered the deposed Catholic English king sanctuary and became his protector.[4]

Parliament swiftly transferred the throne to William and Mary once they had signed off on a Bill of Rights ensuring constitutional and civil-rights protections for Parliament, with the new queen soon leaving governance to her Dutch husband. The Whig Protestant lords who helped orchestrate the coup, ardent opponents of the pro-monarchist Tory Party, proclaimed the seizure of power a "Glorious Revolution."[5] Thus, the usurpation was portrayed as a spontaneous political uprising by united Britons when it was, in truth, a bloodless takeover spearheaded by the Dutch army and navy and a seditious, fiercely anti-Catholic Whig wing of England's Parliament.[6]

The end results of the coup d'état were the security of the Protestant succession, the death knell of royal absolutism, and the establishment of the supremacy of Parliament over the monarchy in England. With the steadfast backing of the Whig aristocracy, the bellicose William III promptly declared war upon France and plunged England into a global conflagration of unprecedented cost. The hostilities would become known as the "War of the English Succession" in England and "King William's War" in English America, and they would drain the treasuries of the belligerent powers for nearly a decade.[7]

The news that England had formally declared war on Catholic France on May 18, 1689, took nearly two months to reach William Kidd and his fellow Anglo-American privateers, who had been busy fighting the Dutch and Spanish aboard the *Sainte Rose* in the Caribbean. Since reports of the war between the European superpowers had first reached them a fortnight earlier, the Protestant Englishmen had been waiting for an opportune moment to side with their king and country and strike the French as licensed privateers.[8]

That moment had arrived today.

For the better part of two decades now, William Kidd had been a roving privateer and merchant seaman sailing to and from the Caribbean, the American colonies, and the metropole of London. As a privateer, he had been legally licensed by various English and French colonial governors, or lower-ranking officials, to attack and plunder the enemy in wartime. Though he preferred to sail with "Englishmen" of his own nation—those who hailed from the British Isles or North American colonies—he had little choice but to serve as an occasional mercenary under French or Dutch colors due to royal betrayals and the constant shifting of European alliances.

He had joined the crew of the *Sainte Rose* back in February 1689 at Admiral Henry Morgan's famous launching pad for patriotic strikes against the Spanish Main: Île-à-Vache, or Cow Island, off the southwestern coast of French Hispaniola (modern-day Haiti). The vessel's crew, mostly French Protestant Huguenots, weren't picky when it came to rounding out their motley roster: experienced sailors were always in short supply, and they welcomed Kidd and his fellow Protestant English salts with open arms. When it came to privateer crews, religion often trumped nationality, and the Frenchmen of the *Sainte Rose* stood closer in allegiance to English-born Protestants like Kidd and his compatriots than to French Catholics, who had driven them and their families from their homeland, across the Atlantic, and into the New World.[9]

Armed with a legal privateering commission from a French Hispaniola official, the crew set out in the *Sainte Rose* in tropical waters to prey on Dutch merchant ships.[10] Like the other seamen, Kidd hoped to become a "gentleman of fortune"—but with a legitimate government commission to back him up. With France then at war with the Netherlands and at peace with England, he opted to take his opportunities for plunder with the French. Like most state-licensed privateers and outlaw pirates in the Age of Sail (1500–1850), the crew's 110 Frenchmen and 8 Englishmen were mostly young, hardy men who knew how to handle a dagger, cutlass, pistol, and musket in violent combat. Privateering—piracy on the high seas made legal and respectable by a simple piece of parchment—was a hard combination of seamanship and waging war that only the rugged and adventurous could survive.[11]

Within a week of setting sail from Île-à-Vache, the *Sainte Rose* spotted a Dutch merchant ship. Kidd and Company promptly seized and transported the Dutchman north to sell their plundered cargo to the pious Puritan traders of New England and outfit for a longer voyage. From Boston, the multifarious crew headed south to a friendlier port for both commissioned privateers and renegade pirates: New York. Here they moored their 16-cannon gunship in the bustling harbor, refitted the vessel by loading up with fine New York biscuit and other provisions, and held council on where to venture next in the war against the Dutch.[12]

The well-liked Kidd, a longtime veteran of the Caribbean and Atlantic trade routes, had made New York his home port since 1688 and knew many people in town, including a certain young and attractive woman named Sarah Bradley Cox, who, regrettably, was married to a Dutch flour merchant twice her age. Kidd and Sarah had a romantic history, and he visited the future Mrs. Captain Kidd during his time in port, where he owned multiple real-estate properties close to the harbor.[13]

After spending a fortnight outfitting the *Sainte Rose* and drinking and carousing in the city, the crew was ready to continue harassing the Dutch and seek their fortune along the West African coast. With the trade winds pushing them along, they sailed across the Atlantic to the Cape Verde Islands, located off modern-day Senegal.[14]

Here they came across seven ships-of-war bristling with cannon, the flotilla commanded by the legendary French captain Jean-Baptiste DuCasse. Over the next few weeks, they fought alongside DuCasse and his 44-gun flagship, *Le Hasardeux*, eventually returning to the Western Atlantic and Caribbean. At DuCasse's request, Kidd and his mostly French crew captured a Spanish vessel, seized all her valuables, and took the gunship as a prize, then joined the commander in unsuccessful assaults on the well-fortified Dutch colonies at Surinam and Berbice.[15]

Then, in mid-July 1689, as the French fleet approached Barbados, Kidd and the other crew members received stunning news: England boasted a new king and had declared war on France.[16] The declaration of hostilities suddenly put Kidd and his cohorts in a precarious position, since they were now armed "Englishmen" operating in the midst of a massive French fleet.[17] But the French *flibustiers* pegged them as selfish mercenaries who cared more about capturing booty than fighting on behalf of king and country. Despite the new hostility between the French and English, neither DuCasse nor the captain of the *Sainte Rose*, Jean Fantin, suspected that Kidd and his seven Anglo-American privateers would have the gumption to steal the ship and sail her to an English colony.[18]

The French soon set their sights on the wealthy island of St. Christopher, which the two countries jointly owned and consisted of profitable sugar and tobacco plantations under enslaved labor. Between

July 17 and 19, 1689, the French fleet of 22 ships and a force of Irish Catholics, tired of their lowly status as the White menial laborers of the English Caribbean, launched attacks across the island. The embattled English population of 450 fighting men and a thousand women and children managed to retreat to the safety of Fort Charles, a solidly built fortress on the coast. Over the next two weeks, the French pounded away incessantly at the English defenders but were unable to dislodge them.[19]

That looked to William Kidd like it was about to change.

He peered over the railing toward St. Christopher, a lush and mountainous volcanic island of sixty-five square miles. The French—led on land by Charles de Roche-Courbon, Comte de Blénac, governor-general of the French West Indies, and at sea by Captain DuCasse—were in the midst of a formidable assault on the island that included 98 of the *Sainte Rose* privateers. The gentle lapping of water against the hull was broken by the far-off crackle of gunfire, and Kidd smelled gunpowder in the tropical ocean breeze of Basseterre Harbor.[20] From his vantage point, the fall of St. Christopher to the French appeared imminent.

Now he and his fellow Britons made eye contact as the small talk and laughter of the preoccupied Frenchmen drifted across the bow and over the blue-green water.[21] He signaled the assault team that they would make their move any minute now, with the tide rolling out and no sign of rowboats returning to the ship. At thirty-four,[22] Kidd was one of the senior seamen and had been voted by the English crew as the leader of the privateer insurrectionists.[23]

In his own day, William Kidd was described as a "hearty," "lusty," and "mighty" warrior of "unquestioned courage and conduct in sea affairs," as well as a man of exceptional physical strength and skill in swordsmanship. Taking part in an occupation where violent hand-to-hand combat was the norm rather than the exception, the tall, robustly built, and pugnacious colonial English-American privateer felt no qualms about killing a sworn enemy in close quarters with sharpened steel and snarling lead pistol shot. He was, in essence, a seventeenth-century U.S. Navy Seal.[24]

The twenty-three-year-old Robert Culliford, twenty-seven-year-old William Mason, and thirty-eight-year-old Samuel Burgess stood poised nearby waiting for Kidd's command to seize the *Sainte Rose*. Some of the other men were standing next to the railing and by the water barrels, pretending to make small talk; others were smoking their long-stemmed pipes, sharpening their knives, and staring out over the railing toward the shore. Although they were all playing their casual, scripted roles to lure their French comrades into a false sense of security, they were tense and alert as they waited to make their deadly move.

All they needed was for one Frenchman to step away to do his daily business, so the numbers would be more in their favor. Soon the opportunity they had been anxiously awaiting presented itself. Kidd felt his heart rate click up a notch, as he saw a French *flibustier* stand up from the game of dice and head toward the "seat of ease"—a wooden plank with a hole near the bow. Kidd scanned the shoreline to make sure none of the troops was returning. The coast was clear. With a mere tip of his head, he now gave the signal to move into position and take out their designated targets.[25]

Discreetly removing their daggers and swords, Kidd, Culliford, Mason, Burgess, Browne, and the others stepped quickly but nonchalantly toward the unsuspecting Frenchmen. For the honor of king and country, but mostly for a new prize ship and the spoils of war that would belong to them and them alone, they were about to betray and kill shipmates who had been their brothers in arms for the past six months. Despite their mixed feelings, they moved in swiftly for the kill, for to hesitate could very well mean failure. If their attempt to dispatch the enemy and steal the ship proved unsuccessful, they would all be summarily executed. And if their adversaries somehow managed to ring an alarm bell or fire one of the cannons, the Anglo-Americans' chances of escape would be slim, even if they managed to eliminate or incapacitate all twelve of the French enemy who had remained behind to guard the *Sainte Rose*.

As it turned out, the Frenchmen never saw them coming.

The Gallic chatter ceased abruptly as the startled enemy seamen, finally cognizant of what was happening, looked up with alarm from their pipes, rum bottles, and games of chance. Kidd and his small but highly motivated squadron pitched into their former Brethren of the Coast and newfound enemies with their stabbing, thrusting, and slashing steel weaponry—dispatching some instantly and wounding others.[26] The lightning quickness of the attack was astounding, and the deck swiftly turned to a confused melee. Bodies flew past in a blur; crimson sprays and mists of blood spurted across the deck; caught-off-guard victims collapsed with loud thuds on the hardwood planking; and primitive-sounding screams and grunts filled the air as England and France made war in miniature aboard the privateer *Sainte Rose*.

The battle soon wound down, leaving the deck drenched with blood. It flowed into the scuppers and turned the shimmering aquamarine Caribbean waters a diluted red. Though outnumbered three to two, the Britons had suffered not a single man killed in the engagement and only two wounded, compared to twelve Frenchmen either killed outright or wounded and thrown overboard to swim ashore. Once they had won the battle and taken control of the ship, they bandaged their two wounded comrades and prepared to make quickly for Nevis before DuCasse and de Blénac realized they had been duped.[27]

Having already been voted captain, the senior sailor Kidd took charge of the vessel. There wasn't time to take up the anchor with the French forces all around them, so the victors chopped the thick anchor cable and hauled on the jib's halyard. Even though the prize vessel lay in less than thirty feet of water, the anchor was embedded in the sandy bottom with around eighty feet of cable laid out. To bring up the anchor with the grindingly slow capstan and winch would take too long: the French navy would be on them before the anchor reached halfway to the ship's hawsehole. With the braided rope cable cut and the sails unfurled, they sped southward along the jagged, sandy coastline and toward the Narrows. This was the two-mile-wide strait they had to cross to safely reach the nearby English-controlled island of Nevis. Kidd and the seven Anglo-American privateers making up his new crew swiftly put a half league (a modern mile and a half) between themselves and St. Christopher.[28]

But they were not home free just yet.

As THE BRISTLING cannons of Fort Charles came into view, Kidd breathed a sigh of relief. The crossing of the Narrows had been nerve-racking, but he and his shipmates had managed to evade the French war fleet and make it to Nevis unscathed. Soon they would sail triumphantly into the English stronghold of Charles Town Harbor with their captured enemy prize.[29]

Prior to being sighted by Christopher Columbus in 1493, the volcanic island of Nevis had been settled for more than two thousand years by Kalinago or Carib Natives, who called the verdant islet rising out of the Caribbean *Oualie*—Land of Beautiful Waters. Over the centuries, the indigenous people had for the most part been wiped out or enslaved by European interlopers from Spain and England. Now the Land of Beautiful Waters served as the colonial capital of the Leeward Islands and the most important island in the English colony due to the high quality of its sugarcane. The lucrative sugar trade was fueled by the Age of Enlightenment's revolution in consumer tastes from the emerging coffeehouses of London, Paris, and Amsterdam.[30]

The *Sainte Rose* passed a long, sandy beach north of the harbor that ran along the western coast of Nevis. Off the larboard beam, the island's central volcanic peak soared more than three thousand feet above the shimmering ocean, its top shrouded in a fleecy swirl of white clouds. At the base of the cratered volcano, an overgrown jungle of evergreen trees formed a collar around the gracefully curved cone; and rising up from the lush greenery Kidd saw several plunging gorges and fumaroles slowly releasing volcanic gas and steam.[31] Beneath Nevis Peak, verdant untamed jungle, sugarcane fields, and plantation homes stretched toward the sparkling Caribbean along a gently sloping plain. Three generations into the future, on this little tropical island of forced enslavement and cane sugar, another legendary and controversial Anglo-American would be born: Alexander Hamilton. William Kidd and the future military officer, patriot, statesman, and fellow New Yorker were much alike. Forced to fend for themselves at an early age, they were both energetic, demanding, and hardworking overachievers, with chips on their shoulders from their tumultuous childhoods as common-born subjects of England in a rigidly hierarchical age.[32]

When Kidd and his men reached the harbor, they dropped anchor in four fathoms (24 feet) of water, across from the town and just north of the fort. Charles Town served principally as an English naval base, slave way station, and profitable sugar-milling operation.[33] Government officials and civilians hurried about the waterfront, while red-coated soldiers stood at the ready at the 26 battlement cannons of Fort Charles.[34]

Soon, a longboat bearing colonial magistrates and soldiers rowed out to greet the new arrivals. Kidd informed the delegation that they had just seized a French prize at Basseterre Harbor and wished to make an immediate report to Colonel Christopher Codrington, the English governor of the Leeward Islands. He was disappointed to learn that Codrington was not presently on the island, though he was expected soon from Antigua. Kidd and his men had hoped to secure a new military commission or "letter of marque," this time from the English Crown, to fight against the French as licensed privateers and to legally seize enemy ships.

After leaving behind a two-man watch to safeguard the *Sainte Rose*, Kidd went ashore with Culliford, Mason, Burgess, and the remainder of the men. For many of the randy privateers, particularly the twenty-three-year-old Robert Culliford, it was time to celebrate their victory by getting snot-slinging drunk and going a-whoring.[35]

Nine days later—on August 7, 1689—William Kidd was summoned to the Crown-appointed colonial governor's office to deliver his official report. He and his fellow privateers had spread themselves between their newly captured gunship and the ordinaries in town, refitting the frigate by day and reveling by night, while awaiting the governor's return and their letter of marque. Colonel Christopher Codrington, commander in chief of all English forces in the Leeward Islands, had sailed from nearby Antigua, slipped through Captain DuCasse's prowling flotilla after a bloody battle at Barbuda against two hundred French and Irish soldiers, and arrived on Nevis earlier in the day.[36]

In preparation for the meeting, Kidd tied back his long, reddish-brown hair with a satin bow and put on his best clothes from his wooden trunk: a long, battered, deep-cuffed velvet coat, knee breeches, silk stockings—and silver-buckled shoes, which he rarely wore. The donning of new clothes, especially those taken from ships' officers or passengers, was one important way in which commerce raiders in the seventeenth century could snub their noses at hierarchical conventions and assert their status.[37] Sashed about his waist were a brace of pistols, and on his hip he brandished his sheathed sword, cleaned of the lingering traces of French blood. At this stage of his career, he likely did not wear a gentleman's wig; but by the time he returned to New York in March 1691 he would wear wigs regularly and be considered a "Gent."[38]

In the one and only portrait produced in his own lifetime, the famous early-eighteenth-century oil painting by Sir James Thornhill first sketched when Kidd went before the House of Commons at age forty-six, he wears a shoulder-length brown wig and bears intelligent and penetrating eyes, full lips poised in a cocksure half-smile, a prominent nose, a high forehead, and the lean yet sturdy frame of a lifelong mariner. He is a supremely confident man, one who does not suffer fools or shy away from a good old-fashioned sword or pistol fight. In contrast, the thirty-four-year-old William Kidd about to meet with Governor Christopher Codrington on Nevis Island in early August 1689 was rough around the edges and not nearly as self-assured.

He walked the short distance to the governor's office overlooking the wide, curving bay. Charles Town was affluent: most of the buildings were two-story, English colonial-style or plantation-style edifices built of a combination of brick, stone, and sturdy tropical wood.[39] The seat of government of the English Leeward Islands was located in the courthouse a block off the waterfront, with second-floor offices for the governor and his council.[40]

When Kidd entered the English governor's *sanctum sanctorum*, Colonel Codrington greeted him cordially. Though the governor was wary of privateers, contending that the authority of their captain "is precarious and his motives dependent on a multitude of uncertain humors which it is next to impossible to reconcile," he was thrilled to have the feisty Kidd and his scrappy sea dogs ready and willing to fight for him. Any squadron of Englishmen hardy enough to seize an enemy ship by force and swiftly dispatch or neutralize all the combatants on board, without a single casualty, was what he desperately needed right now, especially with St. Christopher having fallen to the French.[41]

An able administrator and military leader, Christopher Codrington was the most powerful man in the West Indies and one of the richest planters in the Americas. By the dawning of the Glorious Revolution, he had built up his sugar empire through a combination of business acumen and subterfuge, the latter through the acquisition of neighboring estates, emerging by 1685 as the owner of several of the largest plantations on Barbados, Antigua, and Barbuda. In the process, he had made many of his fellow English gentry envious and gained "a reputation as a ruthless, money-obsessed tyrant, a bully and a philanderer."[42] By 1670, he was also accused of being a "murderer," through the alleged poisoning of one Henry Willoughby, a rival claimant to a neighboring Barbadian plantation that Codrington acquired. Though never formally charged for the crime, Codrington had been forced to leave Barbados under a cloud of suspicion.[43]

His main estate was on his five-hundred-acre sugar plantation in Antigua's Old North Sound division, known as Betty's Hope, but he had a sizable house in the port town of Falmouth as well. He owned the entire island of Barbuda, which had been given to him by England's ruling monarch in 1685 in response to Codrington's ambitious plan to use it to breed enslaved Africans like a horse stud farm to fill the ranks of the field workers on his growing sugar plantations.[44] Like any self-respecting English business tycoon and public official in the late seventeenth century, with the outbreak of war he would use the conflict to patriotically expand the English Empire but also to further his own pecuniary interests. The spoils of war would come in the form of captured booty from French sugar plantations, enslaved Black African laborers, and luscious French concubines, the latter of which would serve the dual purpose of augmenting his prodigious fortune and, with his wife, Gertrude, having passed away in 1670, satisfying his fleshly desires.[45]

After offering Kidd a glass of Madeira, the governor had the animated mariner recount Captain Jean-Baptiste DuCasse and Comte de Blénac's invasion as well as the seizure of the *Sainte Rose* from the French. Based on Kidd's intelligence and his own, Codrington would, eight days later, write a detailed letter to the Lords of Trade and Plantations in London, describing the state of the war and putting "Captain Kidd" into the history books for the very first time in his life:

> On the 7th inst. I arrived here and found a French ship of sixteen guns that had been surprised and captured by the English. She was formerly a privateer manned by a hundred and thirty English and French, but mostly French. All but twenty of them made a descent on St. Christopher, leaving the ship at anchor at Basseterre with twelve French and eight English on board. The last named set upon the French, soon overcame them without the loss of a man and brought the ship in here. She is now fitting for the king's service, her captain being William Kidd. This vessel with my two sloops is all our strength at sea.[46]

The two men sipped their wine and talked some more. Before laying out Kidd's future role as a duly commissioned privateer in Codrington's private Royal Navy, the governor summarized the miserable state of affairs in the West Indies. Kidd already knew that St. Christopher had fallen two days earlier, on August 5. The last of the troops and inhabitants of the English sector of the island were still straggling into Charles Town.

His majesty's redcoats, who hadn't been paid in six years, stumbled out of rowboats and periaugers with black powder on their faces, wearing tattered rags for uniforms. Many of the fleeing English troops and citizens of St. Christopher had lost everything except the clothes on their backs and the few trinkets or coins they had managed to carry with them.[47]

When the island fell, Comte de Blénac, the governor-general of the French West Indies, and his victorious invaders carried out an orgy of drunken pillaging and destruction, carting off whatever loot they could find and hauling the portable plunder aboard their twenty-two warships. During the rampage, they torched the houses of all the English living on the island, except those willing to convert publicly to Catholicism, and seized hundreds of farm animals, leaving many to die. The English half of the island was now a barren wasteland, and the loss of the strategic redoubt to the French proved a crushing blow to Codrington and English interests in the West Indies.[48]

Codrington proceeded to lay out Kidd's terms of service on behalf of the Crown. Before the governor's arrival on Nevis, Kidd and his crew had volunteered to fight as lawful privateers on behalf of His Majesty King William. But like all duly licensed commerce raiders operating under a governmental commission in time of war, they fully expected to collect their fair share of the spoils upon fulfilling the military objectives laid out in their letter of marque—after the deduction of the Crown's tenth, the governor's cut (typically 15 percent), and the up-front costs for outfitting the ship. Because the *Sainte Rose* had been taken in war as a lawful prize by Kidd and his crew and thus was not subjected to condemnation and sale under Admiralty law, Codrington recognized Kidd and his men as the ship's legal owners and agreed to outfit the man-of-war at the Crown's expense—provided Kidd and his crew used it exclusively to fight the French.

Privateering as a seafaring profession for both patriotism and profit has existed at least as far back as the Roman Republic, when General Marc Antony hired "pirates" to fight alongside him in the Battle of Actium in 31 BCE.[49] Privateering ships and the privateersmen who manned them (both are referred to as "privateers") served the function of an auxiliary, cost-free navy that were recruited, commissioned, and unleashed upon the enemy when the resources of combatant European nations were overextended.[50] Indeed, the fledgling United States of America would never have won its Revolution against Great Britain between 1776 and 1783 without its fleet of privateers that captured between 1,600 and 1,800 British prizes—crippling the Mother Country by transferring between £7.4 and £8.4 million ($1.6–$1.8 billion today) into colonial American coffers.[51]

The choice of targets of Captain Kidd and his men, and the sharing of spoils, were spelled out in the formal letter of marque prepared by Codrington, a detailed contract that outlined the conditions of the privateering business arrangement between the English commander in chief and Kidd and his warrior-sailors. The agreement ensured that any captured prizes could be legally condemned and that the war booty would be divided amongst the royal governor, the owners of the ship, the Crown, and the officers and seamen in strict accordance with the written agreement.[52]

Privateers like Kidd were, in essence, licensed pirates under the assumption that "the state had the jurisdiction, the legal authority, the moral legitimacy, and the practical ability to allow or disallow armed commerce."[53] However, in practice, the imperialistic European states in the Age of Sail often lacked legal or moral legitimacy in the eyes of their citizens, and the line between privateers and pirates was often hazy, as the difference between a legitimate versus an illegitimate prize was determined by which side of the Atlantic one happened to live on and constantly shifting European alliances.[54] Thus, as the Atlantic scholar Lauren Benton has pointed out, letters of marque "could be broadly interpreted to permit attacks on a wide range of targets."[55] This legal twilight zone between privateers and pirates made it easier for American public officials and colonists to oppose their English king and his Navigation Acts that severely restricted their oceanic commerce, and to countenance piracy when it was in their economic interests. And as Captain Kidd would soon find out, his own men—Robert Culliford, William Mason, Samuel Burgess, and John Browne—had a far different interpretation of what it meant to fight for king and country and take seafaring prizes than did their patriotic privateer commander whom they had voted to lead them in battle.[56]

At the end of the meeting, Codrington gave Kidd his official sailing orders. He was to outfit his new ship and sign on more men to fight on behalf of the Crown, since the promised Royal Navy fleet was not expected to arrive from London before September (actually, unbeknownst to Codrington, the English fleet would not make landfall in the West Indies for more than nine months, in May 1690).[57] Kidd estimated that he needed seventy more sailors to man the privateer's sixteen carriage guns. Codrington offered to help him round up more seamen with fighting experience and lend him four more guns to bring his total to twenty iron cannons for his majesty's service.[58]

The terms of the commission would be "no purchase, no pay," which was the standard contract for privateers and was referred to by seamen as "no prey, no pay." In its simplest form, it meant wreak bloody hell on enemy shipping and port towns and collect pay in the form of captured booty—ships, cannons, firearms, gold, silver, jewels, textiles, farm animals, produce, and enslaved laborers—whenever and wherever possible. Especially coveted were the Spanish silver coins known as "pieces of eight," which served as legal tender throughout the Americas, Europe, and the Near and Far East and as the primary global currency for trade, carrying the same preeminent standing in financial transactions as today's U.S. dollar. Allowing soldiers and sailors to seize Spanish silver and other war booty as payment for their wartime service allowed colonial governors like Codrington to keep their expenses down, since military salaries and reimbursement by the Crown were routinely delayed.[59]

If a raid was successful, the loot would be shared equitably amongst Kidd, his officers, and crew members, with predetermined ratios based on shipboard position, skill, and length of service. On the other hand, if the expedition was only modestly successful, or failed completely in extracting booty, Kidd and his men might receive only a minuscule share or nothing at all. On a privateer ship, the captain, first mate, quartermaster, and other skilled positions received significantly larger shares than the crew, whereas on a pirate ship the captain and senior crew members typically received only one and a half to three times as much as their crews received. This made pirate ships far more democratic than naval and merchant vessels and somewhat more democratic than privateering vessels, where the captain still retained clear command.[60]

As the meeting came to a close, Kidd couldn't believe his good fortune. Last week, he had been a common seaman scraping out an existence as a *flibustier* for the Frenchies; now he was a privateer captain bearing the king's colors and commanding his own 20-gun ship and crew that he would lead into battle on behalf of the Crown. He must have felt like his heroes Sir Francis Drake and Sir Henry Morgan returning to port as seafaring knights in shining armor. At the same time, it was going to be a daunting task to turn back the French now that they had gained the upper hand in the Leeward Islands. DuCasse and Comte de Blénac commanded a formidable fleet of twenty-two total ships, including eight powerful men-of-war. With that kind of firepower, they could take Nevis, Antigua, Montserrat, and Anguilla in a month's time.[61]

During the meeting, or perhaps in the ensuing days as Kidd fitted out his new warship, the governor, with the captain's blessing, renamed the captured *Sainte Rose* prize the *Blessed William* after England's new monarch and with a nod to the vessel's new commander.[62] William Kidd appreciated the double entendre. He also appears to have at this time bought out the shares in the frigate from William Mason and his other shipmates with his earnings to become the legal owner of the *Blessed William*, which meant that for the first time in his life he was not only a full-fledged sea captain but a ship owner.

Armed with his new commission and 20-gun man-of-war, his world was suddenly filled with hope and promise. When he strutted confidently out of the governor's office on Nevis Island on that steamy hot day of August 7, 1689, Captain William Kidd felt like the King of the New World.

–2–

Fighting for the Crown

In mid-October 1689, Captain William Kidd stood on the quarterdeck of *Blessed William*, squinting into the fading afternoon sunlight. The masthead lookout had spotted a trio of enemy vessels against the verdant tropical jungle backdrop of the island of Dominica. Kidd's orders from Codrington were to sail 315 miles to "Barbados to be furnished with men and ammunition" and "to pick up some French prisoners, especially from Martinique, to give information."[1] He had had no success in his first assigned task of raising troops or securing ammunition from the English colony's stingy government, which was disinclined to lend aid to its fellow Caribbean colonies, and especially Codrington due to the latter's controversial past on the island. But by a simple twist of fate, Kidd now stood poised to achieve his second task and capture some Frenchmen to gather intelligence on Captain Jean-Baptiste DuCasse and Comte de Blénac's battle plans.[2]

The lookout shouted down that the three heavily armed French ships had still not spotted them and were busy loading wood and water. The French, Kidd realized, considered themselves safe in neutral territory and were about to be caught with their breeches down.[3] Grabbing his brass spyglass from its becket, he surveyed the anchored enemy gunships and the lush island behind them. Dominica—inhabited mostly by indigenous Kalinago (Carib) Indians along with a smattering of castaways and runaway slaves—was not controlled by England, France, or Spain.[4] In 1660, the French and English came to an agreement that Dominica and nearby St. Vincent would be left to the Caribs as neutral territory and not be settled by the two European powers. But the island's bountiful timber had recently attracted expeditions of mostly French—and some English—foresters. Kidd had learned that French woodcutters from Martinique and Guadeloupe had set up timber camps to supply their nation's Caribbean possessions with much-needed wood.[5]

Peering through his glass, he was able to differentiate a large brigantine from two smaller sloops next to it.[6] He couldn't believe his good fortune: he truly had caught the enemy by surprise. Clearly, the French had not expected prowling English ships-of-war at the northern tip of the Windward Islands, far from Barbados to the south and Nevis and Antigua to the north.

In the past month, the French had taken not only St. Christopher but also Anguilla, where the victors installed an Irish puppet governor; and they had instigated a rebellion on Montserrat, where the Irish outnumbered the English eight hundred to three hundred.[7] What Codrington and Kidd didn't know was that after the fall of St. Christopher, Captain DuCasse, with eight warships bristling with cannon at his disposal, had wanted to immediately attack Antigua, Nevis, Montserrat, and other English-held islands. But the greedy Comte de Blénac refused and instead returned to the safety of Martinique to auction his loot. By putting personal profit above military exigency, the governor-general of the French West Indies had squandered his tactical advantage and allowed the English of Nevis and the other Leeward Islands to regroup.[8]

Studying the trio of awaiting French prizes through his spyglass, Kidd realized that not only did he have surprise on his side, but also the wind and superior firepower. Deciding to aggressively attack, he quickly informed the captains of the two outfitted sloops sailing under his command, the *Barbuda* and *Hope* belonging to Colonel Codrington, of his battle plans. Then he barked out attack orders to his officers aboard the *Blessed William.*

The deck turned to a flurry of activity. A third of the seamen manned the sails and rigging to close fast on the French vessels, while the other two-thirds dashed belowdecks to join the chief gunner and his gun crew in readying the cannons to open fire.

The crew of the *Blessed William* numbered around a hundred men, mostly veteran buccaneers and merchant seamen but with a sprinkling of young landsmen caught up in the patriotism of the moment. Ethnically, it was a motley collection of mostly White provincial English-Americans acclimated to the New World, newly arrived Englishmen and Scotsmen from the British Isles, and a smattering of Dutchmen, French Huguenots, free Africans, and West Indians. Dressed in eclectic clothing, they looked far more like a band of pirates than a Royal Navy crew, since few owned even a secondhand military uniform. Perpetually on the move, privateers and pirates alike had fewer resources than their counterparts on land and had to take what they could get whenever possible. For weapons, most of the men carried at least one pistol, cartridge boxes, a dagger, and a cutlass for boarding actions and attacking towns.[9]

Unlike many of the seamen under his command, Captain Kidd was an educated man who could read and write and trace his roots to a common but respectable Protestant Christian family from Soham Parish, Cambridgeshire, England.[10] Having gone away to sea at an early age as an apprentice or cabin boy from the port town of Dundee, Scotland, he possessed ample nautical skills developed from the hard experience of a life at sea and thorough training in mathematics and navigation.[11] He also had a little salty roguishness in him from spending the last two decades in the Americas sailing, fighting, and drinking with rowdy, violent, and vulgar buccaneers and merchant seamen. Whether he had in fact served under the most famous buccaneer of all time, Sir Henry Morgan (1635–1688), is conjectural, but there is no doubt that William Kidd had been a young, patriotic English privateer sticking it to imperial Spain by the mid-1670s.[12]

The original *boucaniers* were a group of mostly French commerce raiders that emerged in the first half of the seventeenth century from the landless hunters of wild cattle, boars, and goats in the uninhabited regions of French Hispaniola (modern-day Haiti) and Tortuga, a small island off the northwest coast of Hispaniola. By the 1650s, the original buccaneers had gained significant English and Dutch recruits and soon evolved into Henry Morgan's romanticized, English-heavy pillagers. After Jamaica was seized from Spain in 1655, the colony's governors and merchants hired the buccaneers to discourage Spanish counterassaults and launch attacks from the base of Port Royal to undermine the Spanish Empire. This second wave of Caribbean Sea rovers plundered Spanish vessels and sacked Portobelo, Maracaibo, Panama City, and other gold- and silver-rich cities along the Spanish Main with nationalistic relish and ferocity between 1665 and 1675.[13]

Thus, the term *buccaneer* is not another name for pirate, sea robber, or freebooter. Instead, the moniker originally referred to the roving bands of sailors, dyewood cutters, tobacco planters, and liberated indentured servants of western Hispaniola and Tortuga who dried the meat from the wild animals they hunted on a *boucan*, the French corruption of the word *mukem*, a wooden grill first invented by the indigenous Brazilian Tupí-Guaraní. Because Europeans only knew how to preserve meat with salt, a scarce product in the tropics, French seafarers were keen to adopt local methods for meat preservation, and the term "buccaneer" thus originated from the French, based upon the Tupí-Guaraní word for meat-smoker. In addition to hunting wild animals and selling the valuable hides, these tough, hardy, sharpshooting frontiersmen began preying on small Spanish vessels, with raiding eventually becoming their primary activity. By the 1670s, the English had adopted the term "buccaneer" to refer to all non-Catholic European maritime raiders who plundered the Spanish on land and by sea in the Caribbean to weaken Spain's grip in the New World.[14]

The original buccaneers were, thus, transformed from the band of French-heavy hunter-pirates of Hispaniola into the English-dominant commerce raiders of late-seventeenth-century Jamaica. In waging war upon the Spanish Empire, the buccaneers often deployed as a land force rather than a maritime squadron, using their ships as transports in amphibious assaults upon colonial towns. During these raids, they relied on the support of the local tribesmen of Central America and the Caribbean as scouts, guides, and allied combatants. The swashbuckling tales of these multiethnic English, French, and Dutch buccaneers during Henry Morgan's time, the group to which Kidd belonged, have been well documented by the Dutch-French surgeon and former indentured servant Alexandre Olivier Exquemelin in his legendary *History of the Buccaneers of America*.[15]

At first, these Brethren of the Coast served as an auxiliary navy of patriotic raiders chivalrously defending Mother England's honor against the Spanish Empire and acting as a militant vanguard of Protestant English expansion. But over time, the Jamaican planter aristocracy came to resent having to rely on the Caribbean marauders as their protectors, considering them excessively democratic, free-spirited, and difficult to control.[16] The buccaneers' lifestyle was built upon a surprisingly modern-like, egalitarian political framework "free of the restrictions of an unjust society upheld by a punitive legal system."[17] This homegrown system of "direct democracy" resulted in a unique "brotherhood" defined by honor, trust, integrity, and lending a helping hand to those in need. It played a huge role in nurturing William Kidd's core democratic value system and his well-documented generosity. Indeed, during his seafaring career, he would employ African Americans, Native Americans, East Indians, and Jews as share-earning stakeholders aboard his privateering ships-of-force.[18]

Now, with the French enemy in his sights, the experienced buccaneer Captain Kidd crowded on the canvas and let his newly acquired gunship run before the wind. Standing on the deck nearby were chief gunner Robert Culliford, born in Cornwall, England; colonial New Yorker William Mason, his senior officer and a future captain; and Samuel Burgess, the *Blessed William*'s quartermaster, also a born-and-bred New

Yorker. Like Kidd, all three were educated men who could read and write. He had sailed with them at least since signing the *Sainte Rose*'s articles in early 1689 at Île-à-Vache, and may have known them from New York where he owned property. Also working the deck nearby was the illiterate English commoner John Browne, who at around forty was ancient by seventeenth-century seamen's standards. Browne, who would settle in New York in 1693 along with Samuel Burgess, would serve under Captain Kidd twice in his lengthy seafaring career.[19]

As the 20-gun ship-of-force knifed through the white-tipped waves off the Dominica coast, closing to within a half league of the vessels, Kidd saw the panicked French crews and their Kalinago woodcutters and comrades in arms scrambling about the decks of the three ships. He commanded his chief gunner to roll out the cannons. Below on the main deck, the boarding party stood by the railing, gripped with anticipation, led by quartermaster Samuel Burgess. The men were armed to the teeth with not only boarding knives, cutlasses, muskets, and pistols, but blunderbusses and fuse-lit grenadoes consisting of gunpowder, bits of metal, and fuses stuffed into empty rum and wine bottles. They waved their weapons menacingly to strike fear into the French captains and their crews as well as the Kalinago auxiliaries, hoping to scare them into surrendering without a fight. Privateers and pirates both preferred their enemies to submit without violence through a mere show of force to limit combat injuries and maximize profits.[20] Though patriotic privateers did indeed fight in the name of king and country, they were still mostly in it for the money, just like unlicensed freebooters.[21]

Now Kidd gave the order to fire a pair of warning shots across the bow of the brigantine—a double across her forefoot—demanding that the French surrender right away or suffer the consequences. The first cannon erupted along the starboard gunport, followed quickly by another blast. The shots screamed across the water and over the bow of the brigantine. The French and Kalinago dove for cover as the cannonballs flew overhead and crashed into the thick jungle foliage. The warning shots sent a clear message: yield and strike the colors immediately, without a fight—or all three enemy ships would be blasted to kingdom come.[22]

Convinced that he and his men were about to meet a gruesome end from a pack of bloodthirsty Englishmen bent on revenge for the orgy of violence wreaked weeks earlier upon St. Christopher,[23] the French commander ordered the three crews and their Kalinago auxiliaries to prepare their longboats and dugout canoes to make their escape. Less than five minutes later, the French sailors had tossed basic supplies—food, water, small arms, and medicine—into their boats and beat a hasty retreat ashore, along with the Kalinago, who outnumbered the Frenchmen. Scattering into the tropical jungle, the enemy swiftly vanished from sight.[24]

The boarding parties threw grapnel irons over the side and lashed the three French ships to the English vessels. Once gangplanks were lowered, the boarding parties poured across the bridge and over the rails to seize the enemy gunships. Soon thereafter, the quartermasters and their prize crews had inventoried and ransacked the brigantine and two sloops for their valuables, and Kidd's flotilla—now six ships strong instead of three—was off and cruising out to sea once again.[25]

The privateer fleet returned home triumphantly with the three French prizes in tow, dropping anchor in Falmouth Harbor, Antigua, a month after setting sail.[26] On the way back to port, Kidd recruited Captain Thomas Hewetson, commander of the Royal Navy ship *Lion*, armed with 48 guns and crewed by a 150 men.[27] Colonel Codrington, who had been "apprehensive" with Kidd gone so long, was quite pleased to see him. Not only was he thrilled that his protégé had taken three French prizes without a single loss of life, but he was also ecstatic that Kidd had landed the experienced Hewetson and his reinforcements.[28] Hewetson, who was known by the French as a "*scélérat cruel*" (vicious rogue) and "*soudard*" (old ruffian), was hired on the spot on November 22 by the wealthy commander in chief.[29]

With the scrappy Kidd and Hewetson, Codrington now had two seasoned commanders to take the fight to the formidable Captain DuCasse and his French *flibustiers*.

On the day after Christmas, December 26, 1689, Governor Christopher Codrington held a war council with his top lieutenants: Captain William Kidd; the newly hired "old ruffian" Captain Thomas Hewetson; and a third commander, Captain Perry. The goal of the meeting was to work out the final details of a planned attack on the French-held island Marie-Galante. Itching to turn the tide of the war in the West Indies, the governor believed that the important French possession to the south was as good a place as any to start.[30]

Kidd found Captain Hewetson a colorful character, and the two had become fast friends over the past several weeks and would remain bosom buddies for years to come. In 1688, Hewetson had set off from England with an expedition to the South Sea (Pacific Ocean) to set up a colony on the Pacific coast of South America in Chile. But in a voyage straight from the pages of English novelist Daniel Defoe's *Robinson Crusoe*, Hewetson had been unable to beat through the Magellan Straits and was forced to turn back to Tobago. Here he discovered that the change of regime from the Catholic James II to the Protestant William III had rendered his original commission invalid. To make matters worse, he had suffered the misfortune of losing one of the five English ships under his command in a storm off the coast of Chile, and then another when it exploded from a gunpowder-room accident off Barbados, killing seventy of his seamen.[31]

Following the conflagration, the good citizens of Barbados, instead of coming to the aid of the damaged vessel, demonstrated their loyalty to the naval forces protecting their shores by swarming onto the scene and pilfering as many of the shipborne goods that had survived the blast as possible. Barbadian lieutenant governor Edwin Stede ordered that all the "embezzled goods" be restored but with little result, which enraged Hewetson. Given the difficulties encountered on the voyage and now in port in Barbados, most of his men had deserted. He was planning to sail home as escort to a merchant convoy when Bermuda governor Sir

Robert Robinson issued him a new royal commission in mid-October, giving him a fresh start. After raising a crew of over a 150 "lusty men" for his flagship *Lion*, he was soon recruited by Kidd to join him in Antigua and offer his services to Codrington.[32]

Over rum punches, the war council began and the governor got right to the point. Hewetson would be in overall command of the attack on Marie-Galante. He and his 48-gun *Lion* would be joined by Kidd's *Blessed William* of 20 guns, Captain Perry's *Speedwell* armed with 10 cannons, and Codrington's 2 troop transports, the *Barbuda* and *Hope*. The assault force would consist of 540 men, and the remuneration terms would be the usual "no purchase, no pay." The 61-square-mile island, first sighted by Europeans on November 3, 1493, during the second voyage of Columbus and named after his flagship *Maria Galanda*, was home to more than a thousand French settlers and teeming with rich sugar plantations.[33]

The attack of the English land and sea forces would take place at dawn on December 30. Codrington's objective was to force the French to think twice about attacking Antigua and Nevis. At present, DuCasse controlled the high seas and Codrington wanted to hit the enemy where they least expected it. The French had seized Anguilla and St. Christopher; now the English would retaliate in kind by targeting a small but important French stronghold in the southern Leeward Islands off Guadeloupe. A victory would keep the French at bay while giving the men valuable fighting experience, rally the citizenry of the English-held possessions, and keep the Irish from joining the French in all-out war.[34]

Sitting back in his rattan chair and sipping his rum punch, Captain Kidd quite agreed. He, too, was itching to fight for king and country.

The five-ship fleet set sail from Falmouth Harbor on Saturday, December 28, 1689, on the hundred-mile southward journey to Marie-Galante. The next night, as the attacking force drew closer to the designated French target, the air was gripped with pre-battle tension as the men sharpened their daggers and cutlasses, cleaned their muskets, checked their powder, and made their final preparations for the dawn attack.[35]

The assault fleet reached the island in darkness on the appointed Sunday and assembled near midnight. Well acquainted with the local waters, Kidd instructed Hewetson on where best to lay anchor so that their predawn sail would land them at sunrise at a beach four miles from Grand Bourg, the island's principal town. With the attack plan laid out, the five vessels, bristling with warriors and tremendous firepower, mustered just off the empty beach with their sails furled.[36]

The next morning, the sunlight crept like a stalking feline over the palm trees along the southwest tip of the island and touched upon the anchored gunships. As the first rays glimmered off Captain Kidd's powerful iron carriage guns and brass chasers on the bow and stern, he quietly gave orders to his crew to lower the longboats.[37]

A score of pinnaces from the *Lion*, *Blessed William*, *Speedwell*, *Barbuda*, and *Hope* dribbled into the water. Within minutes, they were loaded with 440 men armed with pistols, swords, blunderbusses, muskets, and pikes ferried in a convoy to shore, leaving Kidd with a hundred men to sail the warships and fire the cannons. The privateer commander sighted his 12- and 18-pounders on the palm trees along the shoreline, where he suspected French soldiers lay in ambush. But he saw no sign of the enemy and there was no resistance on the beach to Hewetson and his men. Once ashore, the "old ruffian" led the powerful land force along the coastal road toward Grand Bourg. Kidd waited to make sure Hewetson didn't come under attack before giving the order to set sail with the fleet for the seaborne assault on the fort and town.[38]

The flotilla moved steadily along the coast toward Grand Bourg. Soon, off the square-rigged *Blessed William* frigate's starboard bow, Hewetson began to encounter small knots of skirmishers. The French soldiers were trying to buy time for the townspeople and other citizens to make their escape to the interior of the island.[39]

Called *Touloukaera* (the Island of Red Crabs) by the Arawak, Marie-Galante was known by the French as *la Grande Galette*—the Big

Biscuit—due to its circular shape.[40] The island's economy was based on the cultivation of sugar, indigo, tobacco, coffee, and cotton—but it was cane sugar that dominated its trade. The French operated over fifty sugar mills on the broad plateau in the center of the island and the surrounding coastal plain. Looking through his spyglass, Kidd located the island's highest peak, Morne Constant, rising over 650 feet above the surrounding ocean and below which sugarcane fields spread as far as the eye could see.[41]

With a strong onshore breeze at their backs, Kidd directed the fleet in a zigzag pattern through the channel leading into the harbor.[42] The French fort had been built into a promontory overlooking the oval harbor. Kidd spotted the black cannon muzzles protruding from the square-cut gunports between embrasures notched into the west- and south-facing walls. The little town a quarter mile west of the gun emplacements consisted of white stucco buildings with red-tiled roofs. Inside the harbor, a dozen or so merchant ships and smaller vessels were anchored side by side, stern in, within pistol shot of the wooden wharf.[43]

He ordered his chief gunner to make ready the cannons. He could hear up the coast the steady *pop-pop* of Hewetson fighting the French rear-guard ambuscades. Entering the harbor, the five-man-of-war flotilla looked majestic yet menacing with its bristling cannons in the gunports and swivel guns peering out at Grand Bourg like eighty black iron eyes. With the heavily armed English warships fast approaching, the civilians at the battlements and beyond scrambled to get out of town as the military forces dashed about the walls of the city and the fort's batteries to man the cannons.[44]

Now Kidd gave the order to open fire upon the fort with the carriage guns. A dozen or more of the heavy cannons from the *Lion* and *Blessed William* rolled out one by one for the bombardment. A moment later, the morning air was shattered by a thunderous, crackling roar. Tongues of flame and smoke jumped from the gunports along the lengths of the attacking warships. The stone ramparts and gunports shuddered upon the impact of the heavy iron projectiles.[45]

The French cannons returned a brisk fire on the five approaching warships. The Britons aboard the hundred-ton *Blessed William* and other vessels hit the deck as lances of cannonade streaked toward them.[46] Several of the cast-iron orbs fired by the French shredded sails, damaged masts and rigging, and splintered wooden rails, but none of the warships in Kidd's fleet was crippled and no crew members appear to have been slain, though some may have sustained injuries. Kidd's seamen kept an alert eye toward the French bastion, since round shot often tore through more than one man during exchanges of heavy cannon fire, causing multiple casualties. Cannonballs also ricocheted when they hit the deck and masts, snapping taut lines and cracking them across crew members like bullwhips.[47]

The warships continued to pound the fort. Belches of fire leaped all down the line, as if from the mouths of dragons. Whistling cannonballs blasted the walls and turrets of the fort, bringing down huge blocks of battered stone with a wrenching crash. The embattled fortress was soon wreathed in a halo of dust and smoke. At the same time, heavy iron balls volleyed toward the ships, flying over the decks and splashing in the water. It was a credit to the French that they continued to put up a fight when they were under such heavy attack on both land and sea.[48]

But they were unable to hold out for long.

The devastating cannonade by Kidd, coupled with the steady advancing and firing of Hewetson's muscular infantry column, proved too much for the defenders. The remaining French troops attempted to rally, but soon abandoned their defensive line and the fortress by retreating into the town en masse.[49] Meanwhile, the townspeople rushed to gather their family heirlooms, money, and jewels, so they could flee along footpaths into the jungle as the rear guard of soldiers were forced to leave Grand Bourg to the mercy of the English invaders.[50]

With the town fallen, Kidd captured a pair of well-stocked merchant ships in the harbor recently arrived from France. Then, just as Grand Bourg was being cleared of its last resistance, he was rowed into the port with Captain Perry to join up with Hewetson and the land force.[51]

After Hewetson, Kidd, and Perry raised a toast to the king's health, the victorious trio held a war council at a dockside tavern. They had gained a measure of revenge for the devastation inflicted upon their English brethren at St. Christopher, but their triumph was incomplete. The French governor of Marie-Galante had escaped into the hills with most of the townspeople and many enslaved Africans, lugging as much gold and silver and as many priceless belongings as they could carry. Though Hewetson and Kidd wanted to get cracking after them, they were hesitant to go off on a wild-goose chase, putting the men in jeopardy, especially since darkness would soon be upon them due to the short winter days. Deep in the interior of the island and far from their established base at Grand Bourg, the English scouting and war party might be drawn into a dangerous trap.[52]

With the sun setting, they proceeded instead to work out the details of the occupation. Hewetson decided to let the privateers spend the night searching for hidden valuables, looting the abandoned homes, drinking captured French wine and spirits, and sleeping in real beds.[53]

The next morning, Kidd and Hewetson were informed that a pair of hiding Frenchmen had been discovered and taken captive. The prisoners soon divulged that Marie-Galante's governor, along with most of the French citizens and their slaves, had retreated to an inland entrenchment some twelve miles north of Grand Bourg. They were without artillery and had only the provisions they could carry and a small herd of cattle. The Frenchmen knew the way and were willing to lead Hewetson and his troops there in return for their lives.[54]

The English invaders once again held a war council. Hewetson and Kidd decided to demand the French governor's immediate surrender and sent a company of men with the captured Frenchmen to conduct a parley. Stalling for time, the governor told the English party through a messenger that he would answer by twelve noon the following day; but when noon of January 1 came and went, he still had not issued a response. The English commanders concluded that it was too risky to chase the French so far from the warships or to chance an ambush along the narrow, dangerous footpaths leading to the hideout. Furthermore, it was rumored that the French had already sent for aid to Martinique.[55] Instead, Hewetson ordered the quartermasters to take a final inventory of the town's booty, load the most valuable goods onto the ships, and torch the rest. They also made a final tally of the battle casualties of the land-and-sea engagement: for the Anglo-Americans, three men had been killed and eighteen wounded, while the French suffered more than twenty men killed, with dozens more wounded.[56]

Hewetson and Kidd's force spent the next four days ransacking the manor houses of the sugar plantations, toting valuables to the loading docks, and heaving them aboard the *Blessed William* and *Lion* by runner and tackle. The English marauders then set fire to the homes and sugar works of the French planters, including the cane fields, outbuildings, and profitable cane sugar in giant casks.[57]

While all this looting and destruction was taking place, the English *boucaniers* who had once hunted wild game on Hispaniola and Île-à-Vache slaughtered the livestock. They slit the throats of the bleating bovines, pigs, and horses until they were smeared with blood. The men slaughtered some ten thousand farm animals because there was neither sufficient time to round them all up and load them onto the ships nor enough space in the cargo holds to sail such a vast payload home. Throughout the five-day slaughter and drinking spree, the crews gorged on fresh beef, cooking it over outdoor *boucan*-like spits and in the abandoned kitchens of their vanquished adversaries.[58]

On January 5, 1690, Kidd, Hewetson, and their victorious band of warriors set sail out of Grand Bourg harbor, making their return voyage to Antigua. Kidd had only a little over half of his crew on board the *Blessed William*, as Hewetson had taken forty of his men and put them onto one of the French vessels Kidd had captured in the harbor. The seven ships, loaded down with rich plunder, set out from port together. However, one of the captured French prize ships became separated from the other vessels. The prize crew, sozzled on French wine and Caribbean rum, fell far to leeward, missed their latitude mark, and were forced to tack their way slowly against the prevailing east-to-west winds to reach Antigua. While this bacchanalian crew was delayed, the main body of Hewetson, Kidd, and Perry made their triumphant return into Falmouth Harbor with cannons saluting.[59]

That night, Captain Kidd, Hewetson, and the nearly four hundred returning crewmen divvied up their designated shares of legally obtained war plunder and celebrated in an orgy of drunken revelry.[60]

Five days later, with the captured French prize ship still not returned and one of Codrington's sloops sent out to bring her in, an unknown ship sailed into Falmouth Harbor. A messenger hurried to the governor's mansion to deliver the disastrous news of another French attack. An English expedition, this one commanded by Sir Timothy Thornhill, major-general of the English Leeward Islands militia, had been sent from Barbados with a regiment of six hundred men to capture the island of St. Barthélemy. But after taking the tiny, poorly defended island with ease, Thornhill was lulled into thinking he might just as easily capture the nearby plum French possession of St. Martins, which boasted not only rich sugar plantations but valuable natural salt ponds. The Barbadian commander and his men quickly found themselves trapped by that ever-present thorn in the English side, the cunning jack-in-the-box DuCasse, who seemed to pop up just when least expected. From the quarterdeck of his 44-gun flagship *Le Hasardeux*, the gallant Frenchman commanded a fleet of three warships, a brigantine, and a sloop. Upon hearing news of the disaster, Codrington summoned Hewetson and Kidd, explained the dire situation to them, and recruited them for a rescue operation.[61]

The rest of the day and that night, the privateer captains refitted their warships and cobbled together a force of 380 men to the patriotic cause, again under "no purchase, no pay." Just before the stroke of midnight and beneath a new moon, the *Lion*, *Blessed William*, and *Speedwell* under Hewetson, Kidd, and Perry sallied forth into the fray once again, to battle the legendary DuCasse and rescue Sir Timothy.[62]

–3–

In Victory and Defeat

Shortly after dawn on January 16, 1690, off the coast of St. Martins, northern Leeward Islands, Captain Kidd felt a thrum of excitement as the French war fleet came into view. Sailing in consort with Hewetson in the *Lion* and Perry in the *Speedwell*, he had packed on the sail canvas all night with the hope of surprising the wily DuCasse anchored at daybreak. Though he and his comrades had endeavored every seafaring trick at their disposal to take the enemy flotilla by surprise, Kidd saw at once that they were too late. With his French lookouts on high alert, Monsieur DuCasse and his squadron of five warships had quickly slipped their cables upon sighting the English fleet and sailed out to give battle.[1]

Standing on the quarterdeck of the *Blessed William* with the sun rising slowly in bright orange on the horizon, Kidd studied the oncoming enemy warships and quickly did the math. The French had the numerical advantage at five to three, but Kidd and his fellow Englishmen had the wind.[2]

Commands resounded across the quarterdeck: Hands to quarters! Battle stations!

The officers and crew dashed about the deck to their designated positions, with most of the men going below to man the ship's full complement of twenty carriage guns. The *Blessed William*'s cream-colored sheets snapped in the strong offshore breeze as the ship-of-war moved steadily toward the enemy flotilla.

It had been two days since the English fleet had sailed out of Falmouth Harbor. Codrington's sloop, sent out to bring home the wayward prize ship on the return journey from Marie-Galante, had failed to locate the vessel in time, forcing Hewetson, Kidd, and Perry to press onward to St. Martins without reinforcements to rescue the embattled Sir Timothy Thornhill and his pinned-down force. En route, they discovered that the French on St. Martins and a group of three hundred Irish refugees had united with DuCasse, bringing the French commander's strength up to a thousand armed men aboard his five ships-of-war. Two or three hundred more were reportedly on their way from St. Christopher "to land and attack Sir Timothy."[3]

Peering through his spyglass, Kidd may have spotted his former commander DuCasse on the quarterdeck of *Le Hasardeux*, sailing at the head of the fleet of three battleships, a brigantine, and a sloop to meet the English attack. If he did, he observed a tall, distinguished-looking military commander with a long Gallic blade of a nose, dimpled chin, intelligent eyes, and a lean physique, bedecked in a black cocked bicorne hat, navy-blue waistcoat with epaulettes and insignia rank in gold shoulder and cuff trim, ruffled shirt and britches, a bright yellow sash about his shoulder, and a sword sheathed in a lengthy scabbard. Born a commoner, like Kidd, in 1646 to French Huguenot parents in the Nouvelle-Aquitaine region of southwest France near the Bay of Biscay, DuCasse had joined the French Royal Navy as a full lieutenant in 1686 and risen swiftly through the ranks due to his skills as a mariner and a bold fighter.[4]

Kidd ordered his chief gunner to make ready the cannons with round shot, followed perhaps by chain or bar shot if they could get close enough. While the heavy, spherical iron balls fired by smooth-bore cannons were used as a long-range anti-personnel weapon and to batter the wooden hulls, rails, and masts of enemy ships, chain shot and bar shot consisted of iron balls linked by a length of chain or solid bar to mow down sailors, slash through rigging and sails, and cripple enemy vessels. Compared to solid cannonball shot, chain or bar shot was inaccurate, with an effective range of a hundred yards.[5]

The five French men-of-war ran out their guns. Swallowing against the knot in his throat, Kidd took in the sun-burnished faces of the hundreds of Frenchmen swarming the decks and counted the total number of cannons. DuCasse had over 120 guns, nearly double the firepower of Hewetson, Kidd, and Perry combined. Not only that, but the French had the better-sailing ships and the more-seasoned crews of *flibustiers*.[6]

Both sides prepared for a traditional line-of-battle sea bout. With each gunship in the opposing fleets following the wake of the vessel ahead at a regularly spaced interval of roughly a hundred yards, the men-of-war would pass each other several hundred yards apart, take aim, and exchange broadsides. If during a pass the ships closed to within effective musket range, approximately two hundred yards, both sides would unleash volleys of small-arms fire, and blasts of chain or bar shot if they could get within a hundred yards.[7]

The English fleet formed a line and continued to sail toward DuCasse and his enemy armada, with Hewetson and his 48-gun *Lion* in the first position, followed by Kidd in the 20-gun *Blessed William* and Perry in the 10-gun *Speedwell*.[8] At this pivotal moment, Kidd must have felt as though everything had led up to today, a life-and-death struggle off St. Martins against the legendary DuCasse in the Year of Our Lord 1690. Since he had been a little cabin boy sailing from the Scottish port of Dundee, he had wanted to fight in a great, bloody sea battle against an able foe—and vanquish him. Right here and now was his chance to play the role of his knighted English seafaring heroes, Sir Francis Drake and Sir Henry Morgan.

Half of DuCasse's 40-plus guns opened up on Hewetson and the *Lion* from his flagship, now broad on the *Blessed William*'s bow. The Frenchman delivered a broadside into the *Lion* at the front of the line. With the advantage of the wind, Hewetson closed on *Le Hasardeux*, narrowing the distance between the two vessels almost to musket range, before returning cannon fire. As the passing line of ships closed the distance, the sniping musketeers on both sides, perched high up in the rigging, tried to pick off opposing officers and crewmen.[9]

Now it was Captain Kidd's turn through the gauntlet. Sailing close to the wind past the line of heavily armed French warships, he waited until he was within effective musket range before unleashing his broadside at DuCasse and *Le Hasardeux*.

The *Blessed William*'s cannons exploded like a crackle of rolling thunder. The gun crews deftly placed the heavy iron shot from the 12- and 18-pounders to rake the Frenchman's three vulnerable mastheads as well as the hull and gunrails as they passed. But DuCasse gave as good as he got, and the railing and salty deck of the *Blessed William* sustained damage from the returning volley. The impact of the cannonballs rocked every timber of the ship and splintered the wood into hundreds of shooting darts, forcing the men on deck to dive for cover.

A naval eyewitness aboard Hewetson's ship described the hot action of the first pass thusly:

> DuCasse gave us his broadside smartly before we fired a gun, and when almost within musket shot we gave him ours; they then opened fire with small arms until they were out of reach, we returning the fire. Having passed him, we received the broadsides of the other four ships successively, which we returned.[10]

The ships "tacked about again" and re-formed the line. This time, the French ships-of-war, being faster vessels and "better manned with sailors," gained the wind.[11] Flames burst from the cannon muzzles as the two sides bombarded each other with broadsides and unleashed small arms. The iron orbs ripped into the rigging and sails of each ship, shredding some of the canvas and splintering wood. Kidd was able to maneuver close enough to fire a deadly round of chain or bar shot, which tore through foresails and eviscerated and maimed French sailors like a terrible tempest sweeping across the deck.[12]

Following the second pass, Hewetson reassembled the English fleet some distance away from the French warships and held a conference with Kidd and Perry. DuCasse had formed up to blockade Sir Timothy Thornhill and his men's escape from the island, which gave Hewetson time to hold the quick council aboard the *Lion*. During the previous night, he had become ill with a fever and was now faring worse. History remains unclear as to whether the man known by the French as *scélérat cruel* formally relinquished his authority to his second-in-command in the fight against DuCasse; but with Hewetson sick, more responsibility definitely fell on Kidd's shoulders.[13]

Thus far, the line-of-battle engagement hadn't been getting them anywhere. DuCasse had the advantage in battleships of five to three, and in a war of attrition Kidd knew that he, Hewetson, and Perry would eventually be vanquished. The French outclassed them and possessed the superior firepower. Although damage was being done to the French, little was being accomplished. Not only that, but Captain Perry and the *Speedwell* were not up to snuff, as the sloop was miserably slow, insufficiently armed, and coming under blistering enemy fire. Never one to lack boldness, Captain Kidd proposed something that two and a half centuries into the future would become a staple of Hollywood swashbucklers: an all-out boarding action.[14]

The veteran buccaneer knew that his rough-and-tumble privateers much preferred close-quarters combat over the tactical, aim-and-fire, count-the-wounded approach of a Royal Navy–style line-of-battle. Furthermore, if his sea dogs could board *Le Hasardeux*, Perry and his snail-paced sloop "would be of good service," whereas at a distance the *Speedwell* could do little since her guns were "too small to do the enemy much harm." It was a Kiddian, devil-may-care buccaneer's move—not a paint-by-numbers Royal Navy maneuver.[15]

With Captain Kidd now in effective command due to Hewetson's illness, the three English vessels tacked way wide to regain the wind. But they failed to outmaneuver the French and were unable to board. For the third time of the day, the ships passed in a line exchanging broadsides. DuCasse landed a pair of well-placed round shots into the *Lion*'s side, and perhaps a shot or two into her sails and rigging. Kidd, too, took a pounding as the *Blessed William* came under heavy cannon fire.[16] Tacking away, Kidd regrouped the fleet and they tried a fourth time to recapture the wind—and this time they succeeded.[17]

Kidd barked out orders to come alongside the enemy flagship and prepare to board. The standard "bloody" red flag, signaling that no quarter would be given unless the enemy immediately surrendered, was run up the rigging. Quartermaster Samuel Burgess, senior officer William Mason, and five dozen armed seamen now crowded the decks, brandishing their cutlasses, flintlocks, fuse-lit grenadoes, and grappling irons, and yelling to intimidate the enemy. They would toss the boarding irons across just before the wooden hulls collided and lash the vessels together amidships to allow the privateers to swarm over the gunwales and onto the opposing ship's deck.[18]

The gun deck sprang to life as well, with the master gunner Robert Culliford loading the guns with cartridges and swan shotpieces of old iron, spick nails, and other lethal odds and ends. The murderous shot would mow down the French like a scythe just before boarding, when the *Blessed William* had neared to within pistol range, or fifty yards.[19]

The *Blessed William* was out front with Hewetson's *Lion* and Perry's *Speedwell* following close astern. The vessels were now at musket range, with the English fleet closing fast. The men waved their flintlocks and steely blades and roared like lions. The boarding action would be a bloody affair, fought in a confined space with nowhere to run or hide.[20]

More orders were given: Hands, grapnels at the ready! Prepare to board! Prepare the guns to fire!

But at that critical moment, a bizarre thing happened. The French let loose a blast of heavy cannon fire at close range and sailed off to the south toward St. Christopher, refusing to engage.[21] Kidd couldn't believe his eyes. But now he, Hewetson, and Perry had the opportunity they had been waiting for.

The three English ships rushed toward the harbor, maneuvering close to shore to pick up Sir Timothy Thornhill and his six hundred trapped Englishmen. But as they began loading the men into the oarboats, the French land forces pinned down the major-general and his remaining men in a red-hot skirmish.[22]

By the time the English had fought off the French land attack, DuCasse had appeared again on the horizon. Kidd was stunned to see that the feisty Frenchman had with him a new ship to bring his naval strength up to six men-of-war. From the looks of the big warship, she was a converted Guineaman slaver, bearing more than thirty guns.[23]

DuCasse had returned with reinforcements.

Even worse, this time the French had the advantage of the wind. DuCasse bore down upon Kidd and Company with a vengeance at full sail. The *Blessed William* and *Lion* sped out of the cul-de-sac harbor, with Perry and the *Speedwell* barely making it out before the French were upon them. Recognizing that DuCasse meant to board them, the three vessels turned to face the French—bearing up and laying by in preparation for a hand-to-hand assault.[24]

It was six powerful French men-of-war versus three undermanned English vessels. Kidd commanded his crew to stand by and prepare to receive the enemy with a broadside and a volley of shot, as a prelude to the enemy boarding action. But, to his surprise, the all-out attack and boarding attempt never came.[25]

At that moment, if Captain Kidd had peered through his glass, he would have seen DuCasse engaged in a heated quarrel with a bewigged French gentleman aboard his flagship, *Le Hasardeux*. Against all military reasoning, the French naval commander was being overruled and denied the opportunity for a major boarding action by one Monsieur Charles de Pechpeyrou-Comminges, chevalier de Guitaut, Governor of St. Christopher—when DuCasse had a nearly three-to-one numerical advantage. The fussy French were *bickering* when they should have been *attacking*.[26]

But the next thing Kidd knew, cannons thundered and the two sides were exchanging broadsides again. At the same time, the French land forces pounded Thornhill on the beaches, forcing him and his men to retreat into the dense tropical jungle. As it was nearly sunset and night would soon fall, Kidd, Hewetson, and Perry sailed once again a safe distance away from DuCasse and the French fleet that was blockading the harbor, and conferred in a council of war. They decided to sail far to the south as if they were giving up on the rescue mission, spend the night in a broad tack to be guaranteed of gaining the wind advantage, and surprise the wily DuCasse at dawn.[27]

At midnight, John Browne and the other dog-tired yet adrenaline-fueled seamen tacked the gunship out to sea. When dawn peeped over the horizon, Captain Kidd found the French at anchor opposite Thornhill's camp, and headed straight for them to give battle. With the sun skimming the waves, Kidd and the English flotilla bore down hard on the enemy, but the French veered off. Once again, the aggressive DuCasse wanted to attack but was denied by the timorous governor of St. Christopher and fifty uneasy French citizens.[28]

With the French backing down again and sailing away toward Anguilla, Kidd and Hewetson decided not to go after them, instead choosing to use the opportunity to snatch and grab Thornhill's force off the island. The three vessels quickly loaded up Sir Timothy's men without a single battlefield casualty despite persistent sniper fire, and set sail for the return voyage home. Kidd was relieved that the only crewman aboard the *Blessed William* seriously injured during the two-day battle was a sharpshooter who, as he was raising his gun, lost part of his thumb to a musket ball.[29]

On January 22, Captain Kidd and the victorious fleet arrived safely at Nevis, having rescued the main English land force in the Caribbean. But with no spoils of war to show for their efforts and patriotism regarded by many of the hardened pirates in the company as something for dupes of the Crown, Captain Kidd's privateer crew was far from happy.[30]

THREE DAYS LATER, Governor Christopher Codrington, Sir Timothy Thornhill, and the planter-merchant elite of Antigua threw a special banquet for Hewetson and Kidd in Falmouth Harbor. A cornucopia of food and drink was laid out for the celebratory occasion, and many toasts were made in tribute to the heroes of the hour. The commoner Captain Kidd had probably never been feted like this in his entire life.[31] For his service on behalf of His Majesty King William III, he was given a significant financial reward in silver, above and beyond his official compensation under his letter of marque.[32]

Of Kidd in the 1689–1690 campaign against the French, Hewetson would echo the sentiments of the citizens of Antigua by saying, "He was a mighty man. . . . He was with me in two engagements against the French, and fought as well as any man I ever saw." Officer Thomas Cooper, who served aboard the *Lion* during the heated action off the coast of St. Martins, would also bestow fulsome praise upon Kidd: "We fought Monsieur DuCasse a whole day and, I thank God, we got the better of it. Captain Kidd behaved himself very well in the face of his enemies."[33]

The man who had been "Captain Kidd" for a mere six months was moving on up—and rather rapidly. With the new gift from Codrington and the citizens of Antigua added to his own personal savings garnered under his privateering commissions over the years, he had now amassed £2,000 worth of personal booty in his cabin and in the hold of the *Blessed William*—a value that three centuries later would be worth $700,000.[34] In the process, he had earned the goodwill of men in high places in an age of authoritarianism, nobility, and patronage.[35]

Though Kidd and Hewetson were riding high, Culliford, Mason, Burgess, Browne, and the rest of the crew were far from satisfied. While the two captains were being feted and financially rewarded for rescuing Thornhill and his troops, the crews of the patriotic armada had received no compensation. Though Thornhill had personally thanked them, Kidd knew they were still bitter about the lack of prize money.[36] He also knew the only solution for their dissatisfaction was to make another Marie-Galante-like raid, and soon. His sailors much preferred easy campaigns against weak forces that surrendered quickly to dangerous open-sea battles.[37]

Until seizing the *Sainte Rose* from the French back in late July, he had never experienced the power of an influential benefactor. But over the past six months, he had learned firsthand just how valuable it was to have such a personal promoter. The sponsorship of influential men like Codrington was critical if he wanted to attain true wealth and prestige in a world governed by birthright and elitism. There was no other avenue open to him, given that the English mercantile and political system was built upon the patronage model.[38]

As historian Robert Ritchie has noted of Captain Kidd's era compared to today, "Every position—menial or great—was in someone's control, and all the associated salaries, fees, and privileges could be used to further the career of relatives, friends, and protégés," as well as to advance one's own career. "The more patronage, the greater power to make or break careers and to build factions or buy loyalty. Patronage was the heart and soul of both commerce and politics." He had made his own luck, true, by leading the seizure of the *Sainte Rose*, but he was also a direct beneficiary of the powerful Codrington.[39] He was captain of his own ship with a small fortune in gold, silver, and other booty in his possession—far more than most people of the age earned in an entire lifetime.[40]

The day after the banquet, Kidd met with Culliford, Mason, Burgess, and perhaps others to hear their grievances. Either aboard the *Blessed William* or in a dockside tavern overlooking Falmouth Harbor, the men held a privateers' council. The crew members were still angry at being thrown into a line-of-battle formation in the name of king and country with no financial return. Furthermore, they were growing agitated with no new money coming in, since many of them had already pissed away their earnings on strumpets and liquor, and they wanted to use the

Blessed William to go off plundering French, Dutch, Danish, Spanish, and Portuguese vessels. Would Kidd lead them as their captain?[41]

Weaned on buccaneer egalitarianism, Kidd sympathized with Culliford and the others, and may have even been tempted to take them up on their offer. How long they debated that night, history has not recorded, but his final answer was "no." He would not turn pirate: he would fight with a legal license as a privateer and adhere strictly to the terms of that license, or not at all.[42]

Did Kidd sense that he might have a mutiny on his hands? He had been fighting with these men as a legally sanctioned privateer for the past year—both for and against the French—and he regarded them not just as his shipmates but as genuine friends and comrades in arms. Taking into consideration all they had been through together, he believed it unlikely that they would take the drastic step of severing ties with him and stealing his ship. All the same, he may have doubled the guard on the *Blessed William* just to be safe.

On the night of February 2, the Buccaneer Boy Scout was rewarded for his principled stand by having his ship stolen from him while he was ashore. After a week with no sign of a mutiny, it is possible that he had let his guard down. Led by the ringleaders Culliford, Mason, and Burgess, some eighty men in total seized the *Blessed William* at anchorage and left him high and dry to go a-pirating. But his mutinous seamen didn't just seize his ship; they also took his hard-earned £2,000 in gold, silver, and other booty, as well as all his arms and ammunition.[43] He was rendered a pauper overnight with nothing but the clothes on his back and the handful of Spanish silver coins, or pieces of eight, in his pockets.

It was a crushing blow; yet it was also a wake-up call. So much for the loyal brotherhood of the buccaneers—he was now forced to go all-in on patronage.

Illiterate but experienced seaman John Browne would later claim in a 1702 deposition that he, Culliford, Mason, and Burgess had run away with the *Blessed William* due to Captain Kidd's "ill behavior" toward them. Like Royal Navy commander James Cook a century later, Kidd was a demanding sea captain, to be sure, but there is not a shred of evidence that he was ever inordinately hard on the men. In fact, Browne would voluntarily serve under Kidd a second time, during their 1696–1699 Indian Ocean expedition. Thus, in his testimony given under duress, Browne took Kidd—who was famous by the turn of the century—down to burnish his own image and save his own skin. Imprisoned in London for piracy at the time and intent on obtaining a Crown pardon in return for giving state's evidence against his onetime shipmate Samuel Burgess, Browne sought to justify the mutiny by putting the blame on his privateer commander. In the end, he was pardoned by the English authorities once he delivered his testimony against his former shipmates.[44]

Kidd was dismayed to lose everything he owned except his distant New York real estate properties, which could not bring him any income in the near term. He went to Codrington and Hewetson to deliver the terrible news. For Codrington, the loss could not have come at a worse time for the war effort. Losing fourscore hard-fighting privateers on Antigua was bad enough, but it was reported that twenty French warships stood ready in Martinique and that Count de Blénac and DuCasse would soon sail to St. Christopher with all the regular troops and seamen under their command. After outfitting their amphibious force, they reportedly planned to attack Nevis.[45]

Codrington and Hewetson both offered Kidd their condolences. Simmering beneath his tricorne, the feisty American colonial wanted to go after the perpetrators immediately. The governor agreed to turn him loose, but first he had to raise a full crew, which would take some time. Codrington believed the mutineers had headed north for the Danish-controlled smuggler's redoubt of St. Thomas. But unbeknownst to the governor, Kidd, and Hewetson, the band of outlaws instead had headed south for the Spanish Main.[46]

Kidd couldn't believe his bad luck. In the past six months, he had gone from a lowly seaman, to a wealthy sea captain and ship-owner, and now back to a down-and-outer with no ship, a skeleton crew, and an uncertain future. Luckily, Codrington had taken a shine to him. The governor allowed Kidd to sail to his home port, New York, to attend to his personal and financial affairs and then return in the spring to once again serve under Codrington. The privateer commander would fight on the governor's behalf throughout much of 1690, for which Codrington would, by the end of the year, reward him with his own privateering gunship—the *Antigua*—after Kidd captured the French barkentine in battle.[47]

But at the moment, on February 2, 1690, Captain Kidd had scarcely a penny to his name, was forced to rely on the charity of Codrington, and needed to drum up eighty hard-fighting seamen. Meanwhile, he learned that his good friend Captain Hewetson would soon sail to Barbados to refit, acquire men, and take the hand in marriage of one Butler Chamberlayne, the daughter of the venerable Sir Edward Chamberlayne of Leicester.[48]

In his official report to London, Codrington would lament the unfortunate hand he and Kidd had been dealt:

> On the 2nd February the privateer-ship [*Blessed William*] ran away from us, being well stocked with arms and manned by eighty or ninety men. They took their opportunity when Captain Kidd (who has behaved himself well) was ashore and have carried off goods of his to the value of £2,000. Most of the crew were formerly pirates and I presume liked their old trade better than any that they were likely to have here. I sent after them, but without success, to the Virgin Islands and to St. Thomas, where it was most likely that they would have gone to water. The loss of the ship and men, which is serious, could not have befallen us at a worse time.[49]

For his part, Kidd would get back on his feet—and resoundingly so. But it would take him almost a year to do so. Only then would he get back into his dear Sarah's loving arms once and for all and find that everything in New York had changed. To his infinite advantage.

PART 2

—

The New York Gent *and* King's Pirate Hunter

–4–

Mr. and Mrs. Captain Kidd

On March 5, 1691, as his new ship *Antigua* approached the narrow neck between Staten Island and Brooklyn from the Lower Bay, Captain Kidd felt powerful emotions sweeping through him. He was finally returning home to New York for good after more than a year and a half of fighting in the Caribbean—and he was doing so as the commander and owner of his own 16-gun privateering and merchant vessel. He may not yet have risen to the pinnacle of the seventeenth-century social pyramid, but this colonial American mariner, born a lowly "commoner" across the Atlantic, had indeed defied the staggering odds to become, in the parlance of the day, a "person of quality."

As he navigated northward toward his final destination, he was thinking not only of his triumphant return, but of his beloved Sarah. When they had last seen each other, the "lovely and accomplished" nineteen-year-old Sarah Bradley Cox had been a widow following the death of her elderly Dutch flour-merchant husband, William Cox, and Kidd hoped she was still unmarried. He had known Sarah since 1688, when he had made the city his home, and by the following year the two had begun a clandestine romantic relationship that resulted in not only a son out of wedlock, following Cox's accidental drowning, but one of the greatest New York love stories of all time.[1]

Born in England in 1670, Sarah Bradley had arrived to New York at the age of fourteen along with her father, Captain Samuel Bradley Sr., and two younger brothers, Samuel Jr. and Henry. Within a year she had wed the wealthy graybeard Cox in an arranged marriage. Due to the moral and religious constraints of the age, the future Mr. and Mrs. Captain Kidd gave their infant son William up for adoption following Cox's death, to Kidd's aunt Margaret Ann Kidd Wilson living in Calvert, Maryland. Support was provided by Kidd's father, Reverend William Kidd, and Kidd's mother, Margaret Mary Deare Kidd, who had settled near Margaret Wilson in Maryland.[2]

But what Kidd was likely unaware of as he sailed into New York Harbor in March 1691 is that a year after Cox's drowning accident, Sarah had been forced, due to her difficult circumstances, to take another husband. By August 1690, Sarah Bradley Cox had married a Dutch merchant named John Oort, an associate of her late husband and "sea captain in regular trade" involved in the administration of William Cox's estate. Unfortunately for Sarah, the estate continued to be tied up in bureaucratic red tape by Jacob Leisler, the acting lieutenant governor of New York, and his political cronies at City Hall. She had married Oort out of desperation to recover her rightful inheritance, but he proved to be a failure in that regard. With firm control over her first husband's estate, Leisler demanded that Oort post a £5,000 ($1,750,000 today) bond to recover Sarah's inheritance, but the Dutchman was unable to meet those draconian terms.[3]

To her dismay, her second husband also turned out to be a ne'er-do-well who displayed the telltale signs of being a gold digger.[4] Unbeknownst to her, Oort had borrowed money to pay their mounting bills and was steeply in debt to several merchants.[5] As if that weren't a heavy enough burden for Sarah, she had been forced to shutter her shop of imported high-end goods following Cox's death, since under the restrictive English law of coverture she had been "covered" by him and essentially been his property; and she also still had to care for her tippling father, who had borrowed money from Cox, and her two teenage brothers.[6]

Whether or not Kidd knew that Sarah was married to another and going through a difficult time, he planned to call upon her once he settled back into his home port. As the *Antigua* passed through the Narrows—or *Hoofden,* as the Dutch called it—between Staten Island and Brooklyn and approached New York Harbor's Upper Bay, he grabbed his spyglass from the becket and scanned his adopted city, nestled on the southern wedge of Manhattan Island.[7] Fort William stood tall in the foreground with its formidable seven-cannon battery. The houses around the fort were constructed of both wood and colorful red, white, and yellow brick and displayed deeply canted, shingled rooftops. Most were of a two- or three-story Dutch design like those of the crowded Amsterdam, to make use of the limited space.[8]

When he reached a depth of eight fathoms, he fired off a cannon salute to the fort and ordered anchors cast. Seagulls wheeled in the sky; children could be seen running toward the shore to welcome the new gunship; and sea lions barked as they leaped off the dark, foliated, Precambrian metamorphic schist and marble outcrops into the water at the island's arrowpoint-shaped foot. After meeting with the customs officials who rowed out to the *Antigua*, he had the oarboats lowered and he and his seamen went ashore.

He carried a shipment of sugar, rum, linen, and spices in his hold to sell in the city, which would help regain his wealth even more. Having recouped a portion of the £2,000 stolen from him and now the owner of his own ship, he looked every bit the part of the successful sea captain as the oarboat pulled up to the Great Dock and he planted his feet on the wooden planking.

He was home at long last.

Unfortunately, after selling off his West Indian goods, he had little time to get settled in. Soon after his arrival, he was recruited by Major Richard Ingoldsby and the town's leading citizens in a plan to dislodge Jacob Leisler and his band of rebels from the fort. Leisler, a fifty-year-old merchant and provincial militia captain of German extraction, had seized hold of New York's government several months after Catholic King James II was overthrown in late 1688 and replaced by William and Mary.[9] In the name of the Glorious Revolution, Leisler and his hardline Protestant followers had led a revolt against the Crown's agent in New York, the Anglican Lieutenant Governor Francis Nicholson. Nicholson fled back to England after Fort James—at the southern end of Manhattan—was seized by a rebellious force on May 31, 1689. The insurgents created a Committee of Safety on June 8 and elected Leisler commander in chief of the militia.[10]

Once Leisler was appointed head of the new rebel government, he promptly renamed the town's military garrison Fort William in honor of England's new king. He felt no love for the city's Anglo-Dutch elite who controlled the levers of power, but what most infuriated him and his following of disenfranchised city workers and small farmers was their slowness in pronouncing on behalf of William and Mary and their refusal to enforce strict Calvinist Protestant orthodoxy. Leisler's battle was with the Anglo-Dutch merchants and government officials at the very top who had served under Nicholson, as well as the Anglican and Dutch Reformed Church leaders who supported them.[11]

The Leislerians' goal was to root out all "papists" and "Jacobites" *and* level the economic playing field, so that the city's wealthy, Catholic-tolerating merchants would no longer control the government.[12] But once in power, Leisler proved remarkably undemocratic himself. He jailed his most outspoken opponents, dissolved the governor's council and replaced it with his favored loyalists, swore in his political cronies to key government posts, imposed a 4% war tax solely on the town's wealthy merchants, and, by December 1689, claimed full authority as lieutenant governor of all New York province.[13]

Thus, Captain Kidd had returned home during "Leisler's Rebellion," one of the most tumultuous periods in New York history. Possessing the most powerfully armed vessel in the harbor, Kidd was once again Johnny-on-the-spot. Major Ingoldsby and deposed governor's council members Frederick Philipse and Stephanus van Cortlandt wanted the privateer who had done "signal service" in the West Indies on behalf of his majesty to be on their side. The anglicized Dutchman Philipse was not only New York province's wealthiest shipping magnate, but one of the richest and most influential men in the American colonies. In the coming months, Philipse, van Cortlandt, lawyer William Nicoll, and other city bigwigs would become huge promoters of Captain Kidd, just like Codrington.[14]

Kidd was swiftly brought up to date on the current state of Leisler's populist insurrection. Not only had the struggle between the Leisler and anti-Leisler factions ramped up in the past month, but the French were pressing southward from Canada with an alliance of warlike, Jesuit-influenced Algonquian and Laurentian Iroquois tribes. Furthermore, the newly appointed royal governor set to replace the "usurper" Leisler, Richard Sloughter, had been blown off course en route from England, run aground in Bermuda, and was only now making his way to the city to take office.[15]

As commander of the governor's advance guard, Major Ingoldsby had arrived two months earlier and made daily requests for Leisler to step down and vacate Fort William. But the Frankfurt-born strongman refused to recognize the major's authority and demanded a royal commission from William III verifying that Sloughter and Ingoldsby were leaders of the lawful government. The architect of Leisler's Rebellion continued to claim that Ingoldsby and his troops were Catholic conspirators who had escaped England and sought to seize the fort and hold New York province for the deposed James II.[16]

Though politically Kidd was a progressive Whig and not a promonarchy Tory, he chose the side of the incoming Tory governor Sloughter and opposed Leisler in the rebellion. He was influenced in his decision by Leisler's withholding of Sarah's inheritance from her, and the lieutenant governor's issuing of a privateering commission to Culliford, Mason, Burgess, Browne, and the other *Blessed William* mutineers, who had sailed to New York in May 1690 after stealing Kidd's ship and committing several piracies in the Caribbean. He was especially angry to learn that he had missed his treacherous old shipmates by a mere two months and that they had caroused about town on his hard-earned money before setting out on a piratical voyage to the Indian Ocean with their commission from Leisler.[17] He also recognized that his chances for patronage and rapid advancement lay with New York's powerful English establishment and wealthy merchants. Having alienated thousands of citizens from Manhattan to Albany, Leisler was on his last legs and a poor horse to back for anyone with aspirations for a future in the province.[18]

By mid-March, Kidd had reconnected with Sarah and taken a firm stand against her sworn enemy, Jacob Leisler. Now it was time to act by rooting out Leisler and his band of militant Protestant renegades hunkered down in Fort William.

On March 17, 1691, Captain William Kidd felt the sleet pelting his face as the *Antigua*'s heavy guns took aim at the star-shaped fort. He stood on the rolling quarterdeck, struggling to maintain his balance as he pointed his spyglass at the wood-and-earthen palisades and stout blockhouse of Fort William. The late winter storm had worsened, with roiling seas whipped with foam crashing against the barkentine's hull, battering her timber and smothering her decks with icy seawater that sent violent shivers and curses through his motley crew.[19]

Shouting over the howling wind, Kidd gave his chief gunner the order to prepare to fire upon the blockhouse. The gunner sighted and re-sighted the cannons in the raging seas and gale-force winds, while Kidd patiently waited. But after more than two hours, the swells and surf inside New York Harbor had turned even more precarious. Wanting to avoid collateral damage, Kidd continued to hold his fire so as not to risk the lives of innocent civilians near the fort.[20]

He moved stealthily into shallower water, closer to the fort, attempting to safely sight the target and wait out the enemy. The slushy snow continued to pile up on his black gun barrels trained menacingly upon the blockhouse. The fury of the storm increased and the ship seesawed in the wind. At some point, he decided that the risk was still too great to fire the cannons with several private homes so near the target, including his lover Sarah's Pearl Street mansion only two blocks north of the fort.[21]

He wished Leisler would just surrender. The man was no longer accomplishing anything, holed up in the fort, and had become a desperate criminal. Earlier that day, Major Ingoldsby and his army of soldiers had encircled the fort in an attempt to force Leisler and his men into action. Leisler's rabble-rouser son-in-law, Jacob Milborne, had issued false declarations in Dutch that the English troops were secretly working with Catholic sympathizers and enslaved Africans to overthrow William and Mary.[22] On edge, Leisler's men had opened fire from the blockhouse, killing one old White soldier and a Black man while wounding seventeen others.[23]

Following Leisler's attack, Major Ingoldsby, along with Frederick Philipse and several of the city's other wealthy merchants, representing the government in exile, summoned Kidd for a war conference. Would he be willing to lead an attack on the fort from the sea, while Ingoldsby assaulted by land? Governor Sloughter was expected to arrive any day now from his circuitous voyage from London by way of Bermuda, and they wanted Kidd to help them clear the way for the legally appointed royal governor. Eager to make his mark in his hometown return and deeming the incoming Sloughter administration as the rightful English government, Kidd readily agreed to the council's request. Just as he had with his influential patron Codrington in the Caribbean, he had appeared at the right place at precisely the right moment in history. He was excited to help restore stability to the city and province while simultaneously aiding his beloved Sarah.[24]

Captain Kidd, Major Ingoldsby, and the city leaders quickly worked out a bold plan to bombard the blockhouse lying just outside the fort. Kidd possessed an ample supply of cannonballs, the manpower, and the ship, but he needed gunpowder and supplies. The wealthy merchants quickly assented and provided him with two hundred pounds of powder and other materials with which Kidd hoped to force the capitulation of Leisler and his holdouts.[25]

Now, with his cannons aimed at the blockhouse, he continued to wait for a clean shot at the target without endangering the townspeople. An hour later, he was rewarded for his forbearance.

Looking through his misty spyglass, he saw that the blockhouse was being evacuated. A dozen or so men marched quickly through the snow from the blockhouse to the safety of the nearby fort. His patience had paid off: he had won the battle without firing a single shot or losing a single man to the fort's big cannons. Leisler, unaware of how much difficulty Kidd was having in lining up his guns, had given orders from the fort to surrender the outlying blockhouse rather than confront Captain Kidd and his powerful 12- and 18-pounders.[26] Leisler was already so angry at the former buccaneer for arriving to New York and taking up arms with Ingoldsby and the city leaders against him that Leisler had complained in writing that Captain Kidd was a "Blasphemous Privateer." When Kidd later heard about the catchy pejorative, he considered it a badge of honor rather than an insult.[27]

The next day, on March 18, Governor Sloughter finally dipped his foresails into New York's waters. But with the storm still raging, the opposing winds prevented his ship, the frigate HMS *Archangel*, from navigating the final leg of the journey into New York Harbor. Once again Johnny-on-the-spot, Kidd sailed several leagues downwind on March 19 and personally ferried the new governor ashore, having his men row Sloughter in on the *Antigua*'s pinnace.[28]

Accompanied by Captain Kidd, Sloughter went straight to City Hall, read aloud his commission as royal governor, and then demanded three times that the fort surrender. Leisler, stalling, sent messengers insisting upon retaining the bastion until he received a written order from the king. Near midnight, Leisler dispatched his son-in-law Jacob Milborne to explain that it was against the rules of military conduct to surrender a fort at night.[29] Growing impatient, Sloughter arrested Milborne and his messengers—but not until after Kidd, irked by the lack of respect shown the new governor, roughed up one of Leisler's confederates whom he found particularly abrasive.[30]

In the morning, Leisler sent a conciliatory letter to Sloughter, disclaiming any wish to further withhold Fort William from him. But he continued to stall by asking clarification on certain points. Fed up, Sloughter ordered Kidd to sail around the tip of Manhattan Island once again and train his iron cannons on the backside of the fort. As the New York privateer sailed into position for the second time in four days, Sloughter dispatched Ingoldsby and his company of English troops and colonial militia to order the fort's garrison to ground arms and march out, promising full pardon to all parties except Leisler and his council. With the pugnacious Captain Kidd again threatening his rear with his big carriage guns, Leisler was forced to surrender.[31]

Afterward, Kidd celebrated at City Hall with the victors. Governor Sloughter and New York's glitterati toasted him and Ingoldsby as the heroes of the hour. Frederick Philipse, lawyer James Emott, and other bigwigs held up their glasses in tribute to the saviors of the city. Also present were Captain Thomas "Whisking" Clark, Colonel Nicholas Bayard, and lawyer William Nicoll, all freshly released from Fort William's prison thanks to Kidd and Ingoldsby. The victory celebration at City Hall officially marked the downfall of Leisler, the release of the leading anti-Leislerians from captivity, and the inauguration of Sloughter's administration.[32]

But it was Captain Kidd and Major Ingoldsby who were the stars of the festivities. The thirty-six-year-old privateer stood beaming in the limelight, once again unable to believe his sudden good fortune. He was a war hero in the small English and Dutch community, even though he had not fired a single cannon.

Was Sarah present at this very first of many downfall-of-Leisler rallies New Yorkers would enjoy over the next month? Most likely she was in attendance, which would have been a gratifying experience for Kidd in his moment of glory. He knew that Leisler's many enemies, including Sarah, had dreamed of this moment of vindication for months. But by the time the celebration was over, he must have also felt a touch of sadness to dampen his triumph, for his beloved Sarah was still not his.

But once again, the two star-crossed lovers would surreptitiously find a way to overcome the stifling conventions of colonial America and be together. Whatever intimacy they had enjoyed in the past, they would find a discreet way to share again.

Following his key role in taking down Leisler, the war hero's star rose quickly. Sloughter and his governor's council, upon which Kidd's new wealthy friends Frederick Philipse, Stephanus van Cortlandt, and William Nicoll served, sent a recommendation to the New York Provincial Assembly to reward him for his role in bringing Leisler and his men to justice. On their recommendation, the assembly voted him £150 ($52,500 in today's dollars, no pittance, plus the remainder of the gunpowder and other supplies he was allowed to keep) "as a suitable reward for the many good services done to this province"—namely, for carrying guns and ammunition to Major Ingoldsby, escorting Governor Sloughter safely into port, and forcing Leisler to abandon the blockhouse and surrender Fort William.[33] The reward he received for his efforts was the largest bounty of any of the participants, including Major Ingoldsby, who was awarded only £100 for his role in the overthrow of Leisler.[34]

Regarded now as a gentleman, the bewigged Captain Kidd swiftly secured a position in the inner circle of the city's economic and political elite. His high standing helped rescue him from the tentacles of the Royal Navy. On March 24, when Captain Jasper Hicks of the HMS *Archangel* press-ganged away some of Kidd's best sailors, Frederick Philipse, William Nicoll, and the other powerful members of the governor's council ordered that the pressed seamen be immediately returned "in consideration of Captain Kidd's services to their Majesties forces, and others of their Majesties good subjects."[35]

Now that he was part of their inner circle, the powerful merchants who sat on Governor Sloughter's council found a way to give him yet another bonus for his privateering efforts. When Sloughter set up a new

Vice-Admiralty court to investigate the activities of Leisler's privateers, Philipse, Nicoll, and the other city leaders instructed the former buccaneer to present a libel case against the *Pierre*. The ship was one of the seven French vessels that Kidd's old crewmates Culliford, Mason, Burgess, and Browne had captured six months earlier off the coast of Newfoundland, using his stolen *Blessed William* and sailing under a privateering commission from Leisler. Captain Kidd's high-powered lawyer friends, James Emott and William Nicoll, argued that since Leisler had not been the lawful governor, then his Vice-Admiralty court had not been legal either. Consequently, the decisions and prize sales of all vessels condemned by Leisler's court should be voided, allowing others to put in claims.[36]

On March 27, Kidd filed a Vice-Admiralty prize court claim against the *Pierre*, one of the five ships carried to New York by the pirate-privateers and condemned by Leisler, who had shrewdly invested in the Canadian expedition. In what Kidd had to have considered poetic justice, the *Pierre* was condemned and sold to Philipse for £500 ($175,000 today). Kidd received another £250 ($87,500 today) that, when added to his privateering and merchant monies, the value of the *Antigua*, and his prime real-estate properties, made him overnight one of the wealthiest citizens in New York. He had not yet fully recouped the £2,000 stolen from him in the Caribbean, but he was well on his way.[37]

It was an exciting time for Captain Kidd. But it was also uncertain, since he still did not have Sarah as his own and the Leisler affair and war with France continued to grip the city. On March 26, a hastily convened grand jury brought Jacob Leisler up on murder and treason charges, along with his son-in-law Jacob Milborne and eight other men from his council. By the morning of April 8, Chief Judge Joseph Dudley had declared a verdict. Leisler, Milborne, and six others were found guilty of murder and treason, while two men were acquitted.[38] In pronouncing the grisly death sentence, Dudley ordered that the men found guilty "shall be severally hanged by the neck, and being alive their bodies be cut down to the earth, that their bowels be taken out, and they being alive burnt before their faces, that their heads shall be struck off and their bodies cut in four parts, and which shall be disposed of as their Majesties shall assign."[39]

While the Leisler affair would divide the city for the next decade, it was a pivotal event for Kidd because it solidified his relationships with several of the city's movers and shakers. He became good friends with two of the chief prosecutors of the trial—James Emott and William Nicoll—with Emott remaining his confidant and legal advocate for nearly a decade. Emott was the top lawyer of 1690s New York, though law as a profession was still in its infancy in the American colonies and the first independent law school, the Litchfield Law School in Connecticut, would not be founded until 1782. During the course of the trial and its aftermath, Kidd also became friendly with New York's new attorney general, Thomas Newton, who would in 1692 serve as king's attorney in the Salem witch trials and in 1699 represent Kidd as his Boston lawyer.[40]

On May 14, two days before the scheduled public hanging of Leisler and Milborne (the only two who would be executed), John Oort died suddenly from unknown causes.[41]

The next day, Sarah filed a letter of administration on her late Dutch husband's unsettled estate with Governor Sloughter, which was officially granted to her.[42]

The day after that—the same day as the scheduled execution—William and Sarah were married and forever became Mr. and Mrs. Captain Kidd.[43]

If all this sounds a little too neat and tidy—a sort of colonial-era film noir—then once again we are reminded that truth is truly stranger than fiction. The quick succession of events in the couple's favor has long seemed suspicious to Kidd biographers. It must be noted that skullduggery on the part of the two lovers makes complete sense, knowing their intimate history together, Sarah's distressed marriage with John Oort, and the depth of Sarah and Kidd's love and commitment to each other. If murder was afoot, it had to have been either a crime of passion in a heated moment, or the classic premeditated love-triangle murder plot.

Which is why the question must be asked: Did the soon-to-be-legendary Captain William Kidd bump John Oort off?

Did he perhaps get into a heated argument with Oort over Sarah and accidentally kill him when it turned physical, or might he have stalked and slain him when they were alone together? Built like a heavyweight prize-fighter, Kidd definitely possessed the physical brute strength and experience in hand-to-hand combat and close-quarters killing (the means), and he also had the motive and opportunity. And in late-seventeenth-century America, there were no trained detectives to conduct a thorough forensic investigation of the crime scene, so the bar for Kidd and Sarah to get away with it was a low one indeed.

For conspiracy theorists, the evidence is highly suggestive of foul play. But then Sarah would have to have been in on at least the cover-up, which is hard to believe based on everything we know about this devout Anglican who insisted in her will that "the funerals of my body are to be only such as shall become a Christian."[44] Furthermore, there is no record of exactly how Oort died. For all we know, he could have suddenly taken ill in an age when people dropped dead every minute from dysentery, typhus, measles, cholera, influenza, and smallpox—and when bloodsucking leeches remained the most widely used medical treatment available.

None of this has stopped speculation from historians, amateur sleuths, and fiction authors that Kidd, or Kidd and Sarah conniving together, may have performed the desperate act.[45] In *The Pirate's Wife: The Remarkable True Story of Sarah Kidd*, historian Daphne Geanacopoulos tantalizes us with the dramatic possibilities:

> Sarah knew that the timing of her marriage so soon after Oort's death was suspicious, that some might wonder if Kidd had something to do with the Dutch merchant's sudden demise. Did he kill him or have him killed so he could marry Sarah? Or, did Sarah, with the help of an accomplice, organize the fatal event so she could marry the man she loved?[46]

In his historical-fiction novel *Sarah*, author Joe Attanasio has Sarah poisoning Oort with a vial of chemicals that she pours into his wine, mercifully killing him in his sleep. The night before, as Kidd and Sarah are plotting, she has initial doubts; but in the end, she goes through with the macabre scheme.[47]

If Kidd and Sarah did perform the diabolical deed, they definitely got away with it. There was some suspicion of foul play at the time, but nothing came of it. Kidd was considered a gentleman and war hero, and Sarah was the "lovely and accomplished" Mrs. Captain Kidd before Oort had even gone cold, a two-time widow who had suffered penury at the hands of the cruel Jacob Leisler and was being rescued by her Prince Charming.[48] Furthermore, Oort was a heavily-in-debt Dutchman with the English back in power, who had died intestate without leaving a will and who had, the year before, joined other New York merchants in a letter to King William III pleading for financial relief to pay off his mounting debts due to Leisler's harsh policies.[49]

Guilty or not, future events would demonstrate that they cared deeply for each other. However, their glorious and long-awaited wedding day would be soaked in blood—foreshadowing both the glittering triumph and dark tragedy of their future married life together.[50]

William and Sarah were married on the morning of May 16, 1691, before Jacob Leisler and Jacob Milborne's afternoon execution, inside the Dutch-built Fort William church where Anglican services were held at the time.[51] The wedding was attended by Sarah's father, Captain Samuel Bradley; her two younger brothers; Kidd's privateer officers and seamen; and William and Sarah's close friends from the affluent anti-Leislerian set. At this stage of his career, Kidd was so highly regarded that the municipal clerk listed the sea captain's occupation as "Gent" for gentleman instead of "mariner" on the marriage license issued that morning.[52] That must have brought a devilish grin to the rough-and-tumble Caribbean buccaneer.

When the ceremony was complete, Sarah was thrilled to finally have her true love at her side and her life back on track. Although her affection for Kidd was the driving force behind their marriage, he also brought her financial security. Kidd owned his own ship, the *Antigua*, as well as several valuable real-estate properties from his privateering and merchant cruises over the past two decades. These properties included 86-90 Pearl Street, just down the street from the newlyweds' mansion at 119-121 Pearl, as well as a fine house and seventy-five feet of ground on Tienhoven Street (currently 25, 27, and 29 Pine Street), another lot on the north side of Pearl Street 150 feet west of Old Slip, and 52-56 Water Street between Old Slip and Coenties Slip. He had also been rewarded by Sloughter and the governor's council with a substantial amount of money for his privateering efforts and his hefty cut in the libel case against the *Pierre*.[53]

Though Mrs. Captain Kidd would eventually bring a sizable estate to the marriage, her money continued to be tied up by Leisler's bureaucratic entanglement, making her new husband the current provider of the bulk of the family's wealth. It was Kidd who paid more than £30 to cover Oort's funeral costs, no small amount of money back then (around $10,000 today). And he vowed to work doubly hard with their lawyer, James Emott, to get her and her family their rightful inheritance back.[54]

Following their wedding and perhaps a lunchtime reception at their Pearl Street mansion, they headed to the Leisler execution site. The scaffold was erected a third of a mile outside the City Wall and Wall Street on the eastern edge of the New York City Common, which is today City Hall Park on the corner of Park Row and Frankfort Street.[55] More than two thousand men, women, and children had turned out on this rainy Saturday afternoon for the event. A public hanging was not only grand theater but a public holiday, and at least half of the free citizens on Manhattan Island and many of the enslaved Blacks and indentured White servants had made their way through the city gates to watch the violent spectacle.[56]

The newly married Mr. and Mrs. Captain Kidd looked up with foreboding at the gallows. Constructed from timbers set aside to shore up the fort, the wooden scaffold bore a pair of nooses, one for Leisler and the other for Jacob Milborne.[57] Governor Sloughter had denied a petition of mercy for the two rebels with 1,800 signatures attached to it, but he had reprieved the other six convicted men.[58] He had also nixed the grisly drawing and quartering, so now the two condemned men would only be hanged and beheaded.[59]

Soon, Leisler and Milborne were "brought to the gallows on a sledge" by the high sheriff and a company of militia. In the drizzling rain, Kidd and Sarah watched the grim pageantry with fascination along with the crowd. The sheriff, the file of bayonet-clutching soldiers, and the two prisoners parted their way solemnly through the crowd standing before the hanging scaffold and wooden ladders leaning against it. The condemned men then climbed their separate ladders to the pair of nooses hanging from the crossbeam. Once they were guided to the upper rungs, the nooses were placed around their necks by the executioner. After laying out the crimes for which the doomed men had been convicted, the high sheriff asked Leisler if he had any last words. The gathered throng became quiet as Leisler now delivered his final sermon from the gallows.[60]

"Gentlemen and fellow brethren, all hope in the grace and fear of the Lord Jesus," he opened with, and then he publicly declared that he had forgiven his enemies, proclaimed his loyalty to William and Mary, defended the Protestant cause, and maintained that all he had ever wanted was to restore order, preserve godliness, and enhance commerce in the province. He admitted that he had fallen short of his goal and took responsibility for his mistakes, which he said were the result of his own ignorance and jealous fear.[61]

The sheriff then asked Jacob Milborne if he had anything to say before his sentence was carried out. Leisler's English son-in-law, married to his daughter Mary, proceeded to glare down at a well-dressed, bewigged gentleman standing in the front row named Robert Livingston. Tilting his chin toward the Albany fur-trader and New York City shipping merchant, Milborne shouted down from the gallows in a booming voice, "I forgive the governor and my judges, but I shall never forgive you, Robert Livingston! For it is you who hath caused the king that I must now die! But before God's tribunal, I will implead you for the same!"[62]

Some in the crowd gave an audible gasp as Milborne continued to glare down at the Scotsman, while others booed and hissed Livingston, who looked aghast as all eyes riveted upon him. The cause of Milborne's wrath was that Livingston had for the past two years been a staunch opponent of both Leisler and Milborne. In response to this rejection, Leisler had canceled Livingston's cozy government contracts up north as clerk of Albany and victualler of the English troops. Falsely accused of treason by the Leislerians, Livingston had been forced to hide out in exile in Connecticut, while Leisler's followers harassed his family and ransacked his home.[63]

After the sheriff tied handkerchiefs about the eyes of the condemned men, they were "turned off" from their ladders. Leisler and Milborne hung suspended in midair, suffocating as they kicked and struggled in a ghastly dance of death. Now Kidd and Sarah saw women fainting, some "taken in labor," and heard the terrible "shrieks" of hundreds of people in the rain-soaked crowd. It was at this point that fights broke out between some of the Leislerians and anti-Leislerians.[64]

Soon, the twitching and kicking stopped.

The hangman cut down the limp bodies. With both men and women now openly wailing and soldiers breaking up the fights, a hooded axeman stepped up to behead the corpses. To his credit, the axe-wielding executioner delivered a pair of clean blows that brought more weeping and moaning from the passionate crowd.[65]

Given that it was their wedding day, one would think that the sight of the heads being unceremoniously lopped off and the keening of the Dutch women would have been a gruesome experience for the newly married couple. But such were the times—so distant and bewildering to us today—that they might not have even blinked as the two men were decapitated and the thick crimson blood gushed down the wooden chopping block, only to be diluted in a pinkish stream in the pouring rain.

Once the prisoners were beheaded, their garments were cut into individual pieces by family members and strands of Leisler's hair were doled out as the precious relics of a martyr. The men's separated heads and bodies were then buried next to the gallows in the unconsecrated ground of a pair of unmarked graves.[66]

When the grim spectacle was mercifully over, Leisler's supporters began to sing Psalm 79 in unison.[67] As devout Christians, Kidd and Sarah knew it well: the passage from the Bible recounted the heathens' destruction of Jerusalem, the biblical Jacob's martyrdom, and God's impending wrath. Leisler's mourners seemed to be warning that God would punish Governor Sloughter and New York's anti-Leislerian faction for the grave injustice they had inflicted upon the city's martyred hero. Of course, none of this was lost on the "Blasphemous Privateer" who had been instrumental in forcing the surrender of the leader of Leisler's Rebellion.[68]

As the mass singing drifted into the drizzly air, people began to move off solemnly in small groups. The newlyweds returned home to their fine Pearl Street mansion feeling, among conflicting emotions, vindication. Finally, they were Mr. and Mrs. Captain Kidd, husband and wife. However, they were not allowed to enjoy their connubial bliss for long, for once again the war hero's services were needed to protect America's shores from French attack.

NINE DAYS AFTER their wedding, on May 25, 1691, Captain Kidd headed out to sea once again, with royal commission in hand, to battle the Gallic hordes closing in from New France to the north. Commissioned by New York's new royal governor to protect the region, he was accompanied by Leonard Walkington, captain of the *Horne*, serving under his command. Their military objective was to hunt down a French privateer named Captain Etienne de Montauban.[69]

Having made a name for himself in the past two years for his exploits in West Africa and the Caribbean, Montauban had been wreaking havoc along the New England coast. Sneaking down from Canada in command of the 16-gun *La Machine*, the fast-moving *flibustier* had most recently ransacked Block Island off the eastern tip of Long Island, captured an English colonial merchant vessel, and kidnapped a Rhode Island harbor pilot, which meant that Montauban intended to continue raiding along the New England coast.[70]

Five days later, Kidd and Walkington spotted Captain Montauban and his vaunted *La Machine* in the hazy distance along the eastern edge of Long Island Sound, and they promptly packed on all sail in pursuit. Coming in at 250 to 300 tons and carrying a crew of 120 to 130 souls, the square-rigged, Dutch-built fluyt bore mostly 12-pounders like the *Antigua*.[71] With two men-of-war bearing down on him, the elusive Montauban crowded on all sail to make his escape. He tore through the white-tipped rollers northeast of Block Island in the direction of Nantucket. The *Antigua* and *Horne* followed, but Kidd and Walkington were unable to bring their guns to bear or seize her in a boarding action.[72]

The daring *flibustier* Monsieur Montauban—whose later adventurous exploits off the west coast of Africa in 1695 would be chronicled by Alexander Exquemelin, author of the popular *The Buccaneers of America*[73]—had narrowly made his escape. But Captain Kidd had fulfilled his military mission in accordance with his licensed commission by driving off the enemy, thereby securing the northeastern coast of English America.[74]

In July, Captain Kidd engaged in another privateering action against the French off the coast of Nova Scotia when he spotted a double-masted brigantine armed with sixteen or more cannons. He was alone now, with Walkington patrolling somewhere farther west. His crew at this juncture was a mixture of mostly White colonial English, Dutch, and Scottish New Yorkers with a sprinkling of White and Black Massachusetts sailors and landsmen. Several of the New Englanders were runaway White indentured servants or Black slaves who had joined his crew to be free share-earning mariners under the standard "no prey, no pay" agreement rather than remain the property of other men. Throughout his Caribbean buccaneering career, Kidd had come into contact with hardy indigenous West Indian warriors and free or runaway Africans in his bouts against the Spanish Empire. These disenfranchised men had earned his respect, as the historical record clearly shows that the New York privateer welcomed men of color into his crews, provided that they were skilled sailors, fighters, or cooks.[75]

Thus, like many mariners who emerged from the buccaneering culture of the late seventeenth century, William Kidd "harbored little intellectual commitment to the racial hierarchies underpinning slavery." At the same time, he was a product of his times and, like most people in his day except the Quakers, he was not philosophically opposed to indentured servitude or enslavement and accepted hierarchal social structures as an inexorable fact of life. However, the common-born sea captain continued to embrace maritime egalitarianism throughout his career and was empathetic toward his fellow seafaring laborers under the privateer and merchant capitalism of the Atlantic world.[76]

Upon sighting the French warship, Kidd computed an intercepting course and chased her down with as much sail as the *Antigua* could bear. With the call to action given, the officers and crew scrambled to their posts. From the quarterdeck, Kidd studied the enemy vessel closely through his glass: three white pyramids of now-taut canvas, men scrambling about the decks and high up in the rigging, whitewater flying out from her bow as she parted through the choppy North Atlantic. A *pavilion blanc* with gold *fleurs-de-lys* may have been suspended from the main truck, indicating that the brigantine was indeed a French commissioned ship-of-war bearing royal insignia.

Soon, he overtook the vessel and pulled alongside within cannon range. The French warship's name would have now been discernible on the escutcheon: *Saint Jean*.[77] Though Kidd was still short of gunners, he took the enemy vessel with minimal damage to either ship. Most likely, he bluffed the French privateer into thinking he was stronger than he was and compelled the enemy to surrender without much of a fight, thereby allowing him to simultaneously seize the *Saint Jean* and her contents and keep his men safe from unnecessary death and injury.

When it was all over, Kidd had himself a newly captured French prize ship that fetched him and his crew around £600 ($210,000 today) at auction upon his return to New York in mid-August. The hero of the hour once again, he did not have to pay customs duties for his prize because the ship and goods were already "paying the king's tenths and the governor's fifteenths."[78]

His reunion with Sarah was joyous. If she was not already with child from their brief honeymoon in late May, she became so swiftly after his return to port. Their first daughter, Elizabeth, would be born in 1692.[79]

Most importantly, by the fall of 1691, Kidd would make the transition from full-time privateer to merchant sea captain. Now that he was a self-made gentleman hobnobbing with the wealthiest New Yorkers, he could afford to turn away from dangerous privateering missions and toward lucrative commerce, hauling cargo to and from Antigua and other islands in the West Indies that he knew so well. The rough-and-tumble buccaneer, now closing in on his thirty-seventh birthday, thus agreed to "settle down" at the request of his wife. From now on, Kidd would make short, reasonably safe trading voyages to the Caribbean, with an occasional privateering mission in the mix as the state of the war demanded, instead of patrolling the North American coast as a full-time licensed privateer.[80]

An amusing quote from Governor Sloughter illustrates how the formidable Sarah was able to exert influence over her headstrong seafaring husband. The hard-drinking New York governor would die on July 23, 1691,[81] but before doing so he would pen a letter to Governor Christopher Codrington, Kidd's former patron in the Caribbean. In a letter discussing Leisler's Rebellion and the war against France on the Albany frontier, he wrote: "I have commanded Captain Kidd for their Majesties especial service here, but hope in a few months he may be with you if his wife will let him."[82]

As Kidd biographer Richard Zacks writes, "That phrase 'if his wife will let him' is playful and surprising in an otherwise serious letter. . . . It implies that Sarah is strong-willed and wants William around and also that this military man loves her enough—at a chauvinist time in history when a husband could legally beat his wife—to listen to her. Codrington probably chuckled thinking of that hard-to-command . . . privateer as a newlywed."[83]

For the next five years, the gentlemanly merchant sea captain would live the most placid and domestically fulfilling part of his life. During this halcyon time when he and Sarah would enjoy the birth of their two daughters, Elizabeth and little Sarah, the happily married couple would finally be together much more than they were apart.

And they would live—and love—during one of the most fascinating, romantic, and overlooked periods in New York history: its very own Golden Age—of Piracy.

–5–

The Red Sea Men

In 1688, when William Kidd made the decision to call New York home,[1] he left behind a crucial clue to his character for future historians. He chose the burgeoning port town on the southern tip of Manhattan Island for a reason—and that was what New York had to offer the Caribbean buccaneer compared to Boston, Philadelphia, Newport, Charles Town, and the other major maritime metropoles of colonial America.

In the late seventeenth century, New York was as open-minded and cosmopolitan a city as existed in the New World, just as it is today. The twelfth oldest continuously occupied European settlement on U.S. soil, it was originally founded in 1625 as the Dutch West India Company trading post of *Nieuw Amsterdam* in the colony of New Netherland to take advantage of the North American fur trade. But in 1664, New Netherland became an English colony when an English expeditionary force captured the Dutch province bloodlessly but at the point of a bayonet. Though the city would remain predominantly Dutch in population and architecture over the next three decades, by the early 1690s the original Dutch settlement had undergone a makeover through anglicization and had grown into one of the most diverse of the English colonies in America.[2]

New York was home to a wide variety of immigrant groups, including not only Dutch and English but French, French-speaking Belgian Protestants called Walloons, Scots, Germans, Swedes, Native Americans, and Jews, as well as hundreds of enslaved Africans and some freedmen. The cultural diversity brought with it a multitude of viewpoints, as did its religious diversity. The mixture of orthodox and moderate Calvinists, Anglicans, Presbyterians, dissident Baptists, and Lutherans to go along with a smattering of Dunkers, Quakers, Jews, Catholics, and African conjurors rendered New York the most religiously pluralistic of the American colonies.[3]

With a babel of languages spoken on the streets, along the docks, and in the bulging warehouses and up-island farms, New York during the final decade of the seventeenth century was a progressive and burgeoning maritime entrepôt. New Yorkers were considered a "factious people" due to the tug-of-war of Leisler's Rebellion and their heterogeneity, but they were also known for playing as hard as they worked and for being more accepting of ethnic, class, and religious differences than other colonies. It is thus no coincidence that in 1692–1693, New Englanders accused by Puritans of witchcraft sought refuge in tolerant New York City and outlying areas.[4]

While Mother England prized New York's "strategic position" on the North American mainland, what impressed—and often shocked—visitors to the burgeoning city of four and a half thousand souls were the many "strange tongues, the multiplicity of houses of worship, [and] the hum of activity at the waterfront."[5] Due to the strong Dutch cultural influence, New Yorkers smoked and drank to excess, gambled and raced horses, felt little guilt about skipping church on occasion, were more sexually liberated than their provincial neighbors to the north and south, and tended not to look down their noses at the English, Dutch, Scottish, and French Huguenot ladies of the night plying their wicked craft on Petticoat Lane just off Beaver Street.[6] Thus, the colonial-era City That Never Sleeps was far more typical "of the later history of the United States than were its sister colonies."[7]

It is for these reasons that William Kidd chose to live in New York. As Kidd biographer Dunbar Maury Hinrichs writes:

> New York was not a one idea town like Boston or Philadelphia, or a planter's paradise such as tidewater Virginia and Maryland were to become. New York was New York, the most liberal-minded, internationally flavored spot Kidd could find on the North American coast. When approached from this viewpoint it is easier to understand why a man of Kidd's character might well prefer New York as a place to live, even though Boston was a more important port.[8]

The city was a place of growing economic opportunity, which was another important reason he selected New York as his home base. The colony possessed the continent's best natural harbor and served as the center of a vast trade network linking the northern and southern mainland colonies, the East and West Indies, and Europe. Captain Kidd and other merchant captains traded many New York products in the English and Dutch Caribbean islands in return for sugar, linen, spices, and rum.[9] The province's key products included animal pelts, woolens, hats, glass, iron, soap, lumber, candles, shoes, cordage, beer, and the Hudson Valley's excellent wheat, milled into Manhattan flour and considered the finest in America.[10]

Although legitimate trade was important to colonial New York, piracy and smuggling played a key role in fueling the economy. Though this was not the reason Kidd selected the city as his port of call, Manhattan's "pirate culture" was not a liability for the former buccaneer, and he maintained cordial relations with many seafaring adventurers of a questionable nature, including Captains Thomas "Whisking" Clark and Giles Shelley, as well as his lawyer James Emott, who represented many commerce raiders and brokers. Kidd liked to go deep into his cups and swap tales with his roguish friends at Lovelace Tavern, Hawdon's Tavern, and other boisterous establishments within spitting distance of the harbor.

However, despite his friendships with men who occasionally skirted the law, and although the line separating state-sanctioned privateering and outlaw piracy was thin and privateers used the same tactics and vessels as pirates, unlicensed plundering without a whiff of nationalistic purpose or military patriotism just wasn't for him. A mere scrap of paper may have separated a buccaneer or privateer from a pirate or freebooter; but to Captain Kidd, most seamen of the age, and imperial English and other European officials, the two were vastly different when it came to the patriotic component, criminal prosecution, and prize-money allocation. The crucial factor that separated privateering from piracy is that privateers had the stamp of approval of the international court system, giving them legal title to seized goods and protecting them from future litigation—while pirates did not.[11]

Like Boston and Newport, the New York of Captain Kidd's day was a thriving coastal port city, trading center, and mariner's town. In the city's homes, taverns, ordinaries, and brothels, there was little that separated Royal Navy sailors, merchant seamen, privateers, outlaw pirates, smugglers, and wreckers (those who pulled loot from sunken ships) in outlook, dress, or comportment—and sea rovers often went from the legal to the illicit trade and back again without batting an eye. However, they almost always "sought out some form of paperwork from political bodies on land to provide the patina of legitimacy for committing violence upon the seas."[12] Whether of a piratical persuasion or not, these adventurers were the colonies' native sons, brothers, husbands, fathers, and uncles—in short, men intimately connected to land-based communities.[13] Many of them were married with families, and not all were young men despite the average ship's crew member being around twenty-seven years of age. Neither were the habitual or part-time pirates among them the throat-slitting, perpetually inebriated social outcasts, waging war against the world, of pulp fiction and Hollywood blockbusters, though a minority did fit that stereotypical description.[14]

By the time Kidd settled down with Sarah and began raising a family, New York was the foremost pirate enclave in the New World. This was after the law-and-order gentrification—some would say demise—of buccaneer Henry Morgan's Port Royal, Jamaica, the so-called "wickedest city on Earth," by the mid-1680s. In Kidd's time, New York and Newport served as the two main entrepôts for supplying the Indian Ocean pirates. The Red Sea Men, as they were known, were some of the most audacious freebooters of all time, but they were far from the first to sail the high seas plundering treasure-laden vessels.

Maritime piracy has existed since at least the fourteenth century BCE, when the Sea Peoples of Asia Minor and the Mediterranean plundered the Greeks, Persians, and Egyptians. Homer, Aristotle, and Thucydides wrote of the predations of these commerce raiders of the ancient world.[15] In fact, piracy is one of the most ancient of all professions and originally was not even regarded as a crime. In ancient Greece, piracy and smuggling were ubiquitous and considered honorable ways of earning a living, and during later Roman times large swaths of the Mediterranean were infested with pirates, requiring extensive naval campaigns to suppress them.[16]

But it is the legendary sea robbers of the Golden Age of Piracy from 1650 to 1730—the era of Morgan, Kidd, and Blackbeard—that have captured the human imagination. Temporally, the Red Sea Men era spanned from 1690 to 1705, in the middle of the Golden Age. Although pirates had sailed into North American ports in large numbers by the early 1680s, it was the Red Sea Men of New York, Newport, and Boston in the 1690s who gave rise to America's biggest economic boom of the late seventeenth century. This second wave of commerce raiders emerged due to a new imperial alliance between England and Spain, which caused the buccaneers to shift their hunting grounds from the Caribbean to the more lucrative Indian Ocean.[17]

Their sailing route from New York and New England ports to the western coast of Africa, southward to Madagascar and the Indian Ocean, and from there back again to the North American colonies became known as the "Pirate Round." While the pirates marauded the vessels of Emperor Aurangzeb Alamgir I, the Muslim Great Mughal of India, laden with gold, jewels, silk, and calico, the pirate-brokers traded arms, powder, naval stores, liquor, and other essentials with the plunderers in Madagascar. Both the pirates and traders returned from Madagascar with their "vast wealth" and were "kindly received" not only in New York and Newport but in Boston, East Jersey, Philadelphia, Maryland, and Charles Town. The Pirate Round became an integral part of the American economy and culture in the late seventeenth century because forward-looking colonial seafarers, merchants, and financiers realized that a large-scale raiding and trading network on the fringes of civilization—involving Arabian gold, Madagascar slaves, and East Indian jewels, fabrics, and spices—could generate gargantuan profits and provide well-paying jobs in defiance of England's Navigation Acts.[18]

The Acts of Trade and Navigation, as they were officially known, were seventeenth-century English laws regulating commerce within England's colonies and between England and her trading partners. They benefited the Mother Country by enhancing the collected customs revenue, increasing commerce for English merchants, promoting English seamen and shipbuilding, and augmenting the Royal Navy's muscle for waging war and challenging competing empires.[19] But to colonial America, the Navigation Acts were trade restrictions that squeezed the economic vitality out of the colonies and ensured that they would remain fiscally underdeveloped by banning trade with foreign vessels and the importation of non-English goods and specie. Because most goods bound to or from colonial America had to go through English ports, the additional customs duties and incidental costs harmfully jacked up prices and drove Americans to pursue illegal means to obtain goods and currency.[20] Because they were considered threats to self-government and common-law tradition, the Acts fomented the first stirrings of early ideas of autonomy and rebellion, providing the foundation for the Stamp Act protests, the Boston Tea Party, and other insurrections leading up to America's fight for independence.[21]

The catalyst for the explosion of the Red Sea trade in defiance of England's Navigation Acts was an enterprising Caribbean pirate named

Adam Baldridge. Fleeing Jamaica after being indicted for murder in 1689, Baldridge sailed east to Madagascar and, within two years, had struck a deal with local Malagasy leaders by setting up a profitable base of operations that supplied the pirates on the island of St. Mary's. The Red Sea market circumvented English maritime laws and created an Indo-Atlantic trading center where goods were bought from and sold to the pirates, who, like the "Pirate King" Baldridge, settled, traded, and intermarried with the population on Madagascar.[22]

The Black African tribal slave traders and White Euro-American pirates of Madagascar and the colonial merchants, brokers, governors, customs collectors, and other public officials in America all acted in concert. While the Black chieftains captured and enslaved tribesmen from rival Madagascar villages for sale and profit, the Red Sea Men brought to the underground marketplace the East Indian textiles, precious metals, spices, and jewels that American colonists were eager to obtain. The Red Sea trade thus infused much-needed gold and silver specie as well as enslaved tribesmen from Madagascar into the depressed colonial economy. At the same time, the trading of Malagasy slaves avoided conflict with the Royal African Company, which maintained its own forts, trading stations, and ships.[23] Because Adam Baldridge and his fellow pirates and merchant brokers had little overhead, they sold cheaply to the American merchants, enabling them to earn a tidy profit. In return, the merchants supplied the pirates with liquor, clothing, shoes, grain, peas, salt, flour, seeds, brushes, combs, paper, gunpowder, and weapons to outfit their distant settlements.[24] They also provided shuttling services for the pirates back home aboard merchant vessels.[25]

In circumventing the Crown's prerogatives, America's colonial governors, customs collectors, and other officials did not consider themselves lawbreakers. On the contrary, they prided themselves in boosting their economies by bringing much-needed specie and trade goods into coastal cities.[26] In fact, Indian Ocean piracy was so accepted that shares in the trading voyages were openly bought and sold in the taverns of New York. Many of these voyages promised a tenfold or greater return for merchant investors. Kidd's anglicized Dutch friend Frederick Philipse, the French Huguenot Stephen DeLancey, and other power brokers who financed these ships sailing halfway around the world, selling provisions and arms to pirates, believed they were simply taking advantage of a new and lucrative business market, since trading colonial goods and obtaining slaves on Madagascar broke no English laws—and neither the Royal African Company nor English East India Company had the legal authority or policing manpower to deny outside trade on Madagascar.[27]

The growth of piracy, along with the material riches it brought to New York in the last decade of the seventeenth century, is the perfect capitalistic metaphor for the Big Apple. For the salty Captain Kidd, New York was indeed a place where "a man who had cut his eyeteeth hanging onto a tops'l yard while trying to fist billowing canvas in a gale, or who had dodged French cannonballs as they slithered and splintered across a canting deck" felt right at home.[28] But even more important to him, the town's merchants, and many of the citizens was that it was a place to make gobs of money. Of the merchants of colonial New York, "it was once said that if they thought they could make a profit by passing through hell, they would risk burning the sails of their ships to try."[29] Everyone from Governor Benjamin Fletcher (1692–1698) on down to the poorest Jack Tar scrabbled to make their fortune, by legal *or* illegal means, it didn't matter much which. Fueled by piracy and smuggling, New Yorkers in the roaring 1690s could count on the old adage uttered by one visitor to the city in 1662: "Next to the freedom to worship God, comes the freedom for all inhabitants to make one's living."[30]

When Benjamin Fletcher was still learning the ropes as New York's colonial governor and the Red Sea trade was taking off, Captain William Kidd was a New York man of affairs who had ample reason to reflect upon his good fortune. He was married to one of the most dazzling socialites in town and had an adorable baby girl to cradle in his ropy seaman's arms. He was widely liked and respected, having successfully made the transition from rowdy buccaneer to gentleman merchant captain, with a multitude of people from different social classes he could count on as friends. He had settled Sarah's heavy debts from John Oort, and on November 18, 1692, his tireless efforts to recover her rightful inheritance had paid off as her estate finally settled, with "quietus granted" by Governor Fletcher.[31]

With Sarah's debt alleviated and their wealth at last combined, Kidd stood as one of the most prosperous men of not only their affluent East Ward neighborhood but of all New York. Under the English law of coverture, he as the male head of family—not Sarah—had £1,900 more in coinage and possessed a multifarious assemblage of costly household items to go along with several new parcels of valuable New York real estate. His and Sarah's multiple homes, vacant land lots, and prime slip locations on Pearl, Water, and Tienhoven (Pine) Streets included what are today some of the most expensive real estate holdings in the entire world, and they also held full title to the valuable 19¼-acre Saw Kill farm in Niew Haarlem at today's 73rd Street and the East River. Their 119-121 Pearl Street mansion where they lived full-time was one of the most elegantly furnished residences on Manhattan Island, with more than a dozen exotic carpets, elaborate hand-carved furniture, and hundreds of ounces of silver plate, candlesticks, and eating utensils that only the very wealthy of the age could afford.[32]

The happily married couple's glazed-brick three-story mansion, with its scrolled dormers and fluted chimneys, served as the perfect navigational beacon for Kidd when he sailed home from his merchant voyages to the West Indies.[33] From the front parlor, he and Sarah had an exquisite view of the Great Dock, New York Harbor, and his 16-gun merchant vessel, *Antigua*, anchored a stone's throw from his front door. Built two generations earlier by wealthy Dutch merchant Govert Loockermans, the house had a high peaked gable roof and was 38 feet across and 48 feet deep—double-wide dimensions virtually unheard of at the time. To cap it all off, the enterprising sea captain had a rooftop crane to haul up merchant goods and supplies into a warehouse on the third story.[34]

One of the greatest benefits of their house was its proximity to the Great Dock, the heart of the city's mercantile trade. It was a two-minute walk to the principal business district with its extensive warehouses, the Custom House, and busy wharves of the Great Dock, or to the *Stadt Huys*, New Amsterdam's first city hall and now the official New York City Town Hall. To a man bred to the sea, a former buccaneer who was now a merchant-ship owner, Kidd could not have lived in a more prime location.[35]

At this stage of their marriage, the "astute and business-savvy" Sarah no longer worked at her shop for imported high-end goods and was a full-time mother, since Kidd had helped her recover her inheritance while himself earning an excellent living as a merchant sea captain.[36] Sarah's ploy to persuade her husband to "settle down" in commercial enterprise instead of dangerous privateering, so he could spend more time with her and their young daughter, had worked. From the fall of 1691 through the spring of 1695, he turned for the most part away from seaborne military expeditions and toward oceanic commerce, transporting valuable cargo to and from the English and Dutch West Indies on shorter and less hazardous voyages. Sarah was ecstatic: it meant more time together with her husband as a family, instead of worrying about his being gone for months on end.[37]

The Kidds during these years cultivated relationships with people who would come to play significant roles in their lives. In June 1693, they sold their lots just down the street at 90 and 92 Pearl Street (Dock Street) to Robert Livingston, who wanted to build a private dock for his merchant business.[38] Soon thereafter, they sold their fine house and seventy-five feet of ground on Tienhoven Street (the present-day 25, 27, and 29 Pine Street) to Kidd's good friend Captain Thomas Clark. Clark, the former privateer and city coroner, who would play a key role in building the city's Trinity Church along with Captain Kidd, was a beloved figure in New York and served on various city councils, including one to help the poor.[39]

Kidd sold these properties partly to finance Sarah's younger brother Samuel Bradley Jr., who sought to strike out on his own. Not yet of age to acquire his own inheritance, the nineteen-year-old wanted to set himself up as a merchant. Kidd staked him to a £140 ($49,000 today) interest-free loan, and before leaving port with his cargo the young man made out his will as collateral for the loan. The document, dated July 5, 1693, and witnessed by Kidd's high-powered friend New York attorney general James Graham, reveals the tremendous bond the two had developed since Kidd had become patriarch of the Bradley family. It also sheds light on Captain Kidd as a nurturing family man. In the will, Samuel refers to him as "my loving brother-in-law [who] hath been very careful of me," bequeathed him one-half of his three valuable real-estate properties and one-third of his "goods and chattels," and named him executor of his estate.[40]

At this time, Kidd seems to have taken the entire Bradley family under his wing. Not only was he beloved by Sarah and young Samuel, but he also became quite close to his father-in-law, the tippling Captain Samuel Bradley Sr. By this stage of his career, Kidd was not only well known around the docks and at the high-society dinner parties, but in the governor's mansion. In fact, the common-born Englishman Kidd had by this time befriended or interacted closely with seven colonial governors or lieutenant governors: Codrington, Leisler, Sloughter, Ingoldsby, Simon Bradstreet and William Stoughton of Massachusetts, along with the current governor, Benjamin Fletcher.

In 1694, Kidd and Sarah celebrated the birth of their second daughter, little Sarah. So, while they watched one daughter grow into a toddler, they had a newborn baby girl by mid-decade for the burly sea captain to snuggle and love.[41]

In October 1694, shortly after little Sarah was born, Kidd solidified his privileged status as a New York civic leader by serving as foreman on a grand jury. The case—*Chidley Brooke vs. Barq Orange Cornelius Jacobs*—involved his friend Robert Livingston, who was charged with trading with the French enemy in wartime. Livingston, the Albany merchant and government official, had been caught red-handed illegally shipping flour, butter, candles, tar, bread, pork, and other supplies to Captain Jean-Baptiste DuCasse, now governor of Saint-Domingue in French Hispaniola. However, although the evidence against Livingston and his powerful New York business partners was damning, the prosecution's seafaring witnesses developed a sudden case of amnesia and refused to offer evidence against Captain Jacobs, Livingston, or the other investors.[42]

Without the testimony of the sailors, the grand jury had no choice but to acquit Livingston and his collaborators. As jury foreman, Captain Kidd returned the group's decision of *Sur proditiore ignoramus*, which meant that the Crown had no case due to lack of evidence. Livingston was grateful to Kidd, believing that he had helped direct the grand jury, pulling him out of a jam; but the New York war hero and burgher had done nothing of the sort, and it was the sailors who had sealed the case in favor of the shady Livingston and his wealthy co-investors.[43]

New York's customs collector Chidley Brooke, who had brought the charges against Livingston, was livid at the outcome. In a scathing letter to the Privy Council in London, he excoriated Livingston for treasonously supporting the French war effort.[44] Indeed, the critical provisions supplied by Livingston and his accomplices had allowed DuCasse to strike a devastating blow against the former buccaneer stronghold of Jamaica back in June. DuCasse's military force of twenty-two vessels carrying fifteen hundred men torched and ransacked a half dozen English settlements, carrying off thirteen hundred slaves.[45]

Piracy and illegal trading were enmeshed within the colonial legal system and played a huge role in the lives of New Yorkers. By 1694, the Red Sea trade and Caribbean smuggling had permeated every rung of New York society. And soon, very soon, even law-abiding Captain Kidd would no longer be able to remain out of piracy's long shadow. The reason was a Red Sea rapscallion named Thomas Tew.

In April 1694, after a sixteen-month privateering cruise to the Indian Ocean, Captain Thomas Tew sailed into Newport Harbor loaded with treasure stolen from the Great Mughal of India and was greeted as a conquering hero.[46] Six months later, Tew, the goateed gentleman from a fine Rhode Island family, strutted into New York in search of a new privateering commission from Governor Benjamin Fletcher, who received him in October like a visiting head of state and shuttled about town with him in his six-horse carriage. One of the first and most successful of the Red Sea pirates, Tew was the talk of the town in his handsome blue jacket with gold lace and a gaudy gold chain around his neck. The East Indian prize he had plundered the year before had netted more than £120,000 ($42,000,000 today) in gold, silver, ivory, spices, gemstones, and silk for himself and his sixty-man crew. Each of his Pirate Round sailors had received a stupendous £1,200 to £3,000 ($420,000 to $1,050,000 today), depending on their shipboard rank and experience level. These were life-changing payouts, far more than most seafarers in the Age of Sail could amass in an entire lifetime. Indeed, Thomas Tew and his scrappy American trailblazers had hit the lottery jackpot of the colonial era.[47]

All of Manhattan Island was excited about the legendary Red Sea Man and his crew's financial success; most colonists cared little that the riches had been obtained through ill-gotten means, since they had been seized from the East Indian Moors, regarded by the Puritans and other colonists as the pagan Muslim enemies of Christianity and civilization itself. Every adventurer within a hundred miles knew that Thomas Tew was in New York to obtain a letter of marque from Fletcher for another lucrative "privateering" cruise to the Indian Ocean. Experienced seafarers, landsmen, servants, and cherub-faced farm boys from Boston to Charles Town wanted in on the high-risk, high-reward venture, with parents and preachers striving "with the fear of the lash and hellfire, to restrain them from joining the bandit Tew and his company."[48]

Though William Kidd refused to embrace piracy, it couldn't have been easy for him to see merchants like his friend Frederick Philipse and sea captains like Thomas Tew rolling in the money from the Red Sea trade. Everywhere he looked—along the wharves, in the shops, taverns, and warehouses, and in the colonial mansions of his wealthy friends and the governor himself—he saw the signs of the mind-boggling riches reaped from Indo-Atlantic ventures. Some of his old crewmates like Samuel Burgess and John Browne, who had returned from the Indian Ocean in early 1693 with £800 ($280,000 today) shares of the booty, were living proof of the fortunes to be made. He saw them often enough at Hawdon's Tavern, Lovelace Tavern, and the other seamen's drinking establishments in town.[49]

Like Kidd, Samuel Burgess and John Browne had settled down, married, and bought homes in New York. Burgess was now captaining vessels for Philipse in the lucrative Madagascar trade, while Browne served as a senior merchant seaman, making voyages to the Straits of Gibraltar and West Indies. Though Burgess and Browne had stolen Kidd's ship and made off with his £2,000 years earlier, Kidd was not one to hold a grudge and seems to have gotten along amicably with the two men, or simply avoided them. Whatever the case, by 1696, Kidd and Browne had clearly patched up their differences, since Browne signed up for Kidd's 1696–1699 Indian Ocean expedition. Both Burgess and Browne were testaments to the riches to be made in the East, and Kidd was well aware of their amazing success stories.[50]

But it was Thomas Tew who truly brought home the glitz and glamour of the Red Sea trade. Kidd knew all about Tew's successful foray to the Indian Ocean in which he personally netted the astronomical sum of £12,000 ($4,200,000 in today's dollars) all for himself. Though history has not recorded whether Kidd and Tew spent time together and became friends, it is highly likely that they socialized at the local New York watering holes and at the lavish parties held at Governor Fletcher's mansion in October and November 1694, when both men were in town. Tew, accompanied by his wife and daughters "dressed in rich silks with glittering diamonds from the Orient," attended the "gala functions" at the Fletchers' impressive home at Fort William at this time. On November 18, 1694, after a month of socializing with the governor and his family and most likely making an acquaintanceship with Captain and Sarah Kidd, the Rhode Islander received his coveted privateering commission and a gold watch from Fletcher in exchange for an up-front £300 gift ($105,000 today) to process the paperwork.[51]

Though the success of Thomas Tew no doubt made an impression upon Kidd, it was when he looked within his own elevated social circle that he must have wondered what his and Sarah's life might be like if he did cross the line into piracy. When he was in port, Sarah and he attended sumptuous parties hosted by not only Benjamin Fletcher and his wife, Elizabeth, but by the Philipses, Bayards, Nicolls, van Cortlandts, DeLanceys, Emotts, Grahams, and other high-society movers and shakers. At these fashionable New York galas, the men typically dressed in silk waistcoats with jeweled buttons, full wigs, and lace cuffs, while the women wore the latest fashions from London: narrow-waisted, floor-length, bright-colored dresses of silk or satin, with a slight décolletage in the front and padded bustles, which plumped out the backside.[52] They talked about the French and Indian attacks up north, the continuing battle between the Leislerians and anti-Leislerians, and how Governor Fletcher and the people of New York province were secretly providing a safe haven for New Englanders accused of witchcraft. But what dominated the conversations were the stories of vast treasure chests full of gold, silver, and precious jewels and bales of rich silks pouring into the colonies from the Red Sea trade.

Thus, Kidd's ears by the spring of 1695 had been filled for three years with tales of the eye-popping riches to be made in the East Indies, relayed to him by the returning Red Sea Men and their merchant benefactors, the latter with whom he and his well-regarded young wife regularly socialized. At some point, he decided he wanted to be more than just a merchant captain making runs for sugar, spices, and rum to the West Indies; and he yearned to serve his country as more than a part-time privateer pestering the French in local waters. Having passed his fortieth birthday, he wanted a new adventure and change in his life that was a step up, if not in money, then in prestige.

There was just one catch: he absolutely refused to become an outlaw pirate.

So he made the decision to sail to London on a trading voyage and, while there, procure a privateering commission directly from the Crown in England—or perhaps even a lofty Royal Navy assignment—in the war against France.[53] It was a combination of the feverish excitement generated by the Indo-Atlantic trade, his getting on in years, his undying patriotism, and his lust for adventure that drove him to pursue his dream at this late stage of his seafaring career. He loved Sarah and his daughters and was very happy in his marriage. He enjoyed his new house, his wealth, his wide circle of friends and colleagues, and his stature as a New York society gentleman. But he wanted to take one last shot at a grand adventure, perhaps to recapture the freedom and excitement of his buccaneering days in the Caribbean. More importantly, he wanted to *be* something more, to accomplish something grandiose and magnificent, and he wanted to do it in the service of king and country.

He procured a letter of recommendation from his friend James Graham, attorney general of New York and protégé of Sir William Blathwayt, the Secretary of War and a wheeler-dealer in imperial patronage in London. Graham laid out the case to Blathwayt for Kidd to be awarded a royal privateering commission based on his extensive skill as a mariner, his bravery, and his devotion to duty as a patriot in King William's War. "He is a gentleman that has done his Majesty signal service [and] has served long in the fleet & been in many engagements & of unquestioned courage & conduct in sea affairs," wrote Graham. "He has been very prudent and successful in his conduct here and doubt not but his fame has reached your parts and whatever favor or countenance your Honor shows him I do assure your Honor he will be very grateful."[54]

Given the inherent dangers, Sarah tried to talk her husband out of the enterprise. Contrary to the chauvinistic era, Kidd was passionately in love with his wife, listened to her, and heeded her counsel. But this time he was adamant: he wanted one last shot at command of a powerful ship-of-force and not just his 16-gun *Antigua* on trips to the West Indies. No longer a young man, he was firmly set upon making his mark.

In early June 1695, with his letter from Attorney General Graham in his pocket, a letter that he hoped would open doors to imperial patronage, Kidd bid a teary-eyed farewell to Sarah, their two daughters, and Captain Samuel Bradley Sr., and set sail for London to make a name for himself. The *Antigua*'s cargo consisted of several hundred bales of cloth that would bring him a nice return in London. He took along with him his brother-in-law, the young Samuel Bradley, now a wealthy, seafaring twenty-one-year-old after having gained his inheritance.[55] Before leaving, Kidd and Samuel deeded the 19¼-acre Saw Kill Farm in New Harlem to Captain Bradley.[56]

The journey took some seven weeks and was a perilous one in the summer of 1695. Scores of French privateers prowled the Atlantic trade routes, and the Muslim Barbary pirates of North Africa scoured European waters for White Christians to serve as galley slaves or sell for ransom. In late July, Kidd safely reached the mouth of the Thames and sailed upriver toward the heart of London, joining the bustling commercial traffic tacking in the direction of Old London Bridge and Custom House Quay.[57]

He and Samuel disembarked at a run-down section of East London called Wapping. Apparently, none of Kidd's Soham or Dundee relatives lived in the city at the time—most had immigrated to Maryland and Virginia to make a fresh start in the New World—so he stayed not far from the docks with distant relatives of his wife: Sarah Hawkins and her butcher husband, Matthew. Sandwiched on the Thames between the naval yards and London Bridge, Wapping was where the maritime caste lived, drank in the scores of dingy taverns, and plied their sea-related trades as sailors, dockworkers, shipwrights, and the like. The neighborhood was a warren of crumbling homes, narrow streets, and alehouses interspersed with grimy warehouses, lumberyards, wharves, and Execution Dock—the notorious place where pirates were hanged before thousands of drunken, jeering Londoners.[58]

As residents of seedy Wapping, Sarah and Matthew Hawkins were not well off by any means, but they greeted Kidd and Samuel warmly and took them in as their houseguests. For the next several months, the Hawkinses would generously provide room and board for the two colonial Americans.[59]

Now in London, Captain Kidd's first step was to sell his bales of cargo. Then it was time to go job-hunting to land his privateering commission—or perhaps, if his remarkable luck continued to hold, a captaincy in the Royal Navy.[60] As it turned out, he would become involved in something far bigger and more dangerous than he could possibly imagine.

–6–

The Scheme of English Lords

Soon after setting foot in the fabled city of William Shakespeare, John Locke, and Daniel Defoe, the metropolis that had begun as Londinium in Roman times, the American rustic Captain Kidd visited the office of Sir William Blathwayt to present his letter of introduction and secure his coveted letter of marque. But when Kidd called upon him, he discovered that the Secretary of War was on a military campaign in the Netherlands with the king.[1] With Blathwayt unavailable to help him, he reconnected with his former comrade in arms from the Caribbean, Thomas Hewetson, who was now a married Royal Navy captain living in London. But he quickly learned from his good friend that the Admiralty had a severe manpower shortage and was not handing out privateering commissions.[2]

Then, on August 8, his luck changed. While walking about town, he bumped into a pair of unexpected New York chums: Captain Giles Shelley and Philip French, a rising merchant in the Red Sea trade and son-in-law of his friend Frederick Philipse. The colonials greeted one another cordially, shared the latest news, and described their reasons for being in London—all of which were to gain economic favor in the "fountainhead of political intrigue." Before parting, Shelley and French invited Kidd to join them that upcoming Sunday for a boat ride upriver to the quaint village of Chelsea. Accompanying them, they said, would be none other than Robert Livingston, who had arrived in London just a few days before Kidd, on July 25, after a harrowing voyage delayed several months by a savage winter storm.[3]

Three days later, on August 11, Kidd met Livingston, Shelley, and French at the dock and sailed up the Thames to Chelsea. Accompanying them was William Carter, a guest of Livingston and friend of the Whig politician Richard Coote, the Irish-born Earl of Bellomont, the newly appointed governor of the Province of Massachusetts Bay, who was also angling to replace Benjamin Fletcher as governor of New York.[4] The reason Livingston had risked a dangerous winter voyage to London was to recoup the £4,000 ($1,400,000 today) the English government owed him for providing victuals to the troops in Albany and other loans.[5]

When they reached Chelsea, Kidd and his fellow colonials went to lunch at a swank tavern before heading out for a walk in the leafy park. They talked about the ongoing war between England and France and the equally vicious conflict raging between the newly ascendant Whigs and reeling Tories.[6] At some point, the subject turned to a topic that would preoccupy the thoughts of Kidd and Livingston for the remainder of the day and deep into the night: the bold Red Sea Men of the Pirate Round and the powerful merchants in New York and New England financially backing them. At the heart of the story was the man who stood poised to replace Fletcher—Richard Coote, the Earl of Bellomont.[7]

Sixty years old when Kidd visited London, Bellomont was a powerful Whig House of Commons member and friend of government adviser and philosopher John Locke (1632–1704).[8] Rising to power through his early support of William and Mary during the Glorious Revolution, Coote had served as captain of horse in the Dutch army and was rewarded in 1689 by being appointed to the peerage as the First Earl of Bellomont.[9] His service to the Crown allowed him to parlay his advantage into the position of lord justice of Ireland and catch the attention of the powerful Charles Talbot, the Duke of Shrewsbury, and other members of the

Whig political leadership, known as the Junto.[10] It was the Junto that had directed the Whig Party, and often the government itself, during the reign of William and Mary, and during the king's individual reign after Queen Mary passed away from smallpox in December 1694.[11]

Though the owner of a fine Dover Street mansion a stone's throw from Westminster Abbey, a noble peerage, and extensive land holdings in Ireland, Bellomont had spent most of his adult life desperately short of cash and remained in scandalously heavy debt for a member of Parliament. With his inherited land mostly non-arable and unable to turn a profit, he found himself perpetually in search of additional sources of income.[12] His "flighty" young wife, Lady Catherine Nanfan Bellomont, didn't help his financial straits; her frivolous spending sprees and mounting gambling debts were the talk of London.[13]

When Kidd arrived in London in the summer of 1695, Bellomont was undergoing a career resurgence. Due to his precarious finances, he had been forced to consider the time-honored escape route from penury for English aristocrats: emigration to America as a colonial official. Secretary of State Shrewsbury recommended him to the king for the governorship of Massachusetts Bay province, arguing that Bellomont's military background made him the perfect overseas commander in chief to defend New England from French attacks. The ploy worked, and not only was Bellomont confirmed to the post on June 14, 1695, but with the help of his powerful patrons Locke and Shrewsbury he would, by March 1697, finagle the governorship of New York when the Whigs were at the peak of their power.[14] The dual postings would provide the dishonored earl with an annual income of £1,800 ($630,000 today), enough money to relieve his debt and sustain a cushy lifestyle for himself and his profligate young wife.[15]

Through William Carter's introduction, Livingston had met with Bellomont the night before the Chelsea excursion, on August 10, at the earl's Dover Street mansion. Unlike the humble-born Kidd, Livingston was able to arrange a visit to the earl because he could trace his family lineage back to A.D. 1124 through the royals of Linlithgow, Scotland.[16]

During the "long conference" with Bellomont, Livingston briefed him on the political situation in New York, and they proved to be two peas in a pod, sharing an obsession with money and Fletcher.[17] Angry at the governor for being slow to reimburse his outstanding loans in service of the Crown, Livingston continued to demand repayment at 8 percent interest, but the cash-strapped Fletcher insisted on using the money instead to prosecute King William's War. Livingston and Bellomont agreed to stay in touch while Livingston remained in London, and to help each other achieve their objectives: Livingston to cultivate influential contacts and regain his fortune, Bellomont to bump up his salary by obtaining the New York governorship.[18]

During the Chelsea excursion, Livingston was keen to know more about the exploding Red Sea trade. Shelley, French, and Kidd were all intimately familiar with the New York–Madagascar connection, but only the former Red Sea Man Shelley had sailed to the East Indies. Livingston listened closely to the three men regarding the great riches being amassed by the privateers, smugglers, and traders of colonial New York. Based upon these discussions and further talks with Kidd later that night, Livingston was bitten by the gold bug and hatched a plot that would allow him to regain his fortune, Kidd to obtain his coveted privateering commission, and Bellomont to add the New York governorship to his Massachusetts posting.[19]

The plan was to somehow obtain an official Crown license that would allow Captain Kidd to hunt down pirates in the Indian Ocean, legally seize their ill-gotten riches, and keep them for not only himself and his crew but for the king, Livingston, Bellomont, and other well-heeled London financial backers. There were two problems with the scheme: the first was that it was desperately risky, and the second was that it was most likely highly illegal. Which, of course, would stop no one—except eventually the voice of reason in the whole affair, Captain Kidd. But even he would be thwarted in his attempts to extricate himself from the dangerous intrigue of Livingston, Bellomont, and their coterie of conniving English lords.

Livingston was both the mastermind and principal executor of the treasure-hunting scheme.[20] Kidd himself would one day refer to him as "the projector, promoter, and chief manager"[21] of what would become not only one of the biggest scandals of the Golden Age of Piracy, rocking "the New World and the Old" and threatening "to tip the subcontinent of India to the Maharajahs,"[22] but "one of the greatest political blunders made by the Whig Party in England."[23]

WITHIN TWO DAYS of concocting his quixotic anti-piracy-for-profit scheme, the energetic Robert Livingston began putting it into action. The first step was to persuade the Crown to commission, finance, and outfit Captain Kidd in a Royal Navy gunship potent enough to make an expedition against the Red Sea pirates.[24] He would sail to the Indian Ocean, aggressively hound the freebooters, and confiscate their illicit treasures before they returned to their home ports in New York, Newport, and Boston. As governor of Massachusetts Bay and hopefully New York (still pending), Bellomont would act as head of the Admiralty court in America for the lawful prizes, and he would share the profits along with Livingston, Kidd, and the king, who would all be entitled to hefty shares of the stolen goods and the prize ships themselves.[25]

William III agreed to the plan, with the proviso that a group of private investors would finance the enterprise instead of the Crown and would give his majesty 10 percent of the proceeds of all prizes taken. As a silent partner, this would minimize his exposure if the plan backfired. Like Bellomont and Livingston, the king was fully aware that the project was not strictly "legal."[26] With his majesty on board, Bellomont set out in search of "persons of consideration"—wealthy members of the Whig Junto—to join with himself, Livingston, and Kidd as partners. In the summer of 1695, the Whigs were at their zenith and Bellomont made his pitch to Shrewsbury and other influential Whigs. He told them that by outfitting Kidd and ridding the Indian Ocean of pirates, they had a golden opportunity to simultaneously line their own pockets and perform a patriotic deed for king and country.[27]

While Bellomont rallied his lordly friends to the cause, Livingston blackened the name of Fletcher. He testified before the Lords of Trade that the governor had misappropriated funds and committed election violations by forcing electors to choose specific representatives and by coercing soldiers and sailors to vote for them. To buttress his claims, he called upon Kidd, Shelley, French, and Samuel Bradley to testify before the Lords on his behalf.[28] The four New Yorkers testified on August 28 and September 14, 1695, but Kidd was a reluctant witness and Shelley refused to testify until slapped with a subpoena. Though Kidd didn't want to testify, Livingston convinced him that if he did, he would position himself favorably with the Whig leadership to obtain his royal commission.[29] Kidd was aware of the reports of Fletcher's questionable election tactics, but he readily admitted that most of what he knew was hearsay, and Fletcher himself would later use the captain's own words—"ye deponent cannot say it was by order from the governor"—to exonerate himself.[30] Based upon Livingston's accusations, the Lords recommended that Fletcher be recalled to answer charges; and an Order in Council was issued, followed eventually by a letter from Shrewsbury removing him from power.[31]

From late August through September, while Livingston was pressing his case to the Lords for reimbursement, he was also working hard to put together his pet pirate-hunting scheme. By October 3, he and Bellomont had assembled a prominent team of Whig Junto financial backers that included Lord John Somers, Lord Keeper of the Great Seal; Charles Talbot, the Duke of Shrewsbury, Secretary of State; Admiral Edward Russell, First Lord of the Admiralty and treasurer of the Royal Navy; and Henry Sidney, the Earl of Romney, serial womanizer and Master General of Ordnance.[32]

On October 4, Livingston delivered the good news that the expedition was ready to proceed, but by then Captain Kidd was beginning to have serious second thoughts.[33] There were several reasons for his change of heart. First, he had never fully trusted the money-grubbing Livingston; and, after seeing him wheeling and dealing to further his own interests the past two months, he was wary of the man. A second nagging issue was that Livingston still had not disclosed the names of any of the partners besides Bellomont. This made Kidd wonder if the furtive Scotsman was withholding other critical details from him. But what irked him the most was that Livingston would not even allow him to meet their lordly patrons in person.[34]

There were also issues regarding the voyage itself. In Kidd's eyes, the expedition would be a challenge to pull off, but it could be done. Yet it was so risky that he wondered if it *should* be done. Pirating from pirates was still piracy in his eyes—and he wanted no part of being a pirate; nor did he want to risk his own life, or that of his crew, to line the pockets of London bigwigs. He had come to the seat of imperial power to obtain a royal privateering commission to fight the French—not to capture and plunder dangerous, hard-to-catch pirates.

Therefore, he said no to the command of the pirate-hunting venture—rather emphatically—to Livingston and Bellomont. Given the huge potential windfalls, the highbrow sponsors, and the time and energy already invested in the enterprise, they begged him to reconsider. But Kidd wouldn't budge. Bellomont then threatened to have him arrested, to seize the *Antigua* from him so he could not sail back to New York, and to have his seamen press-ganged away from him by the Royal Navy if he didn't agree to command the voyage. Not only that, but Bellomont warned that he would "oppress" him in New York when he took office as governor of the province.[35]

Kidd backed down. Confident in his abilities and knowing firsthand from the streets of New York the untold riches awaiting him in the East, he decided to carry out the difficult mission rather than make enemies of Bellomont and the other unspeakably powerful English noblemen, who offered him further assurances "of their support and his impunity from criminal prosecution."[36]

With all concerned parties now on board with Livingston's risky scheme, events proceeded quickly. On October 10, 1695, the three main partners—Bellomont, Livingston, and Kidd—signed the first contract for the expedition. To enable the king's pirate hunter to subdue the "predators of the Red Sea," a well-armed warship was to be built by the partners to Kidd's specifications.[37] As agent for the partners, Bellomont was to obtain an Admiralty commission from the king empowering Kidd as a privateer and authorizing him to attack French and pirate vessels. He was also to secure a government grant authorizing Kidd and the partners to keep the prizes without liability. Bellomont and the four other Whig partners were to pay four-fifths of the cost of outfitting the privateering man-of-war, estimated at £6,000 ($2,100,000 today), while Livingston and Kidd were obligated to pay the balance of one-fifth of the cost in exchange for their cut of the profits. Due to the shadiness of the scheme, Somers, Shrewsbury, Russell, and Romney concealed their participation from public view, and thus only Bellomont's name appears on the original agreement.[38]

Kidd was to raise a crew of a hundred men hired on a "no purchase, no pay" basis. Any captured ships were to be carried to Boston without breaking cargo and delivered to Bellomont, who would have the authority to declare them lawful prizes in court and distribute the profits to himself, the king, and the Whig lords without the Admiralty skimming its normal share. Sixty percent of a prize's value was to go to Bellomont and the other partners, 25 percent to the crew, and the remainder to Kidd and Livingston. As a deal-sweetener, if more than £100,000 worth of plunder was captured, the pirate-hunting gunship would become Kidd's property through clear title. This was not an unrealistic possibility, given that the Red Sea Men Thomas Tew in late 1693 and Henry Every in September 1695 had both cleared over £120,000 ($42,000,000 today). All the same, there was no guarantee that he would even catch sight of a treasure-laden pirate vessel, let alone capture one. If he was somehow unsuccessful, he would have to pay back the costs of purchasing the ship as well as compensate Bellomont for his fronted money.[39] Furthermore, to protect himself and the investors, Bellomont insisted that Kidd sign a £20,000 performance bond ($7,000,000 today), and that Livingston sign a similar bond for £10,000.[40]

Captain Kidd, of course, was not happy that the terms were so skewed against him and in favor of his noble sponsors. However, he had no choice but to proceed with the risky enterprise, since Bellomont had threatened to halt his ship, and to have him and his men impressed, if he tried to escape London. With the initial contract in place, the partners secured the standard letter of marque to combat the French from the Admiralty and then obtained a special grant to hunt pirates through a patent under the Great Seal of England. A warrant for the patent went forward on January 20, 1696; and six days later, on January 26, the great seal was affixed to a second commission by full partner and lord keeper John Somers.[41] The second agreement, addressed "To our trusty and well-beloved Captain William Kidd, Commander of the Ship *Adventure Galley*," authorized him to apprehend and bring to trial four specific pirates—Thomas Tew, John Ireland, Thomas Wake, and William May—along with "any other pirates . . . he might find."[42]

While the commissions were being finalized, Kidd oversaw the construction and outfitting of his new warship. He was assisted by Edmund Harrison, a powerful London merchant who was brought in as a sixth investor when Bellomont failed to produce his designated share (Harrison also paid half of Shrewsbury's share and a portion of Admiral Russell's).[43] The ship that Kidd and Harrison decided upon was a 125-foot-long, 287-ton beast built at Castle Shipyard at Deptford. With 34 cannons, the *Adventure Galley* was well suited for the task of hunting pirates, with only naval warships and the largest merchantmen boasting more firepower. Furthermore, while the gunship was large enough to carry 150 to 160 men, she was still small enough to be careened on a beach and not require a dockyard for maintenance. In addition to having three tall sailing masts, the *Adventure Galley* was equipped with 46 oars, 23 on each side. The banks of long oars along each side of the warship would allow Kidd to attack or withdraw from combat at a clip of three knots in a windless sea in any compass quadrant, a significant advantage over his enemies in becalmed waters.[44]

There was just one problem with the massive gunship. Constructed in a stunning five weeks and leaving drydock on December 4, 1695, the *Adventure Galley* was built too fast and with substandard materials. Pressured by the Admiralty to churn out warships to fight the French, the Deptford shipbuilders not only hastily caulked the planks of the double hull, but they also used shoddy supplies to save costs. As a result, the *Adventure Galley* would literally come apart at the seams within two years of her launch.[45]

In January and February 1696, Kidd purchased and loaded provisions and pulled together a crew with Harrison's help. But before he could set sail, there remained one final agreement: a grant giving the partners the legal right to retain any seized property taken from the pirates. If a ship owner was made aware that his cargo had been confiscated by a third party, he could sue for the goods unless the investors had a protection in place denying him the legal right of recovery. The solution was to draw up a special commission in which the king granted the investors the right to keep all captured pirate goods for themselves on behalf of the Crown.[46]

The final commission was not signed by William III until August 24, 1696, when Kidd was in New York visiting Sarah and his daughters and filling out his final crew; and the grant would not pass the great seal by Somers until May 27, 1697. Because the Whig lords refused to have their names associated with the expedition, the final agreement was signed by Bellomont, Harrison, and four obscure surrogates for the other backers. These anonymous "commoners" in the top-secret mission were Samuel Newton, John Rowley, George Watson, and Thomas Reynolds.[47] Just like Kidd, these voiceless seventeenth-century servants of the powerful Whig lords—with job titles like stable groom and footman instead of lord chancellor and Secretary of State—had no option but to accede to their lordly masters' demands, unless they wanted to find themselves out of work without a reference.[48]

On April 23, 1696, Kidd finally set sail from Plymouth, England, to New York to fill out his full 150-man crew and reunite with his family. Due to the Royal Navy's wartime needs, he was only allowed to recruit seventy men total in England and had to sign up the rest in America. On his homeward journey, he captured the *Sita Gratia*, a French fishing boat loaded with salt and tackle for a season's trawling on the Grand Banks. Kidd carried the French prize with him into New York Harbor, arriving on July 4.[49]

Once Kidd settled in again with Sarah and the girls, he would need to obtain Governor Fletcher's permission to hire eighty more seamen. More importantly, he had to sign up experienced mariners to refill several key positions, since the Royal Navy had impressed thirty of his best sailors before he had even left England. Back on February 28, when he reached the buoy at the Nore, the naval staging waters off the mouth of the Thames, Captain Stewart of the 90-gun HMS *Duchess of Queensborough* had ignored the clear-cut orders of his king, stealing away Kidd's most experienced sailors. Kidd was left with only five mariners and thirty-five landsmen, making it risky to sail his lightly crewed vessel out into a war zone. Fortunately, he was able to appeal to his backer Russell for the return of his seamen. The admiral angrily issued an order on March 20 to Stewart demanding the prompt return of all Kidd's men. Although Stewart returned the same number of sailors he had pirated away, he disobeyed his admiral's order and spitefully chose not to return the *same* men. Though Kidd wouldn't lose his second-in-command, Henry Mead, he was forced to relinquish most of his key officers and was saddled with rotten eggs and landsmen as sailors—or, as one historian put it, the lower-caliber "Navy rejects."[50]

Upon setting anchor in New York Harbor, Kidd was rowed ashore like a visiting head of state for his reunion with Sarah and his daughters, who greeted him at the Great Dock. For Captain Kidd, it was truly good to be home.

How many hours he spent reuniting with Sarah, Elizabeth, and little Sarah as Captain Kidd the husband and father is not known, but it couldn't have been more than a day or two; for soon after his return, he threw himself into raising money for the expedition, recruiting additional seamen, and outfitting his new 34-gun ship-of-force.

His first task was to meet with Benjamin Fletcher. With every able-bodied New York male needed to fight the French on the Albany frontier, he needed to obtain the governor's permission to recruit men for his voyage.[51] Unfortunately, Fletcher knew that Kidd had given testimony against him during his trip to London, and the lame-duck governor was now under a cloud of suspicion—though not yet formally recalled.[52] However, Kidd had a strong hand to win back at least a modicum of goodwill from him. To open the meeting, he offered up the *Sita Gratia* for condemnation in the governor's Vice-Admiralty court, as well as his four captured French prisoners of war. Fletcher was indeed pleased. The fishing vessel was promptly condemned and sold as a legitimate prize of war for £350 ($122,500 today) under Kidd's commission. This entitled Fletcher to 15 percent of the profits ($18,375 today), the king a tenth, and Kidd the remainder of the prize money, which he used to pay his men wages and purchase provisions for his forthcoming voyage.[53] By court order, the *Sita Gratia*'s crew members were sent to Boston in exchange for English prisoners of war held by the French in Canada.[54]

After showing Fletcher his commissions, Kidd politely requested that he be able to recruit the remainder of his crew to bring his ship up to full fighting strength. Though the governor wanted to say no, given Kidd's lofty commission from the king he had no choice but to allow him to drum up men and fill out his ship's roster.[55]

As they parted ways, Kidd knew that Fletcher's days were numbered as governor. The man would be of no help or importance to him a year and a half from now when he returned from his voyage.[56] Which meant that everything was now riding on the English earl who had threatened him—Bellomont—once his lordship arrived to replace Fletcher as royal governor of New York.

THE WORD HAD already spread around town that Kidd was outfitting a voyage and looking for able seamen, but he also posted broadsheets—the seventeenth-century version of Help Wanted posters—advertising his commission and need for additional recruits. Although the broadsheets were circulated throughout the city and into the countryside, few seamen initially signed up.[57]

Not only were many young men up north guarding the Albany frontier, but several ship captains were away at sea in the Indian Ocean with large numbers of New York sailors. With England and the Netherlands at peace, there was also a Dutch privateer in the harbor taking on men.[58] The unfavorable terms of the voyage's division of spoils, slanted in favor of Kidd's lordly backers, were also a factor. To attract more seamen and in defiance of his impractical English investors, he decided to change the *Adventure Galley*'s articles into the more democratic terms he had known as a Caribbean buccaneer. The new terms were not more beneficial to himself, but were far more favorable toward his crew since he flipped the division of spoils, giving the crew 60 percent of the voyage's profits instead of 25 percent. This, of course, correspondingly reduced the share of the backers from 60 percent down to 25, which Kidd supported on principle. Because Bellomont had rammed the mission and its unfavorable terms down his throat and since the noble backers were far away in London, he had probably planned on doing it all along to circumvent the inequitable distribution.[59]

He knew he would be angering his investors by allocating the bulk of the prize money to himself and his crew. But if he was unable to pull together a full 150-man crew to sail the ship and man its complement of 34 guns, there would be no return on investment for anyone. Despite New York's severe manpower shortage, the revised arrangement had the intended effect. By late July, with the news that the

Adventure Galley was fitting out under the standard "no prey, no pay" terms, with a 60 percent take for the crew, experienced seamen and landsmen alike flocked to the city to join up. They came from as far away as Pennsylvania and Maryland, from East and West Jersey, and from up north in Massachusetts.[60] On August 28, Governor Andrew Hamilton of East Jersey apologized in a letter to Fletcher for not being able to supply troops for the war effort, blaming the "great wages" now available to the young men of his province, several of whom "are gone aboard Captain Kidd" with no possibility "to prevail with them to continue in garrison."[61]

The voyage's prospects improved so dramatically that by early August New York merchants were advancing money to strangers from Pennsylvania and elsewhere in exchange for a promised piece of their share in the expedition. Even Kidd's good friend Thomas "Whisking" Clark got in on the action: the ship captain, city councilor, and vestryman at the currently-under-construction Trinity Church loaned money to several sailors for a cut of the prize money.[62] When an additional 90 crew members had signed the articles, including around 60 New Yorkers, the recruiting stopped. By late August, Kidd had 152 men total, which was enough to simultaneously sail the *Adventure Galley* and fire a proper broadside.[63]

While Kidd was putting together his crew, he enjoyed his reunion with his wife and daughters and resumed his role as a man of affairs about town. On July 19, he went with his family lawyer James Emott to look at the construction site for the new Trinity Church and to attend a meeting of the construction committee. The city's first English house of worship was being erected at the corner of Broad Way and Wall Street, and Kidd and Sarah were enthusiastic about the enterprise. When Kidd and Emott arrived for the church meeting, they saw more than a dozen Black and White men hard at work on the foundation and walls of the church under the watchful eye of Dutch master mason Direck Vanderburgh. When they reemerged an hour later, Captain Kidd and his family were the proud owners of Pew Number 4, thanks to the recommendations of vestrymen James Emott and Captain "Whisking" Clark and a small donation from the selling of the *Sita Gratia*.[64]

To assist with Trinity Church's construction, Kidd agreed to lend runner and tackle from the *Adventure Galley* as a pulley system to help the workers hoist up the stones.[65] In July and August, while he recruited his crew and spent time with his family, he worked closely with his old friend Clark, one of the chief managers and suppliers of the heavy stones, timber, lime, and ropes. It would take a massive community effort to build the sacred Anglican church, and the former buccaneers Captain Kidd and "Whisking" Clark were an integral part of the endeavor, along with New York's "ingenuous and well esteemed" as well as very busy "pirate lawyer" James Emott.[66]

Pew Number 4, located near the rector, would bear the inscription "Captain Kidd—Commanded 'Adventure Galley.'"[67] Unfortunately, the king's privateer would never get the opportunity to pray at the church he had helped build, but his wife, Sarah, and daughters would.[68] The latest incarnation of the legendary Trinity Church stands today in the exact same spot where Captain Kidd lent his runner and tackle over 330 years ago.

By late August, Kidd had hired on a full crew under the new terms. He recruited heavily at Hawdon's Tavern and the newly opened King's Arms, the leading anti-Leislerian drinking establishment and coffeehouse on Broad Way. His crew ran the full spectrum of colonial American manhood in terms of age, profession, seafaring experience, marriage, and ethnicity. Of the 152 total sailors who signed up, "21 were mariners, 3 were carpenters, and others had assorted occupations such as surgeon, cook, laborer, joiner, cordwainer, gunsmith, jeweler, and baker."[69] Most were poor commoners without property and less than £5 ($1,750 today) of accumulated wealth. Though the majority were young adventurers with few attachments, Kidd and ten others were married men.[70]

Like Kidd's hometown of New York, the crew was multiethnic. More than two-thirds of the men were of English stock. The next largest contingent was the twenty-five colonial Dutchmen aboard, which is expected given that Netherlanders comprised half of New York's 4,500 White European residents. The remainder of the crew was composed of seven Scots, two Frenchmen, two Welshmen, one African American, and one Algonquian Native American.[71]

Despite the crew's multifarious makeup, the men did have one important thing in common: they saw the venture as a way to get rich quick. In an age when the gap between rich and poor was a chasm, the bulk of the crew did not sign up for patriotism, adventure, to prove themselves to their fathers, or to escape the law, but rather to "make a good voyage," which meant they wanted to see a *significant* financial return on their investment of time and energy. Thus, even though only a handful of Kidd's crew members had done stints in jail or served aboard ships as unapologetic freebooters, the crew's motivation for the voyage was the same as it would have been if all the men were, in fact, *hardened pirates*. The Indian Ocean was a gold rush and they wanted in on it—it was that simple.

The articles Kidd had the crew sign were similar to the democratic buccaneer articles he had used throughout his career. They carried many of the same provisions used by Henry Morgan and described by Alexander Exquemelin in *The Buccaneers of America*. Once the value of any captured booty had been estimated and the investors' shares and expenses of the voyage deducted, the remainder was divided among the officers and crew in accordance with their designated shares based upon their rank and skill level. The agreement included an incentive reward of a hundred Spanish silver pieces of eight for the first man to spot a captured prize ship and several clauses punishing bad behavior.[72] Cowardice constituted a loss of a share, as did drunkenness during an attack. All plunder was required to be handed over: if someone stole for his own benefit, he lost his share. Anyone leading a mutiny or disobeying orders would lose his share and receive punishment based on what the captain and majority of the company agreed was appropriate. Thus, Kidd could not punish his men without the majority vote of his crew. The agreement also compensated seamen for the loss of an eye, leg, or arm by giving them six hundred pieces of eight, while the loss of a finger or toe earned a man one hundred. Finally, the heirs of a dead man collected £20, even if there was no purchase from the voyage.[73]

The departure date was set for September 6, 1696. During his last week in muggy New York making final preparations for the voyage, Kidd spent as much time with his family as possible, while his rowdy crew raised hell at Hawdon's Tavern, the King's Arms, Lovelace Tavern, and every other colonial alehouse on Manhattan Island. As the hours and days ticked down toward the departure date, the *Adventure Galley* was a beehive of activity. Trinity Church pew-holder Captain Kidd took back his block and tackle loaned to the Anglican church and used them to load his warship with food and provisions. Supplies were positioned to ensure ready access to specific materials and preserve the vessel's trim by not overloading the stern and having the bow float too high in the water. Meanwhile, the sails were mended, the ropes coiled, and last-minute repairs made to ensure that she was seaworthy. Kidd took great pride in his new gunship and brought Sarah and his daughters aboard to see her up close and witness him and his busy crew in action.[74]

For the grand send-off, New Yorkers turned out in their Sunday finest all along the shore and in small boats, while trumpets sounded from the *Adventure Galley*'s quarterdeck with all due pomp and ceremony.[75] With seagulls soaring overhead, a New York magistrate read aloud King William III's lawful commissions authorizing New York's beloved leading citizen and privateer commander to hunt down the French and outlaw pirates.[76] When the magistrate was finished, Kidd ordered the two-ton anchor heaved and the crew inserted heavy bars into the capstan. To the rhythm of a seafaring ditty, the sailors pushed round and round like mules turning a millstone, pulling the stout cable and the fluked, wrought-iron anchor up from the salty depths of the harbor. After the crew members delivered their final valedictions to their wives and girlfriends, several of whom proved not to be girlfriends at all but sporting lasses of popular

Petticoat Lane, the deck turned to a flurry of activity as the crew made the ship ready to sail. Bare feet chuffed against the damp wood as fresh canvas sails unfurled and the anchor cable ground out the last fifty feet toward the hawsehole.[77]

Sarah and her husband kissed and hugged each other one last time. Kidd promised that he would come back to her and the girls safely. They both probably had tears in their eyes, as Kidd was an emotional fellow and madly in love with her. Along with the magistrate and preacher, Sarah and the other civilians on board for the grand send-off now climbed down into the oarboats to return ashore.

From the Great Dock, Sarah and her daughters watched as the *Adventure Galley* headed south toward the open sea, accompanied by a Bermudan brigantine and the HMS *Richmond*. The triumvirate of ships made quite a sight as they sailed down the southern end of the East River and fired salutes to the fort. Elizabeth and little Sarah squealed with glee as several big guns at Fort William cracked out a rejoinder, the percussions reverberating across the Upper Bay. The crowd gathered along the shoreline gave a rousing cheer and waved handmade Union Jacks, as flocks of osprey and tern swooped low over the water.[78]

The vessels shook out their sails and pointed their bows toward Staten Island before heading for the smugglers' rendezvous of Sandy Hook, East Jersey, the Narrows, and the choppy waves of the open Atlantic. Watching the *Adventure Galley* slowly shrinking as she made her way southward, Sarah struggled to come to terms that her husband was sailing all the way to the southern tip of Africa and from there to the East Indies, where the toughest and most violent pirates in the world had been feasting on fat, treasure-laden Muslim ships. All she wanted was for him to return safely home to her and her daughters.[79]

If she had been aware of Benjamin Fletcher's assessment of her husband's chances for a successful voyage, she would have been even more worried about his safe return. In his letter to the Lords of Trade shortly after Kidd left port, the embattled governor, set to be replaced by Bellomont and angry at Kidd for testifying against him in London, offered one of the most widely quoted and prophetic statements ever written in the Captain Kidd saga:

> One Captain Kidd lately arrived here, and produced a commission under the great seal of England, for suppressing of piracy. When he was here, many flocked to him from all parts, men of desperate fortunes and necessitous in expectation of getting vast treasure. He sailed from hence with 150 men, as I am informed great part of them are of this province. It is generally believed here, they will have money *per fas aut nefas* [by any means regardless of legality], that if he misses of the design intended for which he has commission, 'twill not be in Kidd's power to govern such a horde of men under no pay.[80]

Thus, Benjamin Fletcher, and apparently many other influential New Yorkers, believed Kidd's crew was made up of, in other words, "pirates." The question was, would the Crown's handpicked pirate hunter be able to keep them in line, or would they slit his throat and steal his ship to go a-pirating?

PART 3

—

The Fateful Voyage

–7–
A Shifting World

Once in the open Atlantic, Captain Kidd steered a well-traveled course used by North American mariners embarking for the Indian Ocean. Taking advantage of the winds and weather systems prevailing in the fall, he plotted a route from New York that followed the westerlies to his first port of call, the Madeira Islands off the northwest coast of Africa.[1]

His final selected officers and crew were a mixture of experienced mariners and raw amateurs who would require crash training on how to sail and fight aboard a warship. At the top of his veterans' list was his longtime New York friend Henry Bullen, a privateer who had fought the French in Canadian waters and would serve as his dependable chief mate. Henry Mead, a literate family man who had sailed with him from London, was his rock-solid second-in-command.[2] The next most important officer was John Weir, a lifelong colonial sailor out of Charles Town, South Carolina. Kidd's loyal friend and drinking buddy at Hawdon's Tavern, Weir was the master helmsman aboard the *Adventure Galley*.[3] Englishman John Walker served as the quartermaster responsible for ensuring compliance with the ship's articles, doling out prize shares, settling disputes between crew members, and punishing those who committed infractions.[4] At the bottom of the officer list was Robert Bradinham, the ship's twenty-six-year-old chief medical officer, who would be drunk most of the time and prove a lousy physician.[5]

In addition to Bradinham, two others of Kidd's most experienced mariners would be thorns in his side during the voyage: chief gunner William Moore and, to a lesser extent, veteran seaman John Browne, his mutinous old shipmate from the *Blessed William*. Moore was a former criminal with two prison sentences to his name, but Kidd overlooked his troubled past and signed him on in New York because he was a sure-aimed cannoneer. In 1683, when Moore had been a mere eighteen-year-old merchant seaman, he was arrested for attacking his captain, Edward Reade of the *Golden Hind*, resulting in a two-year stint in prison. Eight years later, he was thrown in the slammer in Barbados and denied bail because he had confessed to a cellmate that he planned to run away to Martinique and desert to the enemy French.[6]

After returning to New York from Madagascar in 1693 with £800 ($280,000 today) in captured booty, John Browne for the next three years enjoyed his ill-gotten riches and signed on for an occasional merchant run to the Straits of Gibraltar and West Indies. But with his funds nearly tapped out and a wife to support, he wanted to return to the sea for one last big score. Because he was a veteran Red Sea Man, Kidd forgave the crusty old pirate, well into his forties, for his past transgressions and signed him on for a full share in the voyage.[7]

As they sailed across the Atlantic, Kidd and his officers put the crew through their paces, teaching the green landsmen and less-experienced seamen how to handle the sails and rigging, and conducting gunnery exercises so they could handle the cannon on a rolling and heaving deck.[8] One week out of port, the exercises were abruptly curtailed as the lookout spotted a lone sail on the eastern horizon. She turned out to be a disabled English trading vessel from Barbados, headed for London, that had lost her mast and bowsprit in a storm and was struggling to steer her way into an English port. Though giving away precious supplies could imperil his mission to the Indian Ocean, still 7,500 miles distant, Kidd graciously gave the English captain a mast, rigging, and canvas, "for which kindness [the] master gave him a few flour barrels with sugar."[9]

Continuing on to the Madeiras with the Bermudan brig and taking advantage of the Atlantic's prevailing trade winds, Kidd two days later came across another vessel. Thinking she might be French, he immediately called for first mate Henry Bullen to pile on the canvas and give chase. But to his surprise, the ship put up as much sail as possible to make her escape. It was not until three days later that he finally overtook the ship.[10]

After he fired a shot across her forefoot, the vessel hove to and ran up a Portuguese flag. Knowing it could be merely a false color, or a *ruse de guerre*, he needed to inspect the ship's official papers identifying the owners, cargo, and purpose of the voyage. Since ships often carried false flags and multiple sets of "safe-conduct" passes, all that mattered was *which papers* were handed over to a captain rightfully detaining a vessel at sea. Because the nationalities of the ship-owners, investors, captain, and crew made no difference, encounters at sea amounted to games of chance, as captains had to decide which country's papers offered them the best chance to go free.[11]

In examining the "safe-conduct" passes, Kidd found the ship to be a bona fide Portuguese merchantman on her way from Brazil to Madeira, both Portuguese colonies. As England and Portugal were at peace, she was thus not a lawful prize, so he had to let her go. After a tense three-day chase, the two captains parted ways as if they had just shared rum punches at the King's Arms. The Portuguese master generously gave Kidd a roll of Brazilian tobacco and some sugar; the commander of the *Adventure Galley* returned the courtesy by presenting his opposite number with a "Cheshire cheese and a barrel of white New York biscuit" that through a mistake by the steward turned out to be cut-and-dried Long Island tobacco.[12] The Catholic-hating crew didn't appreciate that Kidd refused to seize what they regarded as a legitimate prize of a traditional enemy of Protestant England. But they liked it even less when the *Adventure Galley* and Portuguese ship sailed in convoy together to Madeira Island.[13]

During the journey, there was no insurrection, only grumbling whispers; but for the first time Kidd had an inkling of what was in store for him. His trusted friend John Weir of Carolina informed him of all the bitching and moaning belowdecks across the swaying hammocks at night. Gunner William Moore was the one stirring up trouble, with a handful of others making their dissatisfaction known as well.[14]

Kidd tried to nip the discontent in the bud when he reached Madeira, 425 miles off the coast of northwest Africa. On October 8, when the *Adventure Galley* and the Portuguese vessel reached the capital, Funchal, he stayed in port only one day to prevent anyone from jumping ship while he took on fresh water, food, and Madeira wine.[15] In the past two weeks, the whispers aboard the privateer had grown, to the point where John Weir claimed "the men had some ill design" and requested to leave the *Adventure Galley* at the next port. Kidd refused, knowing he needed to retain as many experienced seamen and loyal allies as possible.[16]

Having crossed the Atlantic, his route from Madeira would now take him down the west coast of Africa, around the Cape of Good Hope, and to the pirate strongholds on Madagascar.[17] On his way south along the well-traveled trade route pioneered by Portuguese invader-explorer Vasco da Gama two centuries earlier, Kidd sailed past the Canary Islands and soon came upon the Cape Verde Islands—the last European outpost before the equator and vast expanse of the South Atlantic. He stopped at the island of Boa Vista and spent four days loading fresh victuals, water, and salt to preserve his food supplies.[18]

From there, he continued south to the rugged volcanic island of St. Iago (today Santiago), another Portuguese possession in the Cape Verde chain, where he and his crew were welcomed pleasantly on October 24 by the island's Catholic African population.[19] During their eight-day layover, he restocked the ship's hold with fresh water, melons, dates, coconuts, oranges, lemons, and bananas, and allowed his men to explore the island's exotic setting and share the company of the friendly female inhabitants. The fresh supplies would take them through the South Atlantic stage of their voyage, which was expected to last two months before making landfall and would be the toughest stretch yet.[20]

For his next hundred miles, Kidd sailed south parallel to the West African coast, before changing course to southwesterly toward the South American coast. As he nudged toward the equator, the trade winds died away and he entered the doldrums, the region of the Atlantic with uncannily calm seas, sudden storms, and light unpredictable air flow resulting from a vacuum between the earth's two contrary wind systems.[21] At around the thirty-degree south latitude, with a sporadic westerly breeze puffing out the *Adventure Galley*'s sails like the breath of a giant, Kidd changed his heading to east and began following the well-traveled route that paralleled the equator and pointed to the Cape of Good Hope at the southern tip of Africa. In early December 1696, nearly six weeks out from the Cape Verde Islands and sailing through a heavy fog toward Cape Town, he encountered the second major challenge of his voyage.[22]

On the morning of December 12, the fog lifted, and the masthead lookout cried, "Sail! A sail!"[23]

Yelling up through his speaking trumpet, Kidd asked how the ship stood and her class. The reply came that she was a well-armed ship-of-force, bearing at least 30 cannons and following their plotted course. The *Adventure Galley*'s nautical position was now around 33 degrees, 48 minutes south latitude.[24] Feeling danger in the air, Kidd snatched his spyglass from the becket and studied the vessel closely for himself. Sure enough, the new interloper was a huge gunship: But was she a man-of-war, or was she an outlaw pirate hunting him down?

Suddenly, four more ships climbed over the horizon. In the endless blue reaches of the South Atlantic, why did this aggressive flotilla seem to be coming after him like Drake or Morgan on the heels of a Spanisher? He huddled up with his second-in-command, the Englishman Henry Mead in his beige waistcoat and periwig, and his New York friend and first mate, the experienced privateer Henry Bullen. Outnumbered five to one, the three veteran mariners quickly reached a consensus that crowding on all possible canvas and making a run for it was the better part of valor.[25]

The deck turned to a flurry of activity as the men scrambled to their stations and piled on sail. With a scorching sun now glinting off the water, they made all possible haste in the moderate but persistent westerly winds. After three frantic hours, Kidd was relieved that all but the lead ship had fallen away.[26]

The chase was now *mano a mano.*

But the infuriatingly obstinate ship-of-force, hugging the *Adventure Galley*'s stern rail and spreading more sail, continued to gain on him. Two hours later, he could make out a Union Jack fluttering high above gunports bristling with more than forty 18- and 24-pounders. He and his officers held another conference. They agreed that they would soon be within cannon range of a fast yet stoutly built Royal Navy man-of-war that significantly outgunned them. The thought of half his men being pressed away from him—as Captain Stewart had done at the Nore and which the English navy was entitled to do under Admiralty law—filled Kidd with dread. Knowing that his entire mission would be in jeopardy before it had even begun, he ordered his men to make one last-ditch attempt to escape.[27]

The veteran John Browne, African American seaman John Parerick, and other sailors packed on canvas like demons possessed, for they would rather jump overboard than be pressed onto a Royal Navy ship of the line. But despite their efforts, they were overtaken by the HMS *Tiger,* captained by John Richmond as part of a four-vessel Royal Navy fleet commanded by Commodore Thomas Warren.[28] When Richmond demanded through his speaking trumpet that Kidd lay by, the commander of the *Adventure Galley* had no choice but to furl his sails and await the remainder of the naval squadron.[29] It was now the prerogative of Warren coming up in the HMS *Windsor* to examine his papers and decide what to do with him and his men.[30]

But Kidd's situation was even worse than he imagined.

Because of a pair of interconnected events—the first taking place the previous year in the Indian Ocean, the second a mere two months earlier in a London courtroom—the world as he had known it when he had sailed out of New York Harbor was no more. Due to the cataclysmic events that had unfolded in faraway India and London, his royal commission from the King of England no longer meant anything, and the king's pirate hunter would soon be branded as an outlaw pirate and villain of all nations.[31]

And it would all be because of a *real* English pirate who happened to be the most notorious Red Sea plunderer of them all.

THE TALE OF the mythical Henry Every began more than a year earlier, on September 7, 1695, back when Kidd was in London. On that infamous day in India's history, the thirty-six-year-old Every closed to within cannon range of a massive Muslim gunship. Spotted ten leagues off the coast of Surat, the *Ganj-i-Sawai*, soon to be anglicized *Gunsway*, was the flagship of Emperor Aurangzeb Alamgir's 25-vessel fleet making its return voyage to India from the annual pilgrimage to Mecca, the most sacred rite of Islam known as the *hajj*.[32] Having sailed from Surat to Mocha and Jeddah on the Arabian Peninsula, where the devout travelers rested before proceeding on foot to Mecca, the royal armada carried thousands of Muslim Indian pilgrims and wealthy merchants who had traded their cloth and spices for coffee, gold, and jewels.[33]

Weighing 1,600 tons and mounting 80 lethal cannons, the *Ganj-i-Sawai* belonged to the emperor himself and boasted a musket-armed guard of 400 royal soldiers to protect the 600 passengers on board.[34] The entourage included the Great Mughal's own granddaughter, her elderly royal servant and guardian, and several important officials of Aurangzeb's court.[35] "It is known that Eastern people travel with the utmost magnificence," wrote Captain Charles Johnson (the pseudonym for the English political journalist Nathanial Mist) in *A General History of the Robberies and Murders of the Most Notorious Pirates*, "so they had with them all their slaves and attendants, their rich habits and jewels, with vessels of gold and silver, and great sums of money to defray the charges of their journey by land."[36]

Henry Every was the former first mate of the *Charles II*. In May 1694, he had led a mutiny after he and his shipmates had been confined to the merchant ship in La Coruña, Spain, with eight months of back pay owed them. After stealing the vessel, Every changed the ship's name to *Fancy* and headed to the Red Sea, where he joined forces with Governor Fletcher's protégé Thomas Tew and other American commerce raiders to form a formidable squadron of six pirate ships.[37] Upon sighting Aurangzeb's precious fleet on September 2, Every and his seaborne raiding force packed on sail and fanned out in pursuit of the *Ganj-i-Sawai* and twenty-four other vessels. The pirates first seized a smaller ship, the *Fateh Muhammad*, liberating her of around £50,000 in gold and silver ($17,500,000 today), before the squadron split up and the two fastest ships, Every's 46-gun *Fancy* and the *Pearl* captained by William May, piled on as much canvas as possible to chase down the *Ganj-i-Sawai*, the largest of the imperial vessels.[38]

The Indians opened fire first. But in an incredibly unlucky twist of fate, one of the *Ganj-i-Sawai*'s starboard guns exploded at the beginning of the fight, spraying the deck with iron shrapnel, porcupining the gunners with "flying splinters," and broiling them alive in leaping flames.[39] Moments after the terrifying explosion, a one-in-a-million cannonball shot lobbed from Every's *Fancy* smashed directly into the *Gunsway*'s two-foot-diameter mainmast, toppling it instantly and disabling the bulky treasure ship.[40] As the *Fancy* pulled alongside the massive flagship, Captain Muhammad Ibrahim Khan and many of the pilgrims fled belowdecks into the hold. Brandishing swords, daggers, and primed flintlock pistols, Every and his screaming band of 113 cutthroats engaged in a classic pirate boarding action worthy of a Hollywood swashbuckler. Meanwhile, Captain May and the *Pearl* swept in for the attack along the port rail.[41]

After fifteen minutes of fierce hand-to-hand fighting, the Muslims struck their colors and surrendered, suffering a loss of twenty-five men killed and twenty wounded. The aristocrat Khan, later accused of cowardice by his fellow Indian survivors, could only hope that the pirates would take the plunder and be on their merry way.[42] But Henry Every and his dough-faced English brigands would do no such thing. After taking Aurangzeb's flagship to the island of Socotra, the pirates ransacked the ship and abused Khan and the other passengers while the ships bobbed together. After torturing the Muslim men to locate valuables, the Christian plunderers violently and repeatedly raped the women on board.[43]

The bejeweled, aristocratic Indian women and dark-eyed Turkish "concubines" were part of Aurangzeb's court, and taking the women against their will was an act of blasphemy against Allah. Dragged up from the ship's cabins to the bloodstained decks of the *Ganj-i-Sawai*, Aurangzeb's granddaughter and the other women were violated in full view of their fellow Muslims. "Several honorable women," writes Indian historian Khafi Khan, "when they found an opportunity, threw themselves into the sea, to preserve their chastity, and some others killed themselves with knives and daggers."[44] The orgy of rape, torture, and plundering lasted three full days and nights. Not only did Every not lift a finger to stop the bestial violence, he took an active part in it, though he claimed not to have personally violated Aurangzeb's granddaughter the Mughal princess.[45]

In the end, Henry Every managed to keep all the plunder for himself and his crew aboard the *Fancy* by swindling four of the other captains out of their rightful shares. This did not include Captain Thomas Tew of the *Amity*, who was not present during the seizure of the *Ganj-i-Sawai* and was, therefore, ineligible along with his men to share in the spoils. Tew had been killed by being disemboweled by a cannonball and his gunship badly damaged while taking a third treasure ship at the same time the *Fancy* and *Pearl* were hunting down Aurangzeb's flagship. Thus, with their shares quintupled from the revised share distribution, Every and his crew made out like princes. The East India Company estimated the seized plunder's total value at £325,000 ($113,750,000 today), which yielded a share of £1,000 plus jewels (around $400,000) for each crew member.[46]

Though popular with his men at first, following his betrayal Every became so mistrusted by his own crew that more than three-quarters of them abandoned him before his return trip to the Americas. The irony is that despite his treachery, he was heralded as a legend in his own lifetime and continues to be the archetypal "Grand Pirate" to the present day. By the fall of 1696, as Kidd was sailing southward along the same West African coastline navigated by Every, *The Ballad of Henry Every* and other romantic poems celebrating the English pirate and his derring-do appeared in London booksellers' shops.[47] Of course, the London ballads lionizing his adventures made no mention of the brutal savagery of Every and his crew lasting "several days as the ships lay becalmed in the Arabian Sea."[48] As the mythology of the man overwhelmed the reality, Every would be celebrated as *The Successful Pirate* in an early eighteenth-century stage play.[49]

For William Kidd, the pirate Henry Every and his attack on the *Ganj-i-Sawai* proved disastrous, for the legitimate American privateer commissioned by the king was about to be falsely compared by the authorities to the notorious English brigand.

News of Every's piracy reached King Aurangzeb months before William III and his bewigged lords of Parliament in London. The Great Mughal and his royal court were outraged by the humiliating capture of the massive 80-gun treasure ship and the atrocities committed against their Muslim women. The Indian king swiftly directed his anger at England and the East India Company (EIC).[50]

The mercenary and monopolistic Company cared little about the fate of the "ravished" women or "barbarously" treated men and was more concerned that the "black cloud at Court" did "not produce a severe storm."[51] But Knight-General and Governor Sir John Gayer, the EIC's top dog in Bombay, and his agents would have no such luck; instead of being quietly swept under the rug, the incident caused a major uproar in

India. When the *Ganj-i-Sawai* limped into Surat, riots erupted in the streets and angry mobs gathered outside the Company's factory to throw stones, break windows, and bust into the fortified compound. To both punish the EIC workers and protect them from the hostile mobs that wanted to string them up, the local governor, Ahmanat Khan, rushed in three hundred Indian troops to take over the English factory, clapped President Samuel Annesley and the other employees in irons, and cut the prisoners off "from communication with the outside world."[52]

Aurangzeb—who was nicknamed the "White Snake" because he had been born with curiously white skin, and whose vast empire stretched from Persia to Bengal—considered all pirates Englishmen and claimed the Company actively conspired with freebooters against local trade. He wanted the *Honorable* English East India Company *dishonorably* removed from India. Only the solemn entreaties from the politically savvy Annesley, the Surat man on the ground, prevented a massive uprising that would have destroyed the English factories and driven the "impure" Christian infidels out of Surat and Bombay forever.[53] To regain Aurangzeb's trust and preserve the valuable East Indian trade, the Company was forced to agree to fully reimburse the Great Mughal for his financial losses, backed with a promissory note of credit from the Bank of England, founded in 1694 to act as the English government's official banker. Annesley also guaranteed that, going forward, the Company would escort the Mocha pilgrim fleet under an armed convoy and pool its vast resources to hunt down, capture, and execute Henry Every and his outlaw crew.[54]

Fortunately for the Company and Crown, the Muslim Indian king received a fat 5 percent customs duty commission on all English imports and had no intention of giving up the lucrative trade when his own profits were soaring.[55] In the end, the emperor who had murdered his own brother Prince Dara and imprisoned his father, Shah Jahan, to secure the Peacock Throne agreed not to force the EIC from India. But he sternly warned that all trade would remain suspended until Henry Every was captured and hanged. However, catching the pirate commodore proved problematic.[56] Despite the efforts of the Board of Trade, Royal Navy, and Company, Every and his men disappeared off the face of the earth. All anyone would ever learn of the "Grand Pirate" was that after ravaging the Muslim fleet, he sailed to Madagascar; then to New Providence, Bahamas, arriving in March 1696; then to Ireland, where he made landfall along the north coast in June 1696; and finally to Scotland. After that, he was never seen nor heard from again, which has added to his remarkable legend as one of the few Golden Age pirates lucky enough to retire as a genuine "gentleman of fortune."[57]

In the end, only a dozen of Every's crew members were captured, after surfacing in the Bahamas, Jamaica, Virginia, Pennsylvania, Connecticut, Carolina, England, Ireland, and Scotland. Of these, only the six pirates rounded up in Ireland in 1696, just before Kidd set sail from New York, would ever be tried in court. To appease the White Snake and restore profitability to the embattled EIC, the Crown decided to stage a government-rigged show trial in London of Henry Every, in absentia, and the six captured crew members.[58]

The trial would prove to be the second major event that would turn Captain Kidd into a wanted man—even though he had committed no crime whatsoever—as he approached Cape Town in December 1696, for by then Henry Every had left in his wake a paranoid distrust and hostility toward all English shipping in the Indian Ocean.[59]

The Henry Every piracy trial without its notorious star defendant was held at London's legendary Old Bailey courtroom on October 19, 1696, when Kidd was in the South Atlantic poised to make landfall in the Cape Verde Islands. With Every still at large in the global manhunt, the trial would showcase the awesome power of the imperial English state and demonstrate just how serious the Crown was in waging war against the Red Sea Men and preserving England's lucrative trade with India. The one thing that could not happen was acquittal. Such an outcome would confirm to Aurangzeb and the world that England truly was a nation of lawless pirates and her American colonies were a pirates' nest that not only aided and abetted these plundering enemies of all mankind, these despicable *hostis humani generi*, but invested in and profited from their heinous acts from Barbados to Boston.[60]

Based upon reams of testimony from the accused and the government's witnesses, lead prosecutor Sir Robert Newton, in snow-white jabot and powdered wig, expertly laid out what seemed to be an open-and-shut case. The facts were beyond dispute: the six mutinous pirates had attacked a vessel belonging to his majesty's good friend King Aurangzeb, jeopardizing mighty England's foreign relations and putting the nation in danger of "impoverishment" through "the total loss of Indian trade." If the accused were acquitted, warned Sir Robert to the all-White, all-male body of English jurors, the greatest Christian nation on earth might very well be driven from India by Aurangzeb's rampaging armies.[61]

The jury retired to consider its verdict on October 30, 1696, as Kidd was taking water at St. Iago. Two hours later, the panel of shopkeepers and tradesmen acquitted all six defendants. They cared little about attacks upon some über-wealthy Muslim emperor and did not agree that the very fate of the English Empire was in jeopardy due to the disruption of East Indian trade. In fact, the jurymen applauded Henry Every and his merry band of "Englishmen abroad" for boldly sticking it to the Eastern pagans after their wages had been withheld by callous English ship owners in Spain. In their eyes, they were not that different from Queen Elizabeth's illustrious Sea Dogs Sir Francis Drake, Sir John Hawkins, and Sir Walter Raleigh.[62]

The wealthy English lords presiding over the trial, who had as much in common with the humble jurors as they did the enslaved Africans who powdered their periwigs, were stupefied by the unexpected outcome. The trial was supposed to be a carefully choreographed, open-and-shut case in favor of imperial England and civilization itself. But now the authorities had a bigger problem on their hands. Mortified by the outcome, the chief justice of the High Court of Admiralty, Sir Charles Hedges, swiftly decided that the decision *could not* be allowed to stand. Not only that, but a new, pro-Crown narrative had to be put forward as quickly as possible before the disastrous word spread that the villainous rogues had been acquitted by the highest court in all of England.[63]

What was the noble and lawful English government's solution? It did what authoritarian regimes throughout recorded history have done: the judges swept the first trial under the rug and held a new one with an all-new jury.[64] Based on the law of double jeopardy, the pirates could not legally be prosecuted in a court of law for the same crime twice. Therefore, Sir Charles, laboring frenetically with his fellow justices over a fast-track forty-eight-hour period, came up with a new legal strategy: the sea robbers would not be indicted for piracy, but for mutiny and the theft of the *Charles II* in La Coruna, Spain.[65]

The second trial began on All Hallow's Eve, October 31, with the firm goal of assuring the noose for the six semi-literate seafarers forced to serve as their own defense lawyers. To make conviction more palatable to the new working-class English jury, this time Sir Charles didn't mention the Great Mughal and recast Every's deeds as the same as robbery on land. The chief justice's arguments hit the perfect note on the second go-round. The London shopkeepers and tradesmen on the jury panel convicted the "mutineers" for piracy on the high seas, likely as much out of fear of contradicting the bewigged, scowling-faced "Right Worshipful Sir Charles Hedges" as any genuine belief in the evidence presented.[66]

The Henry Every trials revealed the huge chasm with regard to piracy between the hard-line Crown and Admiralty on the one hand, and the sympathetic American colonies and average working stiff in the British Isles on the other.[67] But the trials had even more dramatic repercussions for Captain Kidd. With Every still at large and the Old Bailey proceedings at best a Pyrrhic victory for the Crown, the English authorities needed now more than ever to capture a well-known pirate captain and make an example of him. The conviction of six lowly seamen was not going to mollify the Great Mughal; only a huge show trial of a high-profile captain could make up for the failure to capture the widely popular and romanticized Henry Every, who was being compared to Drake and Morgan. Time was of the essence. If Aurangzeb learned that the American colonies were making piles of money from purloined East Indian goods with the explicit knowledge and consent of their governors, the Muslim emperor might very well put an end to the East Indian trade once and for all.[68]

The Henry Every trials were also important for another reason. Although they would not lead to an avalanche of prosecutions, they proved to be the critical dress rehearsal for the greatest piracy trial of all time. The Every proceedings taught the Crown how to enforce the supreme power of the state and harness the power of print media. Not only did the English authorities subvert the rule of law by conducting a second trial predetermined to result in conviction, they controlled the trial record by publishing only the second proceeding and destroying all traces of the public record of the first. In the next big pirate trial, the Crown would not need a second, trumped-up charge of "mutiny" to secure a conviction.

The only remaining question was which notorious pirate captain the Crown would put on trial to play the dramatic role of Henry Every.

–8–

Narrow Escape and False Clamors

As Commodore Thomas Warren brought his fourth-rate flagship, the 70-gun HMS *Windsor*, alongside the *Adventure Galley*, William Kidd winced inside. He had tried valiantly to outrun the English fleet, who were on the lookout for "pirates" and "interlopers" in the wake of the Henry Every affair, but had failed. He now found himself at the mercy of Warren, who with his four powerful warships and one East Indiaman wielded the firepower to blow him out of the water.[1] From his raised quarterdeck, the behatted and bewigged commodore, wearing his immaculately pressed and spotless Royal Navy uniform, hoisted his speaking trumpet to his lips and commanded Kidd to gather his papers and come aboard the HMS *Windsor*.[2]

But Captain Kidd did not reply. Instead, he cupped his hands behind his ears. In the subtle act of defiance, the American privateer pretended he couldn't hear the English commodore. Looking at his officers in disbelief, Warren repeated his order, raising his voice several decibels through the trumpet.[3]

This time Kidd spoke in acknowledgment. Though he desperately wanted to protect his ship and men from impressment by the Royal Navy, whom he knew from hard experience had no qualms about snatching dozens of seamen from privateers and merchant ships, he realized he had no choice but to stand down. While waiting for Warren, he and his men had heard the horror stories from the crew of the HMS *Tiger* of the fleet's harrowing seven-month voyage from London. Not only had the inept commodore lost his way in the South Atlantic, his squadron had drifted aimlessly for weeks and was forced to make a humiliating landfall in Catholic Rio de Janeiro, Brazil, after losing three-hundred-odd crewmen to scurvy—and he was now desperate to replenish his ranks.[4] Even worse, Kidd and his men had learned that "Wrong-Way" Warren was not only a poor navigator but a martinet who cared little about his sailors. During the seven-month cruise, he had forced crew members caught swearing to wear iron neck collars weighing fifty pounds, and his seamen had been on meager rations with limited water while he and his officers feasted nightly and popped bottle after bottle of wine and spirits.[5]

Kidd's men would have much preferred to jump overboard to the sharks than be forced to leave the *Adventure Galley* and sail under Warren and his Royal Navy fleet. Sailors in the English navy not only had to survive cramped quarters, myriad diseases, poor food and pay, and perilous weather, but extreme authoritarianism and draconian physical punishment. Major shipboard offenses such as mutiny, desertion, striking an officer, and cowardice carried the death penalty, while lesser infractions such as insubordination, thievery, or fighting might bring much worse than a heavy neck collar: a hundred lashes with a cat-o'-nine tails or solitary imprisonment belowdecks.[6] Conditions were so atrocious that one English officer declared that the king's ships had difficulty even fighting pirates because they were "so much disabled by sickness, death, and desertion of their seamen."[7] Given that England was a coercive and militaristic yet manpower-short nation constantly fighting wars on the cheap using involuntary labor, the pay was guaranteed to be not only meager but delayed, if it ever was received at all. In many cases, the Royal Navy issued vouchers to crew members that could only be redeemed in specific ports, often out-of-the-way backwaters, to cheat the sailors out of their hard-earned pay.[8] But the worst part was that the Grim Reaper of Death always hovered nearby for the poor wretches forced to serve as "liege subjects of the realm to man Britain's wooden walls in wartime."[9]

Gathering his paperwork, Kidd went aboard the HMS *Windsor*. He took along with him his second-in-command, Henry Mead; his first mate, Henry Bullen; and the forty-six-year-old Jewish jeweler Benjamin Franks, acting as his steward. Though Franks had no seafaring experience, Kidd was generously transporting him to India so he could recover the fortune in gold, silver, and jewels he had lost in the devastating 1692 Port Royal, Jamaica, earthquake.[10] In the commodore's spacious and luxuriously appointed cabin, Warren reviewed Kidd's royal commissions, questioned him about his voyage, and informed him of his own troubles at sea without admitting to his ineptitude. He also told Kidd that he wanted him to accompany his Royal Navy convoy to the Cape of Good Hope and that, to make up for his recent losses, he would need him to hand over between twenty-five and forty sailors.[11]

Under Admiralty law, Warren had the right to take up to one-half of a merchant or privateer ship's crew.[12] But Kidd's commissions were not ordinary licenses. They were issued by the king himself and specifically charged and commanded "all our Offices, Ministers, and other our loving Subjects whatsoever, to be aiding and assisting to you in the Premises."[13] Recognizing the unusually important nature of Kidd's commissions, Warren didn't want to flagrantly disobey the Crown's orders, so he found a way to tiptoe around them by merely *requesting* that the captain relinquish a portion of his crew.[14]

Warren was deluding himself if he thought that losing twenty-five to forty men would not be a devastating blow to Kidd, especially if the privateer commander lost men to scurvy in the forthcoming weeks en route to Madagascar, as had happened to the commodore. Already some of Kidd's crew were showing the early symptoms of the affliction, and their health would only worsen. The disease typically appeared after six weeks to two months at sea due to a lack of fresh food containing ascorbic acid and the resulting loss of collagen, one of the human body's connective-tissue building blocks. Deprived of vitamin C, seamen contracting scurvy experienced serious joint pain; developed ulcers, blood clots, and dark blotches on their skin; and finally suffered through the telltale rotting gums with teeth falling out of the jaw and feverish death.[15] By the late eighteenth century, scurvy was controlled through shorter voyages, fresh produce, and boiled fruits and wine, but in Kidd's era most doctors and seafarers knew little about preventing or treating the disease, and it was blamed on sinfulness or a lack of salubrious land air.[16]

Though Kidd was irked that part of his crew was about to be seized from him, he had no option but to pretend to go along with Warren's plan. He and his men, thus, were held hostage by the Royal Navy in the eastward-moving convoy. "I was on board the commodore's ship," later reported Benjamin Franks, "when he told . . . Kidd he had lost a great many of his men and asked him to spare him some, who answered that he would let him have 20 or 30."[17] But the clever Captain Kidd was merely putting on a front. Though he was polite and deferential, he had no intention of giving Warren a single crewman. However, before making any attempt to escape from the Royal Navy, he had to be certain he could pull it off.

As the two commanders talked some more, Kidd was introduced to the other naval captains. He was also presented to Captain John Clarke of the EIC, commanding the *East India Merchant*. Clarke took an instant dislike to Kidd, considering him an "interloper" in the Company's back yard, though he was forced to acknowledge that his "readily produced" commission was "very authentic under the Great Seal of England."[18] Because of the EIC trade monopoly in place from 1600 until the Deregulating Act of 1694, which for the first time allowed other English firms to trade with India, Company officers like Clarke zealously guarded their oceanic turf and considered any outsiders daring to venture to the East Indies as illegal poachers.[19] Even though Parliament had terminated the monopoly, the Bully Corporation's ship captains, crew, and other agents ignored the two-year-old ruling and continued to harass non-Company seafaring traffic.[20] They impounded so-called "interloper" ships and seized cargoes on trumped-up charges;

imprisoned captains and seamen under harsh conditions; and took part in black-market smuggling, often with the connivance of their superiors in Surat, Bombay, and London. Thus, Aurangzeb was partly right when he claimed that Company men were in bed with pirates and active plunderers themselves.[21]

The meeting ended amicably, despite Kidd's initial defiance in pretending he couldn't hear Warren's order. The commodore graciously invited him to dine with him and his officers that evening aboard his flagship. Kidd accepted. As it turned out, the two didn't just share one meal together—the captain of the *Adventure Galley* would be wined and dined by Warren aboard the HMS *Windsor* every day for the next week. During these festive occasions that slowed the squadron's progress to the Cape of Good Hope from the usual 160 to 200 miles per day to an average of only 135 miles per day, the wine and brandy flowed copiously.[22]

On December 18, 1696, after being forcefully detained by Warren for seven straight days, Kidd was once again invited to dine with the bacchanalian commodore. On this late afternoon extending into the early evening, three and a half months after setting sail from New York, Kidd and the other officers got good and drunk while dining in luxury. Warren reminded his guest that he would soon be taking around three dozen of his men from him, and Kidd again politely asked if in return the commodore might be able to spare him a mainsail. He respectfully reminded Warren, yet again, that he had given his all-important spare mainsail away to a disabled English merchant ship from Barbados early on in his voyage and was in dire need of a new sail. Though Kidd offered to write a letter of credit on his lordly partners for a replacement sail, once again Old Wrong-Way refused.[23]

With tongue in cheek, Kidd then brashly joked that, in that case, he might have no choice but to take a mainsail off the next merchant ship he came across at sea. Some, including Warren himself, probably chuckled at Kidd's wine-induced braggadocio, obviously delivered in jest; others, including the humorless East India Company Captain John Clarke, positively did not. In fact, the sourpuss Clarke would later falsely accuse the captain of "rodomontade and vain glory" and question "the honesty of his design."[24]

More glasses were raised and jokes were made, and, as the dinner broke up, Warren once again invited Kidd to dine with him tomorrow afternoon, December 19. After accepting, Kidd thanked the commodore, bid the other officers goodnight, and stumbled into his rowboat to be ferried back to the *Adventure Galley*. Though drunk as a skunk, he was clearheaded enough to know that he had had enough of Wrong-Way Warren and his coterie of snooty English officers.

Upon his return to the ship, he stepped onto the quarterdeck and peered over the railing. With not a puff of wind, the South Atlantic spreading before him in the moonlight was as flat as a billiard table, and he realized he might not have a better chance to escape. Knowing how unspeakably awful life was in the Royal Navy, his men had been pleading with him to protect them from Warren's impressment for the past several days, and they were on pins and needles waiting to see who would be impressed and who would continue on as free sailors aboard the *Adventure Galley*. As he gazed out at the placid sea, he knew he would be taking a grave risk if he attempted to escape. But he could no longer allow Warren to hold him and his men hostage. His Crown-sanctioned wartime mission was as important as Warren's convoy duty, and it irked him that the bombastic Captain Clarke of the *East India Merchant* had not been asked to contribute *any* seamen to the commodore.[25]

Summoning his first mate, Henry Bullen, he ordered him to put together a crew to man the oars and row the galley away from the Royal Navy fleet. Not a man would be impressed against his will into his majesty's navy, he informed his officers, but they must move quickly if they were to make their getaway. With the bold move, Kidd hoped to win back the loyalty of his hard men like William Moore, who were hell-bent on "making a good voyage" one way or another.[26]

Under the cover of darkness, the *Adventure Galley* stole away in the placid seas, her forty-six oars propelling her quietly eastward. This was the third time in his career Kidd had rescued his men from Royal Navy impressment. The next day, the log of the HMS *Advice* read: "Dec. 19. Last night Capt. Kidd of ye *Adventure Galley* sailed from us so yet in ye morning we lost sight of him."[27]

Warren was furious when he woke up, hung over from yet another night of feasting and heavy drinking, only to see that Kidd was long gone and not even a speck on the horizon. After wining and dining this backwater provincial for a week straight, he felt violated.[28] He swiftly ordered his majesty's *Advice* and *Tiger* frigates to chase down the Houdini-like escape artist and reel him in like a flapping *bonito*. But by this time, Kidd had changed course to southward, choosing to bypass the Cape altogether and head straight for Madagascar. This would, unfortunately, lengthen his voyage just as his men were experiencing the first symptoms of scurvy, and his rigging still desperately needed an overhaul. But he had no choice if he were to assure the safety of his crew and preserve his mission.[29]

Kidd's sailors were indeed grateful to their captain for his signature moment of defiance against the English Empire, and he managed to win back his restless crew's loyalty. Twenty-three-year-old seaman Jonathan Tredway of Boston captured the gratitude of the entire crew when he related that there was "great satisfaction of our people . . . who were fearful that some of them would have been carried away by ye Men of War."[30]

Two weeks later, on New Year's Day, Warren and his English squadron of four warships and one East Indiaman bumbled into Dutch-controlled Cape Town, hoping to find Captain Kidd. When the cheeky American colonial was nowhere to be found, Old Wrong-Way spread deliberate lies about him to blacken his name and turn him into a pariah. In fact, Warren decided—without a shred of proof—that the entertaining guest he had wined and dined aboard his ship *every day for a full week*, the man referred to as the "trusty and well-beloved Captain Kidd" by the King of England himself, was somehow an out-and-out pirate. He and the other English captains quickly spread word that Kidd was an outlaw not only to Dutch officials, but to the captains of the five English East India ships anchored in the bay.[31]

Captain Clarke, who would be a thorn in Kidd's side for the next year and a half, eagerly spread the falsehoods. He claimed that he and the other captains had already come to suspect the New York privateer as a pirate before he "quietly skulked away during the night." Blustering to all who would listen, he maintained that Kidd was a wolf in sheep's clothing who intended to plunder the ships of all nations.[32]

Thus, by early January 1697, with only the first leg of his journey under his belt and Henry Every still at large, Captain Kidd became the new Red Sea bogeyman. Hundreds of EIC representatives would repeat the spurious charges, severely damaging his reputation. "This marked the beginning of the Company's campaign to slander Kidd's name," notes maritime historian David Wilson. "From this moment, Company officials kept a close eye on Kidd's voyage, compiling reports and evidence against him to send back to England."[33]

Even interlopers like the *Scarborough*, anchored in Cape Town Harbor when Warren sailed into port, were terrified of this new Attila the Hun of the High Seas. After hearing the false rumors, the merchant ship's commander, Captain Brown, informed Dutch officials that out of fear of the "arch-pirate," he would wait for a well-armed gunship to accompany him eastward toward Bengal. Allen Catchpoole, the *Scarborough*'s onboard trade representative (supercargo) for the ship's owners back in London, wrote home about the new bogeyman's nefarious intentions based on the growing hearsay. Catchpoole, who held the dubious distinction of having been fired by the Company for embezzlement, claimed that Kidd and his "very stout men" wanted "liquors & sails" and were headed "anywhere for gain"—meaning they would plunder indiscriminately.[34]

The manhunt for Henry Every and the bulk of his crew had been an abject failure, and the "legacy of fear and hatred" that the pirate commodore had left in his wake for all English seamen sailing to Arabia and India had not abated in the past year. Which meant that as Kidd escaped Warren's clutches and made his way to Madagascar, the Royal Navy, East India Company, and Aurangzeb all had a new scapegoat for their venomous retribution.[35]

—

On January 27, 1697, Captain Kidd sailed past St. Augustine's Bay on the southwest coast of Madagascar, dropped anchor off the village of Tulear, and began ferrying his sick men ashore. After three months at sea since leaving the Cape Verde Islands, with the detour around the Cape of Good Hope to escape Warren and his neck collars adding an extra month to reach landfall, the ship was debilitated with scurvy.[36]

Peering through his spyglass upon his approach, he for the very first time studied the Great Red Island that enterprising New Yorkers and other American mariners had transformed into a pirate stronghold and cross-cultural Indo-Atlantic trading center. Luckily, there were no pirate ships at anchorage, for his crew was far too weak to mount an attack or defend the ship.[37] The world's fourth-largest island, Madagascar contained fine harbors and ample supplies of zebu cattle meat, rice, oranges, limes, and other nourishing fruits. Descendants of primarily Indonesians with mixed African and Arabic ancestry, the Malagasy tribespeople were not dark-skinned like the mainland Africans across the Mozambique Channel, but resembled the denizens of the western Pacific archipelagos to the east, with straight hair and café-au-lait complexions.[38] The first Europeans to make contact with the island were lost or shipwrecked Portuguese explorers in the early 1500s. Between these early accidental encounters and when Kidd made landfall in 1697, there was countless Malagasy contact with English, French, Dutch, and Portuguese traders arriving to the island. However, "the Europeans proved unable to establish long-standing ties with the indigenous population" and "the Malagasy resisted all attempts by the sea powers to establish a foothold until the French invasion of 1895." With no central government, the island remained a hodgepodge of separate tribal fiefdoms that fought and enslaved one another and engaged in extensive trade throughout the Indian Ocean region.[39]

The pirates of Madagascar—nowhere to be found upon Kidd's arrival—had established frontier outposts at three principal localities:

St. Augustine's Bay, on the southwest side of the island where Kidd made anchorage; St. Mary's, a small and narrow islet off the humid northeastern coast; and Port Dauphin, the former French settlement on the southeast tip of the island. St. Mary's was the pirate stronghold of the "Pirate King" Adam Baldridge and a growing legion of Red Sea Men, who utilized the island as a base of plundering and trading operations.[40]

Kidd made landfall at Tulear at the perfect time of year and remained anchored in St. Augustine's Bay for a month. The fresh fish, rice, fruit, and meat of the zebu grazing on the seasonally luxuriant grasslands ended the monotony of rancid salted beef and moldy biscuit, enabling his scurvy-ravaged mariners to quickly regain their health. While the men recovered their strength, they refilled the water casks, patched the *Adventure Galley*'s leaks, and provisioned the ship with new salted meat and other fresh supplies. Unfortunately, in February, Henry Mead passed away, likely from tropical disease and scurvy. Kidd would sorely miss the leadership and experience of his second-in-command in the coming months.[41]

On January 29, the *Loyal Russell*, a merchant sloop manned by fifteen seamen sailing from Barbados "laden with rum, sugar, powder, and shot" to sell at inflated prices to Madagascar pirates, arrived in St. Augustine's Bay. From the ship's officers, Kidd discovered that Commodore Warren and Captain Clarke were spreading the word that his commission from the king was a ruse and he was a sea-robbing scoundrel.[42]

Anxious to vindicate himself and acquire fresh sails and rigging not available on Madagascar, he set out northward from Tulear for the Comoros Islands at the end of February. Located near the confluence of the Mozambique Channel and western Arabian Sea, Johanna (modern-day Anjouan) and the other islands in the archipelago served as a prime stopover point on the way to the Indian Ocean and would provide a safe place to careen the galley while Kidd waited for the southwest monsoon between May and September. Before leaving, he warned the *Loyal Russell* to steer clear of the *Adventure Galley*, not wanting to be associated with the pirate-brokers, but the merchant vessel shadowed him as soon as he weighed anchor.[43]

A fortnight after leaving the Great Red Island, Kidd sailed into a roiling tempest. Massive storm waves pounded the poorly caulked seams of the *Adventure Galley*, straining the recent repairs and forcing the crew to constantly man the pumps. Raging torrents of seawater roared across the swaying and canted decks like Niagara Falls; the men clung to the rigging and rails for dear life to avoid being washed overboard. For a week or longer, all the captain and his crew could do was douse the sails, batten down the hatches, step carefully, and keep their fingers crossed that they could ride out the typhoon.[44]

To his credit, Kidd kept the big ship afloat and moving toward the Comoros Islands. Toward the end of March, he awoke to find that the storm had cleared and he was a mere day out from making landfall in Johanna. An hour or two later, the topmast lookout spotted a sail poking up above the horizon.[45] A gunship! But was she friend or foe?

Having the wind, in typical Kiddian fashion he quickly decided to try to take the mystery ship-of-force. Never one to lack aggressiveness, even after being rocked by a savage storm, he ordered Henry Bullen to crowd on the canvas. But, to his surprise, the vessel changed heading and swung her bow directly toward the *Adventure Galley*. Now, that was vexing. Here he had packed on sail, and this strange ship out in the middle of the Mozambique Channel had abruptly altered course to boldly meet him. But then the vessel unexpectedly came about, piled on more sail, and doubled back to the southwest. Now Kidd was truly stumped.

Unbeknownst to him, the unidentified ship was the *Scarborough*, the merchantman commanded by Captain Brown. On board was supercargo Allen Catchpoole, whose exaggerated letter tarring Kidd as a pirate would reach London later that summer. Brown had left the Cape Colony in the company of Captain Clarke in the *East India Merchant* and two other Company ships, but the fleet had broken up in the storm. Thinking the East Indiamen must be behind him, Brown had initially mistaken the

Adventure Galley for his comrades; but, realizing his error, he poured on sail to escape.[46]

Kidd continued to close on the big merchant ship, hoping she might prove to be a French prize showing her heels. Suddenly, the *Loyal Russell* hove into view, making the situation even more confusing. The Barbados sloop had been tagging along since Tulear, much to his consternation, but he had thought he had lost her in the storm. Instead, she had stumbled onto the group and joined the chase.[47]

Kidd closed hard on the *Scarborough*, still convinced she might be a French privateer or pirate ship. But before he could overtake the big merchant vessel, a fourth ship came into view: the *Sidney*, a 40-gun behemoth with a crew of 130 commanded by Captain Gifford. Realizing that one of the accompanying East Indiamen from the storm-dispersed merchant fleet had caught up to him, Captain Brown raced toward the *Sidney* to bring his *Scarborough* under the protection of the powerful gunship.[48]

Now the *Sidney* ran up English colors. The Company's distinct flag consisted of a red-and-white ensign carrying eighteen stripes, with the Cross of St. George in the canton.[49] This was quickly followed by the hoisting of a red commodore's pennant, and Kidd knew for certain it was no ruse. With the pennant, Captain Gifford was announcing his superiority amongst the fleet of ships and claiming rank over the *Adventure Galley*. He expected Kidd to lower his topsails out of deference and stand down. But Captain Kidd wasn't about to submit to a mere trading vessel when he boasted a royal privateering commission from King William III himself. Under Admiralty law, because the *Sidney* East Indiaman did not carry a special government-issued privateering license like the *Adventure Galley*, her captain was out of line to claim supremacy and Kidd was fully justified in his actions—though he was being an irritating stickler for protocol.[50]

Growing impatient, Gifford fired a shot across Kidd's forefoot, attempting to bully him into standing down. Kidd responded by hoisting his English colors and King's Jack and pennant and sending over an officer to explain his royal-backed mission and smooth things over with the captain of the *Sidney*. He also informed Gifford that with his commission directly from the king, he outranked East India Company merchant ships, and he hoped the Company man would be gentleman enough to strike his red pennant.[51]

But Gifford refused. Despite the 1694 House of Commons' termination of the EIC monopoly and opening of the East India trade "to all," he was used to pushing around so-called "interlopers" on his oceanic turf. Fortunately, the two men were able to settle their differences over rank and protocol, and the next day the four ships sailed together into Johanna. However, once they reached the harbor, they went back at it again. As was his right, Kidd requested that Gifford strike his red pennant, but Gifford again refused and this time threatened to board the *Adventure Galley* and haul Kidd off in chains.[52]

The next day, during the tense standoff, two more East India Company ships sailed into Johanna Road Harbor. As luck would have it, one of the merchant vessels was the *East India Merchant* commanded by Clarke, whom Kidd knew had spread lies that he was a pirate. Wisely swallowing his pride, Kidd let the pennant matter drop and, to show his goodwill, he invited Gifford, Clarke, and the other captains to have dinner aboard his ship to patch things up.[53]

They rudely declined this olive branch. But that wasn't enough for the persnickety Englishmen. They sent him an insulting note questioning the "honesty" of his mission and threatened him by stating "that unless he behaved civilly [they] would call him to account." Now that Clarke had entered Johanna questioning Kidd's honor and claiming that he was a wolf in sheep's clothing, the relations between the two parties turned frosty.[54]

Kidd stayed three days in Johanna Road, filling his water barrels and purchasing food. But Clarke and the other captains treated him like a pariah.[55] During the stopover, William Moore and some of his other hard men mingled with the East India Company seamen ashore, telling them that they had come to Johanna expecting to find a lone "East India ship . . . bound for Surat" and that they planned to attack the ship to get what supplies they needed. Clarke twisted these rum-soaked fantasies of a few underlings into a massive conspiracy by Kidd and his entire crew, as if the ship were united in a single piratical vision.[56]

It is at this stage of the Captain Kidd saga that the English authorities and East India Company stepped up their "propaganda campaign" against him.[57] In the wake of the Henry Every scandal, the Junto's termination of the EIC monopoly, and the ongoing efforts to replace the Bully Corporation with a new Whig-controlled entity, a wave of extreme paranoia gripped the firm. Company employees were "suspicious" of every strange ship and captain they came across, because they were afraid of being put out of business. "They were looking for a scapegoat and this contact of Kidd with some of their vessels at Johanna was used as part of their case against him."[58]

On April 4, 1697, after three stressful days in port, Kidd left Johanna Road and sailed "ten leagues" to the nearby island of Mohelia, also in the Comoros chain. His goal was to restock there and careen his leaky ship in peace before making the final push to the Indian Ocean. Though the *Adventure Galley* had been at sea less than one full year since leaving London, the ship was in bad shape and the repairs took several weeks. Unable to lose the *Loyal Russell*, Kidd commandeered the small merchant vessel to assist with the careening process.[59]

Repairing the hull of a large warship was a grueling process, but it was necessary to perform two to four times a year in the tropics. Below the waterline, wooden vessels were vulnerable to the destructive, hole-boring powers of the shipworm or teredo, a warm-water mollusk. These burrowing "termites of the tropical seas" would, if left unchecked, fully perforate a vessel's hull in just a few months.[60]

The first step was to lighten the load of the 287-ton behemoth before she could be hauled over. The munitions, food, water stores, topmast, and ballast were removed from the *Adventure Galley* and stored onshore and aboard the *Loyal Russell*, which was armed with several cannons to protect against attack during the careening process. The large warship was then sailed ashore, flopped onto her side, and heeled over onto her beam ends by the smaller ship using a line running from the capstan to the galley's two-foot-diameter masts.[61] Once in position for cleaning and repairs, the hull was scraped of encrusted seaweed and bottom-clinging barnacles that reduced the vessel's speed, and the exposed planking was inspected by Kidd and his master carpenter. Where the wood planks were weak, rotting, or penetrated by boring shipworms, they were replaced. The final step was to re-stuff the narrow seams between the planking with oakum, a mixture of individual strands of hempen rope and tar, and seal each seam with heated pitch.[62]

It was a tough job—but it was made even more difficult when Kidd's crew became deathly ill from tropical disease. More than a hundred seamen suffered from the outbreak, with around a third of them dying in two weeks.[63] By the time the crew had recoated the bottom, righted the vessel, slipped her back into the water, and reshipped the guns, they had buried nearly three dozen of their deceased shipmates in the sandy soil of Mohelia. Kidd's brother-in-law Samuel Bradley was one of those who fell ill. Although he survived, he was never the same again and had to remain bedridden belowdecks for the remainder of the voyage.[64]

The men had suffered from scurvy, malnutrition, and other shipboard maladies thus far on the voyage, but this infectious disease, believed to be a virulent form of dysentery known as the "bloody flux," was the worst so far. Dr. Bradinham and his medieval therapies proved useless. The men experienced severe diarrhea, belly cramps, nausea, violent shaking, vomiting, and unslakable thirst. In an age where bloodletting, enemas, and sudorifics to purge the "evil" out of the body comprised the state of the art, the twenty-six-year-old surgeon from London administered various medicinal powders and liquid potions that likely did more harm than good.[65]

With the previous loss of his second-in-command Henry Mead at Tulear, and this latest outbreak of disease, Kidd's original force of 152 men was down to below 120 by the beginning of May. Fortunately, he was able to augment his crew with disgruntled sailors from the *East India*

Merchant after Captain John Clarke had subjected them to excessively "hard usage." With his crew members dropping like flies, Kidd was not picky about the fresh manpower, and he invited "four English men, an English boy, two Frenchmen, and a Black" to sign the articles and climb aboard his privateer. One of the Frenchmen, Pierre LeRoy, would go on to serve in the valuable role of interpreter aboard the *Adventure Galley*. The "Black" was sixty-year-old Ventura Rosair of Ceylon (modern-day Sri Lanka), whom the captain hired as his personal cook for a share in the voyage (apparently chief cook Abel Owen wasn't much of a chef). When Clarke learned of his unhappy crew's defection to Kidd in his stolen pinnace, he was furious and sought to further blacken the name of the king's pirate hunter. Kidd was also able to score boatswain Hugh Parrot from the *Loyal Russell*, who had gotten into fisticuffs with his captain but would prove a solid gunner under Kidd.[66]

When his ship was seaworthy again, Kidd sailed back to Johanna for provisions.[67] Desperate to buy sails and stores, and with his money to pay for supplies running low, he tried to obtain a bill of exchange from the King of Johanna drawn from a letter of credit on King William, but was refused. Fortunately, he was able to borrow money from the newly hired Pierre LeRoy and an unnamed French comrade of his to purchase victuals and other supplies.[68]

By early May 1697, with his seasoned crew having regained their health and the galley freshly careened and well-stocked with supplies, he was finally ready to fulfill his mission. He had suffered two Royal Navy impressments, a raging tempest, a tropical disease outbreak, repeated Royal Navy and East India Company slander, a badly leaking ship, and insufficient petty cash from his cheap lordly backers to purchase goods. But now the decks were cleared for him to hunt down Frenchmen and pirates. The southwest monsoon began to flow north by early May and would run through September, pushing all sea traffic toward the Arabian Sea, where Muslim pilgrims and wealthy merchants would be returning to India in late summer, so it was in this direction that Kidd now pointed the *Adventure Galley*.[69]

Kidd was not after the Great Mughal's ships, of course, but rather pirates once they had attacked the fleet and were bogged down with their treasure. Thus, before setting out, he made it clear to his men that they would be making "their course for the Red Sea to cruise for pirates" and would not themselves turn pirate. He believed he could seize a greater haul, with less risk of death and injury, from a pirate ship that had just attacked the Muslim pilgrim fleet than he could by launching an assault on the fortified pirate compound on St. Mary's.[70]

By this stage of the voyage, he knew he was going to have an extremely difficult time keeping his men in line. William Moore, Dr. Robert Bradinham, John Browne, and others had been grumbling for the past month—and the rumbles were growing louder every day.[71] His sailors were becoming desperate to take a prize, any prize. Many of them did not care what colors the ship flew—they just wanted treasure. Thus, his only chance to control the mutinous portion of his crew was to take a legitimate prize—and soon.

The *Adventure Galley* was hardly infested with freebooters; it was simply a matter of expectations, just as Governor Benjamin Fletcher had predicted. The crew had signed on for a Red Sea voyage and expected a handsome return on their investment *per fas aut nefas*—one way or another.[72] Thus far, not one crew member had made a penny and several had been forced to sell clothing to buy supplemental food. Even the sailors who were firmly opposed to committing piracy on the high seas did not expect to go home empty-handed.[73]

–9–
The Pirate Hunter

On the night of August 14, 1697, the Great Mughal Aurangzeb's treasure fleet sailed through the narrow mouth of the Red Sea, the strait of Bab-el-Mandeb known to Arabians and Indians as the "Gateway of Tears" and to European mariners as simply the "Babs." By the next morning, Captain Kidd, who had anchored the *Adventure Galley* fifty miles south of Mocha and patiently awaited the fleet for a fortnight, had deftly slipped in amongst the flotilla. The Muslim pilgrim fleet, some seventeen treasure-rich ships in all, was making its return voyage from Arabia to India.[1]

Peering through his spyglass with the sun rising over the sparkling blue waters of the Gulf of Aden, Kidd could tell by how low the merchant vessels sat in the water that they carried rich hauls aboard. With such tantalizing targets there for the taking, how could there not be swarms of pirates moving into position to ambush the fleet?

Both Captain Kidd and his men needed this legitimate score desperately. The journey from Johanna to the Babs along the southeast coast of Africa had taken a heavy toll on the crew. After returning briefly to Johanna for supplies, they had sailed north around the Horn of Africa and into the Gulf—and in all that time they had not encountered a single

French or pirate vessel.[2] Making matters worse, they were pariahs in the eyes of the East India Company and Royal Navy, and their freshwater supplies were running dangerously low since there were no wells in the area from which to replenish their dwindling rations.[3]

But now, as Captain Kidd blended in with the straggled-out fleet, he could feel his luck about to change. Creeping closer to the lead cluster of treasure ships, he noticed an unidentified vessel of English design broad on his bow. He estimated her at four hundred tons, and she carried thirty-six guns and flew no colors. Whoever her captain was, he seemed to be lying low until the *Adventure Galley* drifted within range, a ploy used by privateers and naval men-of-war to lure an enemy within cannon range before opening fire.[4]

He instructed Master Bullen to keep out of range of her guns, which looked to be 18-pounders. The trusty first mate stepped lively to relay the order to the helmsman; but before he could, the mystery ship threw up an English Royal Navy ensign, a field of red with the Union Jack in the upper left corner, and also a Union flag on the bowsprit's jack-staff.[5] According to New York Dutch crewman Nicholas Alderson and Bostonian Jonathan Tredway, Captain Kidd and the crew were taken aback by the sudden appearance of English colors.[6]

As fate would have it, Kidd's opposite number proved to be one of the most extraordinary mariners of the Golden Age of Piracy. His name was Edward Barlow, commander of the *Sceptre*, an East Indiaman with a privateer's commission like Kidd sent by the East India Company to protect the Great Mughal's pilgrim fleet on its voyage to and from Surat, India. Scanning the horizon, Kidd saw far off in the other direction two more large convoy vessels lingering behind the flotilla and flying Dutch colors.[7]

Born in Prestwich, England, in 1642, and impressed into the Royal Navy, which he detested, at an early age, the fifty-five-year-old Barlow had already spent nearly forty years at sea, a remarkable feat given the short life expectancy of mariners in the Age of Sail. What has made Barlow most memorable in the eyes of historians is the 225,000-word,

575-page journal he kept during his lengthy career, recounting his many voyages and presenting an unvarnished look at life at sea.[8] Not only is Barlow's published work one of the finest sea journals ever written, it is richly illustrated with Barlow's own watercolors of the ships he sailed and islands and ports he visited. In his day, he railed against the bigwigs, especially high-ranking officers in the Royal Navy and his own East India Company, for their profiteering, press-ganging, and overall lack of humanity. In another time and place, he and Kidd would have been bosom buddies, for they were cut from the same humble, hardworking, and egalitarian cloth, yet had to kowtow to the noble-born and powerful to survive in an authoritarian age.[9]

Fifteen months earlier, on May 19, 1696, Barlow had sailed from England as a first mate in Warren's 93-ship flotilla. But en route to India, the *Sceptre* had ditched the ponderous commodore. In June 1697, shortly before his arrival in India, a career opportunity had opened up when his commander aboard the *Sceptre*, Captain Phinney, perished en route to Mocha while guarding the Great Mughal's Arabia-bound pilgrim fleet. With Phinney's death, First Mate Edward Barlow became Captain Barlow overnight at age fifty-five.[10] But he was only a provisional EIC captain, and was thus most anxious to prove himself. Arriving at Mocha in mid-June after Phinney's death, he exchanged his cargo of sugar, pepper, knives, lead, and iron for the bustling seaport's chief commodity, its famous java popular in London's growing coffeehouses, and for spices, dyes, and ivory. While awaiting departure, he discovered that a "pirate ship" was lurking nearby at the Babs—which turned out to be no pirate ship at all but Captain Kidd waiting to hunt down freebooters preying on the treasure fleet. With his convoy duty suddenly a high-stakes mission, the last thing he wanted was to lose the confidence of Sir John Gayer by allowing the fleet to be plundered on his watch.[11]

On this Sunday morning, August 15, 1697, as he and Captain Kidd prepared to do battle, Edward Barlow peered through his Company-issue spyglass and spotted a gap in the Muslim pilgrim fleet he was assigned to protect. Beyond the range of his heaviest cannons loomed a strange-looking ship equipped with forty-six galley oars and thirty-four powerful guns. In his journal, Barlow recounts the opening salvo of their legendary scrap at sea:

> He [Kidd] showed no colors but came jogging on with his courses hauled up, under two topsails, having more sails furled than usually ships carry, namely a mizzen topgallant sail and a spritsail topgallant sail. . . . [H]aving our ship in readiness, we were willing to let him come as near to us as he would, for the Dutch convoy was a long way astern and we had very little wind. . . . And seeing the pirate as near as he intended to come, being almost abreast of us, we presently hoisted our colors and let fly two or three guns at him well-shotted.[12]

Thus, Edward Barlow, presuming the *Adventure Galley* to be a pirate from the get-go, ran up his flag and opened fire on Captain Kidd *first* without provocation, as attested by Barlow and several of Kidd's crew members.[13] If Kidd was surprised to see an English flag hoisted, he was shocked when Barlow ripped loose with cannon not upon his forefoot but *directly at him*—without making any effort to surmise his true intentions. Kidd's royal commission gave him every right to demand the papers and search the ships of a convoy to determine if they were enemy French, pirates, or carrying contraband; and, if they were, he was allowed to take them "in a warlike manner."[14]

The crackling sound of Barlow's heavy cannons filled the air, and blossoms of smoke erupted from the gunports of the East Indiaman. A pair of cannonballs splashed in the ocean off the prow of the *Adventure Galley*, sending up fountains of water. Kidd realized that the captain of the opposing ship had mistaken him for a pirate and withdrew out of range of Barlow's heavy guns as the wind died down even further. Amid the calm waters, he saw her captain lower two longboats that began towing the giant ship toward him.[15]

Soon, the English guns again exploded with smoke and fire.

The cannonballs splashed near the *Adventure Galley*, but the privateer was still just out of range of the aggressive East Indiaman. Kidd still had not taken aim with his guns, let alone fired a single shot in return, which was, of course, *very* un-piratelike. But Barlow was still convinced that he had stumbled upon the next Henry Every, and he was not about to err on the side of timidity.

Kidd was able to put more distance between himself and the East Indiaman. In his journal, Barlow wrote that Kidd "sailed far better than we did."[16] However, in moving defensively away from the aggressive Barlow, Kidd soon found himself within cannon range of a big Moorish, or Muslim East Indian, ship with a great deal of treasure aboard. The vessel, alerted by Barlow's fire aboard the *Sceptre*, now took aim at Kidd, as did several other Muslim gunships.[17]

The muzzles exploded down the line.

Once again, cannonballs splashed all around him and whizzed overhead without Kidd's firing a single shot in return. At this point, if he truly had been a pirate, he must have suddenly become a Quaker like his parents, because he refused to shoot at anybody. But then one of the Moors' cannonballs blasted through his recently repaired rigging.

This was too much for Captain Kidd. Turning toward the gun deck, he called out to his pugnacious chief gunner, William Moore, to prepare his cannons to fire in response to the Indian aggression. As the cannon muzzles rolled out of the square-cut gunports, Kidd ordered him to fire when ready and give the Muslim vessel a taste of iron. By the laws of the day and his royal commission, he had every right to stop and search Moorish vessels and return fire upon them if they unleashed upon him first.

Tongues of flame blasted from the muzzles protruding from the *Adventure Galley*'s gunports. The cannonballs whizzed through the air, catching the Moor in the sail and hull above the waterline.[18]

Captain Kidd's multiethnic crew gave a rallying cheer.

Moore opened fire again. As the blasts echoed across the water, the lascars (East Indian seamen) crouched down behind the railings to make themselves small. Though several cannonballs struck the Muslim ship in the hull and through her sails, they failed to dismast the ship or mow down the sailors or gunners on board.[19]

No sooner had Moore reloaded his cannons for another salvo than the *Sceptre*, towed along by her two oarboats, came again within cannon range.[20]

Kidd now faced a decision: retaliate, or sail away.

At this point of the fight, he was overheard by Dutch seaman Nicholas Alderson saying that it was clear that they were dealing with "an English man-of-war" acting as a convoy to the Mocha fleet and "there was no good to be done" in the confrontation.[21]

Now the colonial New Yorker in the *Adventure Galley* and the Englishman Barlow in the *Sceptre* engaged in a slow-motion contest of cat-and-mouse. As Barlow's men in their two longboats worked feverishly to tug their 400-ton behemoth into range to do damage, Kidd had his crew man the oars and deftly pull away.[22]

Soon thereafter, the wind returned.

With his canvas now billowing, Barlow brought his thirty-six guns closer. But Kidd sailed just out of range and patiently waited.[23] He was not yet prepared to give up on his pirate-hunting mission, so he dared Barlow and the *Sceptre* to come closer while still "having no mind to engage."[24] At the same time, he was frustrated. It was looking more and more as if his and his crew's big payday wasn't going to happen at all, which the men would take hard.[25]

The *Sceptre* inched closer again. Kidd waited until Barlow was almost in cannon range and then, at the last moment, he sailed away just out of reach and waited for Barlow's next move.[26] The elderly provisional captain kept on coming and twice more pulled toward Kidd in a direct challenge, with his cannons firing and men screaming like pirates. Kidd continued with his tactic of creating a gap between the two ships, then furling his lower sails and waiting while the ungainly *Sceptre* crept forward and closed to within cannon range, before again retreating just beyond Barlow's reach.[27]

Finally, near sunset, he realized he was accomplishing little and sailed away for good.[28]

If Kidd was merely frustrated, the soon-to-be ringleading mutineer William Moore and most of the crew were bitter and disconsolate over the fruitless outcome. After weathering eleven grueling months without a single prize and having to withdraw from taking one of the richest treasure fleets in the world, they couldn't believe that their captain had *deliberately* chosen not to plunder the Muslim armada.[29] For not only the nascent pirates, but also for the regular seamen who wanted to make money legally like Kidd, it was as if all their hopes and dreams had just been dashed before their very eyes.

AT ONE O'CLOCK the next day, he called a meeting of the entire crew of 130 men aboard the *Adventure Galley*. Even Samuel Bradley, Benjamin Franks, and the other sickly sailors shambled up on deck from below. As Kidd cleared his throat to speak, he knew he was at a pivotal crossroads in his thus far disastrous voyage. The sunbaked, short-tempered, thirsty men stared up at him through slitted eyes.[30]

He was just as disappointed at their lack of success, he said, but they had to put it behind them and push on if they wanted to make a good voyage. The question was where to go from here, and he presented them with two choices. They could continue to shadow the fleet, keeping a safe distance from the English man-of-war, and wait for a pirate or Frenchman to try to pick off a straggler. Or they could head for Cape St. John on the Indian coast (modern-day Daman) to obtain their riches, for fat French merchant ships routinely sailed those waters.[31]

In accordance with the ship's articles and in the buccaneering tradition, the decision was then put to a democratic vote of the entire crew. As always, Kidd was a stickler for following the articles. The crew promptly voted for sailing to St. John, and the captain set a course for the island.[32]

Twelve days later, on August 28, a sail was spotted along the eastern horizon of the Arabian Sea. Desperate for a prize, Kidd calculated an intercepting path, gave helmsman John Weir the coordinates, and raced toward the potential prize.[33] She proved to be a two-masted, square-sailed merchant "grab" of about 100 tons. Surprisingly, she showed no colors and did not reduce sail or slow down at all. By the time he had closed to within musket range, she was still racing for the Indian coast.[34]

He ordered Moore on the gun deck to put a shot across her forefoot.

The *Adventure Galley* shuddered as smoke spat forth from the bristling cannon like a fuming dragon. The iron orb whistled through the air and sailed across the bow of the grab before splashing into the Arabian Sea. Kidd's rowdy seamen crowding the decks roared their approval and yelled at the ship's dark-skinned Moorish crew to intimidate them into standing down.[35]

This time the grab's captain responded with the appropriate deference. Turning the vessel into the wind, he lowered his topsails, drifted to a halt, and began hoisting colors, thereby surrendering his command. But once again it was a friendly flag. At the sight of the huge English Jack, the crew members, whose spirits had been momentarily raised, let out a heavy groan, as they realized that before them was yet another ship that they could not legally seize.[36]

Through his speaking trumpet, Kidd ordered the ship's captain to collect his paperwork and come aboard the *Adventure Galley*. Captain Thomas Parker of the *Mary* gathered the necessary documents and was rowed over and lifted aboard the galley.[37] After ordering his quartermaster, John Walker, to organize a boarding party and conduct a peaceful inspection of the *Mary*'s cargo, Kidd led Parker to his great cabin, closing the door behind them so they could talk in private.[38]

Once they settled into their seats with a glass of Madeira provided by cabin boy Richard Barlycorne of Carolina, Kidd showed his visitor his commissions and examined the papers of the Englishman. He quickly discovered that Parker was sailing from Aden to Bombay with a cargo of coffee, pepper, and victuals for his crew. The owner of the *Mary* was one Girderdas Rupgee, a local Bombay broker for the East India Company. The ship was Moor-owned, and Parker himself was not an employee of the Company and merely sailed for Rupgee. The affable captain informed Kidd that he had a dozen lascars aboard from the Malabar Coast, including a pilot who knew the local waters. He was also carrying five Portuguese monks from Bombay, along with a Portuguese "linguister." This translator spoke English and several Indian dialects, making him an invaluable specialist in foreign waters on the far side of the world.[39]

The two captains talked for more than two hours. This was Kidd's first opportunity in several months to gather information, so he asked about the local shipping traffic, French and pirate sightings, and the latest news of the East India Company. To their surprise, as they were finishing up, they heard a commotion coming from outside the cabin. Rushing onto the deck with Parker, Kidd was stunned to find quartermaster Walker, chief gunner William Moore, and a dozen other crewmen hauling supplies from the pinnace onto the deck with block and tackle and storing the stolen cargo on board the *Adventure Galley*.[40] Walker and the boarding party hadn't just rowed over to the merchant ship to inspect the hold, he soon learned, but had violated his orders by roughing up the Moorish crew to locate hidden valuables and ransacking the ship. They stole bales of coffee, a large sack of pepper, plumb lines, myrrh, navigation instruments, clothing, freshwater casks, and even the rice of the Moorish crew. They also grabbed two blunderbusses and six muskets, weapons that Kidd knew might be used against him, Henry Bullen, John Weir, Samuel Bradley, and his other loyal crew members in a possible mutiny.[41]

Outraged, Kidd gave the ringleaders Walker and Moore an earful. Calling them a "parcel of rogues," he ordered them to return *everything* they had stolen at once and is reported to have pulled his pistol to back up his demand. He soon discovered that Moore and several others had taken two of the Moorish officers, tied their arms behind their backs, hoisted them up, and beaten them with naked swords to find out where they had hidden their gold, silver, and jewels.[42]

He had Walker organize a new party to return the stolen goods. But unbeknownst to Kidd, they returned most—but *not all*—of the pilfered items, keeping some goods already stashed away in the hold. According to historical records, the crewmen returned two compasses, six muskets, four bales of coffee, all of the crew's water, and several other items but kept, without Kidd's knowing, a portion of the Moors' rice, coffee, and pepper, and the two stolen blunderbusses.[43]

Once order was restored, Kidd decided that for his expedition to have any chance of success, he would need to retain Captain Parker as his local pilot and the Portuguese translator Don Antonio as well. He didn't know the Indian Ocean and needed a pilot to navigate the shoals, reefs, hidden inlets, and bays, as well as to sail safely at night. The translator would help him negotiate with local populations to obtain food and water without conflict. Just as the Royal Navy press-ganged any warm body with a ticking heart into its service—often sending entire families into debtors' prison—Kidd was taking a pilot and translator aboard his ship to ensure a positive outcome in his Crown-sanctioned mission.[44]

While impressing seamen onto a private man-of-war was a move that today seems to smack of illegality, in the rugged Age of Sail it was a common practice that fell well short of breaking the law. Taking pilots, translators, carpenters, coopers, surgeons, musicians, and other mariners with valuable skill sets onto vessels by force or cajolery had a long-standing tradition of legitimacy for European and colonial American seafarers, especially during times of war. As Edward Barlow and Alexander Hamilton, a sea captain and trader in Surat, make clear in their extensive writings, the Royal Navy and East India Company did what Kidd did all the time, and they had no more authority than he did. During his circumnavigation of the globe and unlicensed pillaging of the Spanish Empire, Francis Drake, who would be knighted by Queen Elizabeth I for his exploits, took several European navigators by force including the Portuguese pilot Nuno da Silva, whom he kept aboard his gunship *Golden Hind* for over fifteen months.[45] Early-twentieth-century British lawyer and historian Sir Cornelius Dalton postulates that Captain Parker and Don Antonio may have even been thankful to get "on board a European ship" and "join" Kidd's company, "as others in similar circumstances admittedly did afterward." In any case, neither man would ever file a complaint, testify in court, or publicly utter a bad word against Kidd, suggesting they were compensated and treated well throughout their time aboard the *Adventure Galley*, as da Silva had been by Drake.[46]

At nine o'clock that night, once Captain Parker had gathered his belongings from the *Mary*, the two ships parted and the *Adventure Galley* resumed her eastward trek to Karwar. Two days later, the *Mary*'s pilot guided the merchant ship into the port of Bombay using the pilfered compass Kidd had ordered be returned. The Portuguese monks instantly complained to the authorities about Captain Kidd's "piracy," when only a small minority of his crew was responsible. But they did acknowledge that he had forced his men to return the supplies they had seized (they didn't know that Kidd ordered the offenders to return *everything*, but that they had disobeyed him). From the depositions of Father Rosaro, Dom Gonsalvis, John and Pedro Soaza, and Bart Silva taken on October 10, 1697, at the East India Company office in Bombay, and from the testimony of other eyewitnesses, it is clear that Kidd stood up against the freebooters within his crew.[47]

Meanwhile, the *Adventure Galley* continued south along the coast to Karwar under Parker's navigation, where Kidd laid anchor on September 3. Situated on the southwest coast of India, the port town and trading center of Karwar was one of the second-tier outposts of the Company. There he went ashore to meet with the local agents.[48]

When he arrived, he could tell that they were expecting him.

THE MEETING WAS held on September 4, 1697, at the EIC headquarters office overlooking the sun-drenched Karwar Harbor, three hundred miles south of Bombay. The combination fortress, factory, and warehouse consisted of fortified bastions, rows of menacing cannons, and heavily armed guards to keep the profits from the coastal pepper trade in—and the hordes of heathen Muslims and Hindus surrounding the headquarters out. Seated across from Kidd were Company agents Thomas Pattle and John Harvey. The two immaculately groomed men, who like all English officers in India were attended daily by a small army of Hindu or Muslim servants, were the Bully Corporation's top two representatives in the region. As was his custom, Kidd started out by presenting his two commissions.[49]

Once Pattle and Harvey had perused the documents, they asked Kidd to recount his voyage and what his plans were in the region. He politely filled them in regarding his perilous journey thus far, listing the places he had been and making it clear that he was after Frenchmen and pirates in accordance with his lawful commissions. He hoped the Company would provide him with supplies at a fair price, as laid out in the king's commission under the great seal, and allow him to take on wood and water for the *Adventure Galley*. They brusquely told him that they could sell him no supplies, but that he was free to take wood and water—provided he and his men "behaved themselves."[50] No doubt Kidd reminded them of the king's clause stating "And we do hereby *charge and command* all our Offices, Ministers, and other our loving subjects whatsoever to be aiding and assisting you [italics added]."[51] But Pattle and Harvey were half a world away from London and had no intention of obeying their king's commandments; they didn't consider themselves so much Company men or English subjects as emperors beholden to no one, and they viewed him with suspicion.[52]

When the meeting ended, Kidd shook hands with them and returned to the *Adventure Galley,* anchored in the harbor. Pattle and Harvey would write a scathing letter about him and send it up the chain to Sir John Gayer at his sumptuously appointed Bombay Factory headquarters. In their original letter, dated September 9, they claimed that his "designs" were not "as honest as they should be" and falsely accused him of attacking the returning Mocha fleet. On September 22, they added a damning postscript on the *Mary* seizure, accusing him of outright kidnapping her captain while failing to acknowledge that he had forced his unruly crew members to return the stolen goods.[53]

With morale sinking, Kidd now used only the most loyal men to oversee the wood and water missions, denying shore leave to all but a dozen trusted men. At this point, all but thirty or forty crewmen wanted off the ship altogether or to seize her by force. From what Samuel Bradley and his loyal officers were telling him, the majority of the crew was angry at him for refusing to become a pirate, while the remainder worried that they would soon be forced to turn to all-out piracy by the rogues aboard the ship, whether they wanted to or not.[54]

By the time Pattle and Harvey's letter was sent to Sir John Gayer, a dozen men had attempted to jump ship and several had proved successful. One such deserter was Joseph Palmer, who would later sail with the pirate Robert Culliford, turn state's evidence, and lie on the witness stand against Kidd to save his own neck. Kidd had recently discovered Palmer and seven others trying to steal the *Adventure Galley*'s pinnace and sneak ashore. Fortunately, he had been able to stop them, in accordance with the ship's articles, but with a trio of other seamen he wasn't so lucky.[55] Unlike the others jumping ship, Benjamin Franks, still ill from dysentery and planning to set up his jewelry business in India, had been given permission by Kidd to quit the company and go ashore. But when Franks reached Karwar, every single seaman in the rowing party deserted, including the twenty-four-year-old Jonathan Tredway of Boston. To exacerbate matters, Kidd was informed that Franks and Tredway had sought asylum at the EIC headquarters with Pattle and Harvey.[56]

The Company's new star witnesses were promptly shackled, put under guard, and ferried to Bombay headquarters. Franks, the forty-seven-year-old Jewish jeweler, was under the misapprehension that by cooperating with the English authorities, he would be allowed to pursue his dream of regaining his lost fortune in India. Instead, he and Tredway were locked up as prisoners for several months before being shipped to England in January 1698 to testify before the Board of Trade.[57] They would be held in custody in London until giving their evidence on August 22 of that year. While Franks's testimonials given in India and London have proven to be accurate regarding the chronological events of the voyage, they are wildly off base when it comes to the motives behind Kidd's actions with respect to piracy. The reason is simple: Franks had obtained virtually all his information secondhand, as he remained sick belowdecks most of the time after Mohelia; and he and Tredway misinterpreted many of the actual goings-on aboard the *Adventure Galley* through their ignorance of shipboard politics, since they were inexperienced mariners. Though neither Franks nor Tredway ever called Kidd an out-and-out pirate, they hinted at sinister motives due to the slanted questioning of their EIC captors and their ignorance of the ongoing battle between the competing pirate and non-pirate factions.[58]

In Karwar Harbor, Kidd was soon informed of the mass desertion and realized what a huge mistake he had made in allowing Benjamin Franks to go ashore. Regardless of what he did going forward, he had been branded a no-holds-barred pirate by the East India Company, and there was no going back. Which meant that his mission would now be much more difficult to complete, since he would be turned away from every English outpost in the Indian Ocean—despite the king's directive.

On September 11, 1697, Kidd stood amidships overseeing the returning wood and water shore parties in Karwar Harbor, when an oarboat bearing two tricorne-hatted Englishmen appeared. Kidd did a double take as he recognized one of the men on the boat: it was his former senior officer William Mason, who had stolen, along with Robert Culliford, Samuel Burgess, and John Browne, the *Blessed William* and all his hard-earned money seven years earlier in the West Indies.[59]

It must have taken a great effort for Kidd to hold back his anger at the sight of the now thirty-five-year-old Mason. But he put aside his misgivings and decided to play the courteous host. Kidd knew that Mason had been sent by Pattle and Harvey to inspect his ship and gather evidence of wrongdoing. Therefore, before allowing him and his cohort on board, he made sure that Walker had secured Captain Thomas Parker and Don Antonio belowdecks, keeping the two critical mariners incommunicado from the new visitors.[60]

Kidd invited Mason and his partner, Captain Charles Perrin, to his cabin, along with his first mate, Henry Bullen, so they could share a libation and talk. The New York man Bullen had served as captain of the

Resolution in Mason's privateering fleet off the Canadian coast in 1690, under the privateering license granted by Jacob Leisler. After showing Mason and Perrin his commissions, Kidd filled them in regarding his voyage thus far. He had sailed to Madagascar, Johanna, Mohelia, and the Babs, he told them, but had not encountered any pirates or French vessels. The pirates-turned-Company-agents asked him if he was holding Captain Parker and the Portuguese "linguister" aboard his ship, whom they had learned about from the recent interrogations of Franks and Tredway. Kidd wasn't about to give up a crucial navigator who knew the local waters, or a valuable translator either, so he told them he didn't have them.[61]

He asked Mason to bring him up to date on his past seven years and how he had come to work for the East India Company. In November 1690, after hijacking the *Blessed William* and Kidd's life savings, lawfully capturing French ships in Canada, and being accused by his crew of cheating them out of their prize shares, Mason had left New York and returned to illicit piracy along with Culliford, Burgess, Browne, and the rest of Kidd's old West Indian crew. But during the voyage to West Africa and India, yet another dispute split the crew. After taking several prizes, Mason and eighteen others abandoned the ship at Mangalore, India, in August 1691, and Burgess was marooned in St. Augustine's Bay, Madagascar, in September 1691 for allegedly stealing from the crew as quartermaster. With no other career options open to him, Mason had offered his services to the EIC, for whom he had been working on and off since the fall of 1691. The Company, he told Kidd, took advantage of his knowledge of pirates by having him "negotiate" with them, like a modern-day hostage negotiator. No doubt Captain Kidd had a laugh at that one. That the EIC would hire outlaw pirates like William Mason reveals how desperately the Company needed experienced European mariners.[62]

The next day, Mason presented an exaggerated report to Pattle and Harvey, just as Warren and Clarke had done earlier. The Karwar factors put the finishing touches on their half-written letter and sent it to

Sir John Gayer in Bombay and the other factories. In his report to his bosses, Mason falsely accused Kidd of being a "pirate" and of "fighting with his own men on any little occasion, often calling for his pistols and threatening anyone that durst speak of anything contrary to his mind." He also stated that Kidd's seamen had personally begged him "to take over their command," which was true but not for the reasons Mason claimed. In closing, Kidd's mutinous former shipmate accurately reported that, "They are a very distracted company, continually quarreling and fighting amongst themselves, so it is likely they will in a short time destroy one another, or starve."[63]

From his own personal experience, the ex-pirate William Mason certainly knew about "distracted" and "quarrelsome" companies. But in his report to Pattle and Harvey, he was twisting the facts by taking the position of William Moore and the piratical faction. When he falsely claimed that Kidd was a "pirate" and had "threatened" crew members for merely "speaking contrary to his mind," he was burnishing his own star at Kidd's expense.[64] Mason, of course, never volunteered to his superiors that, years earlier, he had stolen everything Kidd owned, including his ship, because Kidd had *refused* to turn to piracy as Mason had done. The angelic Mason also failed to disclose that he had participated directly with Robert Culliford in the 1690 *Blessed William* mutiny, a compatriot with whom he had sailed as a pirate for years and whom he knew at the very moment (fall, 1697) was violently terrorizing and raping his way across the Orient.[65]

While there is no question that Kidd could be a tough taskmaster, he had thus far on the voyage not laid a hand, lash, or naked sword upon a *single* crew member, as punishment was dictated by the ship's articles and he strictly adhered to the stipulations that did "not allow him to order punishment unless he had a majority of the crew in agreement."[66] In fact, the *only* documented instance of Kidd lambasting his men and pulling his pistol was when Moore and his ruffians seized goods from the *Mary* against their captain's orders and roughed up her lascar crew, a clear-cut violation of the ship's commissions and signed articles.[67] Thus, the bogus claim that Captain Kidd maintained quick-tempered discipline[68] and engaged in "bullying cruelty" toward his crew[69] was a fiction created by the mutinous piratical faction aboard the ship to justify the removal of the single implacable obstacle that stood in their way to committing piracy on the high seas.

Most importantly, the false legacy of Kidd's being some sort of Captain Bligh—the commander of the HMS *Bounty* later known for his cruelty toward his crew, who would mutiny near Tahiti in 1789—is the polar opposite of what we know of his history as a maritime officer who routinely looked out for the interests of his crew, and likewise his history as a loving husband, father, and good and loyal friend to a vast assortment of people. In fact, his well-documented friendships and kindly treatment toward others cut across age, ethnicity, and social stratum, making him extremely tolerant and considerate in what we regard today as a rather unenlightened age.[70]

Like so many tall tales of Captain Kidd—especially stories of barbaric cruelty, piratical villainy, and treasure chests overflowing with gold and silver buried up and down the Atlantic seaboard—the Kidd-as-Bligh myth has its roots in the anti-piracy propaganda campaign of the English Crown and the East India Company. These *Treasure Island*–like yarns of a brutal and mean-spirited Kidd who never existed were created by William Moore and his disgruntled piratical faction, retold and spread far and wide by William Mason, the Royal Navy, and the EIC in the wake of the Henry Every scandal, and still persist today, even in some scholarly quarters, because old myths die hard.[71]

Soon after sending the nosy Mason and Perrin away, Kidd was surprised to see another oarboat rowing out to his ship. His new visitors proved to be a pair of sympathetic English seamen, who informed him that the Portuguese in Goa had fitted out two men-of-war that were at this moment sailing down the coast to capture him.[72]

The Catholic Portuguese in India represented a waning empire pushed aside by the bigger bullies of England, the Netherlands, and France. By hunting him and the *Adventure Galley* down, Kidd realized, the Portuguese hoped not only to exact revenge for the embarrassing capture of their monks aboard the *Mary*, but to take down an English pirate and humiliate Protestant England. With this new information, he had to make a run from Karwar straightaway, or he might be trapped in the harbor.[73]

He immediately called the crew to quarters, heaved anchor, and set sail westward out to sea before turning south. But the next morning, as the sun's first fiery rays glinted to the east, he was shocked to see on the horizon the two Portuguese men-of-war bearing down hard upon him. The warships, bristling with sixty-six deadly cannons between them, already had their guns rolled out and prepared for battle.[74]

Now Captain Kidd's enemies didn't merely want to spread false rumors, arrest, and imprison him—they wanted to blow him out of the bloody water.

–10–

Heart of Darkness

Peering through his spyglass at the two approaching Portuguese men-of-war with their Cross of Christ flags snapping in the brisk breeze, Captain Kidd ordered his first mate, Henry Bullen, to prepare to lay by and hail. The date was September 12, 1697, and the formidable gunships stood off the Malabar Coast, south of Karwar, in the trade-rich Arabian Sea. The bigger of the Portuguese was a massive 44-gun commodore's warship, and the smaller vessel carried 22 lethal carriage cannons.[1]

Bullen relayed the order. The crew, primed for battle, trimmed the sails and laid by in the lee in preparation for hailing. Kidd could have put his men to the oars to avoid a confrontation, but he wanted to know what he was up against.[2] Though the wind was shifty, the Portuguese had the weather gauge even in the modest offshore breeze, and soon the pair of interlopers were abaft his starboard beam. The 44-gun commodore's ship-of-war now stood within pistol range, or 50 yards.[3]

Studying the two Portuguese men-of-war bobbing up and down in the sparkling azure-blue waters, Kidd knew they would be a formidable opponent if it came to a chase, line-of-battle engagement, or boarding action with hand-to-hand fighting. The commodore of the larger ship now raised his speaking trumpet and hailed the *Adventure Galley*. In the morning sunlight, the gunship's powerful cannons looked menacing through the open gunports.[4]

"Ahoy there!" declared the Portuguese commander in execrable English. "From whence have you come?"

Kidd knew that the Portuguese captain was checking to make sure that he was confronting the correct "interloper" and not some English, Dutch, or French East Indiaman. Given the unsupported accusations against him and his ship by the EIC and now the Portuguese of Goa, he decided not to tip his hand and to reveal as little as possible.

"Why, I am from London," he responded through his speaking trumpet, his officers and crew looking on with riveted interest.

"London?"

"Aye, that be from whence I came. And where are you from, my friend?"

"We sail from Goa."

"Goa. Well, I wish ye a good voyage."

"And a good voyage to you, Captain."[5]

Kidd tipped his tricorne hat and the deceptively civil exchange ended right there. But he knew that he had not seen the last of his newfound Portuguese friends.

He ordered all hands to make ready to sail.

Clapping on the canvas, Kidd continued steering the *Adventure Galley* south, paralleling the Malabar Coast famous for its spicy pepper and moisture-laden monsoon rains. The Portuguese men-of-war dogged him all day long, the sight of the white crosses on a black background hounding Kidd and his Protestant crewmen like a pair of pursuing highwaymen. The more adept mariner despite his leaking ship, Kidd soon opened up a gap; but that night the Portuguese piled on more sail, and at sunrise the following day the two pursuing ships-of-force once again had closed to within musket range.[6]

Kidd ordered fore and aft all hands to make clear and ready for the gun crews to fight.

The men mobilized swiftly and precisely in taking up their battle stations. Acting as powder monkeys, fifteen-year-old apprentices Richard Barlycorne and William Jenkins and fourteen-year-old Robert Lamley hand-carried the buckets of gunpowder from the powder magazine to William Moore and his cannoneers.[7]

Now the bigger 44-gun man-of-war—without any warning or request for surrender—rolled out her cannons.[8]

Kidd ordered the men to brace up and prepare to return fire. But just as Moore and his cannoneers began flinging open the gun doors, six of the Portuguese cannons, probably heavy 18-pounders, erupted with a broadside, scoring direct hits on the *Adventure Galley* above the waterline. The impact rocked every timber of the ship, and dozens of seamen dove for cover. Suddenly under heavy fire and enveloped in smoke, flying splinters, and dust, Kidd and Company were forced to duck down low and make themselves small to protect themselves.[9]

He commanded William Moore to return fire.

Chief gunner Moore, Archibald Buchanon, Hugh Parrott, Walter Dorman, and the other gunners quickly went to work. The cannons went off in succession, raking the giant Portuguese man-of-war's three mastheads and gunrail, but causing only minor damage.[10]

In response, the enemy unleashed another series of thunderous blasts, and once again the leaking galley took a pounding. The deck was suddenly hot like a bonfire, with the breath of flame and burning ashes stinging Kidd's eyes and the acrid stench of gunpowder filling his nostrils. Squinting through the smoke, he saw amidships that a half dozen of his men had fallen and were bleeding from splinters of wood strafing them like hundreds of darts fired all at once.[11]

Now the big commodore's flagship was maneuvering in to board him. Kidd must have gulped as he took in the swarthy faces of the Portuguese and the menacing cannons protruding out of her gunports like black ravens of death and destruction. This was no fat merchant ship or Royal Navy fifth- or sixth-rate; this was a massive warship intent on killing him and his men. With nearly two dozen cannons blasting away at him and the giant flagship maneuvering to board him, he knew that survival was the better part of valor.

He ordered Bullen to clap on the wind and get them the hell out of there.[12]

With the vessels continuing to exchange cannon fire, the crew pulled desperately at the oars, piled on sail, and slipped away before the big warship could close and board them. Now the confrontation turned to a deadly game of chase.

Though he was able to pull away from the flagship, he quickly came under fire from the likely 8-pound bow-chasers of both vessels. Unable to inflict mass carnage or sink him, the small Portuguese cannonballs hurled at the *Adventure Galley* proved mostly a nuisance, and then only for a few minutes before he was able to pull away from both ships with his combined oars and sails.[13]

Soon the gap between the *Adventure Galley* and the 44-gun enemy ship had widened considerably. The 22-gun ship, however, remained close on his heels. Unfortunately for Kidd, neither warship looked as though it would give up the pursuit until they caught him.[14]

By midday, still unable to shake the smaller and speedier man-of-war, Captain Kidd made a bold decision. He decided to tack, regain the wind, and stand to the enemy's forefoot to engage the smaller vessel *mano a mano* before the hulking 44-cannon warship could close the gap. Several leagues to the north, the more formidable Portuguese vessel was a white speck in the distance. By the time she could catch up, he hoped to have pummeled her consort into submission.[15]

Helmsman John Weir, his experienced Carolina friend and probably only remaining loyal officer along with first mate Henry Bullen, cranked the whipstaff hard to leeward, turning the *Adventure Galley* into the wind. Meanwhile, the men on the deck pulled at the crosstree spars and released a series of ropes. Kidd kept his fingers crossed. If the move succeeded, he would have the upwind advantage and control the engagement; but if the maneuver failed, the Portuguese would have the weather gauge and could swoop down upon him.[16]

The sails briefly flapped and then, like a well-trained horse turning on a penny, the 287-ton galley swung hard about and shot upwind of the smaller Portuguese ship, gaining the weather. Peering through his spyglass, Kidd spotted his opposite number on the quarterdeck of the smaller man-of-war. The Portuguese captain looked like something out of an Exquemelin adventure tale with his black cocked hat, wolf-gray lieutenant's jacket, and crimson sash and sword about his waist. But he had been cleverly hoodwinked by Kidd into a one-on-one engagement against a gunship boasting nearly twice his own firepower. Realizing that he and his ship were in imminent danger, he began frantically barking out orders to his officers.[17]

As Kidd closed on the Portuguese man-of-war from windward, he waited to give William Moore the order to fire until the *Adventure Galley* had closed the distance between the two ships to fifty yards. Flames then blasted from the muzzles of Kidd's powerful cannons. More than a dozen high-velocity iron projectiles landed in a deadly broadside on the 22-gun Portuguese warship, exploding chunks of the gunwale and tearing across the foredeck as well as amidships, demolishing her foresails, puncturing the skins of hapless sailors, and eviscerating and maiming others.[18]

In response, he heard several booms and whistling sounds. A moment later, a series of explosions ripped through the *Adventure Galley*. Looking amidships, he saw men go down in a blast of splintered wood. But the Portuguese fire was less effective, and the galley had sustained only minor damage compared to the enemy.[19]

He came about again and the cannons discharged, one after another down the line, in a terrific broadside. Just before the impact, Kidd saw many of the Portuguese seamen scrambling behind the railings and taking cover. But they were sitting ducks against the *Adventure Galley* with the wind edge. This time he pounded the other ship. If bar and chain shot was used—as is likely, based on the reported damage—the hailstorm of iron bars attached to chains raked across the decks of the enemy man-of-war like Death's horrible scythe, cutting down sailors left and right and mangling sails, masts, and rigging.

Though clearly taking the worst of it, the Portuguese man-of-war was still able to crack off several well-aimed shots with her cannons. Shuddering from the tremors and earsplitting roar of the big guns on both sides, Kidd had to admire the enemy captain for his courage and tenacity. But the Portuguese were taking extreme punishment, with no help coming any time soon from the 44-gun commodore's flagship.[20]

Then the battle took an unexpected turn: the wind died down. Kidd ordered Walker to man the oars and bring the guns abreast of the reeling enemy. The sea captain who had bested the legendary DuCasse knew he had an opportunity for a knockout blow before the 44-gun man-of-war could close on him. With the bigger gunship still two leagues away, he did not have to fear an attack for some time.[21]

Now Kidd and the Portuguese exchanged fire at half a pistol shot, twenty-five yards, slugging it out like a pair of street brawlers. The *Adventure Galley*'s carriage cannons unloaded again with a deadly broadside of conventional cannonballs followed most likely by a blast of bar and chain shot. This time he succeeded in dismasting the enemy. He also may have unleashed his eight *patereroes*, or small mortars, as well as his mounted brass musketoons that fired five-ounce balls. Possessing the advantage with his forty-six oars, he was able to maneuver the galley into position and aim his small and big guns directly at the reeling and overmatched Portuguese gunship.[22]

Through the gaps in the smoke, he took in the scene of destruction. The Portuguese were taking a terrible beating: sails tattered; shrouds, halyards, and braces torn up; gunwales and decks splintered from cannon fire. More than a dozen corpses littered the bloodied and battered fore and aft decks, while twoscore lay twitching, shaking off the splinters, or crawling for cover.[23] Meanwhile, eleven of his own men had been wounded by the enemy in the two separate bouts, some severely. But to Kidd's credit, not a single man of his had been killed.[24]

With the crew's blood running hot, Walker and a squadron of seamen wanted to board the badly mauled Portuguese ship and take her as a prize.

But Kidd would have none of it. With his usual schoolboy exuberance and a tinge of nationalistic pride, he would later chronicle the sea battle in one terse sentence: "The said fight was sharp, and the said Portuguese left the said galley with such satisfaction that the narrator believes no Portuguese will ever attack the king's colors again, in that part of the world especially."[25] But while he enjoyed sticking it to the Catholics, he knew that England was not at war with Portugal, so he could not lawfully seize the ship as a prize, even though the Portuguese had attacked him first without provocation.[26] Seeing the 44-gun flagship now closing in on him to the north, he disregarded his anti-papist and prize-hungry crew, knowing the men would likely be unmanageable if he allowed them to board the Portuguese ship. He instead set a course for south by southwest, in the opposite direction of Portuguese-held Goa.

Even Pattle and Harvey couldn't help but describe the sea battle in patriotic terms: "Kidd's hardy rogues . . . gave [the Portuguese] more than enough and miserably mauled them before the great ship could come up to their aid. When she came near, Kidd set his sails and made from them leaving the smaller ship so much damaged and with such abundance of men killed and disabled that they were forced to run for Goa with all speed."[27] Edward Barlow described the battered Portuguese gunship limping into port like an old peg-legged pirate shambling down the streets of Port Royal: "[W]e met with two Portuguese frigates who were cruising to secure their Mangalore fleet of rice boats from the pirates, for Kidd a little before had met with one of their small frigates and beaten him sadly. One of them, coming up with us, saw we were a merchant ship and sailed away to his consort without speaking to us."[28]

As Kidd made ready to sail, he ordered Dr. Bradinham to sober up and tend to the wounded and Bullen to deliver a damage report. Though he had been victorious, the *Adventure Galley* was "battle-damaged, sea-ravaged, and leaking."[29] With the pounding from the Portuguese cannonballs having reopened some of the old leaks, he needed to find a safe harbor to perform repairs and careen his ship. He sailed to the out-of-the-way Laccadive Islands off the coast of southwest India, where his eleven wounded men could recuperate and the remainder refit the ship and take on fresh food and water.[30]

One month later, in mid-October 1697, the topmast lookout spotted a sail. Kidd quickly charted an intercepting course, relayed it to helmsman John Weir, and bore down hard. This time the chase ended quickly, but once again it was an anticlimactic ending with no prize following the pursuit. When the ship surrendered by raising English colors, he and his men cursed their bad luck yet again.[31]

Hailing the other ship with his speaking trumpet, Kidd invited her captain to come aboard to talk. Stepping lively, the captain was promptly rowed over to the *Adventure Galley*. He introduced himself as Captain Howe of the *Loyal Captain*, a trading vessel sailing from the Madeiras to Surat. Kidd took him to his cabin to show him his privateering commissions and to exchange the latest news. Howe had brought with him a bottle or two of Madeira and some fine food as *peshkash*, the firstfruits given in tribute to an important person in the traditional Indian fashion. The English merchant captain would later report that he had been "civilly treated" and that Kidd showed him his "King's Commission . . . to which he showed due respect" and made "flattering discourses." Howe was the first Englishman in a long time to treat Kidd with courtesy, and the two men ate, drank, and conversed amiably in the idiom of the mariners' trade.[32]

But what Captain Kidd didn't know was that the chivalrous and oh-so-friendly Howe was a wolf in sheep's clothing. The EIC captain already knew about the New York privateer, having met with Captain Gifford of the *Sidney* months earlier in Johanna, as well as having read various reports regurgitating the slanted Company line about the pirate-hunter-turned-pirate. The last thing Howe wanted was for his ship to be captured, so he came aboard bearing gifts and doling out lavish praise, hoping the "pirate" he had heard so much about would let him go without plundering his ship and torturing his crew. Howe informed Kidd that he was carrying only sugar; and the American provincial, as a gentleman, accepted his word for it. Kidd was able to gain valuable intelligence on local shipping as they lingered over their fine afternoon meal and Madeira provided by Howe.[33]

And then, as had happened six weeks earlier with the *Mary*, all hell broke loose on deck.

Hearing shouting voices, Kidd dashed onto the deck with Howe hot on his heels. There he found William Moore and "nine men that had muskets and other arms" arguing with one of his loyal officers, believed to be first mate, Henry Bullen. He demanded to know what was going on. Bullen quickly explained the tense situation. While the two captains had been talking belowdecks, Moore and several others had mingled with the sailors from the *Loyal Captain* who had rowed over with Howe. One of Howe's seamen revealed that traveling aboard the *Loyal Captain* were some Greek and Armenian merchants carrying silver and diamonds. Upon hearing this, Moore had quickly put together a boarding party and armed them with muskets and other weapons. But as they were about to lower an oarboat, Bullen had confronted them and been attacked for his troubles.[34]

Now Moore looked hard at Kidd. "You ruin us because you will not consent to take Captain Howe's ship," he snarled, his eyes dark and glowering.[35]

Kidd had known as soon as he stepped on deck and saw William Moore that his chief gunner had started the ruckus and was the ringleader.[36]

"I will put you, Captain Kidd, in a way to take this ship and come off fairly without committing a robbery at sea," added one of the Dutchmen in Kidd's crew.[37]

Kidd told them to avast their crazy talk.[38] Cursing and stomping, Moore demanded a parley so they could take a vote of the entire crew on whether to take the *Loyal Captain* as a prize. The gunner declared that if the vote came out in his favor, he would lead the prize crew himself and plunder the merchant ship.[39]

With Captain Howe standing worriedly next to him, Kidd consented to having his quartermaster John Walker proceed with a democratic vote to decide a course of action.[40] The rest of the crew was rounded up and brought up on deck. For the next ten minutes, the 115-odd seamen, most of whom carried daggers and nine of whom brandished loaded muskets, vigorously debated whether to take the *Loyal Captain*. When the final tally was in, two-thirds voted in favor of plundering the English ship.[41]

Moore grinned in triumph. But the victory for the gunner and other mutineers was fleeting. Though the democratic Kidd had allowed the vote in accordance with the ship's signed articles, he still had a lawful commission to uphold. Thus, upon second thought, he decided that he could not violate his legal obligations, regardless of how the vote had turned out.[42] With no marines to back him, he knew he was putting his life in jeopardy by standing up to these desperate men who, if they wanted to, could simply toss him overboard and seize the unarmed *Loyal Captain*.[43]

"No, I will not take her," he protested. "The small arms belong to the *Adventure Galley* and I have not come to take any Englishmen or lawful traders. I have no commission other than to take pirates and enemy ships."[44]

The lead insurrectionist, Moore, made it clear that he and the majority of the men didn't care about their commission. The gunner urged the men to grab the pinnace and board the *Loyal Captain*, as she had but a small merchant crew defending her. He and his band of followers, more than a dozen men, then started to move toward the rail. But Captain Kidd stepped between them.

"If you desert my ship, you shall never come aboard again," he warned them in a gruff voice so everyone could hear. "And I will force you into Bombay and carry you before some of the council there."[45]

Moore and his gang of armed pirates argued vehemently with him, but he stood implacably in their way to the pinnace and reminded them of their signed obligations. Captain Howe stepped in and tried to aid Kidd by swearing that he carried nothing but sugar. Emotions ran high as Kidd struggled to control the armed mob of angry seamen. But eventually the ringleader Moore and others backed down.[46]

The next morning, Kidd, pretending as if nothing had happened, politely dismissed Captain Howe, thanked him for his Madeira wine, and sent him on his merry way. Some pirate, that Kidd—he hadn't plundered a *single* item—but, of course, Howe would never report how Captain Kidd had saved his neck by fighting off fourscore angry pirates. As the *Loyal Captain* set off to the north, Moore and his cranky crewmen leaned over the rail, cursing and yelling insults at Howe and his dark-skinned lascars.[47]

Watching the rude behavior of his unruly sailors, Captain Kidd must have shaken his head in dismay and wondered if he would ever make it home to his beloved wife, Sarah, and their young daughters.

TEN DAYS LATER, on October 30, 1697, Kidd was peering through his spyglass at what appeared to be a fat prize when the vessel ran up friendly Dutch colors. With the crippling heat, half-rations, and widespread frustration aboard the *Adventure Galley*, he once again cursed his uncanny streak of bad luck.[48]

He had Bullen raise English colors and stared down from the quarterdeck at the men. William Moore—once again the mutinous ringleader—was loudly complaining about how they should be taking the Dutch ship. This time, the troublemaker who had done stints in New York and Barbados prisons was not calling for a vote of the whole company; instead, he urged the crew to simply ignore Kidd and attack the trading vessel. Looking down at Moore on his soapbox, with fifteen or so crew members listening and nodding, it was clear to Kidd that many of them were in favor of violating the ship's articles and seizing the Dutchman.[49]

Reaching for his speaking trumpet, he shouted down to the men and warned them to think twice about what they were proposing. "She is our friend," he reminded them, by which he meant the Netherlands was England's ally and they would incur the Crown's wrath if they brought harm to the Dutch vessel.[50]

Moore and his band of malcontents disagreed. With the galley's powerful oars, they claimed, they could easily row into position in the calm seas and fire broadsides into the Dutch merchantman until she surrendered. The only question was who would lead the men.

Once again, Kidd called down and made it clear to Moore and the others that they would not be taking the Dutch ship as long as he was in command. A short time later, the men began defiantly sharpening their knives and cutlasses, checking the pinnace, and gathering in small groups to talk in angry tones.[51]

Kidd again warned them to stop their mutinous talk, as Abel Owen, the *Adventure Galley*'s cook, stepped onto the deck to bear witness to what was about to happen.[52]

"You that will take the Dutchman, you are the strongest, you may do what you please," said Kidd. "If you will take her, you may take her; but if you go from aboard, you shall never come aboard again."[53]

He stopped right there, letting his warning sink in. Moore and the others continued to glower up at him insolently. The chief gunner, by this time seated on the deck with a grinding stone and sharpening a heavy iron chisel, was clearly showing mutinous behavior by openly goading the men to take the other ship, but Kidd had no individual authority to punish him. Though Article 12 of the ship's agreement was clear that mutiny would not be tolerated, the actual punishment was "as the Capt. and major part of the company shall think fit."[54] Thus, Kidd would need a majority vote to have Moore locked up belowdecks or flogged, and he surmised that he would never obtain the necessary votes to punish the popular gunner.[55]

Moore was now telling the men how their captain could legally take the Dutch ship. The men were mumbling their assent and nodding—all out in the open on the main deck.[56]

By this point, Captain Kidd had had quite enough. He stormed down onto the main deck and confronted Moore face-to-face. "How will you legally take that Dutch ship?" he demanded of the gunner.

"We will get the captain and men aboard," replied Moore.

"And what then?"

"We will go aboard the ship, and plunder her, and we will have it under their hands that we did not take her."

It was a desperate plan, a pirate's plan, and Kidd would have none of it. Moore was proposing to capture the Dutch ship, hold the captain and crew as hostages, plunder the vessel, and refuse to let the hostages go until they signed a statement declaring that the *Adventure Galley* had not molested their vessel.

Kidd shook his head adamantly, his blood rising.

"No, we are not taking that ship," he said. "What ye propose is Judas-like, and I dare not do such a thing."

"We may do it; we are beggars already," Moore fired back, clearly trying to goad him.

"Why?" he roared. "May we take this ship because we are poor?"

Moore didn't respond. Struggling to control his rising anger, Kidd began pacing the deck. As he passed Moore, the gunner again looked at him impudently while continuing to sharpen his iron chisel with his grinding stone.

"Ye have brought us to ruin, Captain Kidd; surely ye have."

Kidd stared straight at him, his eyes hard and narrow.

"We are desolate," snarled the gunner. "And it is because of you."

All at once, after more than a year of enduring hardship, privation, and bad luck all around, Kidd felt himself snap.

"I have not brought you to ruin! I have not done an ill thing to ruin you! You are a dog to give me those words!"

Moore gave a dismissive snort and returned to his sharpening. Feeling an uncontrollable, roiling fury, Captain Kidd took up an empty, iron-hooped, wooden water bucket and swung it by the handle, catching Moore flush in the temple.

The gunner fell hard to the deck, his chisel spilling from his hand.

Kidd could tell straightaway that he had struck him harder than intended. Though he had no idea of the extent of his chief gunner's injury, he may have observed a contusion and some blood dripping down his cheek. Several of Moore's mutinous comrades now came to his aid, giving their commander the evil eye. Soon Dr. Bradinham appeared, reeking of strong drink but sober enough, and Moore was lifted up and carried belowdecks.

As they made their way down the stairs and to the gun room, Moore looked up at those carrying him and is reported to have said, "Farewell, farewell, Captain Kidd has given me my last."[57]

William Moore's prognostication proved correct. He died the next day of a fractured skull. He was sewn up in canvas with ballast stones and respectfully cast overboard into the sea after a short prayer.[58]

The majority of the crew would never forgive their captain for losing his cool in such a tempestuous manner. For this act, in the view of historians who cling to the traditional English-Crown and East-India-Company narrative, this is a "Gotcha!" moment where the colonial American privateer shows his true colors as a Captain Bligh–type monster. There is no question that he snapped—but there is also no question that he was pushed to the edge, felt ashamed, and showed genuine contrition for his actions. "I had no design to kill him," Kidd would say under oath of the tragic event. "I had no malice or spleen against him. It was not designedly done, but in my passion, for which I am heartily sorry."[59]

–11–
Quedagh Merchant

Following William Moore's accidental death, Captain Kidd's trials and tribulations only worsened. On November 3, he sailed to the East India Company factory at Tellicherry Road to peacefully gather wood and water—but instead came under heavy cannon fire from the fortified compound and was forced to retreat from the harbor. Angry, disillusioned, and worried about having his own throat slit by his men, he trolled the coastal waters off southern India without spying a single ship for two grueling weeks.[1] It wasn't until November 18 that a sail was spotted. A desperate man with an even more desperate crew, Kidd gave immediate chase.[2]

Nine hours later, he finally overtook his quarry and raised a French *pavillon blanc*, or white ensign bearing gold *fleurs-de-lys* royal insignia, to lure and seize her as a lawful prize. Peering at the vessel through his glass, he saw that the ship was a 150- to 200-ton merchantman, half the size of his 34-gun galley. With the heavily armed *Adventure Galley* flying the white flag of royal France, the ketch hoisted both French and Moorish colors. But, to Kidd's surprise, the trading vessel made no effort to slow down.[3]

He ordered his new chief gunner, Archibald Buchanon, to lob a pair of cannonballs across her forefoot.[4]

A 12-pounder exploded from the larboard gunport, followed quickly by another blast that sent a second shudder through the massive galley. The cannonballs screamed across the bow of the ketch and plunked into the rolling waves of the Arabian Sea. With the French and Moorish flags flapping in the stiff coastal breeze, the opposing captain struck his colors, turned his vessel into the wind, and furled his sails in submission.[5]

Kidd had translator Pierre LeRoy, who had left EIC Captain Clarke at Mohelia due to "hard usage," hail the captain. Kidd handed LeRoy the speaking trumpet, and the French sailor barked out something like "*Salutations, Monsieur le Capitaine!*" through the brass device, and then invited the opposing captain to row over with his paperwork to the *Adventure Galley*.[6]

With the two ships bobbing side by side, the crew of the ketch sent an oarboat over to the *Adventure Galley*. Climbing over the railing, the captain introduced himself as Mitch Dekkar of the *Rouparelle*.[7] Looking him up and down and taking in his accent, Kidd could tell that he was a veteran sea dog and Dutchman, though his command of the French language was solid. With all due formality, Kidd introduced himself in his passable French and, after sending Walker and a boarding party to peacefully inspect the *Rouparelle*, he led Dekkar to his cabin so they could talk in private.[8]

After his cabin boy, Richard Barlycorne, had poured them a glass of wine, Kidd asked to see Dekkar's papers. The Dutch captain handed him an authentic French *passeport* bearing the customary "*De Par Le Roy*"—"By the Order of the King"—and the seal of the Royal Company of France of the East Indies (French East India Company), emblazoned with the royal *fleur-de-lis* in the lower left corner. Kidd was able to decipher most of the words on the passport, which was signed by Jean-Baptiste Martin, director-general of the Royal Company of France. The paperwork stated that Vameldas Narendas, a merchant of

Baroche, intended to send his 150-ton ship, the *Rouparelle*, from the port of Baroche to the Malabar Coast. The passport implored all allies of France to honor the legal document and the vessel's trading mission.[9] Because Dekkar had presented a French pass, Kidd for the first time had the legitimacy he insisted upon as a matter of principle. But even though the ship was a legal prize, he was still uneasy because the vessel was Moor-owned and carrying a Dutch cargo.[10]

Despite Kidd's misgivings, Dekkar insisted that the *Rouparelle* was a lawful prize. His crew, he said, consisted of forty Indian lascars and two Dutchmen. His cargo included two chests of opium, a dozen bales of cotton, two horses, fifty quilts, and the household possessions of an unlucky Dutch official, Governor van Duyn, who was moving from Karwar to Ceylon.[11]

Kidd called back Walker's boarding party inspecting the *Rouparelle* and explained the situation in a meeting of the entire ship. Although the vessel flew a French flag and her captain had presented a French passport, making her a lawful prize, she was still Indian-owned and carried the cargo of England's ally the Dutch.[12] He, therefore, tried to "persuade them to restore the Moorish ship to its owners," reported Samuel Bradley, "but the crew opposed him" and voted overwhelmingly to keep her as a legal prize.[13]

This time, Kidd stood by the democratic vote instead of fighting his men as he had with Howe's *Loyal Captain*. The crew finally had something to show for all their hardship after fourteen months of no pay. The cargo of horses, sugar, and cotton wasn't much, but it was enough to renew hope. The crew, already mutinous and on half rations, would now at least have ample food and drink.

Dekkar, who went by the moniker "Skipper Mitch," switched over to the *Adventure Galley* along with the two Dutch crew members and seven Moors, including a pilot. After all the men Kidd had lost to tropical disease and desertion, and with Samuel Bradley and other crew members still sick and unable to work, he could use the extra deckhands, especially if he encountered pirates and required his full complement of cannons.

Kidd allowed the remaining Indian seamen aboard the *Rouparelle* and the ship's owners to take a pair of oarboats loaded with provisions and row the two leagues to Calicut.[14]

Following the privateer tradition of renaming captured vessels, the crew voted on a new name for the prize ship before setting sail. Some voted for the derisive name *Maiden*, since it was the *Adventure Galley*'s first capture, but the majority of the crew voted for *November* for the month the vessel had been captured.[15]

Having taken an instant liking to the easygoing Skipper Mitch, Kidd appointed him as a key officer to replace the deceased Henry Mead. With his men still surly, bickering, and mutinous, he wanted an outsider without preconceived notions to captain his new prize. He also wanted to off-load some of his worst troublemakers onto the *November*, so he got rid of his heavy-drinking surgeon Robert Bradinham, fractious Royal Navy reject and unsuccessful deserter Joseph Palmer, and several other malcontents.[16]

The two ships sailed south for the smuggler's port of Kalliquilon. For Kidd to keep his crew from open rebellion, he needed to quickly sell the cargo and divide the shares amongst them. By contract, he was not supposed to break cargo before returning to America, but his situation was desperate. To have any hope of success in his mission and making it safely home, he needed to purchase food for his hungry and disgruntled sailors and pay them wages. At Kalliquilon, he was able to sell the horses, sugar, cotton, two chests of opium, and quilts to Gillam Gandaman, a renegade EIC employee, for £150 ($52,500 today). The money was divided up amongst the crew in accordance with their designated shares; though a pittance, it was enough to buy provisions and keep the men from tossing him overboard.[17]

For the next two months, Kidd continued to cruise off the Malabar Coast, but failed to sight a single French or pirate ship. After being cannonaded at Tellicherry and denied wood and water at Calicut by his fellow Englishmen, he now avoided EIC factories and traded with local Indian vessels.[18]

On January 30, 1698, the topmast lookout spotted a distant speck of white twenty-five leagues off Cochin, just north of the southern tip of India. It was a sail that would change everything for Captain Kidd and the mutinous band of pirates he was struggling to control.

He studied the gunship closely as the *Adventure Galley*, flying French colors, sliced through the rollers along the northern edge of the Laccadive Sea. Moor-built and square-rigged, the merchant vessel flew Armenian colors, carried fourteen to eighteen cannons, and was manned by an Indian lascar crew just shy of a hundred seamen.[19]

Closing on her quickly, he came alongside and hailed the massive Indian vessel built in 1683 in Surat, commanding the captain through his speaking trumpet to heave to, lower his topsails, and come aboard. His opposite number had little choice but to submit: the Moorish ship, though enormous, was equipped with only half as many guns as the *Adventure Galley* and a crew of docile lascars to face Kidd's heavily armed sea dogs. As the captain acceded to his request, turning the ship into the wind and lowering canvas, Kidd read the gold cursive inscription on her stern name-board: *Quedagh Merchant*.[20]

He scanned the horizon for the *November*, but the consort was nowhere in sight. He decided to interview the captain and inspect the ship's hold while waiting for the rest of the company to arrive.[21] After ordering English colors raised, he met the master along the railing with Bullen and his French seaman Pierre LeRoy. Looking up at the Union Jack, the *Quedagh*'s crinkly-faced captain presented a French passport and said laconically in broken English, "Here is a good prize."[22]

Kidd would have to confirm that, but he must have already felt a thrill at having finally stumbled upon a bulging merchant ship. With his restive crew looking on like a pack of hungry wolves, he and the Frenchman retired to his cabin along with LeRoy, who would serve as an interpreter if Kidd got in a bind. Kidd showed his guest his commission from the Admiralty to take French ships, while he closely inspected the captain's letter of safe passage. As with the *Rouparelle*, he found the *passeport* duly authentic with the official embossed French seal and once again signed simply "Martin."[23]

But as he began to follow up with questions, the Frenchman made a startling confession. He wasn't actually the captain of the *Quedagh Merchant,* but was merely standing in for the real captain—an Englishman named John Wright. Because Kidd had flown French colors, Wright had sent over his French gunner to play the part of captain of the vessel. Now that he knew the truth, Kidd had Captain Wright rowed over to the *Adventure Galley* and brought to his cabin, so the two men could work out the details of the legal acquisition.[24]

After showing the English captain his Admiralty commission, Kidd questioned Wright over a glass of wine to confirm the details of the French *passeport.* The owner of the *Quedagh Merchant,* Coirgi, was a reputable Indian merchant and ship owner. Wright, it turned out, wasn't just a sea captain but also a Surat tavern owner who had been sailing home from Bengal.[25] Serving under him were two Dutch officers, the French gunner Kidd had already met, and a crew of ninety lascars; he also had eight Armenian merchants on board. The ship had been fitted out in Bengal with an immense cargo: 1,200 bales of muslins, calicos, and other expensive fabrics; 1,400 bags of brown sugar; 84 bales of raw silk; 80 chests of opium; and a hefty load of iron and saltpeter. The wealthy Armenian merchants also carried precious jewels, gold, and silver. They were part of a trading syndicate operating out of Surat and had banded together to hire the *Quedagh* from Coirgi. Helping to broker the deal was a local representative of the EIC named Augun Peree Callender, who was moonlighting to supplement his income.[26]

Wright told Kidd that, based upon his commission, the *Quedagh Merchant* was a legal prize. Kidd understood that, but he was still concerned that a representative for the East India Company had brokered the shipping. The fiercely monopolistic corporation continued to be a thorn in his side that he just couldn't shake.[27]

Despite the circumstances, Kidd got along well with Wright. Unlike the East India Company, the Englishman would never utter a bad word about him. When they were finished talking, the English captain took Kidd and a boarding party over to examine the *Quedagh Merchant* and her rich cargo. They found the ship in an uproar. The Armenian merchants were screaming at the two Dutch officers, the French gunner, and the huddling Indian seamen to put up a fight. When the Armenians spotted Kidd and Wright climbing aboard the vessel, they rushed forward to accost them. Wright informed them that he had no choice but to surrender the ship to Kidd since she was a lawful prize, which was the last thing they wanted to hear.[28]

Now the Armenians went berserk. They shouted at Wright, the Dutch and French officers, and the timid lascar crew to stop cowering like women and protect the ship. Parting their way through the agitated Armenians, Kidd had Wright escort him to the captain's cabin and the cargo hold so that he and his quartermaster, John Walker, could take an inventory of the goods aboard.[29]

The *Quedagh Merchant* indeed proved to be a rich treasure ship. The cargo of fine East Indian fabrics, spices, sugar, opium, iron, and saltpeter on board would be worth at least 480,000 rupees (£60,000 sterling, or around $21,000,000 in today's dollars). Doing the rough calculations in his head, Kidd realized that the booty along with the prize ship would easily triple the investment for himself, Livingston, Bellomont, and the voyage's other backers.[30]

Two days later, the straggling *November* packed with Kidd's most unruly seamen finally appeared. Kidd called a meeting of the entire company and explained the situation to them in the presence of Wright and the Armenians.[31] Although the Moorish vessel was a legal prize, he was still uncomfortable because the ship and cargo belonged to England, albeit indirectly, since the East India Company had brokered the shipping. Thus, he recommended they return her since the seizure of such a great vessel in the employment of the Crown "would make a great noise in England."[32]

As expected, the men grumbled their disapproval.

"Where will you take this ship?" he asked, making one last attempt to talk his crew out of plundering the vessel. "And where will you take the cargo?"[33]

They angrily shouted that they would take the ship to the pirate stronghold of St. Mary's.[34]

The Armenian merchants now became hysterical again. One of them, Coji Babba, stepped forward to speak for the group. He offered Kidd and his rowdy sailors twenty thousand rupees to buy back the cargo, which was a ridiculously low offer for a man with zero leverage and a ship full of desperate pirates ready to string him up from a yardarm. The stingy Armenians were only offering them the equivalent of two thousand pounds sterling when they had thirty to fifty times that amount, as well as the huge captured ship, in their possession.[35]

Walker put it to a vote. It was nearly unanimous in favor of taking the *Quedagh Merchant* as a prize. Clucking their disapproval, Coji Babba and the Armenians begged Kidd to sell them back their ship, but Kidd's hands were tied. Worn down by a hostile crew on the verge of all-out mutiny, he had no choice but to accept the majority vote of the company. More importantly, there was no doubt in his mind that his crew would seize the treasure ship regardless of what he said or did. This was the prize they had all been banking on, and they weren't about to allow their fortunes to sail away on the wind.[36]

He now made arrangements for the *Quedagh Merchant*'s crew to sail and row themselves the twenty-five leagues to Cochin and for him and his three-ship flotilla to head south to Kalliquilon to obtain much-needed food, water, and wood for the 2,500-mile journey to St. Mary's, the destination the crew had decided upon by democratic vote.[37] As the *Quedagh*'s pinnace and oarboats were prepared for the captured prize ship's crew to make their way ashore, he allowed Wright to retrieve his belongings off the ship and purchased from the Englishman a navigational pendulum clock.[38] He could tell that the Armenian merchants resented the cordiality between him and the English captain, but Kidd was a gentleman and that's the way he operated. His foremost priority was not to mollify the hurt feelings of the rich Armenians, but to get his 40 percent share of the lawful booty for himself, Bellomont, Livingston, and the other investors safely home to America in fulfillment of his commission.[39]

The captured boats would transport the Armenians, the ninety lascar crewmen, and Captain Wright and his European officers, along with Captain Thomas Parker and Don Antonio taken from the *Mary* five months earlier.[40] Since he was preparing to leave India for Madagascar and thence home to America, Captain Kidd no longer needed a local navigator or linguist. They would all make it safely to shore; and, unlike the EIC, the two English captains, Wright and Parker, would never express a *single* ill word about Kidd in *any* deposition or testimonial. In fact, Wright would be accused by both Indian and English officials, as well as the *Quedagh*'s Armenians, of being *too* friendly with the colonial American privateer. The Armenians would even spread the false rumor that the English captain "was in league with Kidd and a sharer in the spoils."[41]

Kidd steered his three-ship fleet southeast to Kalliquilon to sell the opium and other goods for Arabian gold. By contract, he was not supposed to break cargo before returning to Boston, but he needed to buy food to victual his 115-man crew. If he didn't give his disgruntled men some wages, he would have no hope of persuading them to carry the two prize ships home to the colonies for delivery to Bellomont.[42]

When he reached the smuggler's port of Kalliquilon, he traded a portion of his bale goods to Indian merchant buyers who queued up next to the *Adventure Prize*, as the *Quedagh Merchant* had been renamed. He sold a significant portion of the opium and several dozen bales of silk, generating almost £10,000 ($3,500,000 today) in gold nuggets and bars, or approximately 15 percent of the legally captured *Quedagh*'s riches.[43]

It was during his stay in Kalliquilon in February that Kidd for the first time crossed the line into piracy—or rather looked the other way as his unruly misfits from Skipper Mitch Dekkar's *November* committed piracy on a European vessel. After seventeen grueling months at sea, he for the first time allowed the seizure of a ship that presented official papers of a nation friendly to England (Portugal) and permitted cargo to be taken from her without making a strenuous effort to give it back.[44]

After Kidd's flotilla halted the Portuguese galliot twelve leagues from Calicut, Kidd had the ship's captain rowed over to the *Adventure Galley*, and they spoke in the usual cordial fashion through the Portuguese interpreter Don Antonio. He learned that the ship, whose name was not recorded at the time or later recalled by Kidd or any crew member who delivered testimony, was bound from Bengal to Goa with a lascar crew of seventy hands and a small amount of goods for the local coastal trade. As the two captains talked, the crew of the Dutchman Dekkar's *November* began ransacking the ship in a reenactment of the *Mary* incident with Walker and Moore.[45] But this time Kidd either didn't lift a finger to stop the fractious crew members under his command, or put up only token resistance and said to hell with it. Dekkar's crew seized from the Portuguese vessel two small chests of opium, four bales of silk, sixty to seventy bags of rice, and some butter, wax, and iron.[46] It was a paltry haul, and if Kidd hadn't become such a notorious figure few would have cared that he had allowed a contingent of his unruly seamen under the command of a sub-captain to plunder a few goods from a Catholic merchant ship manned by Moors. Taking the galliot as a prize, Skipper Mitch towed her from the *November* as an escort ship in the growing flotilla.[47]

Why did Captain Kidd finally look the other way toward piracy after all this time? The most logical explanation is that he felt justified in taking retribution against the Portuguese for the damage to his ship and serious injuries sustained by his crew from the 44-gun and 22-gun men-of-war that months earlier had attacked him. He must have also believed that since he had more than tripled his London backers' return on their investment with the *Quedagh*, he would not be held accountable for piracy in taking such a trifling amount of goods from a hated Catholic ship, though England and Portugal were officially at peace. Finally, he was probably so worn down at this point that he simply gave up fighting his rebellious crew.

Whatever his reasons, seizing the Portuguese galliot was the only true hanging offense of the entire voyage. And that is only if one chooses to believe that the English state held actual authority in Indian waters, since European courts and enforcement agencies did not extend beyond the line (west of the Prime Meridian, south of the Tropic of Cancer). But even if the Crown did possess such authority, Kidd did nothing more than the Royal Navy, East India Company, and privateers of all European nations did on a routine basis. In the 1600s and 1700s, all these commerce-raiding factions had their own agendas and different degrees of "state sanction," but in practice they were inseparable from one another when it came to stopping ships at sea, checking for papers, questioning captains and crew members, pressing key seamen into service, and seizing and plundering vessels. This private *and* state-sanctioned raiding ranged from committing minor acts of "procurement," such as relieving ships of some critical cargo or foodstuffs, or conducting one-sided trade with targeted vessels, to committing major acts of sea robbery involving full-scale attacks and seizures of ships and all goods on board.[48]

In fact, the vaunted Royal Navy in the Age of Sail was often every bit as piratical as the pirates they were supposed to be hunting down and bringing to justice. English naval officers were known to carry on active commerce rather than suppress pirates, embezzle goods from the vessels they halted, abandon their convoys to hunt prizes, and undercut local traders since they "sailed without the expense of wages or victualling." William III distrusted his own navy so much that he routinely had his customs officers "search royal ships because of suspicions they were smuggling gold."[49]

Thus, Royal Navy men in Kidd's era were hardly the saintly *Master and Commander*–like heroes portrayed in books and film. Not only did English naval captains during King William's War take bribes, embezzle goods, and smuggle gold into England, they and their seamen physically harmed civilians, stole livestock, and often refused to pay for the food, liquor, and other goods they consumed.[50] The Royal Navy was even known to lend a helping hand to pirates beyond the line in return for payment. The Surat trader and sea captain Alexander Hamilton reported that Commodore James Littleton and his naval squadron aided Indian Ocean pirates in careening their ships-of-force, "generously assisting them with large blocks and tackle-falls . . . in cleaning the bottoms of their large ships."[51]

The reality is that armed commerce—defensive and offensive—"was the norm at sea, not the exception." Indeed, the vast Atlantic, Pacific, and Indian Oceans in the 1600s and 1700s, inhospitable environments far removed from the clubby comforts of domesticated London, were a dangerous wilderness much like the western frontier that would humble the American explorers Lewis and Clark in the early nineteenth century.[52]

In early March, Kidd was awakened one morning in Kalliquilon Harbor by Richard Barlycorne and informed that five gunships were sailing aggressively toward him. Dashing up onto the quarterdeck, he peered through his brass spyglass at the onrushing flotilla.[53]

The two lead ships were powerful English East India Company merchant vessels. Less than two leagues away and closing fast, they were accompanied by two heavily armed Dutch merchant ships and a Portuguese gunship. The lead East Indiaman was the *Dorrill*, commanded by Captain Samuel Hyde, who had received a tip that Kidd was peddling stolen goods. The second EIC gunship was the *Blessing*, smaller but bristling with firepower. As acting commodore of the flotilla, Hyde's plan was to catch Kidd in the harbor at the crack of dawn, while he and his men were still fast asleep in their hammocks.[54]

But for one of the first times during his fateful voyage, Kidd had a bit of luck on his side. Though Hyde and his Anglo-Dutch fleet had piled on all sail in hopes of launching their attack at sunrise, they had missed their mark by a half hour, enabling the *Adventure Galley*'s lookout to spot the incoming gunships in the early morning sunlight.

Wide awake now, Captain Kidd felt his whole body go into high alert. He summoned Walker on deck and alerted Bullen in the *Adventure Prize* and Skipper Mitch Dekkar in the *November* to the new threat. Barking out commands through his speaking trumpet, he ordered all hands in the flotilla to battle stations and to make ready to sail. Rousted out of their hammocks, the men began hoisting the anchors, hurling tow ropes between the ships, unfurling the canvas, and preparing to get under way.[55]

Amidst all this frenetic activity, Kidd tracked the movements of the East Indiamen approaching like great white sharks. The tension was excruciating as the capstans slowly turned and the anchor cables ground their way through the hawseholes on each ship. The *Adventure Galley*'s 4,000-pound wrought-iron anchor had been set apeak, with the bow riding directly over the anchor so she could make a quick getaway if necessary. But it was still taking too damn long, and Kidd now ordered all ships to cut their anchor cables.[56]

Now the East Indiamen moved in for the kill, attempting to seal off Kalliquilon Harbor.

Kidd realized it was going to be a narrow escape, if they escaped at all. With the sun's morning rays glinting off the water, the *Adventure Galley* caught the breeze and was under way, towing the ponderous *Adventure Prize* captained by Henry Bullen in her wake. But Dekkar and his gang of rebels were having trouble putting the *November* to sea while towing the Portuguese galliot.[57] Kidd barked out orders to make haste or they would any second come under fire. As the vessels grappled to get under sail, Kidd yelled to Bullen and Dekkar that if the ships became separated, they should all rendezvous at St. Mary's.[58]

The East Indiamen pressed closer. The lead attacker, the *Dorrill*, commanded by Captain Hyde, opened fire with her massive guns upon Skipper Mitch and his sleepy-eyed sea dogs in the *November*.[59]

Despite once again being saddled with a leaky ship, Kidd was able to navigate the *Adventure Galley* and the *Adventure Prize* out of Kalliquilon Harbor and make his escape when his attackers had him dead to rights. But the *November* appeared to be trapped.[60]

With the situation looking grim, the Dutchman Dekkar made a snap decision. He instructed the prize crew to chop the braided tow line with an axe and leave the Portuguese vessel behind. With the galliot set adrift, the *November*, like Kidd's ships, was only barely able to escape through the narrow throat of the harbor, with the cannonballs from the attacking East Indiamen splashing all around.[61]

Unable to cut off Kidd and his fleet, Captain Hyde in the *Dorrill* halted the chase and made a beeline for the Portuguese galliot to collect the ship as a prize. Meanwhile, the smaller East Indiaman, the *Blessing*, attempted to pursue at first but soon gave up too. However, the attackers still had an ace in the hole. The faster-sailing Dutch gunships were farther out to sea and in position to intercept the three-vessel flotilla.[62]

Kidd studied the two oncoming Dutch gunships through his glass. As the undermanned *Adventure Prize* lumbered out into the open sea and the crew of the *November* grappled to get her sails just right, the two Dutch gunships looked poised to intercept them. But to both Kidd's and Hyde's surprise, Captain Jan Coin and the second Dutch commander sailed into Kalliquilon Harbor without firing a single shot.[63]

Captain Kidd and his Crown-sanctioned privateering fleet that had crossed the line into piracy had narrowly made their escape.

But following the frantic cut-and-run, Kidd's *Galley*, Bullen's *Adventure Prize*, and Dekkar's *November* were spread out, having veered off in different directions to elude their pursuers. Furthermore, the *Adventure Galley* was once again leaking badly. Her hull planks had been burrowed by teredo shipworms, and her seams were opening up from the combined effects of the tropical-water mollusks and cannonballs. To make sure the ship didn't sink, Kidd "was forced to wind her round with cables to keep her together."[64]

On April 1, 1698, Kidd and the *Adventure Galley* limped into St. Mary's harbor.[65] He was all alone, without the *Adventure Prize* or *November* in sight, as he gazed for the first time upon the long, narrow tropical island covering eighty-five square miles.[66] The pirate settlement on St. Mary's founded by Adam Baldridge was a ramshackle affair in 1698, with "a hut on a hill at some distance from the harbor," a few houses, a low palisade, and a couple of cannons.[67] Inside the harbor, Kidd spotted a single large ship armed with more than thirty carriage guns. As he dropped anchor, he saw a group of seamen lower oarboats from the vessel, row ashore, and dart into the woods like frightened jackrabbits. Now, that was odd.[68]

But he soon discovered—from New England trader Edward Welch and the Malagasy tribesmen living on the island—the identity of the ship, her captain, and the men. The *Resolution* was commanded by his old shipmate Robert Culliford, and the roguish sailors were part of the English pirate's East Indian crew.[69]

Having entered the lair of the notorious criminal who had stolen everything from him eight years earlier for refusing to turn pirate, he realized that a golden opportunity lay before him. Not only could he even an old score, he could wipe the slate clean with the English authorities and East India Company in one fell swoop. But first he had to persuade his unruly crew to help him capture Robert Culliford and haul the outlaw back in chains to Lord Bellomont in America.

–12–
The War on Captain Kidd and Piracy

Between the hanging of Henry Every's crew in November 1696 and the arrivals of Captain Kidd at St. Mary's and Lord Bellomont finally in New York in early April 1698, England ramped up its war against piracy. However, Every was still at large, the pirate base at St. Mary's remained unchallenged by the ineffectual Royal Navy, and America's independent-spirited colonial governors, customs collectors, and citizens continued to "kindly receive" pirates and provide "safe and friendly ports and markets for stolen goods." And yet, although the Crown had shown only mixed results in combating piracy, it had succeeded in laying the bureaucratic groundwork for a major crackdown that would have far-reaching repercussions in the New World—especially for William and Sarah Kidd.[1]

The first step in the Crown's war on piracy took place in the aftermath of the *Ganj-i-Sawai* incident but before the Henry Every trial. Cantankerous Edward Randolph, the sixty-four-year-old English surveyor general of American customs, filed extensive documents on the complicity of colonial governors and customs collectors in profiting from, or turning a blind eye to, robbery on the high seas. His abrasive reports, including his extensive treatise *A Discourse about Pyrates, with Proper*

Remedies to Suppress Them, landed on desks at Whitehall at the same time that news of Tew's and Every's depredations began trickling in from the East Indies. With the threat to the East Indian trade posed by the Red Sea Men becoming a burning issue, Randolph's alarming reports of pirates enmeshed within America's social, political, and legal framework constituted a shocking wake-up call.[2]

The second step in the Crown's war against piracy was the 1696 Act for Preventing Frauds and Regulating Abuses in the Plantation Trade—a restatement and strengthening of previous Navigation Acts that became known as the 1696 Navigation Act—or the Jamaica Act, as it was known in the colonies.[3] The most important change was an attempt to institute Vice-Admiralty Courts in America to try piracy and smuggling cases. Although implementation of the special courts would be delayed and Parliament would not enact the statute until 1700 with the Act for the More Effectual Suppression of Piracy, the 1696 Navigation Act put the Crown's regulatory framework in place, thus laying the groundwork for the 1700 Act that allowed pirates to be tried for the very first time on American soil without a jury trial.[4]

The third action taken by the Crown to suppress piracy was the 1696 formation of the new Committee on Trade and Plantations, more commonly known as the Board of Trade. With the change, the ineffectual Lords of Trade—that laissez-faire Good Old Lords' network based on breeding rather than talent—was replaced by a more rigorous and professional administrative body to deal with piracy and illicit trade.[5] The new bureaucratic entity sought to consolidate the English Empire by compiling and analyzing statistics on imports and exports and by maintaining frequent correspondence with colonial officials on how to effectively control piracy.[6] The creation of the more technically rigorous Board of Trade served notice that England "was no longer a brash, thrusting, new power, but an established and ever more formidable imperial state."[7]

With the testimony of Randolph and others, along with the expanded Navigation Act, the formation of the Board of Trade, and the evidence given at the two Every trials, Whitehall for the first time understood the full extent of its "piracy problem" and proposed solutions. Like American Prohibition and the modern-day War on Drugs, the War on Piracy would never actually be won, but no one could doubt the English government's determination to legally address the growing problem of global piracy. While Kidd was away at sea, the Crown's policy toward piracy transformed from one of benign neglect to active investigation, capture, and prosecution. The new paradigm ensured that there would be a continuing manhunt for Every—and that Captain Kidd would soon become England's Public Enemy Number 1.[8]

In early April 1698, the war on piracy took a decisive turn in faraway India when the Great Mughal went into an uproar over the seizure of the *Quedagh Merchant*. The White Snake's ire came just as Sarah Kidd heard the first snippets about her husband's alleged exploits on the far side of the world, Lord Bellomont replaced Benjamin Fletcher as royal governor of New York and launched his anti-piracy crusade, and Captain Kidd anxiously awaited the arrival of the *Adventure Prize* and *November* at St. Mary's Island.

While news of the capture would not reach Whitehall until August 1698, the incident created a furor within weeks of the seizure at the Great Mughal's palace and East India Company factories. Surprisingly, the first reports reaching Sir John Gayer in Bombay and President Samuel Annesley in Surat were accurate: Captain Kidd had seized the 400-ton *Quedagh Merchant* while presenting an official license bearing the great seal of the King of England. Though this was shocking news, what Sir John and Annesley found most distressing was that the commercial Muslim vessel was leased by important members of Aurangzeb's imperial court, including Muklis Khan, a leading merchant and scion of the Indian nobility.[9]

Once again, trade in the thriving port town of Surat was suspended, outraged Muslim East Indian factions threatened to pillage and burn Company warehouses, and Annesley and his colleagues were placed under house arrest, while imperial Indian regulars held back the infuriated mobs from the fortified factory compound.[10] Soon, demands came from Aurangzeb and his governors for the EIC to provide heavy compensation and convoy protection.[11] Just like in the 1695–1696 Henry Every affair, Indian officials made it clear that they would expel the English traders from the continent if their terms were not met. The *farman*—imperial edict—handed down maintained that since the Company was in league with the pirates, all English, French, and Dutch trade was thereby halted until the *Quedagh*'s investors were fully compensated and vastly improved protective convoys for Indian trading ships were supplied.[12]

In all the uproar, Captain Kidd was no longer an EIC bogeyman based upon flimsy evidence, but could now be promoted as a "notorious arch-Pyrate." Like Every before him, he had seized a ship closely connected to the Great Mughal, which not only placed the East India trade at risk but dealt the Company a devastating financial blow.[13] After the seizure of the *Quedagh*, he "came to personify all of the unknown and unnamed pirates who tormented the company,"[14] which "urged Kidd's capture and punishment to prove that there was no official support for this sort of raiding."[15] The EIC was well aware of the depredations of Robert Culliford, Dirk Chivers, and other ruffians plundering far and wide across the Indian Ocean at the time—but all that Sir John Gayer, Samuel Annesley, and the Great Mughal seemed to care about was Captain Kidd. His name just rolled so easily off the tongue, and it even sounded scandalously pirate-like.[16]

From the safety of his opulent and impregnable island fortress in Bombay, Sir John issued stern orders to his subordinate to resist the Indian blackmail because it would lead to having to pay exorbitant bribes every time a piracy was committed. But Annesley had no choice but to cave in to the Great Mughal, who sent instructions to his liaison officer threatening imprisonment if the man did not return in ten days with either 200,000 rupees ($8,000,000 today) or Annesley and his fellow Englishmen in chains. Under heavy pressure, Annesley was able to persuade Sir John to agree to continued convoy protection and a series of smaller payments to placate Governor Ahmanat Khan and other

Indian officials, with the result that the Company paid out only £5,000 ($1,750,000 today) total in bribes.[17]

Annesley was relieved. "The troublesome business of the *Quedagh Merchant*, God be thanked, we have hopes will be well concluded unless the pirates commit any fresh villainies," he wrote to his fussy boss in Bombay. But to put an end to the dispute, Governor Khan inexplicably pointed the finger at the Danes for the *Quedagh* capture, which irked Sir John immensely. "We had rather he had lay the blame on all hatmen [Europeans] in general than the Danes," he lamented, "for then the French and Dutch would be engaged to extirpate them as well and bear an equal share [of the cost]."[18]

The Kidd affair had blown over, just barely, and India was safe once again for the English East India Company. The hapless Danes received the principal blame for Kidd's seizure, and Sir John Gayer, Samuel Annesley, and their Company factors went along with the charade. With disaster narrowly averted, they returned to their armies of Indian servants and lives of opulence.[19]

But less than one week after the Kidd storm passed, Annesley's brief respite of luxury and fanciful scheming to transform India into the Bank of England came to an abrupt end. The news fresh off the boat was that English pirates had once again captured a fabulously rich Muslim ship. This newest act of piracy would quickly overwhelm the *Quedagh Merchant* scandal, make Captain Kidd an even more wanted man, and further harden the Company's position toward him. The irony is that Captain Kidd had nothing at all to do with the latest seafaring skullduggery.[20] However, he did know the pirate behind the attack. It was Robert Culliford, whom he had exhorted his crew to capture months earlier on St. Mary's.

From the forecastle of the *Adventure Prize*, Captain Kidd lifted his brass spyglass, focusing the barrel on the nearby pirate gunship anchored in St. Mary's harbor. With late afternoon sunlight twinkling across the placid tropical waters, he waited for the last of his 114-man crew to assemble on deck for the important meeting he had called on this May 8, 1698.[21]

He wasn't sure if he was powerful enough to apprehend Culliford, so he had waited for more than a month to launch his attack on his old archenemy. All three vessels of his flotilla—the *Adventure Prize* and *November* prize ships and his 34-gun *Adventure Galley*—had reunited following the grueling 2,500-mile journey from Kalliquilon Harbor to St. Mary's just off the northeast coast of Madagascar. He had chosen prudence over aggressiveness, and tonight he would capture the pirates and seize their ship.[22]

Since Kidd had discovered that the notorious Red Sea Man and his roguish crew had taken up residence on the island, he and Culliford had been hovering in a strategic limbo. It was easy for the two mariners—one a licensed privateer, the other an outlaw pirate—to keep their distance on an island thirty-seven miles long and three miles wide. Not wanting his prey to slip from his grasp, Kidd guarded the entrance to the harbor, ensuring that Culliford could not leave without running the gauntlet of his 12- and 18-pounders.[23]

He continued to stare across the harbor at the *Mocha Frigate*, which had been stolen from the East India Company and renamed *Resolution*. Culliford, his former chief gunner, would be around thirty-two years old now, still a relatively young man. From Culliford's chatty crew members on the island and the gossip Kidd had picked up during the past year and a half in the Indian Ocean, he had learned just how dramatically their lives had diverged since parting ways eight years earlier. While Kidd had served as a legitimate privateer, merchant captain, and pirate hunter since 1690 and was a married New York "Gent" and civic leader with two young daughters, Culliford had lived the life of a wandering bachelor and sea-roving criminal, alternating between hardened pirate, East India Company gunner, mutineer, prisoner in a dingy Mughal prison, and "gentleman of fortune" lounging about with Madagascar women, drinking "bomboo" rum punches and counting his ill-gotten gains.[24]

Culliford also may have been the first known bisexual Golden Age pirate. In the past decade, he had had both consensual and nonconsensual sexual contact with a large number of women: he had had a Malagasy harem on St. Mary's when he wasn't pillaging in the Indian Ocean; and he had "ravished" (raped) many innocent female victims during the course of his piratical career.[25] In December 1697, he and his crew of fifty men had captured and kept eleven Siamese women aboard the *Resolution* for two weeks as sex slaves, before dumping them despoiled and traumatized in southern India.[26] But he also may have taken part in carnal relations with his own sex, as he was reported to have spent much of his time with one "John Swann, a great consort of Culliford's, who lives with him."[27]

As the last of his crew members gathered on deck of the *Adventure Prize*, Kidd stepped forward to the forecastle railing to address John Browne, his sickly brother-in-law Samuel Bradley, and the rest of his motley crew. His second in command, his New York friend Henry Bullen, had died or been murdered by the unruly crew en route to St. Mary's while captaining the *Adventure Prize*, so Kidd was down another critical loyal officer.[28] Since the arrival of the prize ships, his men had been flocking to the shack of the New England trader Edward Welch, the "Little King" who had replaced Adam Baldridge as the top pirate-broker on the island, to buy overpriced American rum and local palm wine. They had also been unlimbering their libidos with the Malagasy women, who shared their bodily pleasures in return for a coveted strip of pretty cloth, a trinket, or a valuable iron nail or two, and feasting on steaks of hump-backed zebu cattle and strange cat-like monkeys called lemurs, which the indigenous tribespeople liked to broil.[29]

Kidd laid out his battle plan. With the full company reunited, they outnumbered Culliford and his parcel of rogues and had the firepower to blast them into submission. Therefore, he proposed taking the *Resolution* by force. Instead of being treated like second-class citizens by the Royal Navy, East India Company, and everybody else, they had a chance to make things right and ensure a good voyage. After all the suffering they had endured since leaving New York twenty months earlier, he made sure that they understood the significant goodwill they would garner if they sailed into Boston and delivered the pirate frigate to Lord Bellomont.[30]

"We have sufficient power and authority to take him and his ship," he said in closing to rally the men.

It was then that a derisive, rum-soaked voice interrupted from the deck.

"We would rather fire two guns into you than one into Culliford!" snarled a disgruntled seaman.[31]

A gruff cheer went up and another man yelled, "If you offer the same, we would sooner shoot into you than into the *Mocha Frigate*!"[32]

Then another angry voice shouted, "Where is our damn money?"[33]

Staring down at the red-faced mob, Kidd must have felt in mortal danger. After two days of lying about, drinking, and romping around with Malagasy women, the men were itching for a brawl. Or perhaps Culliford's crew had convinced them of how much easier and richer life would be sailing under the black flag with a real pirate commodore?

Once again, the men demanded their shares. Kidd tried to talk them out of it. Now was the time to take Culliford, he implored them. They could take his treasure and ship and return home with honor and uncontestable governmental approval.[34]

Now quartermaster John Walker demanded a vote. Kidd relented, but he knew he had already lost. The men weren't just worn out and desperate for their money—they had no intention of risking death or injury to subdue their own countrymen.

Ten minutes later, Walker had the final tally. The vote was 97 to 17 to desert and join over to Culliford.[35] The vote affirmed that the majority of Kidd's crew (85 percent at this point) no longer identified themselves as licensed privateers, but as sea-robbing outlaws willing to tie their fortunes to the unapologetic freebooter Robert Culliford. The transformation was complete, and the only mystery is why the crew hadn't mutinied long before, given the hellishness of the voyage. Somehow, Kidd's powerful personality and indisputable skills as a mariner, navigator, and leader had been enough until this stage of the voyage to outweigh his crew's resentment toward him for all the suffering they had endured at sea and his insistence on honoring his royal commissions. Indeed, Captain Kidd's holding on to his command for seventeen full months from September 6, 1696, to May 8, 1698, is even more amazing when one considers how commonplace mutiny and desertion were in the Age of Sail. In the 1690s alone, the English East India Company lost the *Josiah*, *Gingerlee*, and *Mocha Frigate* to fed-up crews who seized the merchant vessels away from their captains.[36] And a century later, in the 1790s, the British, French, and Dutch navies faced more than 150 single-ship mutinies, as well as half a dozen full-fleet mutinies involving tens of thousands of sailors. The legendary Lord Horatio Nelson had to constantly deal with mutiny within the Royal Navy, and such noteworthy commanders as Ferdinand Magellan, Francis Drake, Henry Hudson, and James Cooke, and the famous pirate commodores Edward Thache (Blackbeard), Benjamin Hornigold, and Charles Vane were all either threatened with mutiny or outright deposed by their crews during the course of their careers, just like Henry Every.[37]

All the same, Kidd couldn't believe his rotten luck. Twice in one lifetime, Robert Culliford had gotten the better of him. He was now a captain with a skeleton crew and without a sailable ship, a career nadir that must have been unfathomable to him given his last eight years of good fortune.

The mutineers continued to demand their shares. The resilient Kidd persisted in putting up a fight, even though it was ninety-seven against one. Distributing the prize money and goods, he said, would be breaking the contract they had all agreed to up front, and he would not split the shares until they reached Boston. Upset but pragmatic as always, he and his ragtag but steadfast group of sixteen loyalists left the prize ship and returned to the *Adventure Galley*.[38] He no longer had any senior officers in his camp except his friend John Weir of Carolina and the experienced gunner Hugh Parrot. The rest of his bedraggled band, which included his brother-in-law Samuel Bradley and his devoted cabin boy Richard

Barlycorne, were either ordinary seaman, young apprentices, or still suffering the effects of the Mohelia dysentery outbreak.[39]

With darkness falling and the rowdy mutineers once again pitching into the wine and rum bottles, Kidd and his loyal outfit armed themselves to the teeth with cutlasses, pistols, and muskets from the galley, rowed ashore, and hiked to trader Edward Welch's fortified compound. Kidd knew the battle was not over. In fact, it was just beginning.[40]

On May 9 and 10, the mutineers ransacked the *Adventure Prize* in a drunken orgy, and Kidd was unable to stop them. They hoisted a hefty portion of the six hundred bales of silk, muslin, and calico and other portable treasures and laid everything out on the beaches. At some point, he realized he had to do something, or he and his loyal band would go home with nothing at all. He put together a squadron of heavily armed sailors and Malagasy warriors rounded up by the helpful New Englander Edward Welch. The armed force marched to the beach, and Kidd demanded that the mutineers stop unloading the bales of goods. Outnumbering Kidd's force three to one, the band of mutineers laughed in his face and swilled more palm wine and rum.[41]

But he wasn't about to wave the white flag just yet, nor would he rely on force of arms. Instead, he used his powers of persuasion. Despite his sharp differences with the mutineers, he somehow managed to persuade them to show him and his men the decency of giving them their rightful shares, by insisting that they stick to their original privateering contract as they divided up the spoils. Under the terms of the voyage, he and his investors were allotted 40 percent of the total haul, and each of his loyal men was allocated anywhere from a half share to a full share, depending on their seafaring experience.[42]

It was a clever ploy. The democratic ex-buccaneer knew that the ship's articles were a powerful tool for ensuring honor among thieves. The signed articles—which kept the captain, senior officers, and crew in check through an enforceable balance of power—accomplished precisely what they were supposed to accomplish. Once Kidd had persuaded his unruly crew to do the right thing and before they could change their minds, he and his loyalists had their rightful shares of the prize goods, including some portion of their 250-plus heavy bales of fine silks, muslins, and calicoes, reloaded onto the *Adventure Prize*, which he now possessed along with the leaking *Adventure Galley*.[43]

But by May 12, once the mutineers realized how little money their bale goods fetched thousands of miles from New York and London, they began pillaging the *Adventures* of anything that did not belong to Kidd, his loyal crew, or his backers. Each bale was worth between £50 and £100 in London ($17,500 to $35,000 today), but were not worth a quarter that amount in the distant black market of St. Mary's Island. Edward Welch made out like a bandit, trading the mutineers quarts of rum for their bales on consignment for a tidy profit.[44]

Kidd and his loyal crew members were powerless to stop the angry, drunken mob that formed once the men realized the paltry sums their East Indian goods brought them. The mutineers sharp-elbowed their way past them and carried away great guns, powder, shot, small arms, sails, anchors, casks, and whatever else they pleased from both ships over the course of several days.[45] At one point, Kidd bumped into Robert Bradinham as he was carrying off the *Adventure Galley*'s surgeon's chest of ointments, medicines, and surgical instruments. When Kidd commanded him to stop, Bradinham shoved his way past him and darted up the stairs.[46]

Eventually, Kidd was forced to barricade himself inside his cabin with Barlycorne, as an armed mob came to steal a treasure chest filled with gold and jewels, which they had discovered that Kidd was hiding. He placed several bales of silk in the room to block the door and laid out several pistols, muskets, and blunderbusses, all charged in case he needed to take out a wave of attackers. From the whispers off the coast of India, his men knew he had around £10,000 ($3,500,000 today) in money and precious stones in a strongbox he was holding for the investors. But what they didn't know was that he had left with Edward Welch on the island a chest containing ten ounces of gold, forty pounds of silver plate, and nearly four hundred pieces of eight as shore money to buy provisions.[47]

For days on end, the mutineers yelled at him to open up and hand over the loot or they would knock out his brains. Over and over again, Kidd refused and told them that if they stormed the cabin, he would blow them to kingdom come. Eventually, the pirates became frustrated and left.

Kidd was worried that they might learn of his chest stored at Edward Welch's hut and seize it from the New England trader.[48] His concern proved well-founded, for soon thereafter they barged in on the "Little King" and plundered him in broad daylight. Shoving Welch and his Malagasy cohorts aside, they grabbed Kidd's chest, pistol-butted off the lock, and seized the valuables. In a final fit of anger, they destroyed Kidd's journal and several official papers in his trunk to keep the record of the voyage from the prying eyes of the East India authorities who had been hounding them for the past year.[49]

The mutineers soon joined forces with Culliford. Pulling him away from his Malagasy harem and his consort John Swann, they informed him that they had deserted Captain Kidd and wanted to sail under his black flag. Skeptical at first, he eventually agreed to lead the pirate fleet and returned to the *Resolution*, anchored in the main harbor just outside cannon range of the *Adventure Galley* and *Adventure Prize*. Once on deck, he called a meeting with his own crew of twenty men (more than fifty had died of tropical disease in the past two months) and the ninety of Kidd's mutineers who volunteered to join him (seven chose to remain on the island with Edward Welch and the friendly Malagasies). Culliford persuaded his new combined crew to get busy careening the *Resolution* so they could ride the northbound winds and attack the returning Muslim Mocha fleet in late summer.[50]

The next day, Culliford and his augmented pirate gang sailed the *Resolution,* stolen from the EIC, to the small, sandy island in the center of the harbor used for careening ships. The crew burned and sank the

150-ton *November* next to the *Resolution* to serve as a platform to expedite the cleaning process, which Kidd knew would be performed primarily by the seven Indian lascars who his mutinous crew had seized from him.[51]

Weeks later, on June 15, 1698, the beleaguered but not-yet-defeated Captain Kidd watched as his adversary Robert Culliford steered the freshly careened *Resolution* out of St. Mary's harbor for the Red Sea. Soon, Culliford and his ship-of-force reached the open ocean, turned north toward the Babs, and disappeared over the horizon. How was it possible, Kidd wondered, that the East India Company, Royal Navy, Portuguese, and everyone else had it out for him—instead of the *real* pirate, Robert Culliford? To make matters worse, Kidd knew that he and his loyal crew would be stuck on the island for four months, until October when the seasonal winds shifted and he could return home, making them sitting ducks for any band of cutthroats sailing into the harbor.[52] Still, if he could carry the *Adventure Prize* to America and present the French passes to Lord Bellomont, he could salvage his mission and once again be reunited with Sarah and his little beauties.

On September 23, 1698, three months after leaving Kidd behind on St. Mary's and six months before Kidd would reach the Caribbean, Culliford seized the massive treasure ship *Great Muhammad*, working in tandem with the Irish-Dutch New York captain Dirk Chivers in the *Soldado*. The 600-ton Muslim merchant ship, owned by the Turks of Jeddah and sailing without EIC convoy protection, proved to be one of the biggest captures of the Golden Age of Piracy, with more than £200,000 worth of treasure aboard ($70,000,000 today).[53]

But just like with Henry Every, there was little honor among the thieves. Culliford, Chivers, and their fellow pirates roughed up, savagely tortured, and took pistol shots at the Muslim passengers to locate valuables and every ounce of gold tucked away—with Kidd's former seamen right in the mix. They also set adrift 150 Muslim men in a small boat without oars, sails, or water, caring little whether the followers of Muhammad died or not. But for the pièce de résistance, the pirates did just as the mythologized Henry Every had done in 1695 by gang-raping their way from deck to deck. They kept "sixty women aboard" and "inhumanly abused" them in a mass frenzy of debauchery, ravishing them "in ye most beastly barbarous manner."[54]

When Aurangzeb and his imperial court learned of the disaster off the coast of Surat, it was a déjà vu of the Every debacle. But the attack also resurrected the Great Mughal's bitter feelings toward Captain Kidd, who was still fresh in his mind and had a name that fell so easily off the tongue.[55] The news of the latest English affront reached Surat on October 4, 1698, just as Kidd was outfitting the *Adventure Prize* on St. Mary's to sail to the Caribbean with the seasonal shifting of the monsoon winds. That once again a Muslim pilgrim ship had been captured and dozens of women sexually violated was regarded as a holy war against Islam, unleashing a never-before-seen religious fury by Aurangzeb and the victimized Turkish and Arabic merchants.[56]

Unfortunately for Samuel Annesley, he received news of the *Great Muhammad* mere days after the Kidd affair had blown over. When reports reached Surat of the capture of "another pilgrim ship as big and nobly patronized as the *Ganj-i-Sawi*" and the rape of sixty Muslim women, the port was immediately shut down to English shipping. Once again, Annesley and his fellow EIC employees were forced to take refuge behind the high walls of the Surat factory.[57]

The Great Mughal and his officials once again exploited the situation to gain a heftier share of EIC profits. In December 1698, Aurangzeb issued a *parwana*, or formal decree, that the three European trading companies were now responsible for fully compensating the victims of piracy and for guaranteeing the safety of all trade in the region. Specifically, the English, Dutch, and French had to pay back the losses from the taking of the *Great Muhammad*, reimburse all future pirate seizures, and take responsibility for all convoy protection throughout the Indian Ocean and Red Sea.[58]

Under immense pressure to capitulate, on January 28, 1699, a haggard Samuel Annesley signed the paperwork agreeing to the Great Mughal's financial-restitution terms and making the Company responsible for future losses in the Indian Ocean extending eastward to Sumatra. Though Aurangzeb was fed up with the rapacious European trading companies in his back yard, he didn't want to lose out on his fat 5 percent customs duties.[59] However, there were now two English trading companies in the East Indies. On March 5, 1698, Parliament had terminated the EIC monopoly and chartered a new competitor that it hoped would replace the century-old firm. With the signing of the Treaty of Ryswick in late 1697, the nine-year war between France and the Grand Alliance of England, Spain, Austria, and the Dutch Republic had ended, but William III had found his treasury depleted and sought a £2,000,000 loan ($700,000,000 today) by putting the East Indian trade on the auction block. A new Whig-run Company, promising the full amount at 8 percent interest, was granted exclusive trade with India by the cash-starved king, with the losing bidder, the Old Company, allowed to continue alongside its upstart rival.[60]

But throughout the battles between the Old and New Companies and between the Great Mughal and the Old Company, neither side lost sight of the fact that Captain Kidd was a central figure in East Indian piracy. He came to be the living, breathing symbol of the most disastrous and unprofitable years in Company history. But what made him even more of a villain was the English government's failure to capture and hang Henry Every and that Captain Kidd had become such a distinctive brand name in his own right. After popping up again and again like a jack-in-the-box during his two-year run in the Indian Ocean, the king's pirate hunter Captain Kidd—not Robert Culliford, Dirk Chivers, or any of the other *real* Red Sea marauders—had the ironic distinction of being the new name and face of global piracy.[61]

With the New Company breathing down its neck, the Old East India Company was desperate to regain Aurangzeb's trust and obtain trading advantages over its rival. To accomplish this goal, the Old Company needed to hang and gibbet a big-name English pirate in London and then rush word of the high-profile execution to Aurangzeb and his imperial court. In the view of the EIC and Crown, Captain Kidd was the sinister rogue who best fit the bill. "Kidd and his accomplices will be brought to very quick and public punishments," boldly proclaimed one Old East India Company factor to Sir John Gayer in Bombay. "We hope this promise will remove any reproach that lies upon our nation."[62]

PART 4

—

Treasure Fever

–13–

The Best-Laid Plans

Late on Saturday Night, June 10, 1699, Sarah Kidd was surprised when her housekeeper, Dorothy Lee, informed her that James Emott stood waiting at the front door of her fine Pearl Street home. The trusted family lawyer had important news regarding her husband and wanted to speak to her in private. Anxiously ushering Emott into the house, she and the bewigged fifty-two-year-old Trinity Church vestryman sat down to talk.

Since her husband had set sail in September 1696, James Emott had been her most reliable source of information regarding the voyage. One of New York's most respected legal figures, who had served as an adviser to several New York governors including Benjamin Fletcher, Emott had kept her abreast of her husband's movements whenever he picked up tidbits from returning mariners or colonial officials.[1] Having received word just this evening via messenger, the lawyer broke the gigantic news to Sarah that her husband had made it back from his lengthy voyage to the Indian Ocean the day before and was waiting for her in nearby Oyster Bay, Long Island. Kidd sent along his love and promised they would be reunited very soon.[2]

Both stunned and elated by the news, Sarah took a moment to collect herself. Emott now produced a letter Kidd had scratched out on parchment. Having already verified the authenticity of the seal and perused the document, Emott handed it to Sarah, who could read but not write, and brought her up to date on everything he knew at this point. Both the letter and lawyer confirmed that her husband had taken two Moorish ships in the Indian Ocean as lawful prizes and resisted his crew in committing piracy. On St. Mary's, a large contingent of his seamen had mutinied, robbed him of his papers, and sailed off with the pirate Robert Culliford. Following the mutiny, Kidd had worked like a dog to pull together a sufficient crew to refit the *Adventure Prize* and sail her safely to the Caribbean. From there, he had sailed back home to New York on a smaller sloop.[3]

After surviving Royal Navy impressment; raging storms; disease; attacks by the East India Company, Portuguese, and Moors; severe thirst and starvation; a full-scale mutiny; and two Atlantic crossings, Kidd had miraculously returned to the colonies with around £40,000 ($14,000,000 today) of treasure and the French passes that proved he had taken the *Rouparelle* and *Quedagh Merchant* legally in accordance with his commission. But on April 2, 1699, when he had arrived on Antigua, he and his men had received devastating news. The Crown, at the urging of the East India Company, had sent an alarm to the West Indies and North American colonies in late November 1698 declaring them pirates and ordering an all-out manhunt to capture and bring them to justice.[4]

Thus, from Emott, Sarah learned for the first time that her husband was a wanted outlaw by the Crown, that the *Adventure Galley* was lost, and that he had managed to sail the *Adventure Prize* to a safe berth in the Caribbean. Leaving the ship in the shallow waters off Hispaniola, he had returned to New York on the *St. Antonio*, which was now anchored in Oyster Bay with £10,000 in gold, jewels, and other treasures of the East. Back in May, he had conducted a trading session at Santa Catalina Island with a consortium of English and Dutch merchants and purchased the Spanish sloop from Henry Bolton, an Antiguan trader and former collector of customs for the Leeward Islands. To acquire ready cash, he had sold off 130 bales of East Indian muslins and calicoes.[5] Before returning home to New York, he had struck an arrangement with Bolton to guard the *Adventure Prize* and its £30,000 worth of East Indian goods and to act as his power of attorney in selling them to Caribbean traders. Kidd, or someone acting on his behalf, would return within three months to collect the unsold goods from Bolton and carry the prize ship north to New York.[6]

Sarah also learned from Emott that her husband planned to deliver his legally obtained plunder to Bellomont for distribution to the investors. But before coming in, he insisted that the royal governor issue him a full pardon along with his ten loyal seamen who had sailed with him originally from New York.[7] Though he had wanted to return directly to New York City to be with her and their daughters, he had discovered that many of his mutinous crew members were already raising hell in town, and so he decided to be more cautious.

On May 26, Kidd's friend Captain Giles Shelley had returned from his second Madagascar trading voyage in the *Nassau* with sixty pirates as passengers, including many of Kidd's former crew members rolling in East Indian loot. The mutineers who had deserted him to rampage with Culliford had reached Cape May, New Jersey, and dozens of them had made their way to New York.[8] Instead of returning home, Kidd had chosen Oyster Bay because of two of his good friends whom he trusted to help him and to keep silent about his whereabouts: Justice White and Dr. Cooper.[9] Once contacted by Kidd, the good judge and good doctor had sent a messenger to New York to deliver Captain Kidd's wax-sealed letter to James Emott.[10]

But there was a catch, Emott told Sarah. Bellomont had left the city three weeks earlier, on May 16, for Boston to administer his office in Massachusetts Bay province and collect his salary, leaving his clumsy nephew, Lieutenant Governor John Nanfan, in charge of New York province in his absence. In New York, explained the lawyer, her husband was a leading citizen who could count on the protection of his fellow

Manhattanites when it came to piracy charges. But in Puritan Boston, he was an outsider in a town becoming less accommodating to commerce raiders of all stripes.[11]

Upon hearing Emott's report, Sarah's excitement that her husband was alive and close by was offset by a sense of trepidation. Having never trusted Bellomont, she was not keen about the captain surrendering himself to the highborn earl, whether in Boston or pirate-friendly New York. Like many New Yorkers, she had come to both fear and despise Bellomont. Since taking office as governor of the province in April 1698, he had made hundreds of enemies due to his dictatorial temperament and stringent enforcement of the Navigation Acts. Because the Red Sea trade brought in much-needed specie and goods that greatly benefited the colony, a powerful group of more than thirty merchants that included the formidable Philipse, Bayard, and DeLancey family networks was already working aggressively in New York and London to orchestrate the governor's recall. The word on the street was that Bellomont's crackdown was causing the city to lose out on a whopping £100,000 ($35,000,000 today) in annual revenue.[12]

Although Sarah felt no love for Bellomont, she knew her husband needed his support. But what neither she nor Emott realized was that the earl remained very much on the side of Captain Kidd. In fact, the day before leaving for Boston, he wrote London praying that his protégé would be declared an innocent man: "I am in hopes the several reports we have here of Captain Kidd's being forced by his men against his will to plunder two Moorish ships may prove true, and 'tis said that near one hundred of his men revolted from him at Madagascar and were about to kill him, because he absolutely refused to turn pirate."[13]

Having laid out the situation for her, Emott now broke some bad news: her younger brother Samuel had become deathly ill during the voyage, and Kidd had allowed him to disembark in the Danish port of St. Thomas to seek medical treatment.[14] Due to Dr. Bradinham's desertion at St. Mary's and pilfering of the medical kit, Kidd had not had either a surgeon or any medicines to treat Samuel or the other crew members during their Atlantic crossing. For two years of the voyage, Sarah now learned, her husband had done everything within his power to keep her younger brother alive, even procuring hard-to-find Goa Stone fever remedies. Invented just a few years earlier in India by Gaspar Antonio, a Florentine lay brother of the Portuguese Jesuits, Goa was a fever medicine consisting of various drugs made up into a hard ball, or stone. In St. Thomas, Kidd had told the crew that if his brother-in-law had to endure another week at sea, he would perish. The men fought him hard, not wanting to risk alerting the authorities, but Kidd persuaded them to allow Samuel to go ashore for treatment, thus saving his life.[15]

Sarah now asked Emott what she could do to help her husband. The lawyer said to pack her and her daughters' things over the next few days in preparation for the reunion with the captain. He stressed that she should bring plenty of money with her and clothing for more than a short visit. Sarah knew what he meant: if the situation turned badly for her husband, she needed to have sufficient resources to remain beyond the reach of the authorities for an extended period of time, or to make a quick escape with him and their daughters.[16]

How, she asked, was she going to be reunited with her husband?

Emott now confided to her that their family friend Captain Thomas "Whisking" Clark would outfit a sloop, pick her and her daughters up within the week, and deliver them safely to the captain somewhere off the northeastern tip of Long Island.[17]

Sarah saw Emott out. Though thrilled to soon be reunited with her husband, she couldn't believe how drastically their family situation had changed since she had last seen him. When she had kissed him goodbye in New York Harbor in September 1696, he had been a legally commissioned privateer backed by the King of England and his top ministers to hunt down pirates. Now he was an accused pirate himself. When he had waved goodbye to her and the girls from the quarterdeck of the *Adventure Galley*, she had been a socialite married to one of the leading citizens in the colony. Now she was a pirate's wife aiding and abetting her on-the-run husband, which meant that all conversations from here on out had to be kept in strict secrecy and she could trust no one but Emott and Clark—for, if the Crown authorities learned of her and her husband's clandestine activities, their family could very well be imprisoned and stripped of everything they owned.

Thus Sarah Kidd on the night of June 10, 1699, was one deeply worried woman, with her life and family hanging in the balance. But history is clear that she didn't think twice about what to do next.

She would stand by her man—pirate or no pirate.

THE FOLLOWING EVENING, a tired but determined James Emott was rowed out to the *St. Antonio,* anchored in Oyster Bay. Accompanied by the messenger enlisted by Kidd's friends Justice White and Dr. Cooper, the lawyer had taken the morning ferry from Manhattan to Brooklyn, then made the hard horseback ride north for Long Island Sound. Captain Kidd stood by to greet them at the railing as they climbed aboard the sloop, with Captain Samuel Wood and Kidd's anxious crew looking on. The *St. Antonio* had been piloted by Wood from Hispaniola to Oyster Bay, as Kidd had been merely a passenger during the journey up the Eastern Seaboard so he could remain incognito.[18]

Of his original 152 sailors who had set out from New York with him in September 1696, only 10 remained. Augmenting his company were two South Sea mariners who had gained notoriety in the last decade as pirates: Flemish captain Edward Davis, a rotund, colorful buccaneer and trader; and grizzled James Gilliam, alias James Kelly, an unrepentant English pirate who had sailed with Culliford and murdered the cruel East India Company commander of the *Mocha Frigate*, Captain Edgecombe, by slitting his throat when Gilliam and a group of abused sailors had mutinied and seized the ship. Davis and Gilliam were among the experienced seafarers Kidd had picked up on St. Mary's, at Tulear, and at the West African island of Annobon for the trip home across the Atlantic from Madagascar.[19]

After Kidd paid the messenger, he and Emott retired to the captain's cabin so they could talk in private. Arrangements had been made with Captain Clark and Sarah for the planned family rendezvous, Emott informed him, but unfortunately Bellomont had sailed from New York to Boston three weeks earlier to assume his duties as governor of Massachusetts Bay.[20] To enlist the aid of Bellomont, they needed to get cracking before Kidd's mutinous crew in New York started flinging about exotic Arabian silver and gold, spouting drunken tales of plundering Moorish heathens, and getting thrown in the slammer. If word got out that their captain had returned to American shores, pressure might be applied to seize Kidd as a pirate in accordance with the Crown's global alert.[21]

What at this point neither of them knew was that word of Captain Kidd's return to the colonies had already leaked, and the Royal Navy was out hunting for him. A month earlier, upon learning that he had crossed the Atlantic to reach the Leeward Islands, the governor of Nevis "had sent out his Majesty's ship the HMS *Queensborough*" in search of him.[22] And only the week before, Colonel Robert Quarry, Pennsylvania customs collector and anti-piracy crusader, had dashed off an urgent message to the governor of Virginia that Kidd had been spotted near Hore Kill, Pennsylvania (today Lewes, Delaware), and to send a pirate-hunting warship northward posthaste to Delaware Bay.[23] Making matters worse, word of his presence in Long Island Sound had already reached Manhattan earlier that afternoon, and soon all of New York province and the New England colonies would know of his return.[24]

Adding to the sense of urgency, Kidd in the *St. Antonio* and his friend Captain Giles Shelley in the *Nassau* were not the only Red Sea Men returning to North American ports in the spring and summer of 1699. Shortly before Shelley's return, Massachusetts pirate Joseph Bradish and his crew of plunderers from their own *Adventure* had made their way from the Spice Islands to Long Island Sound and dispersed like windblown wheat into the New England colonies. Now in mid-June, the entire East Coast was in an uproar over piracy.[25]

Suddenly, pirates were everywhere.

But it was Captain Kidd and his vast treasure of gold, silver, jewels, and rich East Indian silks that captivated the entire Atlantic Seaboard.

The sea captain who hailed originally from Soham, England, but had been weaned as a Scottish sea adventurer, was not only the world's most sought-after "outlaw" but was already the talk of the docks, ordinaries, taverns, and meeting halls throughout colonial America.[26] With absolutely no evidence, Governor Ralph Grey of Barbados had raised the alarm a month earlier that the Public Enemy Number 1 Kidd had a staggering £400,000 ($140,000,000 in today's dollars) in the hold of his "pirate" ship.[27] The easily excitable Robert Livingston, whose eyes glittered with avarice at the mere whisper of Araby silver and gold, again without an ounce of proof, claimed that Kidd had £500,000 in sterling ($175,000,000 today) in his possession.[28] London's most egregious gossip, the former member of Parliament and diarist Narcissus Luttrell, would by November 1699 peg Kidd's treasure or "effects" at a less inflated yet still eye-opening £200,000 ($70,000,000 today).[29]

Kidd and Emott strategized well into the night and eventually decided on a plan of action: the lawyer would go to Boston as an emissary to feel out Bellomont about a pardon and hopefully reach terms on a favorable agreement.[30] The next day, as the *St. Antonio* headed eastward through Long Island Sound, Kidd and Emott continued to plot out detailed legal strategy. Before nightfall, Kidd dropped Emott off in Stonington, Connecticut, where the lawyer began his 65-mile horse ride northward to Boston. For a fifty-two-year-old lawyer in 1699, this was one long, hard journey in the name of justice. But he must have been an adept horseman, for he made it to the City upon a Hill in under thirty hours. Emott reached reputable Bostonian Peter Sergeant's mansion, where Bellomont was staying, late on Tuesday night, June 13. It was well after curfew, and blackness had descended over the quiet-as-a-tomb Puritan town.[31]

After rousting the gouty English earl out of bed, the two men held a lengthy meeting in which Emott pleaded his client's case and tried to arrange for an official government pardon. Though Bellomont disliked the lawyer, considering him his "avowed enemy" and a "cunning Jacobite" because of his anti-Leislerian politics and allegiance to Benjamin Fletcher, he treated him cordially, for the last thing he wanted was to scare off Emott or his client.[32] But he also didn't want to appear too eager to accept the proposed terms. He told Emott that he appreciated why their dear friend Captain Kidd would only come into port if the governor agreed to extend him his majesty's most gracious pardon, but he was "tender of using such authority" because it could tarnish his reputation. He had set a rule never to pardon for piracy without a guarantee of innocence—and without the king's express leave and command. If Kidd could prove his innocence, then he could come safely to Boston and Bellomont would undertake "to get him the king's pardon." He then invited Emott to return the next morning so they could talk some more before the lawyer made the lengthy journey back to his client with the governor's message.[33]

The result of the two meetings was that Bellomont wrote a detailed letter to Kidd inviting him to come to Boston under his protection and that he was open to a pardon. Keen to have a viable go-between in place, Bellomont had Duncan Campbell, the Scottish deputy postmaster of Massachusetts whom the governor and Kidd both knew personally, accompany Emott and hand-deliver the letter to Kidd. Emott and the thirty-two-year-old Campbell then made the journey southward to Rhode Island and rendezvoused with Captain Kidd on the *St. Antonio* off Block Island three days later.[34] But Kidd wanted more reassurance, so he sent Campbell back to Boston on June 17 to obtain a promise of a pardon in writing from Bellomont.[35] After meeting with the governor and his council and pleading Kidd's case, Campbell returned to the *St. Antonio* with a letter dated June 19 stating that if the captain came ashore he would be granted his coveted pardon.[36] After receiving Bellomont's letter but before his wife Sarah's arrival at Block Island, Kidd spent several hours with the deputy postmaster composing a reply stating his agreement to now come to Boston.[37]

Though much of his gold, jewels, and bale goods remained with him aboard the *St. Antonio*, to hedge his bet with Bellomont Kidd also at this time safeguarded a portion of his treasure by stashing it away in various places with trusted friends. On June 15, he met with his old mate Captain Thomas Paine on the *St. Antonio* anchored offshore from the Rhode Islander's waterfront home in Narragansett Bay. An early Red Sea pioneer, Paine was a war hero like Kidd, the son-in-law of the late Rhode Island governor Caleb Carr, and a founder of Newport's Trinity Church, where a plaque today honorably bears his name. Over a tankard of ale, Kidd asked his old friend if he would be kind enough to hold a few gold bars and later dispense it to him, or Sarah, upon request. The sixty-seven-year-old ex-buccaneer, who in 1690 had fought off an invading French fleet that had captured Block Island, agreed to help him out.[38]

Shortly after his visit to Paine, Kidd deposited several more items on nearby Gardiner's Island, a seven-mile-long spit in Long Island Sound that the island's First Nation inhabitants, the Montauk Indians, called *Manchonake*—The Island Where Many Have Died—based on the pre-colonial bloodbath between the coastal tribe and their fierce rivals the Pequots.[39] The 3,300-acre wooded estate was known for its sheltered coves for smugglers and warm hospitality of its red-haired proprietor, John Gardiner.[40] His grandfather Lion Gardiner, a Scottish engineer who built forts in Connecticut, had bought the island from the Montauks back in 1638 for "a large black dog, a gun & ammunition, some rum, and a few Dutch blankets."[41] John Gardiner, who would go on to play an important role in the Kidd saga, was fluent in the Montauk language and employed the indigenous descendants of his grandfather to plant corn and hunt whales for him.[42]

On June 19, six days before his reunion with Sarah and his daughters, Kidd anchored a short distance off Gardiner's Island and had James Emott rowed to the wooden dock. Walking over to the manor house, the lawyer knocked on the door and asked John Gardiner if he might provide a boat to take him back to Oyster Bay, without mentioning that the wanted outlaw Captain Kidd was the one hovering in the 6-gun Spanish sloop offshore. After acceding to Emott's request, two days later Gardiner had his buckskin-clad Montauks row him out in a whaleboat to visit the mysterious sloop, which had been joined by two New York trading vessels.[43] Like their captain, Kidd's crew was anxious about Bellomont and safeguarded their earnings by off-loading four chests and ten bales of muslins and calicoes from the *St. Antonio* onto the two local trading vessels. One of these was helmed by two more of Kidd's old friends: Dutch New York trader Captain Carsten Luersten and his first mate, Hendrick van der Heul, "a little black man [dark-haired Dutchman]" who had served previously as Captain Kidd's quartermaster.[44]

During their friendly palaver aboard the *St. Antonio*, Kidd and John Gardiner took a shine to each other. While peering out at the island's sandy beaches, the giant ospreys soaring overhead, the virgin forests of white oak and wild grapevine, and the stolid bluffs of clay holding fast against northeastern storms, the two hardy Anglo-Americans, who had lived a lifetime on the periphery far from the London metropole, shared a pleasant conversation. The purported "arch-Pyrate" impressed Gardiner with his "charm and friendliness," and Kidd decided to trust the whale-hunting, Montauk-speaking head of Gardiner Manor.[45] Informing his host that he would shortly sail to Boston to visit Governor Bellomont, he wondered if Gardiner would be willing to store goods for him until he returned or sent for them. To a toast of hard cider, Gardiner agreed, and a large quantity of East Indian commodities was rowed ashore by the Montauks.[46]

Kidd also purchased six sheep, a 250-pound barrel of hard cider, and a roasted pig from Gardiner for his forthcoming reunion with his wife and daughters. In return for supplying him for his planned bountiful feast with his family, friends, and crew, Kidd gave Mrs. Gardiner rare and exotic muslin cloth with strands of gold and a clay pitcher full of dried fruits. He also generously tipped John Gardiner's Montauks for their help and offered to pay Gardiner in gold and silver coin for the cider, but his host said the beautiful gifts to his wife were enough.[47] To further show his gratitude, the always-flamboyant sea captain gave the Gardiners and the Montauks a resounding four-gun salute from the *St. Antonio* as he sailed from Gardiner's Island to the nearby Block Island for the reunion with his beloved Sarah and the girls.[48]

On June 25, 1699, an excited but anxious Sarah Kidd took in the sight of her husband standing at the railing of the *St. Antonio*, anchored off the craggy eastern end of Block Island. In the longboat with her were Captain Clark; her elder daughter, seven-year-old Elizabeth; her younger, five-year-old little Sarah; her housemaid, Elizabeth Morris; and friends Edward and Mary Sands, ages thirty and twenty-seven. As the longboat nudged closer, Sarah saw her husband beaming down at her and her daughters. He looked handsome in his waistcoat with nine diamond buttons and a chestnut-colored wig parted in the middle and hanging to his shoulders.[49]

Captain Clark had come through for the Kidd family and delivered her and her daughters the day before to the Sands' New Shoreham home on Block Island. Hailing from a prominent early American family, the midwife Mary Sands was the daughter of John Williams, a powerful merchant who had served as Rhode Island's attorney general and a member of the Massachusetts General Assembly. Knowing that his wife would be staying with their family friends, Kidd had left in the Sands' care, before Sarah's arrival, two 300-pound cannons and a huge stash of ammunition. The big guns would provide not only protection, but a backup supply of firepower in case he needed to change ships and make a quick getaway.[50]

Once the oarboat drew alongside the *St. Antonio*, Sarah and the others were helped aboard by Captain Kidd and his men. Reunited for the first time in two years and nine months, Sarah gave her husband a welcome-home embrace befitting a man who had risked everything to return to her and their daughters and clear his good name. Little Sarah, who had been only two and a half when her father had set sail from New York, explored Kidd's face with her chubby little fingers, touching the sun-burnished skin of this huge, bewigged man she could barely remember. In return, he squeezed his little darlings tight and gave them presents of sugar candy.[51]

Kidd introduced his wife and the others to his crew and to the dapper Bostonian Duncan Campbell, who Sarah learned had been working closely with Kidd and James Emott the past ten days to help her husband secure a pardon from Bellomont in Boston. For the next several hours, the deck of the *St. Antonio* was the scene of a bountiful feast of roasted lamb and pig spiced with nutmeg and cloves, fresh oysters, cabbage, salt, sweetbreads, and much hard cider. At dusk, Kidd and Sarah retired to the privacy of the captain's cabin aboard the sloop, while the Sandses returned to Block Island and Elizabeth Morris minded the children in a separate small cabin. Sarah and her husband made love; and afterward, as they lay wrapped in each other's arms, he filled her in on his activities since his arrival in Long Island Sound. She quickly learned that he had been busy and had safeguarded a quantity of gold and East Indian goods with Captain Thomas Paine and John Gardiner, so that their family had hidden reserves in case things went badly with Bellomont.[52]

It is at this important first meeting between Kidd and Sarah, after nearly three years apart, that she expressed her concerns about Bellomont to her husband.[53] He tried to reassure her by showing the governor's June 19 letter offering a pardon. "I have advised with His Majesty's Council," wrote Bellomont, "and they are of opinion that if you can be so clear as you (or Mr. Emott for you) have said, that you may safely come hither, and be equipped and fitted out to go and fetch the other ship [*Adventure Prize* in Hispaniola], and I make no manner of doubt but to obtain the king's pardon for you."[54] But when Sarah finished reading the letter, she made it clear to her husband that she didn't like the conditional nature of Bellomont's invitation and still didn't trust the man. The clause "if you can be so clear as you or Mr. Emott have said" was, in her view, no small caveat.[55]

Just as Kidd had done with James Emott and Duncan Campbell, the husband and wife now plotted strategy. Together, they decided to further hedge their bets in case Bellomont wasn't as accommodating as they hoped. They decided to return to Gardiner's Island and stash away more treasure for protection against a double-cross. Kidd had in his possession a chest containing fifty pounds of gold and fifty pounds of silver, and he had another chest containing spices, drugs, and fine cloths, as well as bales of muslin, silk, and calico and bundles of costly East Indian quilts. He and Sarah decided to stash a goodly portion of the remaining treasure on the island for safekeeping.[56]

The next morning, June 26, the reunited Kidds sailed for Gardiner's Island. Kidd delivered Captain "Whisking" Clark to shore and buried a chest with forty pounds of gold and four hundred pieces of Spanish silver on the island to protect himself in case Bellomont went back on his word. He also gave John Gardiner a small chest containing Goa Stones, valuable fabrics, rare spices, and other exotic treasures from the East. As an additional thank-you gift to Gardiner and his wife, Kidd gave the proprietor of the island a bag of much-in-demand sugar, which Mrs. Gardiner greatly appreciated.[57]

During his return to Gardiner's Island, Kidd was accompanied by a sloop commanded by Captain Cornelius Quick. Yet another rascally seafaring friend who had come to the New York privateer's aid in his time of need, Captain Quick would transport Clark back to New York with items handpicked by Sarah, including four pounds of gold, forty pounds of silver, eleven small pearls, and other riches. Clark stored the goods in a secret warehouse belonging to Major Jonathan Selleck in Stamford, Connecticut—operating under the prying eyes of nosy Crown officials.[58]

On June 26, Kidd also bid farewell and good luck to Duncan Campbell. The deputy postmaster, who would soon become one of America's first two print journalists along with his brother John, would carry Kidd's letter to the governor accepting Bellomont's invitation to come safely to Boston. Along with the letter, the nattily dressed Scot would deliver a gift to Countess Kate, as suggested by James Emott. The gift to Lady Bellomont was a silver box edged with gilt enamel containing four gold lockets set with diamonds and a large diamond of nearly three carats set in a gold ring. In Kidd's era, such gifts from one gentleman to another, or to a spouse, were not regarded as bribes but as a chivalrous compliment.[59]

Kidd also allowed James Gilliam to leave the *St. Antonio.* The pirate would hitch a ride north on a small sailboat to Newport, where he claimed a friend would protect him. Like Sarah and her friend Mary Sands, Kidd hoped he would never again set eyes upon the leather-faced throat-slitter who had sailed with Robert Culliford; unfortunately, he would not be so lucky.[60]

With his final precautions in place, Captain Kidd and his family set sail for Boston on a lightened *St. Antonio.* On June 30, as they entered Nantucket Shoals, the lookout spotted a sail. It was a Boston-based sloop, which happened to be under the command of yet another old seafaring pal of Captain Kidd: Captain Thomas Way, making a return trip from the Bay of Campeche off the Central American coast. After hailing each other, the two chummy captains talked, and they agreed to sail together around the hook of Cape Cod into Boston, with the local New Englander Way serving as harbor pilot.[61]

Once again, Kidd left goods as a precautionary withdrawal with another old mate to protect against betrayal by Bellomont. As many historians have noted, Captain Kidd's "social network was large and long-standing" with "powerful friends high and low everywhere," but what is amazing is the sheer number of people who risked their own necks helping him upon his return to America from Madagascar.[62] This time, he arranged for Thomas Way to carry goods to Boston for him: three pistols, a balance scale to weigh gold, a Turkeywork carpet, and the pendulum navigation clock purchased from Captain Wright of the *Quedagh.* Fearful that the *St. Antonio* might be seized, he also gave the Boston mariner a bundle of his wife's clothes and the six-pound bag of Spanish silver coins she had brought from New York. He wanted to protect his wife's money and possessions from getting mixed up in his own affairs, and also ensure she had money for a quick escape.[63]

On Saturday afternoon, July 1, 1699, Captain Kidd and his reunited family rolled the dice and sailed into the Puritan stronghold of Boston to meet with Lord Bellomont. The Calvinist bastion ruled by the witch-hanging and slave-owning ministers Increase and Cotton Mather and administered by Bellomont was the largest and busiest port city in North America; but when the captain and his family were rowed ashore, they found the town eerily quiet. Most Bostonians were preparing for the Sunday Sabbath, which began at sunset on Saturday and extended through Sunday night, shutting down the city, with all forms of travel, labor, and leisure activities strictly forbidden.[64]

Word of Kidd's arrival was rushed to Bellomont at wealthy merchant Peter Sergeant's mansion, and soon all of Boston knew he had set foot on American soil. The governor did not greet Kidd in person due to his debilitating gout, but sent along his regards and "ample refreshments" for the new arrivals. He informed his protégé that he would meet with him on Monday following the Sabbath and requested that his crew remain aboard the *St. Antonio* until that time, so they could give their statements regarding the voyage as well.[65]

The Kidds and their tired young daughters walked the narrow cobblestone streets to Duncan and Susannah Campbell's humble abode in the nearby North End. Carrying their bags from the ship, they reached the house just before Sabbath curfew. The generous Campbells made Kidd and his family feel right at home. It was at this time, writes historian Morton Pennypacker, that the Campbells' son, Matthew, was introduced to "the real Captain Kidd" everyone was talking about. "Little Matthew Campbell got first a cane as a present from the big-hearted Kidd, and that was followed by another present of candy. Candy enough for all the young folks in the neighborhood—a ten-pound box of it."[66]

The next morning, Captain Kidd, Sarah, Elizabeth, little Sarah, and Elizabeth Morris attended church with the Campbells to hear Cotton Mather deliver one of his typical hellfire-and-damnation sermons. A seminal figure in colonial American history and true Renaissance man, Reverend Mather played a prominent role in the 1692 Salem witch trials and would go on to conduct pioneering research on plant hybridization and inoculation to prevent smallpox. But in Captain Kidd's day, New England's most famous cult personality, "keeper of the state," and "exemplar of empire" was mostly known for delivering stern morality lessons to the people of Boston, not only on the evils of witchcraft and adultery but on the new hot topic in the colonies: piracy.[67]

On Monday, Bellomont remained incapacitated with gout and was forced to hold his conference with Captain Kidd and the eighteen members of his governor's council at Peter Sergeant's mansion. He was still vexed about what to do about his seafaring business partner, who had by some bizarre twist of fate become the most wanted man in the English Empire.

By law, he was supposed to take Kidd under arrest. Like the other colonial governors, he had received the order from the Lords Justices dated November 23, 1698, to promptly seize the "notorious pirate" with no questions asked.[68] However, he had not posted the order, nor had he relayed the Crown's explicitly clear instructions to his Massachusetts, New York, or New Hampshire councils, whom he continued to keep in the dark regarding his ongoing negotiations with Captain Kidd. He had also not notified any of his councils of the jewels Kidd had given his wife through Duncan Campbell, hoping he could find a way for her to keep them as "snacks"—the vulgar euphemism used by English aristocrats of the day for political tributes. He was withholding this information until he had a firm handle on where Kidd had hidden his treasure, the profits to be made, and the full danger his protégé posed to his career.[69]

Bellomont dreaded the prospect of having to return to London in disgrace due to his connection to Kidd, and he still owed Sir Benjamin Harrison £4,000 ($1,400,000 today) for financing the voyage and other loans.[70] However, he did see a clear way out. In his communications through the go-betweens James Emott and Duncan Campbell, Kidd claimed to have £10,000 with him plus another £30,000 aboard the *Adventure Prize* off Hispaniola. Under this scenario, the partners would clear £34,000 after the cost of £6,000 for building and outfitting the *Adventure Galley* was deducted, which meant that Bellomont would only receive £1,000, or less, once he paid off the £4,000 debt he owed Harrison. But if he arrested Kidd under his authority as vice-admiral in the colonies, he was entitled to a third of any treasure seized. Thus, he could lay claim to around £13,000 ($4,550,000 today).[71]

At six o'clock sharp, Kidd arrived with his sheathed sword fastened at his side, and the meeting began before the blue-tiled fireplace in Peter Sergeant's wood-paneled great hall.[72] Representing the Massachusetts governor's council were the elite Bostonians Captain Wait Winthrop, Judge Samuel Sewall, Bellomont's host Peter Sergeant, and several other councilmen, who had all been fawning over the royal governor and Lady Bellomont for the past month.[73] With his gouty foot propped up on an ottoman, Bellomont thanked Kidd for coming and took a moment to study him as the blue-blooded Bostonians did the same. One of these was Lieutenant Governor William Stoughton, whom the well-connected Kidd knew personally. Bellomont smiled pleasantly at the frock-coated commander and oh-so-politely asked him to recount his voyage from start to finish. Kidd, with equal politeness, informed Bellomont and the council that his journal of the voyage had been destroyed by his mutinous crew on St. Mary's, so any report he gave would be based upon his imperfect recollection.[74] He asked that he be granted time to put his narrative into writing, which Emott had likely recommended to him.[75]

Not wanting to scare Kidd off and never see an ounce of treasure, Bellomont concealed his displeasure behind a polite mask. He believed Kidd's lengthy return voyage from the East Indies to Boston had given him ample time to prepare a detailed account of his undertakings, especially since the captain knew he was regarded by the Crown as an outlaw. With a false air of diplomacy, Bellomont told him he would be given time to provide proper written documentation of the voyage, but for the time being he requested a verbal accounting of the merchant vessels seized and their cargoes.[76]

Still uneasy but wanting to be cooperative, Kidd summarized the voyage between September 1696 and June 1699, while rattling off statistics and pleading his case for his innocence. With regard to the cargo, he reported that he had sailed to New England with a considerable amount of gold and silver in the hold of the *St. Antonio*, along with forty bales of expensive cloth fabrics and five tons of sugar. As to the portion of the treasure still aboard the prize ship in Hispaniola, Kidd said that he had 150 bales of cloth, 70 tons of sugar, 10 tons of iron, 14 or 15 anchors, 40 tons of saltpeter, and 30 guns mounted.[77]

After some further questioning, the meeting wrapped up. Bellomont proposed that they convene again the next day at five o'clock. Kidd was instructed to bring a written narrative of the voyage, along with invoices of all cargo, signed by himself and his officers, as well as a list of his original 152-man crew and the 97 mutineers. Bellomont also declared that he was going to have the deputy customs collector put some government "waiters," or agents, aboard the *St. Antonio* to make sure no goods were off-loaded from the vessel.[78]

Kidd agreed to pull together the requested information and returned to Duncan Campbell's house in the North End. At this point, Bellomont still had not decided whether to throw his protégé to the wolves. Knowing the case could break in either direction, he was biding his time until he knew for certain whether he could obtain the booty for himself in a legitimate—or at least undiscoverable—manner. Whether he would garner a fortune for himself, the Junto, and the king from the Crown-backed voyage now depended on the fate of Captain Kidd, who needed his protection badly.

–14–
The Axe Falls

The next day, July 4, proved very bad for Captain Kidd. His afternoon meeting with Bellomont and the Massachusetts Bay province governor's council did not go well. He arrived promptly at 5 p.m. at Peter Sergeant's mansion along with gunner Hugh Parrott, cook Abel Owen, steward Samuel Arris, and the New York sailors English Smith and Humphrey Clay. The seamen delivered a single sworn affidavit to Bellomont and the council and were grilled along with Kidd about the captures of the *Rouparelle* and *Quedagh Merchant*.[1]

The problem with the meeting wasn't what Kidd's crew members divulged. They described the events surrounding the two legitimate captures honestly. The problem arose when Bellomont pressed his protégé several times for his full narrative, his lading manifests, and his crew lists. After spending nearly three full years at sea and, against all odds, turning an epic disaster into a profitable venture for all concerned parties, Kidd believed he should be given a pat on the back and resented that Bellomont was treating him as a suspected criminal instead of his business partner. Although he had the day before hired thirty-nine-year-old Thomas Newton, one of Boston's most eminent lawyers, the two had not had time to pull together the full narrative and other requested materials.

So, he pushed back. "Kidd did strangely trifle with me and the council," sniffed Bellomont of the meeting. In the end, though, Bellomont did grant him an extension to complete his written account of his voyage.[2]

Following the meeting, Kidd hurried back to Duncan Campbell's house to complete his narrative. Along with the captain, Kidd's legal team now consisted of Thomas Newton; the highly literate go-between Campbell; and his devoted wife, Sarah. With the Kidd family lawyer James Emott having returned to New York City, Team Kidd was now headed by Newton.[3]

Born and educated in England, Thomas Newton immigrated to New England to practice law in 1688 at a time when Boston's Puritan leaders requested that London send "some honest lawyers, if any such in nature exist."[4] Kidd and the London barrister first met during the Jacob Leisler treason trial in 1691, when Newton served as attorney general for New York. After his stint overseeing the Leisler trial, Newton returned to Boston, where he served as prosecuting king's attorney in the 1692 Salem witch trials, working closely with Judge Samuel Sewall, Captain Wait Winthrop, and Lieutenant Governor William Stoughton. In the summer of 1699, these elite Bostonians stood poised to determine the fate of the New Yorker Captain Kidd, just as they previously had the alleged witches. In the controversial witch trials, Newton had written out the indictments, compiled the depositions against the accused witches, and determined the order in which the cases would be heard.[5]

It is in his 1692 role as witch-slayer that we get a glimpse into the soul of the man tasked with sparing the legendary Captain Kidd from the hangman's noose. During the Salem witch trials, Thomas Newton and his successor, Anthony Checkley, the two men responsible for gathering the testimony of the "one hundred accusations of witchcraft," played a pivotal role in sending nineteen human beings—and two dogs—"to their deaths."[6] After being appointed in May 1692 to serve as prosecutor in the Court of Oyer and Terminer for the witch trials, the Anglican lawyer only served in this capacity until July 1692, when he left Salem for a judicial position in New Hampshire, suggesting that he may have come to regret his "part in the trials."[7] Following the contentious witch trials and his time as a justice in New Hampshire and Maine, he returned to Boston and started his own law practice, building up a reputation as one of the "best lawyers in America" in the ensuing years.[8]

While Team Kidd worked well into the night on the narrative, Robert Livingston visited Lord Bellomont. Having learned of Kidd's arrival in New England and with visions of exotic riches dancing in his head, Livingston rode his horse at breakneck speed from Albany to Boston, taking "the nearest way through the woods," and arriving on July 3, the day before his meeting with Bellomont. He desperately wanted his share of the loot and to protect his interest in the voyage, since he had put up significant money and was still on the hook for his £10,000 performance bond.[9]

The forty-five-year-old bean counter stormed into Duncan Campbell's home upon reaching Boston and demanded to see Captain Kidd. Unbeknownst to Kidd, Livingston had weeks earlier written Lieutenant Governor Nanfan, Bellomont's nephew, claiming that he had on board his ship in the Caribbean an eye-opening "half a million sterling" and proposing that Nanfan alert the royal governors to arrest him.[10] Thus, the head of Livingston Manor thought nothing of double-crossing the man he and Bellomont had coerced into leading the voyage in the first place. To placate the frantic and demanding Livingston, Kidd took him on a tour of the *St. Antonio*. He at this time revealed to Livingston that he was holding "forty-pound weight" of gold along with other "goods" at secluded locations in Long Island Sound and elsewhere for the investors. However, he refused to divulge the various locations of the treasure until he received his official pardon from Bellomont.[11]

The next night, July 4, Livingston went to see Lord Bellomont at Peter Sergeant's mansion. He arrived as jittery as a newborn colt, fearing bankruptcy from Kidd's actions. The discussion started off cordially enough, but Livingston soon experienced a panic attack and issued an ill-conceived threat to the governor. In a shrill voice, he demanded that Bellomont tear up Livingston's £10,000 bond guaranteeing Kidd's performance, along with the other contracts. If he did not accede to the request, Livingston would swear "all the oaths in the world" that Kidd would never bring in the prize ship and would deliver Livingston his profits privately, leaving his lordship with nothing.[12] The highest-ranking English official in America castigated Livingston for his "impertinence," knowing that Livingston was putting words in Kidd's mouth and the captain would never make such a threat. But with his suspicions aroused, he wondered if perhaps Kidd had given Livingston an advance payment in gold or goods in return for his support.[13]

Livingston left just as frazzled as he had arrived. When he was gone, Bellomont worked out in his mind what to do about him and Captain Kidd. The two seemed to be conspiring with his handpicked go-between, Duncan Campbell, to embezzle the treasure. Although he was still on the fence as to whether to arrest his erstwhile protégé, his window of opportunity to take Kidd into custody and get his hands on the loot was closing fast. Regardless of what path he chose, he had to disassociate himself from Captain Kidd while simultaneously recovering the treasure and protecting his Whig Junto partners. It was going to be a delicate tightrope act, but the Machiavellian English lord-governor was more than up to the task.[14]

On Thursday, July 6, 1699, Captain Kidd's world turned from bad to worse. Though Bellomont had granted him an extra day to prepare the narrative of his voyage, nothing else went right for him.

When Newton suggested that he give another gift to Lady Bellomont, Kidd had his go-between Campbell deliver a green silk bag containing five pounds of bar gold, worth £250 ($87,500 today), to Peter Sergeant's mansion and request a private audience with Lady Bellomont.[15] Shortly after Campbell left, sometime after 9 a.m., Kidd was summoned to the governor's council chambers. When he arrived at the Old State House, he greeted Bellomont, Lieutenant Governor Stoughton, lawyer Wait Winthrop, Judge Samuel Sewall, and the other council members. This time, Bellomont responded brusquely and demanded Kidd's written account of the voyage, which he said he had wanted delivered in full at nine sharp.[16]

Kidd apologized for not having completed the paperwork. He genuinely believed that he was supposed to submit his narrative by 5 p.m., not 9 a.m. Bellomont requested that he return at 5 p.m. with the completed document and dismissed him. The governor was firm and businesslike but not adversarial, not wanting to tip his hand to what he was about to do. For his own self-preservation, he had decided to issue an official warrant and take Kidd and his men into custody.[17]

When the captain left, Bellomont returned to his office and summoned a select group of his councilors that included Stoughton and Sewall to his chambers. For the very first time, he showed them the orders from the Lords Justices and Secretary Vernon in London—both having been sent an astonishing seven and a half months earlier—ordering colonial governors to place Captain Kidd under *immediate* arrest upon making port in their jurisdictions.[18] Bellomont told the assembled group that he had preferred not to arrest the subject until he learned where he had left his great ship with the bulk of the treasure, but now Kidd appeared "as if he were upon the wing and resolved to run away" and the governor believed it was time to issue a warrant for his arrest.[19]

The council agreed. With a quorum, Bellomont adjourned the meeting and had a warrant drawn up calling for the arrest of Captain Kidd and his men and the seizure of all "their goods and treasure" by a committee headed by Judge Sewall. The gouty earl then had Peter Sergeant's house slaves Mingo and Bristol lug him up the hill two blocks to the Sergeant mansion so he could take his lunch.[20]

While Bellomont was making arrangements for the arrest, Kidd returned to Duncan Campbell's house and resumed working feverishly on his narrative with his legal team. Campbell soon returned, carrying the green silk bag containing the gold bars intended for Lady Bellomont. Kidd's heart sank as the Scotsman gave him the bad news: though Countess Kate had kept the first gift, the enameled box, she had refused today's offering of gold.[21]

The countess's rejection set off alarms not just with Kidd but with his wife and lawyer. Though Sarah may have tried to reassure her husband, she knew the writing was on the wall. It was possible the gift of bar gold was simply too bulky, tacky, or indiscreet, but Thomas Newton also realized that the vise was tightening fast on Captain Kidd. At the very least, his client was *persona non grata.* But would Lord Bellomont really go so far as to issue a warrant for the arrest of his own business partner and pack him off to jail?

Kidd must have felt a strong urge to make a run for it, but he somehow put aside the fantastical thought and returned with Newton to his narrative. However, as they laid out the sequence of events at St. Mary's, St. Thomas, and Hispaniola, he had trouble concentrating and pulled his wife aside to talk in private. He didn't understand why Bellomont was treating him this way, he said to her. The earl had told him that the noble lords would "stifle all complaints" made in England or the colonies and guaranteed that "he himself would prevent all clamors in those parts where he was governor" by condemning all the treasure brought in, disposing of it privately, and "satisfying the owners for such part as should be due to them." Furthermore, Admiral Russell and Lord Romney had promised to stand by him in all his "undertakings."[22] He had been ashore now for several days and he still hadn't met alone with his business partner and sponsor Bellomont face-to-face. If he could meet in private with the earl, perhaps he could resolve the situation. After all, why had he come back home if he wasn't innocent?

Recognizing that a personal appeal to the governor could backfire, Newton and Sarah tried to talk him out of it. But Kidd felt that his honor had been impugned, and that rankled him. Having risen from lowly "commoner" to "Gent" based upon his own merits instead of a noble birthright like Bellomont—a rarity in the caste-driven 1600s—honor meant *everything* to him. Unfortunately, he was too worked up to heed his legal counsel's advice, or that of his wise and supportive wife.

He kissed Sarah and left, his sword bobbing in its sheath and his quiet indignation speeding him along Cornhill Street to Marlborough Street and thence to Peter Sergeant's mansion, where he knew the governor would be taking his midday meal. By the time he reached the front steps, he had worked out in his mind everything he wanted to say. But he was still barely able to control his simmering anger.[23]

What he didn't know was that two men were following him, only a half block behind.

He flung open the front door and barged inside. Hearing Bellomont's voice in the next room, he moved quickly in that direction. But he came to a halt when he heard a noise behind him.

He turned around.

Two men burst through behind him. His face red with anger, Kidd turned and walked on.

"Halt!" cried one of the men. "I have orders to seize you!"

Seeing the man was a constable, he put his hand on the hilt of his sword. Ignoring the order to stop, he turned the corner and darted into the room where he had heard Bellomont's voice.

There, eating lunch at the dining table with a Black servant standing nearby, was his newfound nemesis.

Their eyes met.

Dressed in his scarlet jacket, Lord Bellomont stared at him in terrified shock. "What is the meaning of this intrusion?" his eyes seemed to say.

With all the pent-up emotion of the past three years suddenly erupting, Kidd vented his rage by cursing the man who had first coerced and now betrayed him.

The second man coming up from behind him—whom Kidd didn't yet realize was councilman Thomas Hutchinson, a twenty-four-year-old scion of one of Boston's leading families—rounded the corner and seized hold of his arm, as the constable reached out to grab the other.[24]

"You must surrender yourself like a gentleman, Captain Kidd," Hutchinson said. "Please, we have a warrant for your arrest."

The former Caribbean buccaneer, New York man of affairs, and king's privateer could have drawn his sword, slashed away, and easily overpowered the two Bostonians before dealing with the helpless, gout-ridden Bellomont. But he decided against it.

Captain Kidd—still recognized today as one of the most villainous cutthroats of all time—surrendered as peacefully as a kitty-cat. But as he looked back at Lord Bellomont—the very symbol of the paternalistic English Crown with his stern visage, powdered periwig, and blood-red imperial jacket—William Kidd must have realized that he was about to lose everything.

At Duncan and Susannah Campbell's house, Sarah was beside herself with worry. Her husband had been gone for over three hours now, and she was growing increasingly concerned with every passing minute. It was now after 5 p.m., the time of her husband's appointed meeting with the governor's council, and the account of his voyage still remained unfinished. A voice inside told her that her beloved William was in danger, but perhaps it was just her imagination.[25]

Suddenly, a fierce pounding came at the front door. As she looked up, five men burst into the Campbells' home. The intruders poured into the parlor like a pack of ravenous wolves, with two of the men brandishing swords.[26]

Intercepting the wave of interlopers near the front door, Duncan Campbell demanded to know what was going on. He was addressed by Samuel Sewall, the forty-five-year-old Massachusetts Bay governor's councilor, wealthy merchant, and substantial landowner, who had served as a judge in the notorious 1692 Salem witch trials along with prosecuting attorney Thomas Newton.[27] Presenting a warrant, the skullcapped Puritan judge informed Campbell and Newton that Captain Kidd had been placed under arrest and locked up in the Boston City Jail and that Sewall and his four colleagues had been dispatched by Bellomont to seize all Kidd's possessions.[28]

Judge Sewall and his blue-ribbon panel of prominent Bostonians proceeded to ransack the North End home. Though they did not physically harm Sarah or the others, they were aggressive and threatening as they searched the premises. Lawyer Newton protested on behalf of his client that the ships Kidd had taken were legal prizes and they had no right to seize his client's or client's wife's possessions. But his pleas fell on deaf ears, as did the remonstrations of Sarah and Duncan Campbell.

To Sarah's dismay, the authorities swiftly seized her husband's assets. They also snatched all her and her housemaid's personal possessions. Prying open her traveling chest, they found 260 Spanish pieces of eight, a silver tankard, a silver mug, a silver porringer and spoons, forks, and other silver objects. They also found twenty-five English crowns along with a decorative chain, a small bottle, slivers of silver, a coral necklace, and strips of silk, all of which represented the life savings of Elizabeth Morris. Sarah pleaded with Judge Sewall and his men not to take her and her poor housemaid's possessions. After all, the items had nothing to do with her husband. But the old skullcapped Puritan, though a judicious magistrate with humanitarian inclinations, could not care less about the rights of the wife of a pirate.[29]

A half hour later, as the Boston officials were wrapping up their search, Sarah was relieved that Sewall and his men had not found all the gold and silver in her possession. But then, to her dismay, one of the officials performing a final check examined the rolled-up seamen's bedding kits. He quickly uncovered more than twenty pounds of gold, including the gold bars Lady Bellomont had returned, as well as a bag filled with twelve pounds of silver. Soon thereafter, Judge Sewall and his gang of government ransackers concluded their aggressive raid, which had utterly terrified young Elizabeth, little Sarah, and Matthew Campbell, and left the house.[30]

Sarah was crestfallen. What was she going to do now? They had taken not only her husband's belongings but everything she and Elizabeth Morris owned, and she now had nothing for her and her housemaid to live on or to bail her husband out of jail. With the wrongful seizure of these assets, Sarah realized that her legal status had changed and Bellomont considered her not only "an accessory to a criminal" but believed that all three of them were criminals in their own right.[31]

Bellomont was correct in thinking that Kidd and Sarah would be fiercely loyal to each other, and would write to the Board of Trade on July 26 that an important reason he had not arrested his protégé earlier than July 6 was because he "had brought his wife and children hither in the sloop with him, who I believed he would not easily forsake."[32]

During the raid, other Crown officials rowed out to the *St. Antonio*, impounded the goods aboard, and placed the crew members under arrest. Those unlucky enough to be captured included gunner Hugh Parrot, foretopman Gabriel Loffe, and three cabin boys: Richard Barlycorne, William Jenkins, and Robert Lamley. The rest of the crew and passengers, including Edward Davis and James Gilliam, had already scattered, several heading to New York City.[33]

Thomas Newton, for the moment still the Kidd family's public defender, told Sarah that he would go to the Boston City Jail and finish the narrative. It was possible, he told her, that her husband's arrest was for failing to deliver the report to Bellomont and the council at the appointed time. She prayed that he was right, but the situation didn't look promising.[34]

Lord Bellomont moved quickly to secure and itemize the treasure—the only thing he truly cared about. The money and personal effects seized at the Campbells' house were promptly inventoried along with the crew's gold, clothing, and other possessions seized from the *St. Antonio*. Kidd finally completed his full narrative of his voyage, and it was delivered by Thomas Newton and read aloud before Bellomont and the council that evening.[35]

On the advice of his esteemed lawyers Emott and Newton, Captain Kidd omitted three key incidents from his account: the Red Sea bout with Barlow and the Great Mughal's Muslim treasure fleet in the Arabian Sea, which, though no piracy was committed, sounded too much like Henry Every's 1695 attack; the *Mary* seizure, when Kidd forced Moore and the mutineers to return the goods they had stolen, but they disobeyed his orders and returned only a portion, which was also when he pressed

Captain Parker and Don Antonio into service in Royal Navy–like fashion; and the capture of the Portuguese galliot by Dekkar's *November*. These incidents would not only complicate his story and present him in an unfavorable light, but make him appear complicit with the piratical faction of his crew when he was pointedly at odds with them throughout the voyage.[36]

While he worked tirelessly to recover the treasure, Bellomont continued to keep Judge Sewall and his Boston council in the dark about his connection to Kidd, not wanting them to know that he had "readily invested" in the "dubious venture into the Indian Ocean."[37] He still had not located the sixty pounds of gold, hundred pounds of silver, and seventeen bales of East India goods his business partner had brought with him from the Caribbean, nor did he know the precise location of the *Adventure Prize* near the coast of Hispaniola, with bale goods, saltpeter, and other items worth an estimated £30,000 ($10,500,000 today). With Kidd locked up, Bellomont needed to keep him muzzled so he could uncover all the plunder privately before bringing his American councils into the loop.[38]

With treasure fever gripping his imagination, he sent a servant that night to Boston's waterfront taverns to learn where Kidd might have anchored his prize vessel. His protégé had revealed that the *Adventure Prize* was near Mona Island near Hispaniola, but hadn't been more specific. Though the servant failed to garner intelligence on the ship, he did by a stroke of luck learn about another of Kidd's possible hiding places. He overheard a conversation in which a seaman negotiated to rent a sloop for £30 ($10,500 today) to sail to Gardiner's Island. Deducing that Kidd had hidden goods at the eastern end of Long Island Sound, he realized he had to beat the other boat. He suspected that Kidd's wife, Sarah, or Livingston and Duncan Campbell, or perhaps all three working in collusion, had sent the vessel to recover the booty.[39]

The next morning, Friday, July 7, the governor appointed Judge Sewall and the other four council members who had searched Duncan Campbell's home to form a committee to consolidate and safeguard the outstanding treasure.[40] That same morning, after spending the night languishing in his stench-ridden holding cell, the once "trusty and well-beloved Captain Kidd" awoke as an incarcerated prisoner for the first time in his life. The contrast between his fine waterfront mansion in New York and the cesspool he now found himself in was staggering. His cell was a wooden box with a smattering of dirty straw on the floor to sleep on, a single barred window high up on the wall, and a repulsive wooden slop bucket to relieve himself in. He knew he didn't belong here with the highwaymen, murderers, traitors, blasphemers, and other dregs of Massachusetts, but he had no choice but to gut it out until he could find a way to plead his case or make his escape.

Since being tossed into the slammer, he had demanded several times from the Crown jailer, Caleb Ray, to speak with Bellomont. He wanted to know what crime he was being charged with and the amount of his bail requested by Thomas Newton. But neither the jailer nor the governor would give him an answer.[41] Always a glass-half-full man, he still hoped that Bellomont would come to his senses and realize that he and his men were innocent, that the real pirates were the mutineers who had violated the articles and abandoned him to go on the account with Culliford.[42]

Later that morning, he was summoned by Bellomont, who was desperate to get his mitts on the treasure. To win Kidd into his confidence, the governor served up his most pleasant smile as the shackled sea captain was delivered to the council chamber. But it was all an act. In a bald-faced lie, he now informed Kidd that if the captain told him the truth about the whereabouts of the treasure, he would be sent under Crown custody to retrieve it. At first, Kidd revealed nothing. But Bellomont decided to play his hunch about Gardiner's Island. He told him he already knew the gold was on the island, so if Kidd would tell him precisely where it was located, he would improve his standing immeasurably in the Crown's eyes.[43]

The haggard-looking sea captain, who had gotten little rest the night before, took the bait. Choosing honesty over greed, he admitted to fearing bringing the gold and other goods "about by sea," so he had left them in the custody of the island's proprietor, John Gardiner. Bellomont must have gloated inside at such a frank admission, never suspecting it would be this easy. Now he asked Kidd where the *Adventure Prize* lay. If Kidd told him, he purred, he would allow him to go and fetch the vessel. Kidd mulled it over for a moment, before deciding to take a chance that Bellomont would act honorably and not send him straight to the gallows.[44]

"The ship is left at St. Katharina [Santa Catalina Island] on the southeast part of Hispaniola. About three leagues to leeward of the westerly end of Saona."[45]

Concealing his delight, Bellomont continued with the questioning. Toward the end of the interrogation, the earl asked Kidd about the gold discovered in the bedrolls at Duncan Campbell's house.

"I intended it for presents to those I expected to do me kindnesses," responded Captain Kidd.[46]

For a flicker of an instant, Bellomont might have *almost* felt badly for his fallen protégé. But more likely he congratulated himself for laying the perfect trap. Thrilled that he was finally making headway and indifferent to the suffering of Kidd or his worried-sick wife and daughters, Bellomont sent the prisoner back to jail in his heavy chains. Despite Kidd's forthcoming assistance, the governor continued to keep his former partner in solitary confinement and refused to allow him to have any contact with his lawyer or family.[47]

He was taking no chance that Kidd would escape, as the New England pirates Joseph Bradish and Tee Witherly had done the previous month. Bradish and his crew had been captured earlier that summer, but he and the one-eyed Witherly had escaped from the city jail with the help of a maid named Kate Price. Bellomont, who had just arrived in Boston from New York, sent Algonquin warriors after them with tomahawks in hand. In October 1699, Bradish and his accomplice would be captured once again, this time in Maine, brought back to Boston, and chained up in the Boston gaol, Stone Prison, where Bellomont would soon move Kidd.[48]

The next day, July 8, with mountains of treasure foremost on his mind, Bellomont prepared a letter for John Gardiner. Fighting off the excruciating pain in his right hand from his gout, he scratched off a hasty note with trembling fingers requesting that Gardiner sail promptly to Boston and deliver the chest filled with gold and "other parcels" on behalf of his majesty the king.[49] He signed the letter, applied his wax seal, and dispatched a messenger to ride south posthaste, catch a ferry in Newport, rent a seaworthy boat, and sail to Gardiner's Island to secure the treasure.[50]

He was so very close to getting his hands on the remaining treasure, which uplifted his spirits immeasurably. But as he began to count his potential profits in his feverish head, he only wished he could have it *all* to himself.

–15–

The Pirate's Wife versus the Treasure-Mad Earl

Nine days later, on July 17, 1699, Sarah Kidd read over her petition to Bellomont requesting the return of her "plate and money" and housemaid's belongings illegally seized by the governor. Because she could only read but not write, Thomas Newton and Duncan Campbell prepared the letter from her dictation. With her husband in jail and her family's possessions confiscated by the English earl, she had decided to make an appeal to the man who was no longer her husband's patron, but rather his imprisoner and tormentor.[1]

When she was finished, Sarah approved the letter by dipping her quill into the inkwell and signing the document. She block-printed her initials, SK, between the words "Sarah" and "Kidd." The twenty-nine-year-old New Yorker may not have been able to write her own name, but she was savvy enough to have a legal petition prepared to protect her and Elizabeth Morris's rights. She knew that Bellomont would prefer to deny her any money at all, as she could use it to bribe chief jailer Caleb Ray and the other guards; but she hoped that Judge Sewall, Captain Winthrop, and the other council members would be more sensitive to the violation of her and her housemaid's rights and be willing to restore their lawful property.[2]

Until that happened, though, she had no gold or silver money either here in Boston or in New York to pay her lawyer or purchase food, since she had brought all the family's liquid assets with her, and Elizabeth Morris had been left penniless as well. Furthermore, she knew no one in Boston who could help her besides Newton and Duncan and Susannah Campbell, and access to her jailed husband was restricted, though by this time she had been allowed to visit him two or three times. If not for the generosity of the Campbells, who continued to share their home with her and her daughters, she didn't know what she would do.[3]

After the petition was signed, Sarah personally delivered it to Bellomont and the council, but they would sit on it for more than a week. The day after Sarah delivered her petition, Tuesday, July 18, the increasingly irascible earl learned that Captain Kidd had been spotted in the house of chief jailer Caleb Ray next to Boston City Jail—*completely unshackled.* Kidd had been making his first foray into an escape attempt by befriending and persuading the jailer to allow him to stretch his legs in the jail yard. Whether he was planning to overpower Ray during a walk or to set him up for a bribe is unknown, but Bellomont became apoplectic with rage. Without waiting for the advice of his council, he angrily scratched out an order that Kidd immediately be transferred to Stone Prison, remain shackled in heavy leg irons, and denied any visitors including his wife.[4]

Bellomont had made a clear choice based on self-preservation. In arresting Kidd, he had obeyed the royal proclamation and thus protected himself from the wrath of the newly ascendant Tories, but he had technically violated the investor agreement and risked angering Shrewsbury and his fellow Junto patrons.[5] He was, thus, in a bind. To clear himself, he could either try to exonerate his protégé, a leviathan task the Tories would make out as granting protection in return for a bribe; or he could ramp up his anti-piracy campaign and make an example of Kidd, in patriotic service of king and country. Since the captain's arrest, Bellomont had been carefully following the latter course, knowing that his easiest path to profit and vindication was to destroy his business partner.[6]

Despite the fact that no formal charges had been brought against Kidd, the earl continued his scheme of trying to get his hands on the full £40,000 ($14,000,000 today) that the privateer claimed to have tucked away in the colonies and off the coast of Hispaniola. He believed the total value of Kidd's plunder could even be as high as £70,000 ($24,500,000 today), which would be a significant windfall for himself and the other investors.[7] With this in mind, he began to position himself as the great subduer of a criminal mastermind in his letters to London. "He has without doubt a great deal of gold," he proclaimed to the Board of Trade, "which is apt to tempt men that have not principles of honor; I have therefore, to try the power of dull iron against gold, put him into irons that weigh 16 pound. . . . There never was a greater liar or thief in the world than this Kidd."[8]

By the evening of July 18, *this Kidd* lay shackled in solitary confinement in the soul-sucking Stone Prison, wondering what he had done to deserve the pitiless Lord Bellomont. The massive, drab-gray edifice bore three-foot-thick outer stone walls, dimly lit passageways, filthy cells partitioned off with planking, unglazed windows barred with iron, and doors covered with metal spikes. Those shunted inside its stony walls wasted away on six-pennies-a-day food consisting mostly of bread and water. The prison was a miserable place that struck fear into the hearts of Bostonians. But Kidd's situation in solitary was even worse than normal, given the heavy iron shackles chafing at his wrists and ankles and that Sarah could no longer communicate with him except to call up through the barred window from Prison Lane below.[9]

However, there was one silver lining, Kidd had learned from the other prisoners. The dank Puritan penitentiary was a run-down lockup and far from escape-proof, which meant he stood a decent chance of sneaking or bribing his way out, especially if his wife was again able to visit him and they could concoct a promising escape plan.

While waiting for his messenger to return from Gardiner's Island, the treasure-mad Bellomont, clearly "distorted by mental and bodily pain," began his aggressive campaign to defend his actions and protect the Junto.[10] His July 8 letter to London is a masterstroke of self-promotion as he continued to keep his actions concealed from his councils in New York, Massachusetts, and New Hampshire. At the same time, he portrayed Kidd as a felonious and immoral rogue and Robert Livingston, Duncan Campbell, and New York attorney general James Graham as aiders and abettors, embezzlers, men devoid of honor.[11]

"Never one to stop scheming where his purse was concerned," Bellomont left no stone unturned in his treasure quest.[12] Still without the knowledge of his councils, he went to work outfitting a warship of 300 tons and 22 guns, with a crew of 60, to sail along with the *St. Antonio* to Hispaniola to reclaim the cargo from Henry Bolton and his men left behind with the *Adventure Prize*.[13] The three-month round-trip voyage would cost the government £1,700 by Bellomont's "computation" ($595,000 in today's dollars), a massive expenditure for a mere suspicion. Then fate intervened. He learned that two months after Kidd's departure from Santa Catalina Island, Bolton and his crew had off-loaded everything remaining of value, put the torch to the stripped-down hulk and floated it out to sea, sailed to Curaçao, and sold some on-board goods while arranging the transatlantic trade of the remainder.[14] On the cusp of signing the contract for the 22-gun warship, Bellomont canceled the treasure-hunting mission.[15]

While Sarah continued to press for the return of her and Elizabeth Morris's money and plate, an out-of-breath messenger finally delivered some good news to Bellomont. Sailing in a small boat, John Gardiner arrived in Boston on July 17 to hand over Kidd's gold, silver, jewels, and other goods from Gardiner's Island, with six cloth bales to be picked up later by a ship arranged by the governor.[16]

Fresh off this glorious coup, Bellomont turned his eyes to New York. He had heard that Kidd had off-loaded money and goods to New York merchant captains, and he commanded his nephew, Lieutenant Governor Nanfan, to raid specific houses and arrest "arch pyrates."[17] By mid-July, he had arrested a dozen of "Kidd's Men" and was slowly but assuredly recovering much of the booty—still without his councils knowing of his close connection to Captain Kidd. But the terrible irony was that to avoid scandal and continue to flourish under the patronage of John Locke, Lord Chancellor Somers, and the Duke of Shrewsbury, he would be forced to ship every piece of coin, every speck of gold dust, every precious gemstone, every strip of bale goods across the Atlantic to London. Furthermore, he knew that with a single misstep in the Kidd scandal, he could lose not only his governorship but his friends in high places.[18] Thus, like Captain Kidd, Lord Bellomont was a man in mortal danger.

ON JULY 18, outside the split-granite walls of Stone Prison and Boston Town Hall, Sarah was busy taking charge of the family situation, planning to get her hands on some money. Having been neutralized by Bellomont, she had no alternative but to turn to former pirates and other shady characters to retrieve her husband's stashed-away money.[19]

To tap into Kidd's network, she decided that she would have either Thomas Newton or Duncan Campbell, or both, help her prepare a letter to her husband's friend Captain Thomas Paine. Back in mid-June, Kidd had arranged for the privateer hero of Rhode Island to hold three pounds of gold as insurance to protect his family in case of emergency, and Sarah and her husband had talked about retrieving a portion of it during her last jail visit before his transfer to Stone Prison. Her plan was to have James Gilliam's friend, a veteran sea dog named Captain Andrew Knott, deliver her letter to Paine, pick up her husband's gold, and deliver it to her in person.[20] She only hoped that she could trust the former buccaneer, who had led a checkered career as a mariner and pirate-broker on the periphery of the English Empire.[21]

But before the letter could be drafted, she was arrested that day, July 18, and thrown in the city jail by order of Bellomont. She reportedly fought like a lioness to wrestle herself free from the sheriff and his deputies until they finally overpowered her. In seizing her, the English earl had truly sunk to a new low, for, as historian Robert Ritchie writes, the governor had no reason to toss her into the slammer except to intimidate her.[22] In fact, Bellomont rejected the concept of *habeas corpus* altogether, emphasizing to his colonial American councils that the "Habeas corpus act" was not to be enforced in the colonies and that lowly prisoners should essentially have no rights whatsoever.[23]

Luckily for Sarah, who was every bit as resilient as her husband, she found a way to move forward with her critical letter despite being incarcerated. With the help of Newton and/or Campbell, along with possibly Captain Andrew Knott, she dictated a note from her jail cell for delivery to Captain Paine asking for "twenty-four ounces" of the gold her husband had left with him and instructing him to keep the rest in his custody until she, or her husband, called upon him again.[24]

Now hired by Sarah, Captain Knott that same day mounted a horse, rode south toward Bristol, Massachusetts, and ended up covering around thirty miles, or half the distance, before deciding to spend the night at a farm. The next day, after a long ride and a ferry, he reached Captain Paine on Conanicut Island, Rhode Island, to deliver Sarah's letter. Paine honored his old friend Captain Kidd's request by going into his bedroom and collecting seven gold bars. After weighing them on "a pair of steelyards," or balance scales, he recorded the total weight of the bars at 1¾ pounds (28 ounces) on the back of the letter and took Knott's "receipt for the same."[25]

After the two crinkle-faced sea rovers shared a meal and libation, Captain Knott re-saddled his horse, took the return ferry and the same well-traveled dirt trail he had before, and made his way discreetly to the outskirts of Boston by Sunday, July 23. On the Lord's Day, those performing work, sports, or recreational activities, as well as those traveling in carriages or on horseback, would typically be fined forty shillings or publicly whipped by Boston's city leaders. With the streets of the Puritan town quiet and empty on the Sabbath, Knott waited until the coast was clear after dark before making his way to his house, not wanting to have to pay forty shillings or be thrown in jail by the new sheriff of Nottingham, Lord Bellomont.[26]

Knott's journey to the Rhode Island coast and back had taken him five days. By the time he returned, Sarah had just been released from jail and was reunited with her teary-eyed daughters at the Campbells' home. Sarah and her maidservant collected the gold from the dusty, sore-legged pirate and gave him twenty Spanish pieces of eight for "his pains."[27]

That night, Sarah weighed the gold, using the scale her husband had brought from the *St. Antonio*, which had not been seized by the Boston authorities. Looking at the scale, she noticed that the total weight of the gold bars was short. The next morning, she went to Captain Knott's house and confronted him about the discrepancy, informing him that the "six bars of gold weighed 22 ounces" instead of the 28 ounces (1¾ pounds) she was expecting.[28] The grizzled sea rover told her that he had transported everything that Paine "brought out to him, and upon the road on his way homeward the gold by its weight [must have] broke his pocket, and he lost one of the said bars."[29]

The gold hadn't fallen out of any pocket, Sarah knew, looking the old salt straight in the eye. No doubt, he had transferred one of the bars to his other trouser pocket, thinking she wouldn't know any better.[30] But she decided to let it go, since she now had money again for lawyers, bribes, and meals for her husband, who for nearly three weeks now had been subsisting on mostly bread and water. With gold selling for more than £3 per ounce, she now had nearly £70 (around $24,500 today) in her war chest to combat Lord Bellomont.[31]

Two days later, she put the money to good use by submitting another legal petition to Bellomont and the council:

> Petition of Sarah Kidd
>
> To his Excellency the Earl of Bellomont, Captain General and Governor of his Majesty's Colonies of the Massachusetts Bay in New England etc. and to the honorable Council:

The Petition of Sarah Kidd humbly Showeth

> That your petitioners husband Captain William Kidd, being committed unto the Common Gaol in Boston for piracy, and under straight durance, as also in want of necessary assistance as well as from your petitioner's affection to her husband, humbly prays that your Excellency and Council will be pleased to permit the said Sarah Kidd to have communication with her husband, for his relief, in such due season and manner, as by your Excellency and Council may be thought fit and prescribed, to which your petitioner shall thankfully conform herself and ever pray.

Sarah Kidd
Boston 25 July 1699[32]

In politely asking if she could visit Stone Prison and spend intimate time with her husband, she couched her second petition to appeal to Judge Sewall and the other Congregationalists on Bellomont's council. Knowing that they were true believers when it came to the Bible's matrimonial command to "Be fruitful and multiply," Sarah made sure to point out that since her husband was in need of her "affection," she was ready and willing to peel off her petticoats during any conjugal visits and do her part on behalf of her sacred Christian deity.[33]

Unfortunately for Kidd and Sarah, by this time Bellomont and his governor's council were significantly at odds with each other. On the morning of July 25, Judge Sewall and his fellow blue-blooded Bostonians finally responded to her July 17 petition by coming out in her favor just as she had hoped. They "Advised that Mrs. Kidd making oath that she brought the plate and money above mentioned from New York with her, it be restored unto her. As also that Capn. Kidd and Company's wearing apparel under seizure be returned to them."[34] But the immovable Bellomont nixed it, refusing to honor his American council's advice. Not only did he not want her to have access to funds that could be used by her husband for bribes, he didn't care a lick that the captain and other prisoners had been sweating in the stifling July heat in the same clothes since their arrest by order of Bellomont. Therefore, Sarah's petition was never "Advised and Ordered" by the governor, and the belongings and clothing were not restored despite the council's vote.[35] Still worried that the prisoner might escape, the governor also ordered that chief jailer Caleb Ray and his family be removed from "ye gaol."[36]

But he didn't stop there: he also tried to bully his council into adopting England's harsh anti-piracy statutes. Under Massachusetts law, those convicted of piracy had to make a threefold restitution in damages, but were not punished with death as in England. However, during the July 25 meeting, Bellomont again pointed out that Boston's prisons were overflowing with Kidd's and Bradish's men at "great charge to the country," and he, therefore, pressed hard for conformity with the laws of England and the death penalty.[37]

Samuel Sewall and the other stouthearted Massachusetts Puritans—the grandfathers of Samuel and John Adams—dug in their heels. Bellomont was so disgusted with his American underlings, who seemed to care more about their "inalienable rights" than the "Laws of England," that he disbanded the council before it could vote on Sarah's latest petition. He then petulantly announced that he would soon be leaving Boston to visit his third government in New Hampshire. As one would expect based on his lackluster performance in the New World so far, he would prove no more popular in the province whose revolutionary motto would one day be "Live Free or Die" than he was in New York or Massachusetts.[38]

Before leaving for New Hampshire, Bellomont would scratch out one of his usual diffuse, longwinded letters to the Board of Trade to simultaneously boast about his achievements and justify his treasure-hunting shenanigans. Now that he had been rebuked by his own council, he once again sought clear-cut instructions from Whitehall. He specifically wanted to know "what to do with Kidd and all his and Bradish's crew, for as the law stands in this country, if a pirate were convict, yet he cannot suffer death."[39]

Bellomont's implication was crystal-clear: the gouty English earl wanted to see Captain Kidd hang—and he wouldn't mind *if his little wife, too,* met a similar fate.

Before or shortly after Christmas, Sarah Kidd left Elizabeth Morris and her daughters at their dingy dockside inn, where they had been staying for the past four and a half months, and headed west along King Street in the direction of Beacon Hill. Though mentally exhausted from her family's ordeal, she had a spring to her step since she was about to see her husband, who was once again allowed visitors but still lay shackled in isolation and shivering in his summer clothes in the infamous Boston gaol on Prison Lane. Back in mid-October, Judge Sewall and the council had approved her petition to Bellomont humbly requesting that fresh warm clothes be provided to Captain Kidd and his crew, but once again his lordship chose to ignore his council of American advisers.[40]

Captain Kidd had been confined to one solitary cell or another for five straight months, and Sarah and the girls were in a holding pattern, praying for his release. They were nearly as lonely and isolated as their husband and father. Duncan and Susannah Campbell had been generous in letting them stay at their house, but by late August they were no longer willing to accommodate them and turned Sarah and her young daughters out into the street. The ramshackle dockside inn where they had taken up residence was a far cry from the family's waterfront home on Pearl Street in New York, and they never had any visitors. No one invited Sarah to any social events, and, like Hester Prynne of Hawthorne's *The Scarlet Letter,* she most likely heard gossipy whispers wherever she ventured in the Puritan town.[41]

Sarah would do anything to help her husband, but what could she do? She was a pariah and an unwanted Anglican here in Boston and no longer had access to legal counsel.[42] The esteemed but unprincipled Thomas Newton had deserted her and her husband without warning for a Crown appointment under Bellomont back in early September. To ensure that the Boston lawyer who had played a key role in the Salem witch trials could not be used by Kidd as an advocate to secure his freedom, the governor had appointed Newton to the plum job of king's counsel for the Admiralty courts of Massachusetts, Rhode Island, and New Hampshire. Not only that, but he took the lawyer with him during a lengthy fall visit to harass Rhode Island's pirate-loving governor Samuel Cranston and his public officials.[43] Sarah and her husband were also handicapped because Duncan and Susannah Campbell were no longer allies, their good friends James Emott, Captain Clark, and Attorney General James Graham were far away in New York and could not help them, and Robert Livingston was hiding out somewhere between New York and Albany. Sarah was the only one now, and she felt powerless and deeply frustrated.[44]

Yet she hadn't given up all hope.

Upon her arrival at Stone Prison, Sarah found nearly three dozen accused pirates now stuffed into the stone penitentiary, with more arriving each week as Bellomont scoured the countryside for Red Sea Men trying to quietly blend back into colonial American society. Among the new faces who she may have caught a glimpse of during her visits in the fall and winter of 1699–1700 were James Gilliam, Joseph Bradish, and Tee Witherly, all recently ensnared in the English earl's massive manhunt.[45]

When Sarah arrived at her husband's cell, the door was unlocked by the jailer and she was let inside. She found Captain Kidd lying with chattering teeth on a foul bed of straw on the cold floor, wearing the same thin summer clothes he had been arrested in back in July. He rose to his feet, laboring under the burden of the sixteen-pound leg irons binding his ankles, and kissed and hugged her tight.

During this late December 1699 visit, Kidd and Sarah hatched an escape plan. Talking in whispers so as not to be overheard by the jailers, they decided to have Elizabeth Morris visit Kidd's friend Captain Thomas Clark to retrieve the gold given to him in June at Gardiner's Island. Hiding out in Stamford, Connecticut, to remain out of the long reach of Bellomont, the well-respected New Yorker "Whisking" was holding around £8,000 ($2,800,000 today) of Kidd's money and valuables in the warehouse of Major Jonathan Selleck, and at this point he was the lone remaining fence for Kidd's legally seized plunder. Kidd proposed that Sarah use some portion of the £8,000, perhaps as much as a quarter, to buy off the chief jailer and keep the rest to live on. But what neither Kidd nor Sarah knew was that the bloodhound Bellomont was already hot on the trail of the Clark-held plunder. Having estimated its value at an inflated £10,000 sterling ($3,500,000 today), he was desperate to get his hands on it for himself and his fellow noble investors.[46]

After the husband-and-wife team sealed the deal with a kiss, Sarah returned to her dockside inn and made the necessary arrangements with Elizabeth Morris. In one of the coldest New England winters on record, the hardy English spinster rode a horse all the way from Boston to Stamford, 175 miles, and met with Clark, who had taken refuge in Connecticut to escape the wrath of Bellomont.[47] But when she requested the money, Captain Clark refused to give her a single penny, though he let her down as gently as possible. He had already been arrested once under the orders of Bellomont back in September, he explained, and had been grilled by Bellomont's nephew, Lieutenant Governor Nanfan, and his heavy-handed Crown officials. To protect his longtime friend Captain Kidd, during his interrogation he denied receiving any goods from the *St. Antonio* and claimed that the New York trader Cornelius Quick had given him only money and valuables from "Madame Kidd," which could not lawfully be seized by Bellomont since they were not pirated goods. But the dogged English royal governor still had him spooked. Clark was afraid if he gave Morris any money, Bellomont would have him locked up again—only this time he would throw away the key.[48]

The maidservant made it clear that without the money, Captain Kidd and his wife, Sarah, had nothing with which to pay bribes to the jailers and were, therefore, doomed. Clark was sorry, but his hands were tied. In fact, Clark was so fearful of the earl that he had already reached an agreement to deliver all the goods to Bellomont, which, of course, he did not tell Elizabeth Morris. He had promised to do so on one condition: that Kidd would be in irons on a prison ship bound for England when he relinquished the goods.[49] Clark had sealed the deal with his lordship back in late October, after the initially resistant Connecticut governor, John Winthrop, had finally caved to the earl's demands. Thus, "Whisking" didn't actually betray his good friend until after being pressured by *two* colonial governors.[50]

When Elizabeth Morris returned from Stamford to Boston to report the devastating news, Sarah was disconsolate. Her family's situation had turned from precarious to utterly hopeless, and she prayed she could keep her daughters from knowing just how low their mother and father had fallen. It was looking more and more as if the Kidd family would never be made whole again.

Meanwhile, in the ice-cold Stone Prison, Captain Kidd was even more miserable than his wife. Shivering away the winter in solitary confinement was bad enough, but he had to endure the pious hectoring of Puritan Boston's televangelist-like Cotton Mather. On January 20, 1700, Reverend Mather, who had been unctuously fawning over Bellomont since his arrival, delivered a forceful sermon to Kidd and the other "Pyrate" prisoners from Jeremiah 17:11 on the topic of ill-gotten gains. "He who gets Riches and not by right," Mather sternly preached, "leaves them in the midst of his days and in his End shall be a Fool." Though the North End luminary was genuine in his desire to heal the scourge of piracy, he also at this time admonished wayward sailors for what he called the "Special Vices of the Sea." These included not only the sins of unlicensed plundering and thievery but drunkenness, whoremongering, cursing, and gambling.[51]

Captain Kidd, who could have desperately used a good stiff drink and the warm conjugal affection of his beautiful young wife, was neither comforted nor impressed by Cotton Mather's ministerial instruction—for in his own eyes, he was and always would be an innocent man.

On Saturday, February 3, 1700, the fourth-rate warship HMS *Advice*, captained by Robert Wynn and carrying a crew of 197 souls, dropped anchor in Boston Harbor. The ship destined to convey Captain Kidd to London for trial had completed the Atlantic crossing in five short weeks, after the HMS *Rochester* had been crippled by winter storms and been forced to return to England in early December.[52] Upon setting anchor in the harbor, Wynn was rowed ashore through bobbing chunks of ice. The weather had turned bitterly cold in the past two days, with vast swaths of seawater freezing in place near the shoreline. Upon reaching the dock, he shivered his way up the snow-covered streets of the City upon a Hill to meet with Bellomont. After presenting his commission, he delivered to the governor "his packets"—the latest correspondence from Whitehall.[53]

In perusing his correspondence, Bellomont was exhilarated to receive high praise from London for his crackdown on piracy. Now not only would his reputation survive the Kidd affair, he was looking like a hero and might even profit financially. The English authorities were especially pleased with the voluminous written documentation he had thus far provided. He had sent back several packets of materials, including Kidd's narrative of the voyage; the French passes taken from the *Rouparelle* and *Quedagh Merchant*; the depositions of John Gardiner, Duncan Campbell, Robert Livingston, and several crew members; and Bellomont's correspondence with Kidd luring the privateer into Boston.[54]

Because the Kidd scandal implicated the king and his lofty lords, Captain Wynn was under strict orders to bring the prisoner home to London completely incommunicado. No one was allowed to talk or send correspondence to the New York privateer, and he was not allowed to write letters to anyone, including his wife. The English government was treating him with a paranoia and severity usually reserved for traitors, regicides, and captured foreign potentates.[55] Bellomont ordered Wynn to come to Peter Sergeant's mansion every morning and remain on call throughout the day until the HMS *Advice* set sail, so Kidd and the other prisoners could be loaded onto the ship for departure to London at a moment's notice. He also commanded Wynn to have his carpenters and metalworkers prepare the *Advice* to receive up to fifty total prisoners.[56]

While Bellomont made arrangements for Kidd and the thirty-one other alleged pirates to be shipped to England for trial,[57] Captain Kidd and Sarah forged ahead with their latest escape plan. She had informed her husband of the arrival of Captain Wynn and the HMS *Advice*, so they knew their time was running out and they had to make their move. The critical first part of the plan called for Sarah to sweet-talk or bribe the jailer to remove Kidd's irons that had been chafing his ankles for the past six months. Kidd contributed to the scheme by complaining about the pain in his legs from the heavy irons. It is not certain what combination of the pleading, the bribery, or the sweet-talking was the factor, but on Thursday, February 8, the jailer took off Kidd's iron shackles to alleviate his discomfort.[58]

Then the escape plan entered the second phase. Sarah's job was to find a way to enable Kidd to physically sneak out of his solitary-confinement cell. The two most promising alternatives were loosening or filing through the heavy iron bars, or picking the lock, so that he could slip out undetected late at night. There was no time to spare, with the king's ship having arrived.[59]

They made plans to escape on February 13, five days in the future. This would give Sarah time to make all the arrangements for the jailbreak. At this point, the best option seemed to be smuggling in tools so that he could saw through the iron bars. James Gilliam had used an iron crowbar and metal files during his attempted escape back in December, but he had made too much noise and was caught before cutting through the last of the iron bars at his cell window.[60] Sarah's second option was to persuade the jailer, who she knew was a considerate man since he had let her husband out of his irons, to set Kidd free for a price.

As the Kidds implemented their long-shot escape plan, Bellomont tended to his severe gout inflammation and fretted at Peter Sergeant's mansion. He was desperate to get Captain Kidd and the other prisoners out of Stone Prison and onto the HMS *Advice* so he would no longer be responsible for them. In his letter to the Board of Trade, he wrote that he was "very uneasy for fear they should escape" and nervously joked that he would give £100 ($35,000 today) if they could be magically stuffed overnight into Newgate Prison in London. Unfortunately, the frigid New England weather and accumulation of ice in the harbor made loading the prisoners onto the ship and sailing across the Atlantic impossible.[61] Bellomont was worried that the *Advice* would become frozen in a block of ice, or the growing sheet would crush the hull and it would be impossible to ship the prisoners to London until late spring.[62]

Meanwhile, Team Kidd continued to move forward with the secret escape plan, still scheduled for Tuesday night, February 13. At Stone Prison, Sarah and her husband made their final arrangements. With the mission worked out, she returned to her dockside inn, where she had to prepare for not only her husband's prison break but for their family to sneak out of Boston to some safe haven in New York or southern New England, where they had trusted friends who could help them remain out of reach of Bellomont.[63]

At this time, the snowstorm abated and the weather warmed. The harbor's ice sheet melted and huge drifting blocks began hammering the sides of the *Advice*, as Bellomont had feared. The ship was now anchored in the gap between Castle and Spectacle Islands. Soon a gigantic iceberg several hundred feet long and half as wide rammed into the ship, driving it toward Spectacle Island and beaching it like a giant whale.[64]

Unaware of the rampaging icebergs, Team Kidd worked to bring the captain to freedom. On the morning of February 13, Kidd had been out of shackles for five straight days. But despite her best efforts, Sarah had not been able to smuggle in a file, or to make an approach to the chief jailer with a bribe that had a reasonable chance of success. Nor was she able to put together a more aggressive jailbreak with Andrew Knott or some other rough New England mariners who would be sympathetic to her seafaring husband's plight. Kidd had done his part to gain the jailer's sympathy and remove his shackles, but he hadn't been able to persuade him to allow him to leave the cell.[65]

Unfortunately for William and Sarah, that Tuesday morning Bellomont sent a man to check on Captain Kidd. When the earl learned that his fallen protégé was unshackled and moving about his cell, he erupted with volcanic rage. He demanded that Kidd be re-shackled and set the date for him and the other prisoners to be loaded onto the HMS *Advice* for Friday, February 16. He told no one about his plans but his council secretary, Isaac Addington, and the officers who would round up the prisoners, once again keeping his Massachusetts council in the dark.[66]

At dawn that Friday, the high sheriff and an armed force of deputies arrived at Stone Prison to forcibly remove Kidd and the other prisoners from their cells and load them onto the HMS *Advice*. How many went peaceably and how many put up a fight is uncertain—but Captain Kidd did not go quietly. Making good use of his powerful frame, he punched, kicked, elbowed, head-butted, and perhaps even bit a nose or two when his captors came to his cell to unshackle him from his wall bolt. Sharp words were exchanged, and it took a half-dozen men, or more, to wrestle him into submission and carry him out of the Stone Prison, despite the heavy chains binding his hands and feet. When the now-sweaty Captain Kidd realized they were taking him to the Royal Navy man-of-war anchored in the harbor, he knew what his chances of survival were if he went aboard—and he again fought his captors like a wildcat. But eventually he was subdued and stuffed into the *Advice*'s longboat.[67]

Still clothed in his thin, foul-smelling summer garb, he ached that he couldn't bid farewell to Sarah and his daughters before being loaded onto the prison ship. Once the oarboat steered through the floating ice and reached the 118-foot-long frigate, the prisoners were hauled like potato sacks up onto the deck. While Kidd was chained up in isolation in a low-ceilinged, windowless cabin in steerage, James Gilliam, Joseph Bradish, and Tee Witherly were chained together in the gunroom, which had been converted into a giant jail cell.[68]

By the time Sarah awoke at a seaside inn with Elizabeth and little Sarah, her husband had been dragged out of Stone Prison and was shackled aboard the *Advice*. It pained her that he had spent nearly eight months in Boston's two dismal prisons without being charged with a single crime. But she was even more crestfallen when she learned that he would now be shipped off for a probable show trial and grisly hanging in London, and she and her daughters would not even have the opportunity to bid him a proper farewell.[69]

However, the prison ship did not set sail immediately. There were repairs to be made to the yardarms, tiller, and sails, victuals to store on board, and the treasure to hoist on deck and stow away shortly before departure. Headed for London was a vast supply of gold, silver, jewels, Goa Stones, muslins, calicoes, silks, and other exotic valuables from the East—the sum total of everything seized from Captain Kidd, his many helpful friends, and his loyal seamen. The treasure included not only the haul from the East Indies but the illegally confiscated personal property of Sarah and Elizabeth Morris.[70]

Bellomont also needed time to pull together the remaining documentation for the Crown and prepare correspondence for Shrewsbury and the other backers to justify his actions and set himself up for the future.[71] "I hope East India Goods and Treasure that's sent will amount to £20,000 [$7,000,000 today]," he wrote to Shrewsbury, "which will reimburse everybody if the King will consent it shall be so; for I doubt Kidd will be proven a pirate, and then the King's grant will be necessary."[72] He also conspired to have James Gilliam's £3,000 ($1,050,000 today) in gold and jewels treated separately from Kidd's treasure and to have Sir Edmund Harrison cut out of his share of the profits so Bellomont could have more for himself. "I am told that as Vice-Admiral of these seas, I have a right to a third part of them," he wrote to his London business agent, Sir John Stanley, as well as Shrewsbury. "If the rest of the Lords come in for snacks I shall be satisfied; but that Sir Edmund Harrison should pretend to a share of what was not taken by Kidd is very unreasonable."[73]

Because the legal case against Captain Kidd for piracy was so shaky, Bellomont sought a way to ensure that his onetime protégé would be found guilty so that he and the other Whig investors would not be called into question. He came up with just such a strategy to buttress the prosecution's case against Kidd following his interrogation of seaman Joseph Palmer, whose July 29, 1699, Rhode Island deposition accused Kidd of piracy and the accidental killing of William Moore. Traveling with friends, Palmer had arrived in Boston from Rhode Island and surrendered himself to Bellomont on February 21, five days after Kidd was stuffed aboard the HMS *Advice*. During their meeting, Bellomont became enamored with the pirate. He was particularly taken by the young man's respectable demeanor and liked that he was friends with "substantial people" from Westchester north of New York.[74]

Bellomont recommended to the authorities in London that Joseph Palmer testify against Kidd for the killing of gunner William Moore. The governor believed that a strong case could be made for murder instead of merely manslaughter and that, if Palmer would testify, he would be granted the king's most gracious pardon. Bellomont notified Shrewsbury's man, James Vernon, that Palmer's sister was traveling to London: "She could easily persuade [her brother] to tell the whole truth," he wrote, "and a frown from you will make her endeavor it."[75]

Captain Kidd was held in solitary confinement on the HMS *Advice* in Boston Harbor for three straight weeks. Counting Kidd, there were now thirty-two accused pirates, including Joseph Palmer, and four enslaved Africans imprisoned aboard the London-bound frigate.[76]

Upon learning that her husband was being held captive aboard the HMS *Advice*, Sarah set about trying to visit him so she could say goodbye. But Bellomont would not allow any visitors aboard the vessel. Saddened but undaunted, she sought out Captain Wynn, hoping that he might be more sympathetic. She was able to introduce herself one wintry afternoon shortly before the ship's departure as he was leaving the governor's mansion.[77]

She told him that she was upset at not being able to visit her husband since he had been taken aboard the prison ship, and that she and her two daughters were very sad that they couldn't say goodbye. She then made a humble request. Would Wynn allow her and her daughters just five minutes to bid farewell to their husband and father and send him off with their love and a note to remember them by? He was innocent, she pointed out, and he deserved the right to say goodbye to his family, whom he might never see again.[78]

Before Kidd had been stuffed in his cold iron shackles aboard the *Advice*, she and her husband had decided that it would be best if she, Elizabeth, and little Sarah remained in America if he were taken as a prisoner to London. Not only did Kidd want to ensure their safety, but he couldn't bear the thought of his wife and daughters seeing him disgraced in irons in the atrocious Newgate Prison or Marshalsea Prison, or to see him on trial for his life before a courtroom of hostile Englishmen salivating at the prospect of his swift conviction and gruesome public hanging.[79]

Though Captain Wynn appears to have been a sympathetic figure, he was far too afraid of incurring the wrath of Bellomont to honor Sarah's humble request. He regretfully informed her that he had been commanded by the governor to guard Captain Kidd as a "close prisoner" with no visitors or letters, and that he could not violate his military orders by allowing her to visit or deliver a message to her husband, despite the fact that he was under heavy guard.[80]

Unwilling to be dismissed when her husband's life was on the line, Sarah reached into a leather pouch, retrieved a golden ring, and pressed it into Wynn's hand. The Royal Navy officer explained that he could not accept gifts and tried to give the ring back to her.[81]

But the stalwart Sarah wouldn't take it back. She requested that Captain Wynn keep it, and all she asked in return was that he treat her husband with kindness on the long oceanic journey to London. Once again, he protested that he could not accept any gifts.[82]

Feeling the emotions welling up inside her, she drew closer and looked the Royal Navy man right in the eye. "Captain, I must insist you keep the ring as a token until we meet again," she said. "On the day you bring my husband back to me."[83]

And with that, Sarah Kidd walked away and into the pages of history. Not yet thirty years old, she had stood resolutely by her man for the past nine months, sailing with him and their daughters aboard the *St. Antonio* and living in a repressive Puritan citadel that was utterly alien to her, with no friends at all once Duncan and Susannah Campbell booted her and her family out onto the street. Like her husband, Captain William Kidd, she had been abandoned by everyone once she became tainted and expendable, including her Boston lawyer who went over to Lord Bellomont, and she had even done a stint herself in the dank city jail. Yet never once during the interminably long, bitterly cold, and desperately lonely winter had she wavered in her support of her beloved husband, or in her belief in his innocence.

A day or two later, on March 10, 1700, the HMS *Advice* set sail from Boston Harbor for London and the trial of the century. A trial, in fact, that has been hotly debated for the past *three* centuries.

PART 5

The Trial *of the* Century

–16–
The Corporation of Pirates

On April 2, 1700, as the HMS *Advice* sped eastward across the tempestuous North Atlantic, England prepared for the long-awaited arrival of Captain Kidd. The news that Bellomont had captured the "American rogue" had reached the London metropole in August 1699; and with Kidd expected to arrive any day now, everyone in the city from King William III to the lowliest commoner in rags awaited his arrival with bated breath.[1]

The English authorities and East India Company knew that their very futures rested on the fate of Captain Kidd. On March 16, the House of Commons petitioned the king, asking that Kidd "not be tried, discharged, or pardoned until the next session of Parliament" to allow time to prepare the case against him and ensure his conviction.[2] He had been expected in February, then March, and by early April he still had not arrived at the mouth of the Thames. Not since the days of the Elizabethan Sea Dog Sir Francis Drake had a returning "pirate" so dominated the politics of London.[3] The air of excitement was further stirred by London's two top competing newspapers, the Tory *Post Boy* and the Whig *Flying Post or The Post Master*, both of which reported that "the notorious Pyrate

Captain Kidd" and more than two dozen of his fellow freebooters were expected shortly in England.[4]

The inflated estimates of the value of Kidd's treasure contributed to the heightened anticipation. While most Londoners were no longer gullible enough to believe that his booty was worth the £400,000 to £500,000 previously reported ($140,000,000 to $175,000,000 today), the estimates were still high. The latest reports coming out of the city still pegged the total value of "Capt. Kidd's" treasure at an eye-popping "£200,000" ($70,000,000 today), making Captain Kidd the hottest topic of the day.[5]

The London where the trial of the century was about to take place had changed dramatically since Kidd's last visit to the English capital. When he had shipped off to New York from England in April 1696, the Whigs had held the grip on power, the Junto had been untouchable, and King William's War had been in full swing. Now, four years later, the nine-year war had come to an anticlimactic end and the political winds in England had shifted back to the Tories.[6]

For Captain Kidd on the eve of his arrival in London, the political rift between the Whigs and Tories did not bode well. Not only did the Junto no longer wield the power it had when he had set forth on his voyage, but several ministers had been hounded out of office by the Tories, and those that remained continued to face scrutiny. Due to health issues, the Duke of Shrewsbury had retired in 1698 as Secretary of State, leaving his subordinate, Sir James Vernon, as his replacement. Admiral Russell, knighted Lord Orford two years earlier, had been forced to resign as the First Lord of the Admiralty and treasurer of the Navy for exploiting his governmental authority and lining his pockets with gold. Only Lord Chancellor John Somers and the Earl of Romney, who in his unimportant role of master of ordnance was not specifically targeted by the Tories, retained the same governmental positions they had held four years earlier.[7]

For the past year and a half, Kidd's highbrow English backers had been following their American protégé's movements with growing concern, keeping their fingers crossed in the hope that the rumors coming out of the Indian Ocean were untrue and wouldn't tarnish them. The key investors in England—Shrewsbury, Somers, Romney, Orford, and Harrison—had first learned of Kidd's seizure of the *Quedagh Merchant* in August 1698, when the EIC received correspondence from Sir John Gayer and others. Given the shifting political winds and Tory resurgence, they were particularly anxious about how they would be linked to the controversial Captain Kidd, the pirate base at Madagascar, and American trade violations. That is, if their *actual* names were ever publicly revealed.[8]

By a stroke of luck, throughout 1698 and most of 1699, no one discovered their involvement in the affair. But the English nobles knew that the clock was ticking and it was only a matter of time before their names would be publicly disclosed. Once news of the *Quedagh* seizure reached London, the Tories and Old East India Company began a whispering campaign about the true identities of the voyage's backers. The gossip in London's posh clubs, smoky taverns, and august halls of Parliament claimed that Kidd had been sponsored by well-connected men at the highest levels of the English government. No one except the investors knew that printed on Kidd's commission were the names of four lowly servants standing in for Shrewsbury, Somers, Orford, and Romney.[9]

With a steady stream of information on piracy coming in from Edward Randolph, Bellomont, and captured Red Sea Men, the calls for Kidd's head grew louder. The Old East India Company and Tory leadership in the House of Commons realized that they had a huge political scandal in the Kidd affair: they sought to bring down the Junto and at the same time put the blame for the proliferation of Indian Ocean piracy squarely on the North American colonies, thus absolving the EIC of responsibility.[10] Shrewsbury and the other backers soon recognized the full danger posed by the accused pirate and that they must take steps to protect themselves, as it was clear that the Tory directors of the Old Company sought to retaliate against them for terminating their profitable monopoly in India and creating a New Company to replace the Old. Sir Edmund Harrison was ordered to gather the official documents relating to the venture, since the Tories planned to bring the issue of East Indian piracy before Parliament and produce embarrassing revelations linking the Junto to Captain Kidd.[11]

In early December 1698, the partners met in secret at Lord Chancellor John Somers's London mansion, Powys House, and mapped out a strategy. They decided that if Harrison was confronted by the Tories in the House, he should be proactive by revealing the participants and should not try to hide anything. On December 15, Somers reported the meeting in a letter to Shrewsbury, anticipating the threat posed by the Tories. "We hope there can be no crime," he wrote, "though perhaps we may appear somewhat ridiculous. We also intend to inform some of our friends of the circumstances of fact, that they may be . . . prepared to speak to it."[12]

When news of Captain Kidd's arrest reached London in the late summer of 1699, it spread like wildfire from the Tory and Whig newspapers and the rumor mill of Narcissus Luttrell, the former member of Parliament and diarist known as the "master of hearsay." With Kidd captured and piracy taking center stage in Whitehall politics, the names of the backers were uncovered in November by the doggedly persistent Tories. The stunning news that Captain Kidd had been supported and financed by lofty stalwarts of the Whig Junto provided the party of William Blathwayt with a powerful weapon to bludgeon their foes.[13]

At this point, the king's once "trusty and well-beloved Captain Kidd" became not only a political puppet in the clash between the Whigs and Tories but the lead actor from central casting in the battle between the Crown and defiant American colonies. Like the Henry Every scandal, the Kidd affair revealed fracture lines between England and the "rebellious rabble" across the Atlantic that would within the next century spark revolution.[14]

On December 1, 1699, the Kidd issue was raised in the House of Commons, and soon the scandalous actions of his financial backers became the focus of the debate.[15] The Tories, with the backing of the Old Company, led the assault on the Whigs and singled out Somers for criticism, since as lord keeper he had conferred the Crown's stamp of approval on the enterprise. The Tories grumbled that Kidd had "plundered with a commission under the Broad Seal" from Somers and had been encouraged to commit piratical acts by his Whig backers. They wanted the commission declared void, arguing that the illicit goods did not legally belong to the pirates and were, thus, not grantable to a third party, by which the Tories meant the king and Whig Junto investors.[16]

To resolve these thorny issues, the House required several days to review the official communications. That night, Kidd's secret backers met once again at Somers's Powys House to determine what papers they needed to submit and how best to position themselves to avoid disaster and ensure that Captain Kidd would be the only one to take the fall. At this important meeting, the Duke of Shrewsbury's replacement as Secretary of State, Sir James Vernon, was present.[17] Eight years older than Kidd at fifty-four, Shrewsbury's protégé would now play a key role in the affair.[18]

During the December 1 meeting attended by Vernon, Somers argued for total transparency. The lord chancellor preferred that there be no delay in coming forward with the list of who stood behind the names on the commission and had "fitted out the ship" as well as "what they paid toward it." With Vernon acting as the Junto's representative before Parliament, Kidd's backers now decided to present every scrap of paper they had produced in the risky venture and to acknowledge their and the king's involvement.[19]

Amazingly, they never discussed the onerous fate of Captain Kidd—except for how it might adversely impact the Junto. Not once did they consider that he might not even be a pirate, nor did any of them propose supporting him, or at least looking into the veracity of the allegations against him. They *assumed* he was an eager and willing brigand and considered him expendable. Not only was he an embarrassment to the Junto, the English nation, and God Almighty, he posed a grave risk because of what he knew, and they were desperate to distance themselves from him.[20]

At noon on December 6, the House reconvened. The Tories moved to declare the original grant "illegal and prejudicial to the trade of the kingdom" and claimed it was a contravention of an Act of Parliament making it illegal to give away a felon's property until after conviction.[21] To exonerate the Junto, Vernon presented a heavily biased account of the Kidd affair, putting all the blame squarely on the king's privateer by claiming he had "turned pirate."[22] But what the Tories cared most about was the evidence of Kidd's backing by Lord Chancellor Somers and the other Whig ministers. However, the Whigs undercut the Tory arguments by focusing on property rights. Under the law, the Lord Admiral was granted plunderers' captured goods in the name of suppressing piracy, just as manor lords were granted felons' goods. If Kidd's commission to seize pirates was considered unlawful, the long-standing system of English property rights had to be illegal as well.[23]

The debate continued in a seesaw battle for nine straight hours. By 9 p.m., many of the Tories had left. Most being wealthy lords with comfortable estates, they did not wish to bite off the hand that fed their prosperity by attacking property rights. In the end, the Whigs carried the vote 189 to 133 in a pivotal victory. The final verdict found the commission legitimate and the goods grantable to the Crown.[24]

In April 1700, the talk of Parliament and all of London lay shackled in irons aboard the HMS *Advice*, just off the southwest coast of England. Kidd's home for the past month's travel had been a windowless, freezing cold cabin in steerage.[25] Though he still hoped for the possibility of acquittal, he knew his prospects were grim. With his backers having abandoned him and the English Empire out for blood, the American privateer was acutely aware that he was engaged in a David vs. Goliath struggle against the Mother Country he had once been honored to serve but now abhorred.

Late on Friday night, April 5, a messenger arrived at the Admiralty office in London to breathlessly report that Captain Kidd had arrived on England's shores. The clerk on duty ordered that the message be delivered posthaste to Secretary of State James Vernon. Awakened from his bed, the toothless English bureaucrat quickly perused the communiqué and immediately began scratching out a lengthy letter to the Duke of Shrewsbury, which he would finish and send along the following afternoon.[26]

In his long-winded letter, Vernon informed his patron that the HMS *Advice*, carrying Captain Kidd and "about thirty pirates" as well as "the plunder that had been recovered from them," was headed toward the mouth of the Thames. His foremost concern was that Kidd might not arrive to London before the end of the parliamentary session in a week's time. If this happened, it would be difficult to keep him incommunicado from the nosy Tories, since the next session would not take place for a year. Instead of being swiftly tried and executed, Kidd might be interviewed and coached *by the opposition* on what to say to save himself from the hangman's noose.[27]

Terrified that the accused might bring down the king and lordly Whig investors, Vernon arranged a hasty meeting on April 6 with Admiral Russell (Lord Orford) and others. They wanted Kidd to be interviewed quickly by the Whig leadership before the House of Commons went home and, if that was not possible, they wanted him kept muzzled and inaccessible to the Tories. But Vernon discovered that Captain Kidd couldn't be interviewed until the next parliamentary session, and his scheme quickly fell apart.[28] Orders were then sent to Wynn aboard the HMS *Advice* commanding him to proceed to the Downs and meet with the yacht to transport Kidd to Greenwich. Marshal John Cheeke of the High Court of Admiralty was assigned to sail in the second-rate *Royal Katherine* and intercept Wynn and Kidd in the *Advice*, which reached the Downs on April 10. Cheeke arrived the next day. Perhaps expecting Kidd and his gang of "cutthroats" to break their chains and seize the ship, he was backed by a small army of more than thirty redcoats. He needn't have bothered: Kidd was seriously ill from being stuffed into the ship's stagnant-aired hold and living mostly on biscuit, beer, and water for the past month.[29]

After nearly three stressful years at sea followed by nine straight months of incarceration under solitary confinement, he was "unfit to face the ordeal before him."[30] However, despite his faltering health, he had worked like a dog the past month to put together his legal defense for his trial.[31] In Boston, Bellomont had denied him ink, quill, and paper in Stone Prison to prepare for trial, worried that he might exonerate himself by implicating his lordly backers. But on the HMS *Advice*, Captain Wynn supplied him with writing materials and allowed him to prepare documents. For this, Captain Kidd could thank his wife, Sarah, for having given Wynn her gold ring in early March.[32]

Not one to lack resolve in the face of adversity, Kidd was as prolific as William Shakespeare, producing in four weeks a mountain of written material. He wrote letters to friends and lawyers living in England and to the two Junto backers he had met in person, Admiral Russell (Lord Orford) and the Earl of Romney. Along with his letter to Orford penned on April 11, 1700, from the Downs, he enclosed a copy of his official "Protest."[33] In the document, he laid out his case and defended his actions at sea:

> I know not what is generally thought of me, nor what is alleged against me, but I do assure your Lordship I have done nothing but what is punctually declared in the said protest, wherein if anything be accounted a crime, 'twas so far contrary to my sentiments that I should have thought myself wanting in my duty, had I not done the same. I am in hopes that your Lordship and the rest of the honorable gentlemen my owners will so far vindicate me that I may have no injustice, and I fear not at all upon an equitable and impartial trial, my innocence will justify me to your Lordships and the world.[34]

When the *Advice* reached the Downs, Kidd entrusted his lifesaving letters for Orford and Romney to Captain Wynn. The fair-minded captain had treated him respectfully during the voyage and Kidd trusted him. But he did not trust Wynn enough to hand over the two dozen pages–plus of his legal defense. These he carefully sewed into the lining of his waistcoat.[35]

The *Royal Katherine* anchored next to the HMS *Advice* for the transfer of prisoners. With a solemn Royal Navy drumroll echoing across the water, Cheeke and his file of armed soldiers boarded the *Advice*, took Kidd and the other ragged prisoners into custody, and hoisted them in chains into their yacht. With the prisoners shackled belowdecks, the *Katherine* sailed up the Thames for Greenwich, accompanied by Captain Wynn. It is at this time that Vernon concocted another scheme to have Kidd brought speedily before a special Whig cabinet council for interrogation, where Somers could listen and control the subsequent narrative. But his plan backfired when the House of Commons ended its parliamentary session and the Admiralty ruled that the prisoner would be interviewed by the Lords of the Admiralty and not members of Parliament or the Ministry.[36] Due to the end of the session, Kidd would be shunted away for the next nine months in either the noxious Newgate Prison or Marshalsea Prison, with a high probability of dying a slow and agonizing death long before getting his day in court.[37]

To provide cover for the Junto, Vernon also at this time made the unilateral decision to maintain an unprecedented level of government transparency by having Bellomont's letters and other correspondence read before the Admiralty. But what he failed to foresee was just how vile and avaricious Bellomont would come across in defending his actions and persecuting Kidd.[38] From Bellomont's correspondence to his London business agent, Sir John Stanley, and Shrewsbury, what the dirt-broke English earl with the expensive young wife appeared to desire most of all was *more money*, which he believed he was entitled to by noble birthright.[39]

It was Bellomont's letters about cutting Sir Edmund Harrison out from his rightful share of Kidd's treasure, his entitlement to a third of Gilliam's loot as colonial vice-admiral, and his proposal to hand out "snacks" to Somers, Shrewsbury, and the other Whig lords that drew the most eye rolls from Admiralty officials. As the earl's indiscretions were laid bare, he looked more and more like a greedy pirate himself, especially when he went on to "propose that the partners acquire a new grant for the king for Kidd's treasure" and when he "asked Vernon to solicit a present for him from third parties."[40] But his most astonishing revelation was his firm conviction that "the greatest liar and thief of them all," Captain Kidd, would not even "be proved a pirate" in a court of law and would gain acquittal.[41]

At dawn on Sunday morning, April 14, a sick and demoralized Captain Kidd was made presentable aboard the *Royal Katherine* anchored at Greenwich so he could be brought ashore in London and interrogated by the Admiralty. Thoroughly frisked by Marshal John Cheeke, his clothing was inspected, and he was forced to empty his pockets to make sure he wasn't smuggling in a concealed knife or lockpick. But during the pat-down, Cheeke instead discovered in the sewed lining of Kidd's waistcoat the twenty-five pages of carefully prepared legal-defense documents.[42]

Having spent the past month preparing the materials to save his life, Kidd refused to give the papers up. In fact, having been cut off from humanity for nine straight months without being accused of a crime and knowing that he was about to be paraded about London in shackles like a monster, he put up a fierce fight just as he had at Stone Prison. Despite being dreadfully sick with fever, he punched and elbowed and kicked and head-butted his assailants, fighting like a chained bruin at London's Bear Gardens with a half-dozen armed soldiers tearing at him like snapping pitbulls.[43] "His shackles dented the oak door jambs; he bloodied the guards; and then he passed out in a sweaty clammy heap. A few moments later, Kidd awoke, queasy and feverish."[44]

But Kidd's next act surprised even John Cheeke. "After he recovered from the fit he had," relayed the marshal to the Admiralty after seizing Kidd's life-or-death papers, "[Captain Kidd] took out a piece of gold and gave it to [my] deputy and desired him to send it to his wife, for that he believed he should die, since his papers were gone."[45]

So, Captain Kidd gave away his last coin on earth to his dearly beloved back home in America, realizing that his contest against the Goliath English Empire was already over. The deck was too stacked against him. As Kidd biographer Richard Zacks writes, it was "a remarkable gesture, an act selfless, demented, lovelorn. One gold coin could support him for a month or more in prison."[46]

Captain Kidd, deathly ill and knowing that his chances of clearing his name were virtually nil, wanted to end it all right then and there. "If I'm condemned, I hope to be shot and not suffer the shameful death of hanging," he said to the deputy. He then asked the stunned Englishman if he would be so kind as to hand over his knife, so that he could take his own life and thereby preserve the only thing that mattered to him besides his dear family: his honor.[47]

But the deputy and Kidd's other captors refused to allow him to control his own fate.[48] Gentleman Marshal John Cheeke was under strict orders to bring Kidd in alive.[49] Neither the Whigs nor the Tories, neither the Admiralty nor Parliament nor even King William himself, wanted Kidd to die *quite yet*. He needed to be cross-examined about every aspect of his voyage and his marching orders from the Whig Junto—before he would be allowed to die in public shame.

At 3:30 p.m. on Sunday, April 14, 1700, a chained and feverish Captain Kidd was unloaded from a private barge to the waterside stairs near the Admiralty's new building next to Whitehall Palace. From there, he was transferred to a sedan chair and carried under "strong guard" by a "file of soldiers" to a conference room bearing a group of solemn, scowling-faced English aristocrats wearing leonine periwigs.[50]

All the Admiralty big shots were there to interrogate him, including the Whig John Egerton, Third Earl of Bridgewater and First Lord of the Admiralty; the Tory Sir Charles Hedges, chief judge of the Admiralty, who had instructed the jury in the second Henry Every trial to *ignore* the presumption of innocence so the previously acquitted seamen could be promptly found guilty and hanged; and Admiral Sir George Rooke, a Tory member of Parliament and avowed enemy of Lord Orford. Led by Sir Charles, the wolfish assemblage proceeded to grill Captain Kidd during two separate interviews over a seven-hour period.[51]

Once again, not a single one of the officials, whether Whig or Tory, considered the possibility that Kidd might be innocent. Instead, Sir Charles bulled ahead with accusatory question after accusatory question, while his colleagues chimed in occasionally; or, as the Admiralty Board preferred to describe it, they examined Kidd "as to the several piracies laid to his charge." Kidd kept to the narrative he and his legal counsel had developed, omitting the Red Sea, *Mary*, and Portuguese galliot incidents that would complicate his story. At the end of the first session, around 8 p.m., the sick and exhausted prisoner signed his deposition and Sir Charles was asked to leave the room.[52]

It was during the second session that the thornier political issue of the Junto's involvement in the affair was broached. The Tory Board members were interested in the activities of the Whig partners, and the burning question in their minds—and all of London's—was whether these lordly gentlemen had violated their office and hired him to commit piracy. Everyone involved in the affair—from the youngest cabin boy aboard the *Adventure Galley* to the king himself—was by this time considered by the Tories to be part of a nefarious criminal cabal known as the "Corporation of Pirates." Kidd gave a bland and accurate account of his financial backers and the cost of outfitting the *Adventure Galley*. He had worked closely with Sir Edmund Harrison in fitting out the ship, he said, but had met Lord Orford (then Admiral Russell) on only two occasions, one of which was a private meeting, and the Earl of Romney (Harry Sidney) only once. He admitted to never having met Somers or Shrewsbury, but he had been in the duke's office on one occasion, where he had seen Bellomont, with Robert Livingston's proposal in his hands, discussing the expedition with James Vernon, Shrewsbury's senior secretary at the time.[53]

At 11 p.m., the Admiralty Board wrapped up the proceedings. Once again, Captain Kidd affixed his signature to the deposition, and both testimonials were now signed and embossed with official hot-wax seals. The Admiralty secretary was ordered to keep the signed and sealed document safe, while officials arranged for Kidd's incarceration in London. As the tired clerks wrapped up the final paperwork, Captain Wynn of the HMS *Advice*—sans the keepsake golden ring Sarah had given him, which he had already turned over to officials—came before the Admiralty Board and delivered Kidd's legal defense papers written aboard the *Advice*.[54] Wynn had already handed over Kidd's letters intended for Orford and Romney to the Lords of the Admiralty when the *Royal Katherine* stopped in Greenwich. Unfortunately, these life-or-death letters never reached either of the two key backers the New York privateer had met with in person and who had guaranteed his protection along with Bellomont.[55]

Captain Kidd's testimony was to be held unread until the next session of the House of Commons, which meant he would remain in one life-sucking hellhole prison or another for at least a year. It was at this time that the decision was made to hold Kidd as a "close prisoner" and commit him to the toxic Newgate Prison instead of the Marshalsea, the Admiralty's customary destination for alleged pirates awaiting trial. Having embarrassed the English state and East India Company, he was regarded as a political prisoner rather than a civil or military one by the Crown. While he was fated to rot away in Newgate, all the other prisoners shipped from Boston to London were confined to the far more tolerable Marshalsea.[56]

At the awful Newgate, Captain Kidd would once again be held in solitary confinement, subsisting mostly on bread and water, and would be allowed a physician only if he could afford one (he was penniless and could not, nor could he afford supplemental food). He would be given ink, pen, and paper to write—but only to the Admiralty.[57]

Kidd had to die, of course, but it had to be by the noose in a grand London spectacle to show the Great Mughal and those recalcitrant American provincials that the English Empire was *deadly* serious about its war on piracy. The Henry Every scandal had been an embarrassment to the nation and a Pyrrhic victory in the courtroom; this time around, the Crown would leave nothing to chance.

With his seven-hour ordeal mercifully over, Kidd was escorted by Marshal Cheeke and his file of now-tipsy soldiers, who had been drinking heavily since dropping Kidd off at 3:30 p.m., back down to the Admiralty barge on the Thames. Two hours later, he was delivered downstream in irons to the dreaded Newgate Prison—a black, five-story stone hulk brandishing a giant pair of shackles above the gateway. Captain Kidd—once a strapping and robust "Gent" with a beautiful young wife, two wonderful daughters, and dozens of good friends who cared deeply for him—was now all alone in the world.[58]

The massive door opened. Kidd, Marshal Cheeke, and the file of soldiers were instantly assaulted by the stench. The rank odor filled Kidd's nostrils like a plague, and it was only with great difficulty that he fought back the urge to retch. The vile smell was in fact made up of several different odors: the rotting corpses of prisoners whose families had not yet raised sufficient money to have them "released"; human excrement from long-unemptied chamber pots; foul body odors from unwashed humanity; dead vermin; the unrelenting London dampness; and stale tobacco and woodsmoke. The stench hung over the English prison like a cloud of death.[59]

At Newgate, Londoners kept a safe distance, not only to avoid the stink, but because they might be doused with refuse from emptied chamber pots from upper windows. The place was so unsanitary that most physicians of the era refused to even set foot inside the prison.[60] A hundred and twenty-five years into the future, in 1825 after decades of British prison reform, a prisoner at Newgate would still say of the place:

> I have here unjustly suffered so much, and seen and heard so much, that I am not as I was. My nature has become changed and hardened against my race. I feel myself let loose from all the ties of society and that I have lost almost all the feelings that belong to humanity.[61]

They were greeted by one Mr. Fells, the keeper of Newgate, a greedy Englishman who had been making out like a bandit for years extorting money from desperate prisoners, and who ruled his fiefdom with an iron fist just like Bellomont. The goal of Fells and his jailers was not to rehabilitate prisoners, but to extract as much gold and silver as possible from them before their release or execution. Cheeke presented his orders to the keeper, who closely examined them before allowing the marshal and his prisoner to set foot inside the prison.[62]

Fells knew all about Captain Kidd and the "Corporation of Pirates" from the *Post Boy* and other London newspapers. Like modern-day tabloids, the news media of the day had been telling wildly inaccurate tales of Kidd's exploits for more than a year now. Knowing that Captain Kidd was important, and having heard the stories of his vast treasure, Fells selected a particularly heavy set of iron chains for his new guest. The time-honored scam for the keeper of Newgate was to make a prisoner so uncomfortable in his heavy shackles that he would be desperate to pay handsomely, or, in the lexicon of the age, to proffer a "garnish" to have the painful iron devices removed. Once Cheeke unlocked the Admiralty irons, Fells clamped a much-heavier pair of Newgate shackles about Kidd's wrists and ankles.[63]

Captain Kidd, who by now was close to passing out from his ill health, the putrid stench, and exhaustion from seventeen straight hours of transport and interrogation, shambled forward, his cold irons clanking miserably into the night. Ten minutes later, he was unceremoniously stuffed into a bleak cell in the Condemned Hold in the cellar of the prison. Though he was used to severe deprivation from his many years at sea, even he must have been shocked at the dreadful repository in which he found himself. The cell was a claustrophobic, windowless dungeon with a cold stone floor, a single unemptied slop bucket, and a wooden cot with no mattress, sheets, blankets, or pillows.[64]

He collapsed onto the dingy wooden cot, his hefty shackles chafing his ankles. The iron door clanged shut, the bolt clicked home, and he found himself all alone in pitch black with the only sound in the sepulchral darkness his own labored breathing.

–17–

Stacking the Deck

During his first three weeks of close confinement, Captain Kidd shivered alone in his dank prison cell in constant darkness. He was not allowed to take air or exercise in the outdoor yard available to most prisoners. His human interaction was restricted to jailkeeper Fells, who remained convinced that his famous prisoner had amassed a great fortune.[1] The two men haggled daily over removing the chains, with the stubborn American refusing to pay his English tormentor the standard extortion fee, even on future credit. With no service from Fells, Kidd's cough, fever, chills, and headaches worsened to where he lay semi-comatose twenty-four hours a day, quivering and hacking and slowly dying.[2] Miserable and angry at his ill treatment, he petitioned to have his chains removed and be allowed to take exercise in the prison yard. But the Admiralty refused to budge on anything except releasing him from his heavy iron shackles.[3]

Knowing that he had to establish contact with the outside world to survive, he persuaded Fells's deputy jailer to locate three Londoners whom he hoped would help him recover his clothing chest that had been removed from the HMS *Advice*. He sent word to his wife's relatives Sarah Hawkins and her butcher husband Matthew, who had put him and Samuel Bradley up in 1695–1696; and also to a gray-haired fishmonger named Blackburn, a relative of Sarah's first husband, William Cox. Forced to call upon a landlady, a butcher, and a fishmonger to plead his case before the Admiralty, Captain Kidd had indeed fallen to an all-time low.[4]

On May 7, 1700, landlady Sarah Hawkins of Wapping came before the Admiralty Board to petition that Kidd's "trunk of wearing clothes & bedding" be returned to him, so he wouldn't die of exposure in prison. Mr. Blackburn of Thames Street, meanwhile, humbly asked if he "might have the liberty to speak with Captain Kidd" at Newgate since the man seemed to be doing rather poorly. The Board replied to both, with typical bureaucratic obfuscation, that its hands were tied.[5]

On May 13, the deputy keeper informed the Admiralty that "Captain Kidd was troubled with a great pain in his head, and shaken in his limbs, and was in great want of his clothes."[6] To avoid the possibility of premature death, which would strip the English state of its show trial and public-hanging spectacle, the Lords of the Admiralty reluctantly ordered that the ailing prisoner's trunk of clothes and bedding be returned to him.[7] The Board also declared that Kidd's relations Sarah Hawkins and Mr. Blackburn would now be allowed to visit him in the presence of Fells or his deputy. Furthermore, since Captain Kidd was "very much indisposed in his health," they could give "their assistance in supplying him with necessaries and money." They could also bring a doctor to treat him—as long as they paid for it themselves.[8]

In early May, Captain Robert Wynn of the HMS *Advice* was notified by the Admiralty that two of his men had attempted to visit Kidd at Newgate. After looking into the matter, Wynn reported back that his chaplain and the chaplain's servant, who had befriended the captain and were concerned about his deteriorating health during the transatlantic crossing, had tried to visit him but had been rebuffed by Keeper Fells. Both the Admiralty and Fells were under strict orders from the Crown not to allow anyone with access to high-ranking public officials anywhere near the famous prisoner.[9]

Due to the Crown's paranoia, Kidd did not receive his first visitor until mid-May, more than a month after being stuffed into solitary. On this day, Sarah Hawkins was led by Fells through the dark stone corridors of Newgate to the ailing prisoner's cell, holding a vinegar-soaked rag to her nose to overcome the stench. She found Kidd pale, shivering, semi-delirious, and racked with a terrible cough. The once-robust sea captain was on the cusp of death.[10] To soothe him, she covered him with a blanket, held his hand, and informed him that she had arranged for a doctor. This recorded visit by Sarah Hawkins was the first loving care he had experienced in three months, since his wife Sarah's last visit to his cell in Boston's Stone Prison.[11]

Over the next few months, Kidd gradually recovered his health while the Admiralty interviewed witnesses who might be willing to testify against him, reviewed documents, and put together its case to prosecute him and his crew members. Despite his dismal incarceration, he went to great lengths to help two of his officers' widows in their attempts to recover money owed them by the Admiralty. His second-in-command, Henry Mead, and officer William Beck had died early on the voyage, before any of the alleged piracies had been committed, and Kidd came up with a way for their spouses, Elizabeth Mead and Gertrude Beck, to recoup money from their husbands' auctioned goods, which had been unlawfully seized by Bellomont in Boston. In November, with Kidd's assistance, the widows prepared a petition before the Admiralty to recover their husbands' money, but were refused. Desperate, they petitioned directly to the king. Though their request was read to him in person, he declared that it was not in his power to grant them the money and they must apply through the requisite courts. On the cusp of debtors' prison, Elizabeth Mead pressed her claim in the High Court of Admiralty, but lost the case and was shunted away into prison just like Captain Kidd.[12]

Soon, another gloomy English winter began, and, as the days dragged on in the cold stone prison, Kidd's health again deteriorated. He continued to pepper the Admiralty with complaints regarding his denial "of liberty of the Gaol" that other prisoners enjoyed and his toxic environment under solitary confinement. In his December 30, 1700, letter to the Lords of the Admiralty, he laid out his case for humane treatment, knowing that his only leverage was the threat of premature death. After reviewing the petition, the Board decreed to Keeper Fells that Kidd be allowed to walk around Newgate "to air himself" when accompanied by the keeper or "one of his officers."[13]

After eight months of close confinement and a year and a half of total captivity under atrocious conditions, he was finally allowed access to the outdoor yard. But he still could not talk to anyone except Sarah Hawkins and the other sporadic visitors to his cell. Though he was still physically barely holding on, had not been charged with a crime, and had no access to any written records or legal counsel, "his constitution, long attuned to the rough life at sea, kept him alive."[14]

On February 10, 1701, King William III called his Fifth Parliament in his eleventh year of sitting on the English throne. The Whigs had narrowly lost the election and the new Tory-controlled House of Commons was thrilled at the opportunity to humiliate the Junto. Now in a position to control the Kidd affair, the Tories and the Old East India Company could finally put the infamous outlaw up on the national stage and force him to answer the burning question: Had he been hired by the Whig leadership—the nefarious "Corporation of Pirates"—to commit licensed acts of piracy?[15]

Rotting away in Newgate, Kidd soon received word that Parliament was back in session and ready to bring him before the House of Commons. Recognizing that he was being set up to take the fall for his lordly backers, he wrote to the Admiralty on March 20 requesting that he be allowed to talk in private with legal counsel and be permitted use of "pen, ink and paper" to prepare his defense.[16] The House permitted the writing materials but refused to restore his previously granted 20-shilling weekly stipend, which prevented him from hiring legal counsel to build his defense.[17]

In late March, he was ordered to testify before the House along with Coji Babba, the Armenian part-owner of the *Quedagh Merchant*, whom the Old Company had brought all the way from India to press its case for the goods taken from the 400-ton behemoth. The authorities had also rounded up Henry Bolton, the sleazy Antiguan merchant who had received Kidd's goods and put the torch to the *Adventure Prize.* Captured in Jamaica and returned to England, Bolton had dealt with part of the treasure, making him an important eyewitness to strengthen the case against Kidd, who was about to become the first alleged pirate ever to testify before Parliament.[18]

On Thursday morning, March 27, 1701, Captain Kidd was finally released from solitary confinement for his much-anticipated date with the House of Commons. Escorted down the stone stairs in his iron shackles, through the heavy door, and beneath the ornate gateway by Keeper Fells and a squadron of heavily armed soldiers, he squinted against the gloomy early spring sunlight as he set foot in the outside world for the first time in almost one full year.[19]

With his chains clinking and clanging against the stone pavement and hundreds of curious onlookers swarming like vultures, he marched in a humiliating procession through the narrow streets toward Whitehall Palace. The chains binding his ankles and hands underscored to the celebrity-obsessed public the danger he posed to the English nation. The procession slowly made its way west on Holborn, then south via Charing Cross, heading from Newgate to St. Stephen's Chapel. All along the way, the mob continued to press in around him and shout out his name. Once delivered to St. Stephen's Chapel, he took his place before the bar to await the House of Commons debate.[20]

More than four hundred House members turned out for the electrifying spectacle the Tories hoped would bring down their Whig rivals. While the relevant documents were placed on the table in the middle of the room, the periwigged political luminaries chattered in gossipy patters throughout the dignified chamber. Like Captain Kidd, Coji Babba was there to give his testimony, but Henry Bolton was nowhere to be found. Since presenting his written deposition on February 4, the shady Caribbean trader had managed to raise bail and flee London.[21]

Once it was certified that Kidd's testimony, given the preceding April before the Admiralty Board, and the other papers were in order, the transcript of the private interview was unsealed and read aloud before the packed House. The Tories sought to answer the burning question of whether Kidd had followed secret orders from Somers, Shrewsbury, Orford, and Romney to commit piracy. Their endgame remained the same: to use the Kidd scandal to impeach the Junto. But as the transcript was read, it quickly became apparent to the esteemed members of Parliament that the "notorious arch-Pyrate," as the London rags were all calling the king's privateer, had never committed piracy at all, or at least that he was certain in his own mind that he hadn't.[22]

In his testimony to the Lords of the Admiralty, Kidd did not waver from what he had told Bellomont in Boston. He vigorously maintained that he had never been under secret orders to act as a pirate and that he had, in fact, hunted down pirates and England's enemy the French until his unruly crew had mutinied.[23] The Whigs in the gallery breathed a sigh of relief, for they recognized that their Junto brethren had nothing to fear from Kidd's written deposition. But as Captain Kidd himself prepared to take center stage for his in-person testimony, they had to wonder if, after rotting away in the atrocious Newgate Prison for the past year, he might name names to save his own neck. Especially if the Tories had managed to sneak inside the prison and offer him a bribe. The rumor circulating around London was that if Kidd agreed to help the Tories by painting the Whig lords as "dishonorable rogues" and by playing the part of the duped victim in the "Corporation of Pirates," he would escape the hangman's noose.[24]

After the preliminaries were undertaken and Coji Babba's petition on the capture of the *Quedagh* was read aloud, Captain Kidd was ushered into the chamber.[25] Though he had spruced himself up for the occasion, he was a shell of the man who had visited London a half-decade earlier. As maritime historian David Cordingly writes, "[T]he first and only pirate in British history to have to explain his actions before the assembled Members of Parliament, [Captain Kidd] was hardly in a fit state to do so. Depressed, disheveled, and suffering the ill effects of two years of imprisonment in horrendous conditions, he must have been a pathetic sight."[26]

Kidd once again presented his narrative of the voyage; it was virtually identical to his two previous depositions given under oath. The Tory House members shouted down questions to him, goading him to turn on his powerful Whig promoters, but he refused to take the bait. He stood by his earlier testimony delivered to the Admiralty Board that he had never met Somers or Shrewsbury, but had met Orford twice and Romney once. When the roles of Sir Edmund Harrison, Lord Bellomont, and Robert Livingston were broached, he identified them simply as the principal organizers and managers of the expedition.[27] The speaker then dismissed Kidd from the Commons chapel to allow the expedition-planning documents, Bellomont's letter luring Kidd into Boston, and Kidd's reply to be read before the House before recalling Kidd for more testimony. But upon his return, the colonial American sea captain stood firmly and consistently by his two previous accounts.[28]

By this point, virtually everyone in the chamber wanted to send him straight to the gallows. To the Whigs, he was merely an annoyance; but to the Tories, who had pinned their hopes on the mud he would sling at the Junto, he was an extreme disappointment who had made them look like utter fools. They had counted on Captain Kidd to be their weapon to bring down the "Corporation of Pirates," but all he did was make a convincing case that he had grappled mightily to adhere to his commissions and serve the Crown. Though his Whig Junto patrons had left him high and dry, his testimony cleared them of wrongdoing as well. Now that he had been brought before the House, his backers were content to leave their discarded protégé confined to his lonely prison cell at Newgate.[29]

Perplexed and disgusted, the House ordered the shackled Kidd remanded back to Newgate. The following day, the House reviewed the documents of the "Corporation of Pirates" and then debated the legality of whether the Crown could grant away pirated goods before conviction. The debate went on until eight o'clock that evening when the question of the legality of the royal-backed enterprise was put before the parliamentary body. The vote was close, 198 to 185, but the Whigs prevailed. The House, despite a slender Tory majority, upheld that the grant was legal, and Somers and the Junto could once again breathe a sigh of relief.[30]

On March 29, the House of Commons voted that "Captain Kidd may be proceeded against according to Law," and the next day another round of unnecessary theatrics occurred in the Kidd saga.[31] A sketchy rumor claiming that the accused desired to come clean about the Junto to save his own neck was reported to Sir Edward Seymour, a rabid Tory House partisan. Kidd had been visited at Newgate by a coffee man named Mr. Kistdale, who had come to the prison to collect the seven shillings Kidd owed him for liquid refreshments at the Court of Wards coffeehouse. Under close watch by Keeper Fells, Kistdale told him, "You are a fool to hang for anybody, and you might certainly save your life if you can say anything against Lord Orford or Lord Somers." In response, Kidd responded vaguely: "I will hang for nobody. I am resolved to speak all I know."[32]

The next morning, March 30, without notifying Kidd of his plan, Kistdale delivered a handwritten note to Sir Edward Seymour, informing him that not only did Kidd have more to say, but that he was prepared to *tell all* about his lordly Whig backers. Thrilled at the prospect of lowering the boom on the Whigs, Sir Edward quickly arranged for Kidd to make a second appearance before the House of Commons the very next day.[33] On Monday, March 31, the slavering Tory waved Kistdale's letter like a battle flag and read aloud before a packed gallery that Captain Kidd had requested a second appearance before the House. Upon this news, House Speaker Robert Harley issued a warrant to Keeper Fells to deliver the prisoner. With the gawking crowds gathering and the coffeehouses buzzing, Kidd was brought in again for questioning without having any idea why he had been summoned. Seymour tried to intercept him for a hasty tête-à-tête before his appearance, but as Kidd was escorted into the building a pair of Whigs rushed forward and whisked him into St. Stephen's Chapel.[34]

Captain Kidd once again found himself standing before a hostile House. With the flair of a veteran stage actor, Speaker Harley demanded to know why he had requested a second appearance before the noble body. The New York privateer, who had looked forward to getting another crack at exonerating himself by answering the House's queries, was flummoxed and politely informed them that he had not requested the meeting, had not prepared any statement, and had no new revelations.[35]

Infuriated, the House ordered Kidd back to Newgate. Thoroughly embarrassed for having trusted the word of the Court of Wards coffee man and in need of a scapegoat, Sir Edward Seymour blamed Kidd for the fiasco. "The fellow is a fool as well as a rogue," he was soon overheard blustering to a colleague, "and I will never credit what he shall say hereafter."[36]

With Captain Kidd the biggest story in town, there were some who regarded him as a hero for refusing to turn on his backers to save his own skin. Bishop Gilbert Burnet, for one, admired Kidd for his courage:

> [H]e accused no person of having advised or encouraged his turning pirate [and] said he had no orders but to pursue his voyage against the pirates in Madagascar. All endeavors were used to persuade him to accuse the Lords; he was assured that if he did it, he should be preserved; and if he did not, he should certainly die for his piracy: yet this could not prevail on him to charge them.[37]

Kidd even drew praise for his discretion from Whigs closely connected to the Junto. Josiah Burchett, Secretary to the Admiralty and a former Whig member of Parliament, proclaimed in his history of the Royal Navy that it was to Kidd's infinite credit that he did not break down under the government pressure, especially when one considered the "great industry which was used to prevail with him to impeach some

Noble Lords who were concerned in fitting him out, with a Commission under the Great Seal."[38]

On the way back to his cell, Kidd was once again hounded by a London mob. Not only did he draw gigantic crowds wherever he went, he continued to be the source of "unprecedented coverage" in the emerging press of the day. Even before he had been shipped in chains from Boston to London, he had regularly been featured in the Tory *Post Boy* and Whig *Flying Post*, as well as other newspapers, for his alleged predatory exploits. He had been making headlines since late 1697 when news first reached England that he had "turned pirate," and within months of his arrest in Boston in July 1699 he was known as "the Wizard of the Seas."[39]

The public was conflicted between a proletarian sense of fascination and sympathy for the common-born "criminal" and a nationalistic, pro-Crown desire to see justice done and to witness the grand spectacle of a public execution. But what Londoners were most fascinated with was his alleged transformation from the king's patriotic privateer to a villainous pirate and the reports of his massive treasure dispersed and hidden all around the world.[40]

Having learned its lesson during the Henry Every trial, the English state went out of its way to control the public perception of the Kidd narrative through "media manipulation" to ensure his conviction and hanging. In the newspaper reports of the day, the pro-government journalists framed the English authorities as resolute, fair-minded, and powerful, while Kidd was painted as a terrifying hardened criminal condemned to a dreadful but well-deserved fate. The Crown was portrayed taking "firm action" against the "notorious prisoner" to whom "no person is admitted to speak," while Kidd was often described as wearing "irons" and "hand cuffs" and being "under a strong guard." By firmly controlling the newspaper narrative, the English state put the humble-born American colonial in his place as a lowlife felon, violent menace, and traitor to his most gracious king and Mother Country.[41]

In early April, still languishing in Newgate, Kidd was finally informed that he would be going to trial on May 8. He immediately wrote the Admiralty, requesting that his allowance money be restored and that he be sent the crucial documents to properly defend himself in court.[42] Still worried that the prisoner would find some way to miraculously escape justice, the Admiralty Board refused to cough up a single penny—until the night before the trial. However, three weeks before the trial, on April 16, the House of Commons did agree that Kidd could have copies of his commission and other papers needed for his defense.[43]

Two days later, on April 18, the captain submitted an itemized list to the Admiralty of the documents needed for his defense. The House clerk, Paul Jodrell, and the Admiralty's secretary, Josiah Burchett, cooperated with Kidd's request and sent Fells at Newgate all papers made available to them.[44] But without any money to pay for lawyers, Kidd was still at an extreme disadvantage. Knowing that he was being railroaded, the once-again penniless sea captain wrote to the Admiralty on April 21 requesting that he be allowed to use "some part" of what Bellomont had seized from him to pay for his defense, but his request was denied.[45]

Kidd's itemized list of the documents in his letter to the Admiralty included his original commissions and sailing orders, the communications between Bellomont and himself, his bond and orders from the Admiralty, and the French passports taken from the *Rouparelle* and *Quedagh Merchant*.[46] While he did receive a bundle of paperwork from Burchett, he discovered that he was missing several critical documents. The most important were the two missing French passes, but Kidd was also very upset not to have received Bellomont's letter sent to him from Boston, instructions relating to his commission from the Lords of the Admiralty, and a "blue-skinned" book naming the *Adventure Galley*'s owners and "their proportions of money" as well as "the ship's accounts." Correctly surmising that the critical materials were being withheld from him, he dashed off a letter requesting the conspicuously missing items, especially the French passports that he wrote were the "cornerstone" and "justification" of his defense. But in the end, the French documents and other critical papers had mysteriously disappeared, and neither Burchett nor Jodrell could find them.[47]

Bellomont's correspondence was especially important because it highlighted the Whig Junto's involvement, documented the existence of the French passports, and anticipated their effectiveness in securing Kidd's acquittal.[48] Sent by Bellomont to London in late July 1699 with the first wave of documents, the vital French passports had been delivered to the English authorities on September 26, 1699, and publicly read before the House that December and entered into the Commons Journal. However, although the Admiralty's secretary, Burchett, controlled the records, he did not keep them exclusively at Admiralty House and allowed government officials to take them to their offices or homes to review in private. The materials, thus, had passed through the hands of several officials and did not have to be formally signed out. These two factors made them ripe for being stolen or carefully hidden by corrupt members of Parliament, the Ministry, or the Admiralty.[49]

Clearly, the French passports should have been available to Captain Kidd in the spring of 1701, as they were found in 1910 by treasure-hunting American historian Ralph Paine, tucked away in the records of the British Board of Trade. Instead, the handwritten French documents were deliberately withheld from Kidd for his trial.[50] As Atlantic scholar Lauren Benton notes with a trace of sarcasm, this "misplacement" certainly proved quite convenient for the English authorities.[51] For more than two centuries, some British historians were skeptical of the existence of the French passports—until the *American* Paine unearthed them in London and in the process discovered a 210-year-old English conspiracy to seal the fate of William Kidd.[52]

That the crucial evidence was withheld from Captain Kidd to ensure his downfall is beyond dispute. Thus, the only question is what English official, or cabal of English officials, was responsible at the time for withholding the critical records and thus stacking the deck against him. The consensus amongst historians is that Secretary of State James Vernon is the culprit, as multiple lines of evidence point to him.[53]

As the Whig Junto's primary fixer, Vernon clearly had motive and opportunity. Not only did he keep Somers, Shrewsbury, Orford, and Romney continuously abreast of the developments in the Kidd case, but he actively sought to protect them at every turn, as revealed by the Secretary of State's extensive—indeed one might say obsessive—correspondence regarding the Kidd affair.[54] Furthermore, not only did he have full, unsupervised access to the papers, but he kept many of them in his office and he recognized their importance to Kidd's defense. Bellomont himself had informed Vernon of the two passports he had secured, and both men knew that not only would Kidd base his defense on them but that these French papers would likely get him off. Finally, the two passes discovered by the American sleuth Ralph Paine in 1910 were found deeply buried in the records of the Board of Trade, the archives of which by the twentieth century had been combined with those of the English Secretaries of State.[55]

Thus, Vernon either deliberately withheld the documents until after the trial had passed and later sneaked them into the Board of Trade records, or he buried them deeply in the Secretary of State files and they were later combined with the Board of Trade records.[56] But did he act alone, or under the orders of Shrewsbury and the Junto? The British pirate scholar Joel Baer believes the suppression of the French passports was most likely "the doing of Secretary of State James Vernon at the behest of the Junto."[57] In the first Henry Every trial, the working-class London jury had been reluctant to convict Every's seamen based on evidence similar to the Kidd case, and Vernon and Co. decided not to take *any* chances this time around.

When he was informed of the disappearance of the crucial life-or-death evidence, Kidd justifiably went ballistic. Though he understood that England would likely never allow him to walk free, he didn't want to fight with both hands tied behind his back. Quickly learning to represent himself and hoping to level the playing field, Kidd sent repeated requests to the Admiralty for the crucial documents that he believed were being withheld.[58]

One of these urgent letters was submitted in late April to Sir Robert Harley, Tory Speaker of the House. By this time, ten days before his trial, Kidd was finally allowed to meet with a lawyer. He would have two of them: Dr. William Oldys and Mr. Lemmon, both veterans of the court and both Tories. Their first action was to petition for Kidd to have money to pay their defense-lawyer fees and to recommend that the accused write to Speaker Harley to plead his case. Oldys and Lemmon were granted £50 ($17,500 today), but the sum was suspiciously not delivered until the night before the trial. With Kidd seeking help from a Tory politician and Tory lawyers, it was clear that he had given up on his Whig backers.[59]

In his letter to Harley, Kidd for the first time took a swipe at the sponsors of his voyage. "I did not seek the commission I undertook," he wrote, "but was partly cajoled, and partly menaced into it by the Lord Bellomont, and one Robert Livingston of New York . . . who only can give your House a satisfactory account of all the transactions of my Owners." Kidd went on to call the withholding of the French passports to ensure his conviction "barbarous" and "dishonorable."[60] Based upon Bellomont's unscrupulous character and previous threats toward him, Kidd earnestly believed that he was the one who had withheld the evidence in order to secure his downfall. In this plausible inference he was wrong, of course, as the earl had sent the passes, along with the rest of the papers, to London in late July 1699. Although Vernon was likely the culprit, Kidd was correct in identifying that an English government conspiracy was afoot when he said, "I must be sacrificed as a pirate to salve the honor of some men who employed me and who perhaps if I had been one—and they could have enjoyed the benefit of it—would not have impeached me upon that account."[61]

While Kidd struggled to assemble his arguments in ten measly days, the prosecution put the finishing touches on the case it had been preparing against him *for the past year*. An English Court of Judicature liked to have two eyewitnesses friendly to the Crown to obtain a conviction, so the Admiralty in Kidd's era typically selected two seamen for their intimate knowledge of the prizes taken and their willingness to betray their shipmates. After interrogating a dozen or more of "Kidd's Men," the Board decided upon Dr. Robert Bradinham and Joseph Palmer as the Crown's star witnesses.[62]

It was either them or Kidd—and to cheat the hangman, Bradinham and Palmer put forward a false narrative that neatly shifted all the blame to the Crown's primary target, Captain Kidd, thereby absolving themselves and the other mutinous crew members of wrongdoing. After taking a dozen or more merchant ships on Kidd's orders, they claimed, they had gone to St. Mary's, where Kidd had voluntarily divided the loot, befriended Robert Culliford, and cruelly deserted his crew to make their own way home.[63]

Joseph Palmer was interrogated by the Admiralty on April 15, 1700. He immediately spun a tale at odds with his testimony given in Newport on July 29, 1699. Press-ganged into the Royal Navy before the Kidd expedition, Palmer was one of the naval rejects who had been foisted upon Kidd by Captain Stewart in March 1696, after Stewart had wrongfully seized Kidd's men at the Nore and was forced by Admiral Russell to return them. Now in his early thirties, Palmer came across to both Bellomont and the Admiralty as articulate and presentable, which made him a strong candidate to turn state's evidence against Kidd and ensure a conviction.[64]

Robert Bradinham, the heavy-drinking surgeon aboard the *Adventure Galley* and later the *November* until he defected to Culliford, had, like Palmer, returned to America from Madagascar with Kidd's friend Captain Giles Shelley, aboard the *Nassau*. He was later arrested in Philadelphia for piracy and shipped to England, arriving at the Admiralty office for questioning on February 1, 1701. To save himself, Bradinham agreed to prepare and sign a statement claiming that Kidd had personally ordered and committed numerous acts of piracy and that the crew had merely followed his explicit orders. Delivering his full testimony to the Board on February 4, he came across as somewhat refined and intelligent like Palmer, and he had no criminal record up to the date of his arrest in America.[65]

For their willingness to turn against their captain and his loyal crew members and help secure convictions, the state's star witnesses were both promised a royal pardon. By April 30, 1701, the Admiralty prosecutors had met "about perfecting the indictment" with their two already-perjured witnesses, whom Kidd would not know had been handpicked to testify against him until he stepped into the courtroom. The trial was scheduled for May 8.[66]

Knowing that his day in court was fast approaching and that the deck was heavily stacked against him, the New York privateer wrote a remarkably honest and impassioned letter that he planned to deliver to the English court. With his back against the wall, he made clear what he thought of Lord Bellomont, his wobbly-kneed English backers who had abandoned him to his fate, and the clearly rigged English judicial system in which he now found himself.

> If ye design I was sent upon be illegal, or of ill consequence to ye trade of ye Nation, my Owners who knew ye Laws, ought to suffer for it, and not I, whom they made ye tool of their covetousness. Some great men would have me die for salving their Honor, and others to pacify ye Mughal for injuries done by other men, and not myself, and to secure their trade; but my Lord! Whatsoever my fate must be, I shall not contribute to my own destruction by pleading to this Indictment, till my passes are restored to me. It is not my fault if I admit myself a pyrate as must do I plead without having those passes to produce.
>
> Let me have my passes, I will plead presently, but without them I will not plead.
>
> I am not afraid to die, but will not be my own Murderer, and if an English Court of Judicature will take my life for not pleading under my circumstances, I will think my death will tend very little to the Credit of their Justice.[67]

In his outpouring of emotion, it is clear that Captain Kidd no longer saw himself as an Englishman. In writing of an "*English* Court" and declaring that his death "will tend very little to the Credit of *their* Justice," he has distanced himself from and renounced the Crown and, in the process, has made the complete transformation from a loyal English subject to a colonial American citizen acting in defiance of the English Empire.

It is also evident from his letter that he knew his fate was already sealed. Though he still held a tiny shred of hope that by some miracle he might receive a royal pardon, he knew the odds were overwhelmingly against any such merciful intervention. But the scrappy American from New York was still game for the challenge, for the stubborn Captain Kidd had vowed to himself that he would not stop fighting until he had had his last dance.

The dance of death.

–18–

Premeditated Murder by Wooden Bucket

On Thursday morning, May 8, 1701, Captain William Kidd stepped warily into the Old Bailey, the legendary London courthouse adorned with august symbols of Admiralty power.[1] He wore a navy-blue tailored jacket, a cream-colored cravat, a trim waistcoat, and a shoulder-length blond-brown wig that accentuated his ruddy cheeks, keen brown eyes, and prominent nose. But the gentlemanly attire he had managed to cobble together to look his best in court could not conceal the physical and emotional ravages that he had endured during his extended Age of Enlightenment incarceration.[2]

Entering the courtroom, Kidd couldn't help but be awed by his imposing surroundings. The Old Bailey truly was a "palace of justice," with the ornate Silver Oar of the Admiralty and a plethora of national symbols displayed in the various heraldic crests, colorful flags, and inscriptions on the walls.[3] Beneath a great crest bearing *Dieu et Mon Droit*, the English sovereign's motto "My Divine Right," sat the Admiralty's chief advocate, Dr. Henry Newton, a veteran of the first unsuccessful Henry Every trial; Sir Salathiel Lovell, the cantankerous, antediluvian court recorder with the nickname "Obliviscor of London" due to his absentmindedness; and five veteran Crown prosecutors. The prosecution team, eager to swiftly dispatch the nuisance Captain Kidd, all wore full-bottomed and freshly powdered periwigs, lush scarlet robes, and hoods lined with either taffeta if they were Oxford alumni, or white ermine if they called themselves Cambridge men.[4]

Kidd was accompanied by six of his loyal seamen who had refused to go a-pirating with Robert Culliford and three of the mutineer-pirates. Of Kidd's loyalists, the teenagers Richard Barlycorne, William Jenkins, and Robert Lamley stood next to gunner Hugh Parrot, veteran foretopman Gabriel Loffe, and cook Abel Owen. The three mutineers who had gone over to Culliford were the unlucky Irishman Darby Mullins and veteran mariners Nicholas Churchill and James Howe. They all looked like death warmed over and smelled like month-old codfish after their lengthy stints in Marshalsea Prison.[5]

After nearly two years of languishing in one solitary confinement hell-hole or another, Captain Kidd's opportunity for vindication had finally arrived, though he knew acquittal was a long shot. For his defense, he would continue to follow the expert advice of his four lawyers to date: James Emott and Thomas Newton in America, and now Dr. William Oldys and Mr. Lemmon in London. The highly competent Oldys had extensive courtroom experience in "pirate" cases. A graduate of New College, Oxford, where he served as a fellow from 1655 to 1671, Oldys had served as advocate of the Admiralty under King James II in the late 1680s and as the lead counsel in the 1694 trial of eight of the former Catholic king's privateers. Putting the law above the selfish interests of the Crown, the maverick lawyer refused to prosecute James's duly licensed seamen as pirates and was "summarily dismissed" by William III.[6]

Even though Captain Kidd had the experienced Dr. Oldys and truth on his side, the odds of a courtroom victory when he stepped into the Old Bailey were exceedingly long. In criminal trials in the Golden Age of Piracy, the Crown and Admiralty were both participant and referee, with the ability to impose the rules and direct the proceedings heavily in favor of the prosecution. The presiding justices in Kidd's era were appointed by the Crown and, thus, beholden for their careers to the patronage of the king, who dismissed or promoted them based upon their ability to deliver verdicts favorable to his majesty (indeed, the principled Dr. Oldys was "fired" by the Crown for this very reason). The end result was that the judges spent most of their time prodding or bullying the jury into adopting the Crown's position and recapping the evidence in a theatrical manner that forced jurors to render a guilty verdict, leading to a noose for the defendant.[7]

Being at the mercy of conservative activist judges was bad enough, but Kidd also had to defend himself without the aid of counsel, except on narrow points of law. Furthermore, he was denied the right to give evidence under oath, and none of his fellow seamen could testify on his behalf if indicted for the same offense. This meant that his cabin boy, Richard Barlycorne, who had witnessed firsthand virtually every event aboard the *Adventure Galley*, could not give testimony regarding his captain's repeated resistance to committing piracy. Though defendants could submit physical evidence and call witnesses, it still fell upon their shoulders to call and examine their own defense witnesses, cross-examine prosecution witnesses, raise procedural questions, and deliver opening and closing arguments without any help from a defense lawyer.[8]

The final major liability for Captain Kidd was that the "course of courts" of the day made it difficult for defendants to present a coherent case for an alternative to the "prosecutor's tale of malice in thought and deed."[9] During the course of a state trial, the story of the accused would not be told by the defendant but would come in bits and pieces through the Crown's biased version of events—told and retold in the indictment laid out by the prosecutor, in the eyewitnesses' testimony, in the prosecutor's closing arguments, and in the presiding judge's summation. Instead of being presented Kidd's side of the story in an orderly fashion, the jury would hear snippets of his defense only during cross-examination and in the defendant's final words.[10] Because cases were so heavily skewed in favor of the prosecution, most trials in this period lasted less than a full day. Even when twenty or thirty seamen were tried, they rarely lasted more than two days.[11]

Thus, on May 8, 1701, when Captain Kidd stepped into the Old Bailey, the atmosphere hung heavy not only with the majesty of the English state and edge-of-your-seat tension, but with the stultifying prejudice of the Crown. The preliminaries had already been completed. The court had brought forth six separate indictments: one against Kidd for the premeditated murder of William Moore, and five against Kidd and the nine other crew members for piracy on the high seas. The leader of the prosecution, Dr. George Oxenden, had also already read the king's commission empowering the court to act and empaneled a grand jury of seventeen White Englishmen. Unfortunately for Kidd, Oxenden happened to be not only perhaps the leading civil lawyer of the day but a Whig member of Parliament and the nephew of the East India Company's late governor of Bombay.[12]

Now, as Kidd set foot in the courtroom with the other accused seamen following the trial preliminaries, he immediately proceeded to shake things up. When the rheumy-eyed "Obliviscor" Sir Salathiel Lovell, the clerk of the court, asked him to hold up his hand and be sworn in, Kidd brought the proceedings to a standstill by requesting something that today we take for granted: he asked that his legal counsel be allowed to speak to a matter of law.[13] In an era when accused "pirates" were not allowed active representation by lawyers in court, Captain Kidd wanted to change the rules of the game to give himself a fighting chance. He requested that his lawyers be allowed to speak on his behalf and that the trial not commence until he was granted his French passports that would exonerate him, for he firmly believed that the papers being deliberately withheld from him were the key to his fate.[14]

For fifteen minutes, Kidd and his legal team argued back and forth with the clerk of arraigns, court recorder, and prosecutors. But in the end, they were forced to capitulate to the Crown's demands and proceed with the trial despite the lack of the crucial French passports. The clerk called "All rise" and, with grandiose formality, the sixty-three-year-old Sir Edward Ward, Lord Chief Baron of the Exchequer, and five more of England's most distinguished judges paraded into the courtroom and took their elevated seats overlooking the chamber.[15]

The clerk of arraigns now read the first charge against Kidd—which was not for piracy, as the beleaguered captain and his legal team expected, but for the premeditated murder of his chief gunner:

> The Jurors for our sovereign lord the king . . . present that William Kidd . . . not having the fear of God before his eyes, but being moved and seduced by the instigation of the devil . . . did make an assault . . . upon one William Moore in the peace of God . . . with a certain wooden bucket . . . [and] did violently, feloniously, voluntarily, and of his malice aforethought, beat and strike the aforesaid William Moore in and upon the right part of the head . . . giving [him] one mortal bruise. . . . How sayst thou, William Kidd, art thou guilty of this murder, whereof thou standest indicted, or not guilty?[16]

Kidd stood there completely stunned. Premeditated murder "by the instigation of the devil" with "malice aforethought" using not a pistol or sword but a *wooden bucket*? The charge would have been laughable if it hadn't been so gravely serious. It was clear that the prosecution had sprung the murder charge on him at the last second to catch him by surprise and ensure the noose. He had been taken into custody in Boston for the crime of piracy, not murder, and had been sent to London for trial because piracy was not a hanging offense in America, but murder was. If he was supposed to be a murderer, why had no notice of this charge been given to him in Boston "unless it were to prevent him from preparing his defense and getting his evidence ready"?[17] Most historians agree that it was preposterous for him to be "tried at once on an indictment for murder sprung upon him a few moments before . . . and be forced on the spur of the moment without conferring with any legal adviser, to conduct his own defense."[18] After two years of imprisonment and countless depositions, it was shocking enough to learn for the first time that he would be tried for the inadvertent killing of mutineer William Moore. But the Crown wasn't content with a mere manslaughter charge; to ensure a date with the hangman, it was necessary to indict him for premeditated murder.

After recovering from his initial shock, Kidd entered his plea of "Not guilty."[19] It is important to note that the Moore incident—while admittedly impulsive, excessive, and regrettable on the part of Captain Kidd—did not constitute an actual felony at the time, especially given that the victim was leading a mutiny. By law and custom, captains in the Age of Sail were granted broad and unchallenged authority in the management of their crews[20] and "it was the rarest occasion when a sea captain would be put in the dock for the murder of a member of his crew."[21] Thus, as many legal scholars have noted, the Crown's evidence against Kidd for premeditated murder was weak, but the piracy indictment was even feebler, as Bellomont himself recognized.[22] It was precisely because "the piracy case seemed so shaky that it was decided to try Kidd first on a murder charge."[23] Because the authority of sea captains was so vast, the prosecution knew that it had to prove "malice aforethought" to make the murder charge stick. If Kidd could prove to the jury what had actually happened—that he had struck Moore with the bucket in a moment of passion during an ongoing mutiny, accidentally killing him—that would be "justifiable homicide" instead of murder.[24]

Once again, Kidd's lawyers argued for the trial to not proceed until their client was granted his French passports and other papers necessary for his defense. But after a vigorous debate, Lord Chief Baron Edward Ward, a staunch Whig with close ties to the East India Company, ordered the trial for murder to proceed since it was not dependent upon the missing French passes, which did not bode well for Kidd.[25] Three members of the prosecution team—the king's solicitor-general Sir John Hawles and the Crown lawyers Mr. Knapp and Mr. Coniers—now followed one another in rapid succession to sketch out what must have been an unprecedented crime in the annals of human history: *premeditated murder by wooden bucket.* To drive home the fiction that the killing was premeditated, Hawles roared that Kidd "gave him this blow whereof he died" without "any provocation," while Coniers claimed that Kidd had abused poor innocent William Moore and killed him in a "barbarous" act with "no manner of provocation."[26]

With the Crown's narrative laid out for the jury and no rebuttal allowed for Kidd, the Crown called its two star witnesses, seaman Joseph Palmer and tippling surgeon Robert Bradinham. Two of the Crown's prosecutors, with a helping hand from Lord Chief Baron Ward, led Palmer first through the Moore incident, feeding him leading questions to present the accused in the worst possible light. Palmer started out truthfully by recounting how Kidd had confronted Moore on the deck of the *Adventure Galley*, but from there the lies multiplied exponentially. He claimed that Kidd had falsely accused the saintly gunner of trying to trick the innocent and law-abiding crew into turning pirate, despite the well-established fact that Moore was the clear-cut leader of the insurgents and they were eager and willing mutineers who required no cajoling. In Palmer's slanted retelling, Moore denied the outrageous charge, the two men got into a heated quarrel, and Kidd smacked him on the head with the bucket, from which he passed away the next day.[27]

With the basic facts and several outright lies put into the jury's ears, the prosecution set Palmer up to deliver the *coup de grâce* by asking him if Kidd had struck Moore "immediately after" their argument.

"No," replied Palmer. "He walked two or three times backward and forward upon the deck before he struck the blow."[28]

This well-rehearsed exchange between the prosecution and the witness was important because the Crown wanted to prove that Kidd had paced the deck before he struck the blow, which would preclude a sudden rush of uncontrollable anger (manslaughter) and thus clear the way for a full murder rap.[29] It is critical to note that Palmer's testimony directly contradicted his deposition taken in July 1699 in Rhode Island. Back then, the young freeman from Westchester had reported under oath that "Capt. Kidd in a *passion* struck his gunner . . . with an iron bound bucket, which blow he lived not above twenty-four hours after, but *I was not upon ye deck* when ye blow was struck [italics added]."[30] Because Kidd wasn't given sufficient time to prepare his case and was denied several critical documents, he was unable to use Palmer's contradictory deposition for his defense to show that the Crown witness was lying under oath and hadn't even been present during the Moore incident.

When the prosecution was finished, Justice Ward turned the state's witness over to Captain Kidd. Bereft of trial counsel, he now had to conduct his own cross-examination of the king's perjured testifier.[31] His only courtroom experience had been his brief time as a jury foreman in the Livingston and Chidley Brooke case way back in 1694. Unfortunately, his lack of legal training would quickly show.

Captain Kidd: "The [Dutch] ship was a league from us, and some of the men would have taken her, and I would not consent to it, and this Moore said I always hindered them making their fortunes. Was that not the reason I struck him? Was there not a mutiny on board?"

Palmer: "There was no mutiny, all was quiet."

Captain Kidd: "Was there not a mutiny because they would go and take the Dutchman?"

Palmer: "No, none at all."[32]

Kidd appeared flummoxed by Palmer's outright perjury. It is at this critical moment, when Kidd was still struggling to find his bearings as a first-time defense lawyer, that the prosecution cut in and attempted to call Bradinham to the stand.[33] But one of the jurors and the lone fair-minded justice on the panel, Sir John Powell, sensing that the prosecution was unfairly pushing Kidd around, broke in to ask questions of their own. The fifty-six-year-old Powell, a veteran Whig appointed Baron of the Exchequer in 1691, had a reputation as a humane and prudent judge of high moral character. Based upon the questioning of Powell and the sympathetic juror and Kidd's follow-up, the trio managed to demonstrate that Moore had been the ringleader of two separate mutinies. The first had occurred during the seizure and subsequent release of the English ship *Loyal Captain* commanded by Captain Howe; the second, two weeks later when a Dutch ship was sighted, Moore and the other mutineers wanted to take her, but Kidd staunchly refused, and he and the chief gunner got into an argument.[34] The evidence in the case from the various reliable eyewitnesses clearly indicated that Moore had upbraided Kidd in the altercation for not allowing "the mutineers to have their own way," which had "ended in the fatal blow."[35]

But there was a problem. Though together Justice Powell and Kidd managed to get Palmer to admit that the deponent had prevented the *Loyal Captain* from being seized by the ringleader Moore and the other mutineers, the Crown still managed to create the false impression that the *Loyal Captain* incident and Moore's death were unrelated and that the mutiny had been over for two weeks.[36] The prosecution also pushed hard to demonstrate premeditation by having Palmer emphasize that Kidd had "struck" Moore with the bucket by holding the "premeditated" weapon in his hand by the strap instead of merely throwing the bucket at him.[37] But Palmer couldn't have known this because *he hadn't even been on deck* when the fatal blow was struck. Unfortunately, Kidd didn't know that Palmer hadn't been present to witness the Moore incident and he, therefore, did not challenge him on this point.

With no way to refute the wildly exaggerated testimony, Kidd called three of his loyal crewmen as witnesses: cook Abel Owen, cabin boy Richard Barlycorne, and gunner Hugh Parrot. Unlike the well-rehearsed prosecution, he had no idea what these wildcards who had rotted away in the Marshalsea for the past year would say. But he had no choice but to roll the dice with them, for under courtroom law he could not refute Bradinham and Palmer's tall tales directly using his own testimony.[38]

Kidd started with Abel Owen, hoping to establish that mutinies had taken place both before and at the time of the Moore incident and that the death had been accidental. Even with help from Justice Powell, Owen proved a disastrous defense witness. With regard to Moore's mutiny being the reason for the inadvertent death blow, Owen made it clear that part of the crew was mutinous and for piracy, but the captain "would not give consent to it." This honest assessment looked good for Kidd, but the cook's testimony quickly broke down when Lord Chief Baron

Ward confused him by forcefully declaring that the supposed mutiny had occurred a month before Moore's death. With an eye toward the prosecution, the chief justice ensured that the word "mutiny" was restricted to the actual rebellion against Kidd during the taking of the *Loyal Captain*, and did not include the later plotting by the ringleader Moore and the mutinous portion of the crew with the Dutch ship in close proximity.[39]

Next up was seventeen-year-old Richard Barlycorne. The cabin boy swiftly backed up Kidd's narrative of the two mutinies, but once again Barons Ward and Hatsell picked apart the young Carolinian's defense. By the end, Kidd's apprentice was so confused that the only mutiny he could account for was the one that happened during the seizure of the *Loyal Captain*. Desperate to help his captain who had treated him well, Barlycorne then insisted that Moore had been sick for a month before the incident and that Kidd's blow was not the cause of his death. Bradinham was called to the stand and easily refuted this, making the boy look like an overreaching partisan "trying to press the point" to rescue his captain.[40]

By this stage of the trial, Captain Kidd and his crew had established reasonable doubt for premeditated murder and made an imperfect but still strong case for justifiable homicide on the grounds of mutiny, but Lord Chief Baron Ward would further muddy the waters and ensure that the jury reached no such conclusion. In an effort to discredit the Crown's witnesses, Kidd asked Barlycorne whether Bradinham was "in the mutiny." The cabin boy quickly answered "Yes." But once again Ward quickly shut him down by stating that there was no evidence of "a mutiny at this time," thereby ensuring that Kidd couldn't score any points with the jury.[41]

Thwarted yet again, Kidd called Hugh Parrot as a witness. The gunner, too, quickly made it clear that there were mutinies both during the taking of the *Loyal Captain* and two weeks later during the encounter with the Dutch ship and Moore incident, that Kidd had struck Moore because he "was in a passion," and that the defendants were all telling the truth. Without any pre-trial preparation or lawyer coaching, the stories of Kidd, Owen, Barlycorne, and Parrot were all in agreement, but the

Crown wasn't about to allow them to make a coherent case. When Kidd asked the gunner whether Bradinham was "in a mutiny" aboard the *Adventure Galley*, Chief Justice Ward grumbled that it was immaterial and snapped at him to get on with his defense.[42]

But Captain Kidd was not to be bullied. He was able to get Parrot to explain that Moore had repeatedly incited mutinous piracy aboard the *Adventure Galley* and that the accidental killing of the chief gunner was the result of a dispute between the two men over Kidd's refusal to seize the *Loyal Captain* and the Dutch ship two weeks later. But Ward was having none of it, and he and the other pro-Crown activist judges again quickly shut down the defense.[43]

Knowing that he was being railroaded, Kidd now jumped in to give the last word. "I have no more to say, but I had all the provocation in the world given me," he said. "I had no design to kill him. I had no malice or spleen against him."

Not wanting to end on such a forthcoming note, Ward quickly snapped, "That must be left to the jury to consider the evidence that has been given. You make out no such matter."

A sympathetic juryman, unconvinced of the Crown's unassailable case against the alleged premeditated killer, asked if perhaps Kidd had done anything to "cure" Moore's wound. But the impatient Lord Chief Baron stopped the question in its tracks: "He is to be tried according to law," the angry justice bristled. "The King's evidence hath been heard, and he has the liberty to produce what evidence he can for himself. Will you put him to produce more evidence than he can?"[44]

Bullied into submission, the sympathetic juror shrunk back in his seat and made no reply. Captain Kidd then said the heartfelt words that have echoed down the centuries.

"It was not designedly done, but in my passion," he said earnestly to the jury, "for which I am heartily sorry."[45]

The English baron didn't care for such sincere contrition in his courtroom. In his summation, he made sure that the American colonial's apology would have no chance of resonating with the jurors and that they would have no option but to rule in favor of the prosecution.[46] "His insistence that Kidd's wielding the bucket was an 'unjustifiable act,'" observed prominent New York legal scholar Richard Morris, "amounted to instructing the jury to find the prisoner guilty of murder."[47]

Seeing the writing on the wall in his crash course in English courtroom procedure, Kidd pleaded with the court for permission to present character witnesses regarding his patriotic service to the Crown during King William's War against France. But the Lord Chief Baron snapped at a bewildered Kidd that he was too late. The chief justice had already presented his summation and the case was in the hands of the jury, who then left the courtroom for their deliberations on the murder charge.[48]

WITHOUT A BREAK, the court moved on to the next case: the piracy charges against Captain Kidd and nine others for the seizure of the *Quedagh Merchant*. But just before the beginning of the first of three piracy trials, Dr. William Oldys and Mr. Lemmon quietly stepped out of the courtroom and mysteriously did not return either that day or the next.[49]

Were they recalled or coerced into standing down by the Crown or Junto? Did they abandon Kidd to his fate because they realized his case was a losing cause, or because they felt it would harm their careers? Or were they disgusted by Justice Ward and the Crown's heavy-handed control over the proceedings? Unfortunately, history is silent on these questions. But there is no question that the vanishing act of Captain Kidd's legal team must have left him profoundly dejected. Dr. Oldys was not only the most experienced defense lawyer in all of England for "piracy" cases, but the ex-Admiralty advocate was an original thinker and courtroom articulator who possessed the moral courage to put aside his political, religious, and royal motivations in a judicially challenged age and be "above all else . . . a man of the law." It was for these reasons that Kidd had wisely selected the stellar defense lawyer in the first place, and he now had no one to help him in the greatest fight of his life.[50]

While he desperately scanned the room looking for his defense lawyers, the clerk announced that he and the nine others in the dock were charged with committing piracy upon the *Quedagh Merchant* on January 30, 1698. The accused seamen all pleaded "Not Guilty," the jury was selected, and the courtroom crier announced the traditional "Twelve good men and true, stand together, and hear your evidence."[51]

Dr. Henry Newton, the advocate for the Admiralty who had been embarrassed losing the first Henry Every trial, proceeded to paint Kidd as the devil incarnate along with his degenerate crew, spewing the same type of vitriolic hyperbole used in the Salem witch trials and Every trials. Kidd's criminal actions, he snorted, "had rendered his name, to the disgrace and the prejudice of the English nation, [as] deservedly detested [and] he was now looked upon as an arch-pirate and the common enemy of mankind."[52]

Halfway through the long-winded speech, the door to the courtroom opened and a court officer announced that the first jury had reached a verdict. It had taken the twelve Englishmen a full hour to come to their decision, which was a lengthy amount of time for courtroom deliberations in Kidd's era. The clerk of arraigns ordered Captain Kidd to raise his right hand as the first jury reentered the chamber in the middle of the second trial.[53]

Clerk of Arraigns, to the jury: "Look upon the prisoner. Is he guilty of the murder whereof he stands indicted, or not guilty?"

Jury Foreman: "Guilty!"[54]

–19–

The Innocentest Person of Them All

Hearing the decision, Kidd felt as if he had been punched in the gut. Meanwhile, up in the gallery, his friends Colonel Thomas Hewetson and Captain Giles Shelley were rendered speechless. The lifelong mariners knew that convicting a sea captain of murder for striking an accidental lethal blow to a mutinous crewman was unprecedented. After nearly two years of incarceration under horrifying conditions, where he had had nothing to do but play out his forthcoming trial in his head over and over again, Kidd couldn't believe that it had taken the English justice system all of four hours to try him and condemn him to death. The shock of the verdict was severe and it took him a half hour to recover his senses. Thus, at the beginning of the first piracy trial following the return of the murder verdict, Kidd appeared "tired of mind and body"[1] and "to have lost his focus."[2]

Picking up where he had left off without skipping a beat, Dr. Newton continued with his embroidered Crown version of the fateful voyage. He falsely claimed that Kidd had been chummy with Robert Culliford on St. Mary's and had not even tried to capture the known outlaw who was now, in yet another twist of Kiddian irony, being held in custody in Newgate Prison.[3]

After Robert Culliford's return to St. Mary's in late 1698 with Kidd's mutineers, carrying a rich haul of treasure from the seizure of the *Great Muhammad*, he had found Kidd long gone. A half-year later, in August 1699, four English warships had sailed into the harbor to deliver an important message from the Crown. To Culliford's surprise, he and his men found themselves offered a royal pardon, which the pirate commodore promptly accepted. However, despite the pardon, he was arrested in late July 1700 upon his return to London and locked up in the Marshalsea, where he managed to post bail and was set free but recaptured on October 17 and stuffed into Newgate. With his pardon ruled invalid, Culliford was to be tried for the piracy of the *Great Muhammad*, but like Bradinham and Palmer he would strike a deal with the Crown to turn state's evidence.[4] As the piracy charges brought the court hearing to its second day, on May 9, Captain Kidd would come face-to-face with his old nemesis at the legendary Old Bailey.

Now Kidd listened as Newton rambled on about how he was a vicious cutthroat who had been in league with Culliford on St. Mary's. The Admiralty prosecutor claimed that at first Culliford and his pirate crew had feared that Kidd "was come to take and hang them," but that he quickly assured them that he'd "rather his soul should broil in hell than do them any harm" and that he "would be true to them." Instead of "taking Culliford," Newton claimed, Kidd lavished him with "money and ammunition, two great guns and shot, and other necessaries to fit him out to sea, that he might be in a condition the better to take and seize other innocent persons."[5]

Virtually all of this was poppycock, of course, but Newton was hell-bent on building upon the momentum of the guilty verdict and manipulating the "public sphere" through the court record, as was done in the second Every trial.[6] After calling for the jury to find Kidd guilty of injustice to "the English nation,"[7] the Crown once again called forth Bradinham and Palmer to back up the pack of outright lies and minor exaggerations, carefully sprinkled with some undeniable truths to lend the proper verisimilitude. The Crown's prosecutors first led Bradinham through a detailed account of the voyage. To put his captain in the worst possible light, the surgeon, taking well-practiced cues from his lawyers, made the Red Sea incident with Captain Barlow and the Great Mughal's treasure fleet into a piratical act (it wasn't); claimed that Kidd had cruelly kidnapped Captain Parker and the Portuguese linguist Don Antonio of the *Mary* (they never filed *any* complaint against Kidd, and impressing skilled seamen was standard operating procedure in the Age of Sail); and stated that Kidd, not William Moore and the mutineers, had barbarously tortured the detained supercargo, seamen, and passengers of captured vessels (Kidd must have been shocked at the brazenness of the prosecution to make such outlandish claims).[8]

Afterward, Palmer was called to the witness box. His examination was similar to that of his fellow perjurer; however, he slipped up at one point and accidentally mentioned the critical French passport taken from the *Rouparelle*. Contrary to the claims of the prosecution, they were *not* a figment of Kidd's imagination.

Joseph Palmer: "[Captain Kidd] took her under French colors, and hailed her in French; and this Monsieur LeRoy was to pass for captain, and he showed his French pass, and—"

He was stopped right there as Coniers jumped in quickly to contain the damage. "Give an account of his personating the captain," interjected the Crown prosecutor. "Who ordered him to do so?"

Palmer: "Captain Kidd . . . and they hailed him in French, and he came aboard, and he had a French pass."[9]

So, despite his extensive pre-trial coaching by the prosecution, Joseph Palmer slipped up *not once but twice* by testifying under oath that he had seen with his own eyes one of the two French passports Kidd and his lawyers had been making such a fuss about. Yet, for some inexplicable reason, no one in the courtroom appeared to notice this momentous revelation except the prosecution, which quickly covered it up.[10]

Soon thereafter, Palmer went in for the kill. Telling his most egregious lie of the first piracy trial, he claimed that Kidd and

Culliford—the man who had stolen everything from the accused a decade earlier—had never been adversaries at all but, in fact, had been bosom drinking buddies on St. Mary's.[11] The testimony, though contrived, proved damaging. In actuality, Kidd and Culliford had never come within a hundred yards of each other while on the island; but, most importantly, there is *no logical reason* they would have been on friendly terms or that Kidd would have given Culliford men, weapons, and critical supplies *without receiving anything in return*, especially after Culliford had stolen his *Blessed William* and hard-earned £2,000 at Antigua in 1690. The two mariners were enemies, and the only way Kidd could benefit from Culliford was through his capture. Which is precisely what the privateer commander attempted; but his mutinous crew refused, as testified by multiple reliable witnesses who did not turn state's evidence.[12]

Kidd returned to the topic of the missing French passports. Though he knew at this point that justice would be denied him here in England, he still fought to establish their presence, knowing that without this crucial evidence he stood no chance of exonerating himself, at least in the eyes of history.[13] As Kidd biographer Dunbar Maury Hinrichs notes, despite the "monstrous perversion of justice," Captain Kidd "was still defending his life, his name, his honor."[14]

Captain Kidd, to Lord Chief Baron Ward: "I ask him [Palmer], whether I had no French passes."

Palmer: "Indeed, Captain Kidd, I cannot tell. I did hear him say, that he had French passes, but I never saw them."

Captain Kidd: "And did you hear nobody else say so?"

Palmer: "No."

Captain Kidd: "I had a commission to take the French, and pirates; and in order to do that, I came up with two ships, that had French passes both of them. I called you all a-deck to consult, and did not a great many of the men go aboard? Did not you go? You know, Mr. Palmer, I would have given these ships to them again, but you would not. You all voted against it."

Palmer, cleverly deflecting the question by pointing to the Armenian merchant Coji Babba in the courtroom: "This man offered you 20,000 rupees for the ship, and you refused it."

Captain Kidd: "Did not I ask, where will you carry this ship? And you said, we will make a prize of her. We will carry her to Madagascar."

Lord Chief Baron Ward: "What was that pretense of a French pass that was onboard the *Quedagh Merchant*?"

Palmer: "I saw none."

Captain Kidd: "But you have heard of it."

Palmer: "I have heard of it, but never saw it."

Justice Powell, sympathetically: "Captain Kidd, can you make it appear there was a French pass aboard the *Quedagh Merchant*?"

Captain Kidd: "My lord, these men say they heard several say so."[15]

This was a crafty maneuver by the neophyte legal practitioner, though it ultimately failed to work. As American legal scholar Alan Dershowitz writes, "Kidd, like other intelligent defendants, managed to circumvent [the court's] restrictions by a clever ploy, well-illustrated in the transcripts of these trials. By conducting the cross-examination himself and by loading the questions with factual assertions, Kidd managed to present his own account of events [i.e., the presence of the French passes] without actually testifying. . . . The real injustice lay in the fact that the French passes did, in fact, exist."[16]

Kidd then called Captain Edward Davis to the witness stand to verify the existence of the French passports. The crusty old buccaneer had wrangled with the Crown before: he was tried but cleared of piracy charges in return for donating £300 ($105,000 today) toward the building of a college in Virginia in 1692, which would become The College of William & Mary. Although Davis testified that he was aware of the French passports, the judicial activist Ward quickly undercut his testimony by asserting that he could not know for sure that the passes had "any relation to the *Quedagh Merchant*." With a cue from Kidd, Davis then tried to circumvent Ward's bullying by explaining how crewmate Captain Elms had told him that the documents were indeed the French passports in question. But unfortunately, the testimony still went for naught. Davis—who had sailed with both Captain Kidd and the legendary pirate William Dampier, bestselling author of *A New Voyage Round the World* and the toast of the London literati—was forced to admit that he did not know with absolute certainty the relation of the French papers to any particular ship.[17]

One of the critical arguments that the Crown justices and prosecutors took advantage of was that Kidd had not condemned either the *Rouparelle* or *Quedagh Merchant* in any prize court. On several occasions, Ward and others reprimanded him for not condemning the ships as lawful prizes, as he had done with the French banker in New York in 1696. Kidd had reasoned that he could not bring his two legal seizures into a prize court because of the "mutiny in my ship." But he failed to make clear that there were no Vice-Admiralty Courts in India at the time; that his official instructions from Bellomont and the investors were to take his prizes to the North American colonies; and that he had been on his way home to America with the vessels to have them judicated as lawful prizes when most of his men mutinied on St. Mary's.[18]

Ward delivered his charge to the jury, rehashing the Crown's talking points in a fiery oration worthy of Cotton Mather. He focused his wrath on the *Adventure Galley* articles (standard democratic privateering articles, which Ward made out to be pirate articles); Kidd's cozying up to Culliford (never happened); and the taking of the *Quedagh* (a legitimate prize carrying a French passport).[19] The Lord Chief Baron's summation was "long, eloquent, and tendentious,"[20] with a mixture of outright lies and more subtle but equally damaging exaggerations taking up half of the seven typewritten pages in State Trials, Volume 14. But Ward's slickest judicial maneuver, a true *coup de grâce*, was when he undercut the accused's best defense, the French passports, in what he knew was a bald-faced lie. "As to the French passes," he sniffed, "there is nothing of that appears by any proof, and for ought I can see, none saw them but himself, if there were ever any."[21]

The jury retired for its deliberations. With the momentum all on the side of the prosecution, this time the panel of shopkeepers and tradesmen took only a half hour to return a verdict. Each juryman was identified by name and polled whether the verdict was unanimous.[22]

Clerk of Arraigns to the jury, after asking Kidd to raise his right hand: "How say you, is he guilty of the piracy whereof he stands indicted, or not guilty?"

Jury Foreman: "Guilty!"

Kidd shook his head, rankling inside. The question was then asked in reference to each of the other nine defendants. The three young apprentices were cleared of the piracy charge, since they had had no choice but to obey their masters, while the other six were found guilty. Captain Kidd, who now stood as the most famous convicted pirate of all time, lay under two miserable death sentences.[23]

By the end of the second trial, it was late afternoon and Kidd was disgusted and exhausted. The court proceeded to indict him and the other nine defendants on four more counts of piracy. These included the piratical seizure of the *Mary* (where Kidd forced Moore and his gang to give back what they had stolen); the *Rouparelle* (French passport); an unnamed Moorish ketch (likely either did not happen, or involved Dekkar's *November* acting alone since it was sailing independently from the *Adventure Galley* at the time); and the unnamed Portuguese galliot (a clear-cut piratical act by the *November* but Kidd's role remained ambiguous). The court was then adjourned until eight o'clock the following morning, Friday, May 9.[24]

With his head hanging low, the demoralized American colonial shambled back to Newgate in chains along with the other odiferous condemned men. But with nothing left to fight for except his honor, he would come out swinging the next day against the English Empire like a back-street New York brawler.

WHEN CAPTAIN KIDD entered the Old Bailey the next morning, Lord Chief Baron Ward was nowhere to be found, and neither was the lone voice of impartiality on the judicial panel, Justice Powell. After being condemned to death twice over and stewing all night long, Kidd had lost the last thimbleful of respect he had for Mother England and was one bitter and angry man who no longer had anything to lose. In his mind, English justice was a joke *and* a lie. On this historic day, May 9, 1701, he had decided that if he did nothing else, he would turn the tables on his perjured accusers and shame the Crown judges for posterity. Today, he would show the packed gallery who he believed were the real scoundrels.

The trials for the piratical seizure of the *Mary* and *Rouparelle* were similar to that of the *Quedagh Merchant* the day before. Once again, new juries had to be selected for each trial, so the testimony from Bradinham and Palmer had to be repeated. This time it was prosecutor Knapp who led the jury through the major events of the voyage. Bradinham went first, regurgitating the same pack of lies carefully sprinkled with some truth from the day before, but Kidd quickly went on the attack.[25]

He hammered Bradinham for testifying against his fellow shipmates when he had taken a share of the *Quedagh* prize money, being drunk belowdecks most of the time aboard the *Adventure Galley*, stealing the surgeon's chest, and voluntarily joining Culliford to commit acts of piracy.[26] Palmer was then called to the bar to rehash the neat-and-tidy narrative devised by Crown prosecutors. Kidd pointed out several inconsistencies in his testimony as well, providing ample support for his arguments. But with the Crown-appointed justices continuing to act as agents for the prosecution, he was still unable to raise significant doubt in the jurors' minds.[27] By this time the other seamen, too, had had quite enough of the English state's duplicitous stage show, with even young apprentice William Jenkins snapping at one of the perjurers, "How can you attest these wicked lies?"[28]

Desperate for some way to break through to the jury, Kidd called the Royal Navy officers Colonel Thomas Hewetson and Thomas Cooper as character witnesses. Kidd had fought with them in the Caribbean against the French, and he had remained good friends with Hewetson over the years. Hewetson, anxious to help his old friend, came right out before the prosecution could disrupt his train of thought and stated under oath that Captain Kidd had been "a mighty man" fighting alongside him in the West Indies a decade earlier. "He was with me in two engagements against the French, and fought as well as any man I ever saw. We had six Frenchmen to deal with, and we had only mine and his ship."[29]

"Do you think I was a pirate?" Kidd then asked him.

Colonel Hewetson: "I know his men would have gone a-pirating, and he refused it, and his men seized upon his ship. And when he went this voyage [to the Indian Ocean], he consulted me, and told me they had engaged him in such an expedition; and I told him he had enough already, and might be contented with what he had. And he said, it was his own inclination, but my Lord Bellomont told him, if he did not go the voyage, that there were great men, and they would stop his brigantine in the river, if he did not go."

Justice Turton: "If he had kept to the honest design of that expedition, he had done very well. Did you apprehend that his intention in that undertaking was to be a pirate?"

Colonel Hewetson: "No, my lord. He told me his business was to go a-cruising, and surprise pirates."

Solicitor-General Hawles: "Did he tell you he had no such design?"

Colonel Hewetson: "Yes, he said he would be shot to death before he would do any such thing."[30]

Kidd then called naval officer Thomas Cooper to the stand. He, too, testified to Kidd's valor in the West Indian campaign fighting the French: "I was aboard the *Lion*, and this Captain Kidd brought his ship from a place that belonged to the Dutch, and brought her into the king's service at the beginning of the war, about ten years ago; and he took service under the colonel; and we fought Monsieur DuCasse a whole day, and, I thank God, we got the better of it; and Captain Kidd behaved himself very well in the face of his enemies."[31]

Four character witnesses appeared to speak on behalf of Captain Kidd at his trial, all of them Royal Navy men or auxiliaries. In addition to Colonel Hewetson and Officer Cooper, Kidd had called Captains Humphrys and Bond, with whom he had fought against DuCasse in the Caribbean, as character witnesses the day before. Captain Humphrys stated under oath that Kidd "had the applause" of Governor-General Codrington in the "late war," while Captain Bond confirmed that he had been "very useful" against the French in the West Indies.[32] That these four naval officers took the time and trouble to come all the way to the Old Bailey and speak on his behalf, knowing full well that to do so was not only unpopular but might jeopardize their naval careers, was a testament to their character—and Captain Kidd's. The problem was that his heroic actions fighting DuCasse and the French naval forces had happened more than a decade earlier. As Captain Charles Johnson (pseudonym of journalist Nathanial Mist) wrote, Colonel Hewetson "gave him an extraordinary character . . . but this being several years before the facts mentioned in the indictment were committed, proved no manner of service to the prisoner on his trial."[33]

Through much of the third trial, Captain Kidd kept his eyes fixed accusingly on his perjured ship's surgeon.[34] "Kidd found Bradinham particularly repulsive," noted one historian.[35] Toward the end of the trial, he accused the heavy-drinking officer who had stolen the *Adventure Galley*'s medical kit of lying to save his own neck, but the Crown's justices once again struck back immediately.

Captain Kidd: "Mr. Bradinham, are you not promised your life to take away mine?"

Justice Sir John Turton: "He is not bound to answer that question. He is very fit to be made an evidence for the king. Perhaps there can be no other than such as are in his circumstances."[36]

With the dagger driven in deep, Turton now longwindedly summed up the third trial (and second for piracy) for the jury. Once again, Kidd and the other accused seamen were branded "Hostes humani generis, the enemies to all mankind," and the summation was gift-wrapped so that the twelve jurymen had no choice but to render a guilty verdict.[37] Kidd and six of his sailors were found guilty of piracy on the high seas, while young Barlycorne and the other two apprentices were ruled not guilty for being mere servants to their shipboard masters.[38] Captain Kidd was now under three sentences of death—with one trial remaining.

The fourth trial was for piracy against both an unnamed Moorish ship four leagues from Calicut in late December 1697 and the unnamed Portuguese galliot twelve leagues from Calicut in early February 1698. Once the jury was impaneled, Kidd challenged the court. The Crown, low on jurymen and hardly concerned about fairness toward Captain Kidd, had tried to foist several jurors upon the court who had already brought home a guilty verdict in the murder trial. Even in Kidd's day, this was considered prejudicial, and the embarrassed court was forced to produce several new jurors.[39] The prosecutors then gave their opening statements and led Bradinham through the fourth retelling of the incidents, on behalf of the new jury.[40]

When the good doctor finally got to the Moorish ketch that Captain Kidd had supposedly seized four leagues off Calicut, a ship in which Bradinham and Palmer could neither recall a name nor a captain yet meticulously listed the "thirty bales of sugar-candy, tobacco, sugar, and myrrh," Kidd erupted.[41] Recall that at this point of the voyage, in the winter of 1697–1698, the *November* (captained by Skipper Mitch Dekkar and aboard which Bradinham and Palmer served) often sailed independently from the *Adventure Galley* (captained by Kidd); and by February 1698, she would sail independently of both Kidd's *Galley* and the *Adventure Prize* (captained by Henry Bullen before his suspicious death in March). Many scholars maintain that all Kidd did was trade with the Moorish ketch, or, if she was captured, that the seizure was performed by the *November* acting alone, since Kidd had put Bradinham, Palmer, and other troublemakers aboard this vessel.[42] Most importantly, there is no record of a Moorish ketch being taken by *any* eyewitness except the two perjured mutineer-pirates who sailed with Culliford. Furthermore, the East India Company, which kept detailed records of captures at sea within its sphere of influence, never reported the taking of *any* Moorish ship by Captain Kidd in December 1697, nor did the

Company report a *single one* of the nine-to-twelve other unnamed Moorish vessels Bradinham and Palmer *claimed* Kidd seized off the Malabar Coast.[43]

Bradinham and Palmer's lies, repeated over and over again, truly made Kidd's skin crawl. Toward the end of the third piracy trial on the second day, he roared at them, "Because I would not turn pirate, you rogues, you would make me one."[44] What is fascinating about this angrily delivered line is that it encapsulates Captain Kidd's entire frustrating case in a nutshell. The New York privateer had refused to take part in piracy in 1690, and he did so again in 1697–1698—because he was not an outlaw pirate and had never had any aspirations to be a pirate, despite his admittedly roguish buccaneering background.

However, despite his anti-piratical by-the-book nature, he was technically on the hook for the Portuguese galliot seized by Dekkar and the *November*, where he either looked the other way or plain gave up challenging his crew. He knew he bore at least some responsibility for his unruly seamen's actions since he had not lifted a finger to stop them when they boarded and pillaged a vessel friendly to England. According to Joseph Palmer, the haul from this small Catholic prize ship amounted to "two chests of Indian goods, two chests of opium, some rice, butter, wax, and iron."[45] Compared with the booty taken from the *Quedagh Merchant*, this was a trifling sum indeed. But in this case, Palmer appears to have given an accurate description of what was taken from the ship, as the seizure of the Portuguese galliot was independently verified by the East India Company and other deponents besides the two perjurors.[46]

By late in the fourth trial, Kidd was so disgusted with the sham proceeding that he refused to play along with the Crown's one-sided morality play. "It signifies nothing to ask any questions," he chided the justices. "A couple of rogues will swear anything."[47] Moments later, when it came time to present his defense, he said simply, "I will not trouble the court any more, for it is a folly."[48]

After Justice Turton gave the usual heavily biased summation, the jury retired for its deliberations. This time, the contingent of White working-class Englishmen returned a mere ten minutes later. Kidd and three others—the unlucky Irish mutineer Darby Mullins and the loyalists Hugh Parrot and Gabriel Loffe—were found guilty. After surviving three piracy trials, the three young apprentices would be eligible for release, pending payment of their prison fees.[49]

It is at this stage of the historic trial, late in the afternoon of the second day, that something remarkable transpired. As the chatters of the spectators navigated through the gallery upon the reading of the individual verdicts, and while Hewetson, Shelley, and others sympathetic to Kidd quietly groaned, the barred door leading to Newgate Prison opened, and in walked none other than Robert Culliford, along with two other accused pirates. They stood indicted for the taking of the *Great Muhammad* in the fall of 1698.[50]

Kidd couldn't believe his eyes. Standing shackled before him was the man who had destroyed his life two times over. He had not seen his nemesis since June 1698, when Culliford had sailed out of St. Mary's harbor with ninety of his crew members for the Red Sea. As Kidd watched Culliford saunter into the chamber like a game rooster, he wished he had been made aware that his former first mate had been incarcerated in London for months, for he would have called him to the stand to refute Bradinham and Palmer's lies. Now it was too late. The Crown, having obtained its conviction of him and his men, did not care a whit about Culliford's version of events.[51]

Kidd quietly watched as Culliford entered his plea of not guilty for the *Great Muhammad* attack, and, a moment later, for the seizure of the *Satisfaction,* for which he was also indicted.[52] After everything Kidd had been through, it would now be some consolation to have a front-row seat and witness Culliford's conviction. But then a bewigged lawyer entered the courtroom, spoke a moment to the chief justice, and rose to the bar to announce before the spellbound gallery that his client Robert Culliford wanted to change his plea. The judges agreed to accept the retraction. Following his lawyer's instructions, Culliford changed his plea from not guilty to guilty on all counts, claiming that he had surrendered to Captain Thomas Warren (the nephew of Commodore Warren) on St. Mary's under the proclamation of pardon.[53]

It was a gamble, but to take advantage of the king's most gracious pardon Robert Culliford had to plead guilty, admit to being a pirate, agree to testify later against other pirates, and then keep his fingers crossed that the Crown would not go back on its word by rejecting his protection under the king's proclamation. Ironically, he would eventually be called upon to testify against his and Kidd's old shipmate Samuel Burgess, who worked for Frederick Philipse and would by July 1701 be charged with illegally trading with pirates on Madagascar.[54]

With Kidd and the other exhausted defendants forced to sit there and watch, Culliford and the other accused men were swiftly tried and found guilty. However, the "judgment against Culliford was respited." Kidd was stunned when he saw that his nemesis was the only one, besides the apprentices, who would walk away from the Old Bailey as a free man. However, he had scant time to ponder his miserable fate as the clerks moved Culliford to one side, while Kidd and the other convicted pirate prisoners were paraded to the bar in the Crown's final act of retribution against him and his seamen.[55]

The sentence was delivered by the esteemed advocate for the Admiralty, Dr. George Oxenden:

> You the prisoners at the bar, you have been severally indicted for several piracies and robberies, and you William Kidd for murder. You have been tried by the laws of the land, and convicted; and nothing now remains, but that sentence be passed according to the law. And the sentence of the law is this: You shall be taken from the place where you are, and be carried to the place from whence you came, and from thence to the place of execution, and there be severally hanged by your necks until you be dead. And the Lord have mercy on your souls.[56]

Crestfallen at the outcome, embittered by the unfairness of it all with the unrepentant pirate Culliford going scot-free, and thinking of how horrifying and financially ruinous his judgment would be to his dear wife and daughters, Captain Kidd now gave the last word, scoring for himself and posterity one last mini-victory "over the machine dead set on killing him."[57]

"My Lord, it is a very hard sentence," pronounced Captain Kidd for the history books. "For my part, I am the innocentest person of them all, only I have been sworn against by perjured persons."[58]

And with that, the trial of the century was over.

–20–

The Snap of the Rope

The day after the trial, May 10, 1701, the Crown moved forward aggressively with plans for Captain Kidd's high-profile execution. The Admiralty's advocate, Dr. Oxenden, met with the king regarding the trial and its verdict. With the final word on the fate of England's condemned, William III held the royal prerogative to bestow clemency upon those he wished. But as he studied the list of convicted men, he gave the thumbs-down for Captain Kidd, along with John Eldridge and the unlucky Irishman Darby Mullins. Meanwhile, the remaining prisoners would be kept in suspense, praying for "the royal favor" at Execution Dock that might or might not end with a hangman's rope.[1]

If Kidd thought he could live out his final days in quiet seclusion, thinking back with fond remembrance to all the good times he had shared with Sarah and the girls, he was in for a rude awakening. He would now be pestered endlessly by a God-fearing charlatan in the Cotton Mather mold. His name was Paul Lorrain, and as the so-called "Ordinary of Newgate" he was the chaplain responsible for the spiritual comfort of the prison's condemned inmates during their final days on earth. Having previously served as a copyist to Samuel Pepys, the Secretary to the

Admiralty, he had for the past three years made his living not so much by praying for the souls of Newgate's condemned prisoners, or giving them religious instruction, but by profiting from their grisly deaths.[2]

A French Huguenot and self-described "presbyter of the Church of England," Lorrain steadfastly held the office of Ordinary of Newgate from 1700 to 1719—amassing a fortune of £5,000 ($1,750,000 today) by peddling the intimate details of the final days of imprisonment and last dying words of England's most notorious criminals. As one of the perks of his office, he held a lucrative monopoly on the publication of his "official" *Accounts of the Behavior, Confessions, and Dying Words* of Newgate's condemned prisoners. His *Accounts* presented hastily cobbled-together biographies of the criminals, the confessions of their sins since they were *always* presumed to be guilty, and their last dying words prior to execution at Tyburn or Execution Dock.[3] These popular broadsheets sold in the thousands to a voracious London reading public with "a taste for sensational crimes." Usually hawked the day after a public execution, they were affordably priced between three and six pence, according to length—with most of the money pocketed by the entrepreneurial Frenchman.[4]

Lorrain's primary mission was to break the criminal by forcing him to confess his sins and salve his immortal soul, thereby robbing "him of his autonomy" and preventing "the sort of bravura performance that, indeed, all too often occurred at the gallows."[5] Not surprisingly, he was sometimes met with scorn. One Scottish pirate "famously threatened to kick him downstairs,"[6] and a skeptical playwright snarkily referred to Newgate's prisoners as "Lorrain's Saints," based on the chaplain's remarkable ability to obtain guilty confessions and rehabilitate lapsed Christians.[7] His success in peddling death eventually led to competition from professional writers like Daniel Defoe, the author of *Robinson Crusoe*, *Moll Flanders*, and *The King of Pirates*, the latter about the mythical Henry Every.[8] Though he claimed not to be interested in profit, Lorrain changed publishers at least five times during his career and published his broadsheets earlier and earlier following an execution to beat his competition to the punch.[9] He also took out advertisements in the Tory *Post Boy* and other newspapers, warning his readers against "sham papers" and alerting them when his reliable "true accounts" would come out in print.[10]

For Paul Lorrain, Captain Kidd represented a gold mine. As historian Robert Ritchie writes of the huckster of death, not only did his infamous new prisoner give the chaplain the opportunity "to bring a tormented soul into proper condition to meet its maker, such a famous criminal also meant a substantial opportunity for a big sale of his account." In fact, Lorrain had already arranged for a special advertisement promoting the forthcoming last dying confession and hanging of Captain Kidd in the *Post Boy*, to preemptively strike at the competition before the publication of his actual *Account*.[11]

Lorrain's first visit with the New York privateer and his convicted seamen occurred on Saturday, May 10, the day after the final piracy trial. Still smarting from his courtroom debacle, Kidd was in no mood to listen as Lorrain admonished him and the others to examine their villainous lives and repent their terrible crimes. Over the next week, Lorrain continued to hound him and the other ten men to confess their sins before God. While the sad-sack Irishman Darby Mullins and the other seamen would all eventually succumb to Lorrain's fervent exhortations and outright bullying, Captain Kidd continued to insist on his innocence and rebuffed him at every turn. In response, the Ordinary of Newgate claimed that the convicted "pirate" had a "hard, unmelted heart." The two argued back and forth all week, until Kidd, to get Lorrain to stop harassing him, finally agreed that if he did not receive a pardon through the intervention of his sponsors or by order of the king, he would confess at "The Hanging Tree."[12]

On Saturday, May 17, the Admiralty issued a Latin precept setting Kidd and the other condemned men's date with the hangman for May 23, at Execution Dock in Wapping.[13] While the gallows at Tyburn was the "ultimate location of punishment and site of state power," Wapping was where the Admiralty projected England's maritime authority. It was here, along the banks of the Thames, where all pirates, both the famous ones like Captain Kidd and the not-so-famous like Henry Every's six convicted "mutineers," made their final speeches and engaged in "the Marshal's dance" for the amusement of a rowdy, inebriated, jostling London mob.[14]

The next day, May 18, on the morning of the Sabbath, Captain Kidd found himself sitting in the Condemned Pew of Newgate Chapel, surrounded by gawking Londoners who had paid Lorrain handsomely to watch the celebrity pirate conduct his final prayers before his grisly public hanging. The Ordinary of Newgate, feeling the momentousness of the occasion as the Wapping endgame drew near, chose to preach from Ecclesiastes 12:13 to the packed house. The overarching theme was that the fear of God made men wise and allowed them "to obtain thereby both a present and eternal reward." For the afternoon sermon, Lorrain hammered home a New Testament lesson from 2 Corinthians 5:10, which he directed specifically at the sea captain and the other prisoners. All men must "appear before the Judgment Seat of Christ," he exhorted them, "so they would return to God with their whole heart; and so obtain their great pardon sealed before they were called to the great Bar of God's justice." The Ordinary concluded by commanding Kidd and the others to follow through with their "indispensable obligation" by owning up to their sins, making abundantly clear "the severe wrath and terrible judgment of God which would most certainly fall upon them as sinners unless they speedily and sincerely forsake[d] their evil ways and repent[ed]."[15]

Newspaper accounts of the period suggest that Kidd was at peace in his final days, despite his anger over his undeserved fate and Lorrain's badgering. One broadsheet proclaimed that he didn't seem "to be in any way terrified or afraid at the approaches of death." In truth, Kidd thought about his wife and daughters almost constantly. What troubled him most of all were "the sad tidings" and ill treatment his wife would receive from her fellow New Yorkers due to his notoriety, as well as the financial suffering she, Elizabeth, and little Sarah would be subjected to by the Crown from his conviction and hanging as a felonious criminal.[16]

The date of execution—Friday, May 23, 1701—finally arrived. In the morning, Kidd was herded along with the other prisoners into the chapel.

Lorrain took a final crack at arm-twisting him, along with the other condemned men whom the cranky chaplain believed had given tepid confessions, to come clean regarding their heinous crimes and repent. After delivering his second sermon in the early afternoon, he then left Kidd and set off for Execution Dock to make final preparations.[17] Later that day, the Ordinary of Newgate, who got Kidd's backstory mostly wrong in his *Account of the Behavior, Confessions, and Dying Words of Captain W. Kidd*, chronicled his final "exhortations" given to the American colonial:

> I was afraid the hardness of Captain Kidd's heart was still unmelted. I therefore applied myself with particular exhortations to him, and laid the judgment of God against impenitent and hardened sinners, as well as his tender mercies to those that were true and sincere penitents, very plainly before him. To all which he readily assented and said that he truly repented of all his sins, and forgave all the world.[18]

Captain Kidd had merely told Lorrain what he wanted to hear to get him to stop harassing him. For a few hours later, when the two men met again at "The Tree," the self-described "innocentest person of them all" was no longer in a forgiving mood toward the English Empire that had destroyed him and his good name. While he was willing to "forgive all the world" to appease Paul Lorrain, he was not about to take responsibility for offenses far more attributable to others than himself, or to plead for forgiveness for imaginary sins.[19]

At the scaffold, he would tell the whole world just what he thought of English justice and who he believed would stand as the real rogues before the judgment of history. Now, by the blood of his heroes Drake and Morgan, the entire world would finally hear his true story, the one that had been suppressed at the Old Bailey.

This time, he truly would not stop fighting until he had taken his last dying breath.

At a quarter to two that afternoon, the key of Keeper Fells ground into the iron lock of Captain Kidd's cell for the final time. To build up the suspense, the London morning newspapers claimed Kidd was offering £10,000 ($3,500,000 today) in return for a tell-all about his Junto backers and the sparing of his life.[20] From his cell, he was taken under heavy guard by Keeper Fells and his men to a trio of waiting horse-drawn prison wagons. As he emerged from the prison gates, he and the other nine prisoners were swarmed by a howling mob of Londoners gathered on the street to accompany them on their westward procession to Execution Dock.[21]

Once he and the other prisoners were stuffed into the wooden, steel-barred, black-draped wagons, the grim procession formed up. The Admiralty officials, the sheriff of London, and his deputies took positions in front of, behind, and next to the prison wagons. As the crowd pressed in all around Captain Kidd, the English officials and an armed guard struggled to keep the rubbernecking public at bay. Once the raucous crowd was brought under control and the ten condemned men were secured, the procession moved out.[22]

In the vanguard rode the Admiralty's deputy marshal in an open-topped carriage, carrying over his shoulder the silver oar symbolizing the august authority of the Lords of the Admiralty. Behind the lead carriage came the powdered and bewigged John Cheeke, Marshal of the Admiralty, mounted on horseback, and other Crown officials. Following in the three black-draped wagons were Captain Kidd and the other prisoners. The mounted sheriffs and deputies preceded and followed the prisoners. The procession headed toward the City of London and the hanging scaffold three miles away, situated along the eastern foreshore of the Thames in Wapping.[23]

The parade of English officials and condemned wretches clattered down the dirt and cobbled streets, flanked and trailed by a growing crowd that plied Kidd and the other prisoners with rum, whiskey, and beer. The solemn cortège and carnivalesque procession of followers headed down broad Cheapside flanked by tall buildings, past St. Paul's

Cathedral where refurbishing was still in progress after the Great 1666 Fire, past the Royal Exchange and the pump at Aldgate, past the East India Company headquarters on Leadenhall, and finally along the Minories toward Tower Hill, where the huge stone fortress with its square battlements stood resolutely by the Thames.[24]

Soon the procession rumbled down through Wapping, the squalid seamen's neighborhood. As the prison wagons rattled over the cobblestones of Catherine Street toward Execution Dock, Kidd saw the pleasure boats jockeying close to the north shore and ferrying people to prime locations for witnessing death. He was only a stone's throw from where he had lived in 1695–1696 when he had sailed to London to obtain his privateering commission. One last time, he took in London Bridge steep with the tall buildings along its great piers and the late-afternoon sunlight glinting off the Southwark rooftops.[25]

He soon reached Execution Dock. A huge crowd stood waiting on the narrow streets, Wapping Stairs, and the wide foreshore, a tidal mud flat that at high tide would become submerged. The foul smell of the polluted river and tenements rose to his nostrils. He looked up at the gallows, his last podium to vent his anger and tell his story. The scaffold—a single horizontal wooden crossbeam held up by two vertical beams and a raised platform—stood on the muddy river bottom below the high-water mark. The hanging platform was sturdy enough to hold the doomed men, the executioner, several magistrates, and Paul Lorrain.[26]

The funereal cortège came to a halt before the muddy flats beyond the last tenement along the fetid Ratcliff Highway. In grim silence, the ten condemned men climbed down from the wagons. Paul Lorrain stood next to the gallows with the other ministers, ready to guide the convicted men through their last moments on earth. During the Golden Age of Piracy, large numbers of people flocked to public pirate executions, but the turnout for Captain Kidd was unprecedented. The crowd was an eclectic mixture of merchants, military officers, ministers, and shopkeepers rubbing elbows with drunken sailors, dockworkers, apprentices, barkeeps, housewives, laundresses, and street urchins. A hefty percentage of London's criminal underclass rounded out the events: highwaymen, pickpockets, prostitutes, "harpies who preyed on pig-tailed Jack Tar ashore," and hooligans who got cheap thrills flinging dead dogs or cats covered in excrement into the crowd.[27]

The last-minute royal pardons arrived just as the ten condemned men assembled at the foot of the gallows. Admiralty Marshal John Cheeke stepped forward and cut out the six prisoners whom the king had spared: three of Kidd's loyalists—Hugh Parrot, Gabriel Loffe, and Abel Owen—and three who had mutinied over and gone a-pirating with Culliford: Nicholas Churchill, James Howe, and Robert Hickman (John Eldridge had been pardoned the night before). That left Captain Kidd of New York to be hanged with the luckless Irishman Darby Mullins and two French corsairs, Jean DuBois and Pierre Mingueneau, sentenced from another piracy trial. Slowly, the four men set to die climbed the stairs of the gallows. After standing each of them under their nooses, the executioner pinned their elbows behind them, fastened ropes about their wrists, and looped the nooses around their necks.[28]

It was now a quarter to six in the evening.

Addressing the crowd, the marshal recited the crimes, gave the order of execution, and then stepped aside to allow each of the condemned men to make their final speech. The crowd hushed as an orangish-red glow bathed the Southwark rooftops across the Thames behind Captain Kidd, Darby Mullins, and the two Frenchmen. The Crown expected the condemned to make the usual repentant remarks at the gallows: one part admission of guilt, another part warning to the sailors in the crowd to steer clear of piracy and wickedness. The goal was for them to *condemn themselves* in their own words. This would reaffirm the English state's position that the trial and sentence were just and fair, and that those found guilty were criminals who had sinned against not only England but God Almighty, and were now publicly repenting.[29]

But sometimes executions did not go according to the Crown's neat and tidy script. Regarded as popular heroes by much of the public and especially the lower classes, pirates and other spirited rogues could turn their solemn date with the hangman into a final act of triumph, which Lorrain and the Crown deplored. With eight special execution days per year, the English authorities found it appalling when pirate executions became celebratory pageants that encouraged the emulation of sea robbery instead of serving as a deterrent.[30]

Darby Mullins went first with his speech, followed by the French pirates. The sad-sack Irishman from Londonderry gave the Crown, Admiralty, and wealthy of London the penitent narrative these powerful interests wanted to hear. He issued a warning to sailors "to avoid covetousness and all vain and idle company, lest ruin and misery overtook them before they were aware."[31] This made Lorrain ecstatic. The two Catholic Frenchmen, scrawny and disheveled in their prison rags, had nothing to say.[32]

Then came the moment the crowd had been waiting for, and everyone hushed before the well-dressed sea captain in his clean waistcoat, breeches, and chestnut-colored wig. Well-lubricated but "in full possession of his faculties," the feisty American colonial didn't care what Lorrain or the English Crown expected of him and proceeded to make abundantly clear to the rowdy crowd precisely what he thought of English lords and English justice.[33] In a booming voice filled with righteous indignation, he stated for the record that he was an innocent man and that his trial at the Old Bailey had been a travesty of justice. He denounced Bradinham and Palmer as liars who had relied on hearsay. He blamed his mutinous crew and his highbrow English backers for contributing greatly to his fall, singling out the double-crossing Lord Bellomont and Robert Livingston as particular villains. His Junto backers had promised to support him, he said, but instead had turned out to be the traitorous instruments of his ruin. He stated that the killing of William Moore had been a crime of passion committed under provocation and was not a premeditated act, and that he felt badly for his actions in that regard. His fiery oration from the gallows wasn't the full historical reality, of course, but his version of the events and motivations of the key participants hewed *very close* to the truth. His claim that Bellomont and the other backers had maliciously betrayed him was his least accurate indictment, as he was more the victim of collateral damage of the English Empire's far-reaching commercial aspirations in India, war on piracy, and political battle with her independent-minded American colonies than the object of a targeted campaign of personal betrayal.[34]

There were many in the crowd who found his words to be not only brutally honest but deeply moving, and they cheered when he took down the high and mighty. Paul Lorrain was not one of those cheering. He hectored Kidd to admit to the gathered multitude that God had righteously brought him here to the gallows. It was not too late to repent, the chaplain urged him; but while Kidd was ready to repent his sins in general, he was not about to kowtow to the Crown and make up lies that he was a cold-blooded murderer and outlaw pirate. But he did toss the preacher a bone by proclaiming his "confidence in God's mercy through Christ" and that he would die on the scaffold "in charity with the World" by forgiving the iniquity of those who had perjured themselves at his trial to spare their own necks. Still, it wasn't enough for Paul Lorrain, who would write grumpily of Kidd in his final *Account*, "He left little doubt that he felt more sinned against than sinning."[35] The London *Post-Angel* was even more caustic: "Captain Kidd was such a hardened wretch [that] at the gallows he was unwilling to own the justice of his condemnation."[36]

Lorrain now led the four men in a short prayer, joined by the other divines on the platform. Afterward, Kidd declared that he had a final thing or two to say to the crowd. He warned that all seamen, especially captains, should exercise great caution in private and public affairs and beware of the false promises made by greedy men in high places. He then expressed profound sorrow about leaving his beloved wife a widow and his children fatherless and "told those around him to send his love to his wife and daughters."[37]

Once the hangman and his deputies secured the nooses and made sure the men's bonds were fastened tight, they descended the elevated platform via the ladder with Lorrain. It is at this point that the Frenchmen muttered prayers in their Gallic tongue and Darby Mullins, with tears in his eyes, called out, "Lord have mercy upon me! Father have mercy upon me! Sweet savior of the world have mercy on me!"[38]

Captain Kidd just stood there resolutely, staring out at the crowd and taking in the scene one last time. Even with a noose around his neck, he looked as hardy and tough as New York granite.

A nearby church bell tolled six o'clock.

The hangman and his assistants in death jerked away the wooden blocks from under the hanging platform and the four men dropped less than a foot and started kicking with their unbound legs. The crowd surged forward, feeling a rush of excitement at the sight of the bodies in their death throes, thrashing at the ends of the constricting ropes.

But something was wrong.

Instead of four kicking bodies, there were suddenly only three. For the rope attached to the neck of one of the condemned men had not been able to carry his weight and had snapped, with the body falling heavily upon the ground.

Lo and behold, it was Captain Kidd.[39]

A cry of surprise mingled with morbid fascination and exhilaration rose up from the crowd as the prisoner lay bound, dazed, gasping for air, and suddenly stone-cold sober upon the ground. Meanwhile, Darby Mullins and the two Frenchmen kicked their legs furiously in their death struggle. The crowd of English men, women, and children screamed and cheered at the grotesque spectacle, like a Roman mob applauding a gladiatorial contest.

To the roar of the bloodthirsty Londoners, the sheriff and his deputies grabbed Kidd and picked him up off the ground. English tradition held that when a rope broke at a public execution—a rare but not unheard-of occurrence—it was considered an act of God and the condemned were often reprieved. But as the Kidd case involved English politics at the highest levels, the American sea captain would not be so lucky.[40] It took a little time for the hangman to clear away the broken-down platform and prepare a new rope. They also had to locate a new ladder and set it up along the scaffold. The featured star of the attraction now had an extra ten minutes of life, but that would be all.

Sensing a golden opportunity, Paul Lorrain now moved in for the kill and begged the hangman to allow him to obtain a final confession from Captain Kidd from the ladder once it arrived. He would convince the "arch-Pyrate with the unmelted heart" to admit the justice of his sentence and repent his sins before God Almighty and all of London.[41]

When the ladder was delivered, the hangman climbed up it, slung a fresh noose over the bar, climbed back down, and propped the ladder against the scaffold post. Then he prodded the now-recovered and surprisingly calm Captain Kidd to mount the ladder and guided him to the top rung. Having received permission to speak with the condemned, Lorrain climbed up several rungs until his head was at the level of Kidd's waist. From this vantage point, the Ordinary of Newgate listened to Captain Kidd's last dying words.[42] These he reimagined in his head and thence on paper to fulfill his pro-Crown agenda, published the next day in his *Account*.

> But here I must take notice of a remarkable accident which then did happen . . . the rope by which Captain Kidd was tied broke, and so falling to the ground he was taken up alive, and by this means had opportunity to consider more of that Eternity he was launching into. When he was brought up and tied again to the tree . . . I showed him the great mercy of God in giving him unexpectedly this further respite [and] press[ed] him to embrace . . . steadfast faith, true repentance and perfect charity, which now he did so fully and freely express . . . declaring openly that he repented with all his heart, and died in Christian love and charity with all the world. This he said, as he was on the top of the ladder (the scaffold being now broken down) and myself halfway on it, as close to him as I could,

> who having for the last time prayed with him, left him with a greater satisfaction than I had before, that he was penitent.[43]

Like so many of the unreliable narrators in the Captain Kidd saga, Lorrain was only half-truthful, and was imparting the moral lesson he knew the Crown wanted London's working-class masses to hear. According to the more-accurate and less-polemic rival broadsheet publication from that historic day—*A True Account of the Behavior, Confession, and Last Dying Speeches of Captain William Kidd, and the rest of the Pirates that were executed at Execution Dock in Wapping, on Friday the 23 of May 1701*—Captain Kidd's final prayer was for his wife, Sarah, and their daughters.

> [Captain Kidd] expressed abundance of sorrow for leaving his wife and children without having the opportunity of taking leave of them, they being inhabitants in New York. So that the thoughts of his wife's sorrow at the sad tidings of his shameful death was more occasion of grief to him than that of his own sad misfortunes.[44]

Once Lorrain climbed back down to the ground, the executioner kicked out the ladder and this time sent Kidd to his maker. The American sea captain expired just as a blood-red sun set over London Town and the gently rippled waters of the Thames.[45]

With his "important work" completed and commerce beckoning, Paul Lorrain dashed off to the printer to publish his *Account* before the "sham papers" of his rivals. The four bodies were left to dangle as the massive crowd slowly began to disperse. By the time darkness had fallen over Execution Dock, the boisterous mob had broken up and the myriad vessels in the river had sailed off in the sunset.[46]

The sheriff's deputies waited until the crowd was gone to cut down the bodies and chain them to wooden posts driven into the mud flats.

There the corpses would remain until the tidewater had ebbed and flowed over them three times. A guard was posted to make sure no sympathetic seamen, or grubby profiteers who sold cadavers to surgeons for dissection, sneaked in at night to steal the soggy corpses.[47]

With the long-anticipated execution now complete, the teeming masses and English authorities alike began a saturnalia of celebration. "Execution Dock day ended with an orgy of boozing, debauchery, whoring, guzzling, and gluttony," and, at Wapping, "Hangman's Fair began and lasted till far into next day's dawn."[48] In the post-execution celebration, Marshal Cheeke and his Admiralty deputies got sloppy drunk, charging more than a hundred stiff drinks to their government expense account "at a Tavern in Wapping and at the Horne Tavern."[49]

That evening, to show his support for the Whig lords and celebrate the end of the man formerly known as the "trusty and well-beloved Captain Kidd," King William III dined at the mansion of one of Kidd's prominent backers, the Earl of Romney. How many times glasses of wine were hoisted to celebrate the demise of Captain Kidd was not recorded, but there must have been several toasts to his death. The Admiralty was so giddy with the successful outcome that it sent an express letter to India, via the HMS *Royal Bliss*, alerting the Great Mughal that mighty England had executed that villainous cutthroat and destroyer of imperial trade Captain Kidd.[50]

Three days later, with three tides having washed over the bodies, Captain Kidd's bloated white corpse was unchained by Deputy Tom Sherman and his men, hefted onto an Admiralty barge, and transported twenty-five miles downriver to Tilbury Point. Here the gibbet—an iron-banded cage shaped like a human body—constructed by the government-contracted blacksmith James Smith awaited. After being removed from the barge, the wet, slimy, and decomposing corpse of Captain Kidd was carried up a long flight of stone stairs and coated with tar. The tar ensured that the body could remain suspended in the gibbet for as long as possible without disintegrating or being picked clean by scavenging birds.[51] The corpse was then squeezed into its custom-fit iron cage, which lay open on the ground, with "the head set in a metal harness to ensure that the skull remained intact upon the torso" so the standing human form would be a recognizable "terror to all that saw it" upon the Thames.[52]

On May 27, 1701, Captain William Kidd was hoisted in his gibbeted iron cage at Tilbury Point, where his body would remain for the next twenty years. The Admiralty's orders required that his body be placed "so that he may be most plainly seen," and those orders were carried out in an act of early-eighteenth-century state-sponsored terrorism. Seagoing men, women, and children from a multitude of countries, sailing to and from the trading metropolis of London, would for an entire generation have no alternative but to gaze upon Captain Kidd's tarred, chained, rotting, and bird-pecked corpse gently swaying in the sea breeze and lashed by the rain.[53]

Captain William Kidd—more than any other sea captain in the Golden Age of Piracy—would serve as the English state's "grisly warning to other would-be pirates" of the fate that awaited them if they pursued the short but merry life of a marauding freebooter.[54] The great irony, of course, is that Captain Kidd—even more so than his knighted heroes Sir Francis Drake and Sir Henry Morgan—was, as historian Philip Gosse declared over a century ago, "no pirate at all."[55]

–21–
Afterword

Kidd was a Man of such undaunted Spirit,
He'd face Hell-Gates, and all the Devils in it,
Were't possible to steal a Golden Prize
Did so bewitch his Heart, and charms his Eyes!
When on the Seas proud Waves he boldly rid,
All stroke to fly the Great and Mighty Kidd
So terrible was He, where e'er he came
To Rob, or Plunder, that his very Name
Wou'd cause a Trembling Fear and Dread in those
Who were his Friends, as well as his Foes.[1]

In the end, the same English Empire that had transported Captain William Kidd back to London and interrogated, incarcerated, tried, hanged, tarred, and finally gibbeted him—at *huge* government expense—restored only a fraction of the goods to Coji Babba and his fellow Armenian merchants and refused to cough up even a penny for the desperate privateer wives Elizabeth Mead or Gertrude Beck. The claim filed in the High Court of Admiralty maintained that Coji

Babba and the merchants had lost £60,000 ($21,000,000 today) from the *Quedagh Merchant* capture. Putting up roadblocks, the Admiralty requested official documented evidence of wrongdoing committed against the Armenians in Persia, Bengal, and Surat, delaying the settlement of the case until November 21, 1704, more than three years after Kidd's trial.[2] In its final ruling, the Admiralty took more than 90 percent of the proceeds, or £6,472, "to cover Kidd's trial expenses as well as storage of his belongings."[3]

Thus, when presented with a golden opportunity to return the stolen goods to their rightful owners, the English Crown felt no qualms about seizing the bulk of the money and goods and leaving the Armenian merchant and his fellow investors with less than 1 percent of the estimated £60,000 value of the cargo. Refusing to give up, Coji Babba filed a claim in Chancery Court for a portion of the £6,472, but was thwarted yet again by the immovable English Empire.[4]

At this point, the lordly and well-connected directors of Greenwich Hospital entered the picture with a plan to get their hands on the contested "pirate" money and put it to beneficial use. Pressing forward with a claim, they soon received Admiralty approval to put the tainted money toward completing the hospital, located southeast of London on the Thames. The construction of the Christopher Wren–designed sanctuary for the care of maimed, broken, and destitute naval seamen had begun in 1696, but by 1704 it still remained unfinished. With the death of King William in 1702, Queen Anne ascended to the throne and wanted Greenwich Hospital to serve as a symbol of the Royal Navy's importance to the nation. She, therefore, signified her willingness to turn "the effects of the Pyrate Kidd" over to the hospital. The queen used a 1705 Act of Parliament to dispose of the "residual estate" of Captain Kidd, donating the £6,472 "gift" in her name to complete the construction of the new facility. With this windfall, the directors bought the house, park, and gardens of Colonel Sidney of Greenwich, the nephew of Kidd's backer the Earl of Romney. Thus, in another twist of Kiddian irony, the "notorious arch-Pyrate Captain Kidd" made possible the creation of Wren's splendid

Greenwich Hospital, which is still visible today on the Thames, much as he had contributed to the building of the legendary Trinity Church overlooking the Hudson in New York City.[5]

Upon Kidd's death, his worst fear came true, and his beloved wife and daughters were treated just as atrociously by Mother England as Elizabeth Mead, Gertrude Beck, and Coji Babba. On August 4, 1701, nine weeks after his gruesome public hanging, Sarah received a knock at the front door of her house at 119-121 Pearl Street, and a New York official notified her that her husband had been executed in London on May 23. Since Captain Kidd had been "attainted as a pirate," the official presented her with a signed warrant for the confiscation of her husband's estate. Under English law, she owned nothing as the widow of a pirate and was cast out onto the street, along with Elizabeth, little Sarah, and housekeeper Dorothy Lee.[6]

She promptly waged a fierce legal battle against the Crown, arguing that the properties and household possessions had been acquired from her first and second husbands, William Cox and John Oort, and from Captain Kidd prior to his alleged piratical acts. Unfortunately, the case would drag on through the courts for more than two years. At this stage of her life, she was thirty-one and Captain Kidd had become a cautionary folk antihero whose exploits were recounted from Carolina to Maine in *Ye Lamentable Ballad of Captain Kidd* and other wildly inaccurate but entertaining ditties. Since Kidd had sailed from Boston in irons in March 1700, she had struggled to put her life back together while living quietly in the city with Elizabeth and little Sarah; but times were hard, as many of her New York friends ostracized her.[7] Her only consolation was that Trinity Church honored the Kidd family's ownership of Pew Number 4, allowing her and her daughters to regularly attend church services in return for her husband's generosity to the community back in 1696. The pew was right up front near the rector and bore the inscription "Captain Kidd—Commanded 'Adventure Galley.'" Unfortunately, Captain Kidd never had the opportunity to pray with his family at the church he had helped build and that stands today as one of New York City's greatest links to its historic past.[8]

Sarah grieved for her beloved sea rover for more than two years—far longer than for her first two husbands, and a lengthy time for a widow to remain unmarried. As a fallen woman, she needed a male head of household to survive in a perilous colonial world devoid of any social safety net. On November 4, 1703, she took Christopher Rousby as her fourth husband. Rousby—a stable, politically connected New Jersey merchant who owned the 19¼-acre parcel next to the Sawkill Farm—apparently found her social grace and beauty more important than her connection to the most "notorious arch-Pyrate" ever to sail the seven seas. On May 2, 1704, Queen Anne granted back to Sarah and Rousby the title to the Pearl Street mansion, where she and Kidd had lived with their two daughters; the Wall Street house owned by her brother Samuel Bradley, who never recovered from his illness acquired on Mohelia and died in 1703; and all of Sarah's household possessions.[9]

With Rousby, Sarah gained a second chance at life. For her daughters' sake, she tried to put Captain Kidd and his notoriety behind her. She changed Elizabeth and little Sarah's last name from Kidd to Rousby, and there would be no mention of the surname Kidd in her will. Over the next several years, she had three boys with Rousby: Christopher, named after her fourth husband and his antecedents; Henry, named after her youngest brother, who had died in 1693; and William, named after her beloved sea captain, whom despite all her hardships she had never forgotten and for whom she still retained an affection. When she signed her will on November 1, 1732, at age sixty-two, she was finally able to write her own name.[10]

Sarah Bradley Cox Oort Kidd Rousby died a moderately wealthy widow on September 12, 1744. By this time, she had moved back to New York from New Jersey and was living in her old home on Pearl Street where she had lived her best years with Captain Kidd. In her will, she specified that she should be buried as a Christian, bequeathed her wedding ring to her eldest Rousby son, Christopher, Jr., and declared that all her houses and lands were to be sold and the proceeds given to her remaining Rousby children and her grandchildren. Fittingly, she is buried today in the churchyard of Trinity Church on Wall Street in Manhattan.[11]

So, WHO WAS Captain Kidd *really* and what is his *true* place in history? Ultimately, my ninth-great-grandfather is hard to pin down, as he is a man of many contrasts. He has to be regarded as a colonial American hero for his full body of work as a patriotic privateer in the war against France, guardian of the North American coast, merchant sea captain building up a new democratic nation, and dedicated family man, civic leader, and friend to a vast number of his contemporaries. But he also possessed more than his fair share of character flaws and at least some of the roguishness of the classical antihero, which is what he remains most known for today.

The debates over Captain Kidd's true character, his rightful legacy in the Golden Age of Piracy, and the secret locations of his wildly inflated buried treasure have continued unabated since the late seventeenth century—and show no sign of letting up. Even before his execution, he was transformed from a courageous yet mundane sea captain into a mythical legend and global sensation, and he stands today as an American icon immortalized in the works of Washington Irving, Nathaniel Hawthorne, Edgar Allan Poe, Robert Louis Stevenson, and artist Howard Pyle, while arguably more successful or more dastardly pirates like Thomas Tew, Henry Every, and Robert Culliford have long been forgotten except by pirate scholars and aficionados.

Maritime historians, writers of all stripes, and the general public still vigorously debate whether he was ever a pirate at all, precisely when he "turned" pirate, whether his trial was fair, whether all of his treasure has been found, and his proper place in history. Though the real Captain Kidd would have loathed being labeled as one of the most notorious villains of all time, he would have been delighted at being a continuing hot topic of conversation for over three hundred years and counting. As

British pirate scholar Patrick Pringle noted, "It is unlikely that he will ever be displaced as the Great Pirate."[12]

The challenge with Captain Kidd has always been in stripping away the myth and propaganda, exposing the lies of the various unreliable narrators, and not succumbing to the traditional rigid "villain" or "martyr" concepts. Much like Alexander Hamilton, Captain James Cook, Colonel George Armstrong Custer, and General George S. Patton Jr., historians tend to either love Kidd or hate him, and they assemble their facts and ignore the ones they don't like accordingly.

Researchers who don't care much for Captain Kidd and consider him nothing more than a second-rate, guilty-as-charged pirate have a familiar and predictable *modus operandi*. They ignore or give perfunctory treatment to a dozen or more historical events in Kidd's life that a growing number of Atlantic historians believe are critical to his story and illuminate his true character. These events include his valiant pre–Indian Ocean years fighting the French, when he took a firm stand against piracy that would later be repeated in the East Indies; his vast network of friends from all social classes; his role as a leading New York citizen; his close and loving relationship with his fiercely devoted wife, Sarah; his incredible generosity over the years to those in need; his fair and just treatment toward people considered low in the social hierarchy of the day, including African Americans, White indentured servants, Native Americans, and Jews; his well-established buccaneer egalitarianism and strict adherence to the standard democratic privateering articles of his age; his ability to turn the other cheek in Christianly fashion; the fact that he was strong-armed into accepting command of the Indian Ocean expedition by Bellomont; the many democratic meetings he held with his crew during his voyage to the Indian Ocean; the fact that Bradinham and Palmer lied extensively under oath and that Kidd was on antagonistic terms with his old nemesis Robert Culliford as soon as he sailed into St. Mary's harbor; and his many well-documented attempts to prevent his mutinous crew from committing piracy.

At the same time, there is no question—none whatsoever—that he was no saint and was stubborn as a mule; that he could be nearly as hard a taskmaster toward his crew as Royal Navy commanders like James Cook or Horatio Nelson; that he was politically naïve; and that he was not a fully "innocent" man, despite the fervent arguments for his martyrdom and innocence by some historians and his many supporters in Great Britain and the United States who continue to actively campaign for him to receive an official pardon from the British government. Even by the sketchy standards of his era, he was guilty of at least one act of piracy during the Indian Ocean expedition, or at least of failure to lift a finger to prevent his crew from committing piracy; and, possibly but not definitively, one count of manslaughter in a fit of passionate rage. In the judgment of history, then, William Kidd no more deserves to be "draped in robes of spotless white" or to stand as "the perfect gentleman and the complete martyr"[13] than he does to be called "the world's greatest liar and thief" or a "villain of all nations."

In many respects, Captain Kidd is uncannily similar to the legendary Scottish American naval commander John Paul Jones, hero of the American Revolution and "Father of the American Navy." Like Captain Kidd, Jones was patriotic, resolute, ambitious, hard-fighting, tireless, an outstanding seaman, and, on occasion, violent-tempered, leading to the killing of a mutinous sailor with a sword. But unlike Kidd, he was never prosecuted, and he was later caricatured as "Paul Jones the Pirate" by the British over whom he had been victorious. Yet today Kidd is recognized as a fiendish arch-pirate, while Jones is a national treasure. As a London magazine proclaimed in 1874, Captain Kidd "did some queer things, no doubt, but he was hanged for doing them, whilst so many who did infinitely worse than he died in their beds in the odor of sanctity, and, according to all the rules of fair play, ought now to be suffering a good deal more than he."[14]

It is for these important reasons that most modern scholars lean more toward Captain Kidd as a gray-shaded hero, or at least admirable and scapegoated antihero, than the unfounded caricature of the villainous arch-pirate, brutal thug, or vacillating privateer-turned-pirate widely accepted before the French passports were unearthed by Ralph Paine in 1910. Thus, it is Paine's contemporary, the British legal scholar Sir Cornelius Dalton, who has captured the essence of the real, honorable, yet flawed Captain Kidd, when in 1911 he wrote:

> This worthy, honest-hearted, steadfast, much enduring sailor, a typical sea captain of his day, seems to have done his best to serve his country and his employers [under] very difficult circumstances. His fatal mistake which brought all his sufferings on him was that he yielded to the solicitations [and] intimidations of personages of higher rank than his own, who for their own ends induced him against his better judgment to embark on an impossible enterprise. . . . For his pains, after giving himself into custody in reliance on the word and honor of his chief employer, a Whig nobleman, he was ignominiously executed and hung in chains, after nearly two years' close incarceration, and has ever since been held up to execration as the arch-pirate, who left behind him untold hoards of treasure. . . . It would be difficult to conceive any wilder misrepresentation of the poor man's doings.[15]

What makes Captain Kidd important today is not merely his remarkable "rags-to-riches, back-to-rags" story but how many people were profoundly affected by his actions and how entrenched his myth has become in popular culture. As Robert Ritchie and Mark Hanna have observed, the Kidd story is compelling and dynamic because it involved "such a broad range of imperial political actors, including Armenian merchants, Caribbean governors, East India Company factors in India, New York City jack-tars, and even King William himself."[16] In Kidd's own day, he was a luminary of the media and popular culture, the hot topic of "the courtrooms and coffee shops of New York, Boston, London, and India."[17] London printers reeled off at least five accounts of Kidd's trial proceedings, and four broadsides were circulated at the time of his public hanging at Wapping in addition to Paul Lorrain's.[18] His body was barely cold when the popular ballad "Captain Kidd's Farewell to the Seas" was published on the streets of London and swiftly dispersed to the American colonies. In fact, the ballad was so popular in America that it would be sung and reprinted into the twenty-first century. A torrent of Captain Kidd books, broadsides, and pamphlets followed soon after his execution, the most famous of which were the wildly popular *A Dialogue between the Ghost of Captain Kidd, and the Napper in the Strand* (1702) and, much later, the widely distributed *The Dying Words of Captain Robert [William] Kidd* (1790).[19]

By the late eighteenth century and into the early nineteenth, Captain Kidd had secured his place in the pantheon of American folk heroes as "our maritime Kit Carson and Jesse James."[20] As Robert Ritchie writes, "A young country without a mythic past filled with heroes such as King Arthur, Roland, or Siegfried, the United States reached out to its margins to use frontiersmen, whalers, and buccaneers as suitable characters for national literature. Washington Irving, Edgar Allan Poe, James Fenimore Cooper, and others found them useful [and] Kidd's legend was very much a part of this evolution." Captain Kidd also began to appear in novels, such as Joseph Ingraham's mid-nineteenth-century works *The Spanish Galleon, or the Pirate of the Mediterranean: A Romance of the Corsair Kidd* and *Captain Kyd, or the Wizard of the Sea: A Romance*. During the 1840s and 1850s, Kidd was transformed into a romantic figure who captured and had a torrid love affair with the Great Mughal Aurangzeb's daughter.[21]

But in the 1700s and 1800s, most scholars and laypeople still considered him a colorful outlaw through the wild stories that told of a swaggering pirate, with tens of millions of dollars' worth of buried treasure still to be found from Asia to the Caribbean to Newfoundland, or in his hackneyed English Empire–scripted role of the "turned pirate" that continues to the present day.

In the 1820s, American newspapers published stories claiming that Captain Kidd had constructed a subterranean hideout in

Kiddenhooghten, New York, or "Kidd Heights" near Dutch Albany, where he stashed away fifty boxes of gold for a rainy day. By mid-century, the myths of his vast hidden caches of gold and jewels had spurred treasure-hunting expeditions from Maryland to Nova Scotia. Fortune hunters claimed to have discovered these long-buried troves of treasure in virtually every state along the Eastern Seaboard, with gold and silver literally washing up on the shores of the Hudson. Others reported to have found sealed bottles containing letters and treasure maps scratched out by Kidd himself.[22] At this time, several companies began scouring the lower Hudson River Valley for Captain Kidd's lost treasure, and his undiscovered fortune became linked with the supernatural.[23]

For the past two hundred years, treasure hunters have claimed an occult connection to the privateer. "Scholars have well established that the prevalent use of folk magic and divining practices in New York and the New England states for the search of buried treasure was motivated by Captain Kidd's legend."[24] When one reads the countless tales of Captain Kidd's unrecovered treasure from the nineteenth century to the present day—featuring treasure chests guarded by headless men, guardian dogs with red eyes, monster horses, enormous crows, and magical rings that deflect bullets—one cannot help but wonder if all this insanity is my ancestor's revenge for the miscarriage of justice that brought him to his inglorious demise at Wapping in 1701.[25] As recently as the 1950s, a newspaper reported an American expedition in search of "the £1,000,000 pirate's treasure of Captain William Kidd"—despite the fact that the largest estimate in Kidd's own lifetime was Robert Livingston's exaggerated appraisal worth half that amount.[26]

In the treasure-hunting mania, it was only a matter of time before the con artists entered the fray. The most famous scam of all time had to do with the Kidd-Palmer charts. These were four of Kidd's alleged maps pinpointing the location of his treasure in the South China Sea. The Kidd-Palmer charts were discovered in 1929 by Hubert Palmer, a retired British lawyer and antiques collector. After Palmer's death, the maps were bequeathed to his housekeeper, Elizabeth Dick, who brought them before the British Museum in London to be examined by cartographic expert R. A. Skelton. When Skelton verified that the maps were legitimate, a frenzy of speculation around the legend of Captain Kidd cranked up once again. Fly-by-night outfits began promoting treasure-hunting expeditions to the South China Sea using the Kidd-Palmer charts. Of course, Kidd never made it that far east during his fateful voyage, but that hasn't stopped successive generations of treasure-mad Lord Bellomonts from having a go at the pipe dream that keeps on giving.[27]

The gold rush created by the Kidd-Palmer charts eventually suffered a serious setback in 1951, when a fraud report was filed with Scotland Yard against one James Brownlie, who had advertised an expedition to the South China Sea in search of Kidd's buried treasure reportedly worth £100,000 using the illustrious charts. As leader of the expedition, the British P. T. Barnum–like huckster managed to sign up two gullible adventurers, who invested over £1,500 (around $68,000 today) in the hokey enterprise. When they sued him for fraud, Brownlie was forced to postpone the expedition due to "bad weather" and "necessary repairs." He then claimed that he would finance the expedition himself, but soon canceled the South China Sea adventure for unspecified reasons.[28]

Scores of investment companies and adventurers have scoured not only the South China Sea but Madagascar, the Caribbean, and the North American Atlantic Seaboard in search of Captain Kidd's much-exaggerated treasure and his sunken ships (*Adventure Galley* and *Quedagh Merchant*). One of the most bizarre took place in 1983, when American thriller writer Cork Graham and a British adventurer and struggling actor named Richard Knight teamed up in the quest for Captain Kidd's buried treasure off the Vietnamese island of Phú Quốc, located two hundred miles west of Saigon. Knight claimed to be in possession of a map passed down from his grandfather that gave the precise location of Captain Kidd's buried treasure. However, the two goofy treasure hunters were apprehended by the Vietnamese authorities in their speedboat before even reaching the X-marks-the-spot treasure site. They were promptly convicted of trespassing in Vietnamese territory and assessed a $10,000 fine. In a Kiddian twist, they were imprisoned for eleven months in solitary confinement, with only three hours of exercise per week, until they were able to pay their fines.[29]

Thankfully, the legendary Captain Kidd has also generated some serious scientific research. In 2007, the *Quedagh Merchant* (*Adventure Prize*) was discovered on the sandy sea bottom off the coast of Catalina Island in the modern-day Dominican Republic. Though underwater archaeological investigations have not uncovered Kidd's purported billion-dollar treasure, the shipwreck site—a "Living Museum of the Sea" open to the general public—has to date yielded twenty-six cannons, three large anchor crowns, piles of scrap iron from the ship's hold, and other important archaeological artifacts that help further reconstruct the true Captain Kidd story.[30]

To this day he stands as one of the most well-known, popular, and controversial figures in world history, with countless books, short stories, articles, ballads, and songs written about him (as well as rock bands, pubs, restaurants, streets, and hotels named after him). There are a large number of websites on Captain Kidd, including more than a few with helpful tips on where plucky treasure hunters can find his long-lost fortune. In the U.S. alone, legend still places buried chests of Captain Kidd's treasure in a multitude of locations in Connecticut, Maine, Maryland, Massachusetts, New Jersey, and New York.

However, Captain Kidd's contribution to history is not limited to his "romantic myth of the flamboyant pirate" or his "treasure rumored to be scattered all over the world."[31] More important is his role in planting the seeds of rebellion against the English Crown that would grow into a full-fledged revolution by 1776. Captain Kidd was not merely a leading New York citizen who helped build Trinity Church, nor was he just a courageous privateer commander in King William's War against France and an important member of America's first unofficial Coast Guard. His story—as much as any other between the settling of Jamestown and the American Revolution—symbolized colonial American defiance against the English Crown and its Navigation Acts. Though his Indian Ocean voyage led to his tragic downfall, his story brought to light the huge disparity between England's and colonial America's definitions of privateering versus piracy, foreshadowed the widespread American resistance to England's economic policies that would climax during the Revolution, and underscored the symbiotic relationship between America's seaborne commerce raiders and landed communities.[32]

In his own lifetime, he did not think of himself as a proto-revolutionary at war with the English Empire, though when imprisoned under atrocious conditions and denied a fair trial from 1699 to 1701 he came damn close. But like the American colonists who dumped three hundred–odd chests of East India Company tea into Boston Harbor on December 16, 1773, Captain Kidd was every bit the patriot fighting to protect his country from her enemies at the time, the French, as well as an incipient revolutionary fighting against Mother England and her draconian Navigation Acts.

The spectacular irony is that Captain Kidd has won a posthumous victory over his English foes. The same powerful forces that destroyed him have made him a staple of popular culture and sanctified his historical legacy in a way he never could have imagined. And let us not forget that the rope around his neck broke on May 23, 1701. If British and colonial American folklore, as well as the supernatural ghost stories of Irving, Poe, Hawthorne, and Stevenson, are to be believed, then the rope giving way on that fateful day was an act of divine providence. Perhaps God Almighty was sending a message that he truly was "the innocentest person of them all" after being "sworn against by perjured persons" and having the deck illegally and unfairly stacked against him by the English Crown. If so, then it is Captain Kidd who has had the last laugh on us all.

Despite his many flaws and the fact that he was not a 100 percent innocent man by the legal standards of his age, I have come to love the old seafaring rascal, my ninth-great-grandfather Captain William Kidd, who remained resolute in his convictions, true to himself, and fiercely devoted to his wife, Sarah, and their daughters until the bitter end.

Acknowledgments

In writing this book, I am pleased to have the opportunity to thank the innumerable talented individuals and scholarly institutions that helped bring the true story of my swashbuckling ancestor, Captain William Kidd, to fruition. First and foremost, I would like to thank my literary agent, Max Sinsheimer, for playing a modern-day Maxwell Perkins by taking my original 1,050-page tome that covered virtually every personal event in Captain William and Sarah Kidd's lives in exhaustive detail and converting it into a workable manuscript for today's mainstream publishing industry. I would also like to thank up front the prominent maritime historians and authors Dr. Robert Ritchie, Benerson Little, Dr. Rebecca Simon, and Dr. Guy Chet, who were kind enough to read an earlier draft of the book and give important pre-publication endorsements that greatly aided in securing a high-quality nonfiction history publisher, Diversion Books. Without the generosity of spirit of Dr. Ritchie, Mr. Little, Dr. Simon, and Dr. Chet, all of whom are mini-legends in their own right, this four-year-long research project might not have seen the light of day.

I would like to thank Dr. David A. Boyles, Jack R. Gaines Emeritus Professor of Chemistry of the Department of Chemistry and Applied

Biological Sciences of the South Dakota School of Mines and Technology, for his game-changing genetic genealogical research on William and Sarah Kidd. During our extensive communications over the past four years, he patiently explained arcane concepts like "shared cluster analysis" and "triangulation" to me, and has in the process helped make a major contribution to the true Captain Kidd story by quantitatively verifying the early William and Sarah connection and improving upon our knowledge regarding the Anglo-Scot, Virginia, and Maryland Kidd genealogical families.

At Diversion Books, I would like to thank Evan Phail, Keith Wallman, Clara Linhoff, and Scott Waxman for their tremendous efforts in supporting, editing, producing, and promoting the book in its various incarnations; and Shannon Donnelly for her invaluable assistance in in marketing and publicity. Evan Phail, in particular, provided invaluable editorial recommendations that resulted in dramatic improvements to the text of *Captain Kidd.* I would also like to thank copyeditor Phil Gaskill, proofreader Michael Fedison, and managing editorial assistant Amy Martin at Neuwirth & Associates, who went above and beyond the call of duty during the various stages of editing and production. A special shout-out also goes to cover designer Jonathan Sainsbury for the impressive jacket and to the cartographic team at Mapping Specialists for creating the outstanding maps of Captain Kidd's 1696–1699 Indian Ocean voyage route and other key maps of Kidd's old stomping grounds in the Caribbean and the Indian Ocean.

The key libraries, archives, and organizations that provided much of the primary source materials for this book and who deserve special thanks include the National Archives of the United Kingdom, Public Records Office, at Kew outside London; the New York State Archives and New-York Historical Society; the Gilder Lehrman Institute of American History; the Massachusetts Historical Society; the Henry E. Huntington Library in San Marino, California; and Adam Matthew Digital Limited.

Though this book is first and foremost a scholarly work based upon primary sources, I would like to acknowledge five secondary references that proved indispensable in helping me put together the Captain Kidd story and to tip my hat to the authors behind these important works. I have already paid tribute to the legendary Roy Ritchie—who, quite fittingly, finished reading my manuscript in a driving rainstorm not far from Wapping where Kidd was hanged in ignominy—but I must thank him again for his landmark book, *Captain Kidd and the War against the Pirates*, and also for generously giving me an endorsement for the final book. That Ritchie's 1986 tour de force still remains to the present day the starting point, road map, or framework of contention for every "pirate" book on the planet is a testament to his pioneering contribution to Atlantic research and colonial American history. I would also like to thank the wonderfully irreverent, highly accurate, and always entertaining Richard Zacks, author of *The Pirate Hunter: The True Story of Captain Kidd*, as well as three of his deceased predecessors who had such a profound influence upon his interpretation of Captain Kidd as well as my own. These twentieth-century experts on all things Kiddian are the multifarious New Yorker and decorated WWI veteran Dunbar Maury Hinrichs (*The Fateful Voyage of Captain Kidd*), the quirky British journalist Harold Wilkins (*Captain Kidd and His Skeleton Island*), and British legal scholar Sir Cornelius Dalton (*The Real Captain Kidd: A Vindication*). In short, Zacks, Hinrichs, Wilkins, and Dalton have all gotten the Captain Kidd story right by probing deeply into the primary sources and getting inside Kidd's head, and by exposing and ruling out the unreliable English Crown and East India Company narrators who clearly had a political axe to grind.

I would also personally like to thank my wife, Christine, for her invaluable assistance on the Endnotes and Bibliography, and, even more importantly, for her long-standing moral support and putting up with a "pirate" for the past four years.

Lastly, I want to thank all my readers and anyone and everyone who actually purchased this book, as well as my loyal fans and supporters who have helped promote this work and others over the years. You know who you are and, as always, I offer you a Mile High Salute.

Endnotes and Bibliography

Because historical records on the legendary Captain William Kidd extend back to the late 1680s, the combined Endnotes and Bibliography for *Captain Kidd: A True Story of Treasure and Betrayal* comprise virtually an entire book in themselves. Therefore, to view the extensive Endnotes and Bibliography that includes archival manuscripts, newspapers, and other primary and secondary printed and digital sources for *Captain Kidd*, please visit www.diversionbooks.com/books/endnotes-captain-kidd/.

Or scan here:

About the Author

Samuel Marquis is the ninth-great-grandson of legendary privateer Captain William Kidd, and is the #1 Denver Post bestselling and award-winning author of *Blackbeard: The Birth of America*, among eleven other American nonfiction-histories, historical novels, and suspense books, covering primarily the period from colonial America through World War II.

Marquis works by day as a VP–principal hydrogeologist with an environmental consulting firm. He lives in Louisville, Colorado, where he and his wife raised their three children.